Windows® Runtime via C#

Jeffrey Richter
Maarten van de Bospoort

PUBLISHED BY
Microsoft Press
A Division of Microsoft Corporation
One Microsoft Way
Redmond, Washington 98052-6399

Library of Congress Control Number: 2013952561
ISBN: 978-0-7356-7927-6

Printed and bound in the United States of America.

First Printing

Microsoft Press books are available through booksellers and distributors worldwide. If you need support related to this book, email Microsoft Press Book Support at mspinput@microsoft.com. Please tell us what you think of this book at http://www.microsoft.com/learning/booksurvey.

Acquisitions Editor: Devon Musgrave
Developmental Editor: Devon Musgrave
Project Editor: Carol Dillingham
Editorial Production: Curtis Philips, Publishing.com
Technical Reviewer: Christophe Nasarre; Technical Review services provided by
                Content Master, a member of CM Group, Ltd.
Copyeditor: Roger LeBlanc
Indexer: Lucie Haskins
Cover: Twist Creative • Seattle and Joel Panchot

Kristin, words cannot express how I feel about our life together. I cherish our family and all our adventures. I'm filled each day with love for you.

Aidan (age 10) and Grant (age 5), you both have been an inspiration to me and have taught me to play and have fun. Watching the two of you grow up has been so rewarding and enjoyable for me. I am lucky to be able to partake in your lives. I love and appreciate you more than you could ever know.

—JEFFREY RICHTER

Jeff takes a break while his family computes.

To Jules and Joris. You guys have taught me so much. The two of you have been inspirational, each in your own particular way.

To Brigitte. For your tireless optimism, energy, love, and unwavering support.

—Maarten van de Bospoort

Maarten and family celebrate the publication of his first book.

Contents at a glance

Contents

What do you think of this book? We want to hear from you!

Microsoft is interested in hearing your feedback so we can improve our books and learning resources for you. To participate in a brief survey, please visit:

http://aka.ms/tellpress

Chapter 7   Networking   145

Chapter 8   Tile and toast notifications   183

Chapter 11 Windows Store — 247

What do you think of this book? We want to hear from you!

Microsoft is interested in hearing your feedback so we can improve our books and learning resources for you. To participate in a brief survey, please visit:

http://aka.ms/tellpress

Foreword

No kidding! Take your seats, everyone, so we can get started. If you haven't a clue what is being discussed, you need to put this book down. Go back to the book store and buy Jeffrey Richter's *CLR via C#, Fourth Edition* (Microsoft Press, 2012). Really, you need it anyway. Then after you read the Foreword, you may join us!

If you're short on time, here is the CliffsNotes version: in Jeff's previous two books, he vowed to never write another one. Well, here we all are again. No more empty promises. Jeff will probably write another book. After so many years of his lies about stopping, I can no longer support them. We are all here for the intervention. How much more can be said, right? I mean, aren't there literally thousands of pages of stuff written on this already? Jeff claims that because Maarten came up with the initial research and prose, Jeff was cowriting the book, so it doesn't count. We all see through this ruse. This is not our first rodeo.

Maybe you all can't appreciate Jeff's humble origins. He was never fully understood by his family. His parents didn't believe there was a future in computers and hoped he would "get over it" and find a real career. When he quit his first job to write a book, they could not believe you could make a real living if you didn't wear a tie every day. His mother never got over the fact that he wore jeans to work. His grandmother held a book of his in her hand and then decided that "windows" meant he dressed the mannequins at Macy's. Like he was an expert on shopping and merchandising at the mall. I am not kidding; this is true. Let me just tell you something Jeffrey is not an expert on, and that is malls and shopping. So maybe that is why he must continually write, explaining over and over the importance of technology—this is just to justify his life to his family. It is the only explanation I can come up with.

The amazing thing is this new book does have stuff about the Windows Store! His grandma would be so excited—finally, she can go shopping for something in a store that has to do with Windows. Hopefully that will provide the validation he needs.

I will warn you. Jeff is becoming a bit of an old timer. Oh, it's true. While I was trying to understand this book (which of course I don't), he couldn't stop himself from harkening back to the day. When programs were real programs. They did meaningful things, like run medical software and financial software. Now we have *applications* and even that word is too complex, so we call them *apps*. They are available for $1.49, and they do things like pass gas or make a flashlight. There is nothing mission critical about this. Jeff feels a little like a sellout—with all his skills, the best he can do is try to create an app that will outsell Pet Rescue. He then talked about how this book will make programming so easy. Windows 8.1 is so clean and smooth. There is not the same level of intensity to programming for it.

Although, between you and me, there is a little secret that should be shared. Under full NDA, just because we are friends. Jeff wrote a few of these apps for the Windows Store, and they were rejected. So maybe making a flashlight is not so easy, huh?

Really, this whole book thing is not even necessary. I mean, now you can hear him with WintellectNOW's on-demand video training. It is like a lullaby—you can turn on Jeff's videos anytime you need the comfort of another human's voice. Reading is just a silly old-school skill that we used to need. Now we have the Internet and video feeds. So whenever you have issues with your code, you can invite Jeffrey into your office for a little lesson. If you happen to need a nap at the same time, well napping is one of the 7 habits of highly effective people.

So, with Windows 8.1 released, a new paradigm is in place. Jeffrey is clearly in front of this situation. He has his fingers on the pulse (or at least the touch-sensitive screen) of this situation. Who knows, someday he may even get me to update to this new version of Windows.

I would like to close with some thoughts from some old (I mean, *longtime*) friends, his business partners and fellow Wintellectuals.

John Robbins says:

> *Jeffrey and I go way back. Back to the time when Steve Ballmer had hair and modern applications used this amazing technology called a "Windows message." When Jeffrey started development with Windows, you were doing really well if you could get two programs running at the same time. After some detours through Windows XP and the like, you could run dozens of applications concurrently. Windows 8.1 brings us to the future of modern applications where you can run two side by side.*

Jeff Prosise says:

> *One of our favorite Jeffrey-isms: "This code is so bad, I feel sorry for the compiler that has to compile it!"*
>
> *Jeffrey has an admitted inability to build user interfaces. Ergo Jeffrey-ism #2: "There is no UI problem that can't be solved with a command prompt."*

And in closing, Mark Russinovich, author of the cyber thriller *Zero Day*, says:

> *I have known Jeff since 1997 when he heckled me during a talk I*
> *was giving. He had a point, though, so we've been friends ever since.*
> *Jeff has come a long way since I first started mentoring him and he*
> *continues to impress me with his ability to solve Portal 2 puzzles.*

I hope you all enjoy this book! I am patiently awaiting the return of my husband.

Kristin Trace (Jeff's wife)
October 2013

A typical father-and-son LEGO project.

Introduction

The Microsoft Windows operating system offers many features and capabilities to application developers. Developers consume these features by calling Windows Runtime (WinRT) APIs. This book explores many of the Windows Runtime APIs and how to best use them from within your own applications. An emphasis is placed on using WinRT APIs from Windows Store apps. Windows Store app developers will also find a lot of architectural guidance as well as performance and debugging advice throughout all the book's chapters.

In addition, since many WinRT APIs are available to desktop apps too, much of this book is also useful to desktop app developers. In particular, desktop app developers will get a lot from the chapters that cover files, folders, streams, networking, toasts, and the clipboard.

Although WinRT APIs can be invoked from many different programming languages—including JavaScript, native C++, and Visual Basic—this book focuses on consuming them from C# because this language is expected to be the most-used language for consuming WinRT APIs due to its popularity with Microsoft-centric developers and the enormous productivity the language provides. However, if you decide to use a different programming language, this book still provides a lot of information and guidance about the WinRT APIs, and this information is useful regardless of the programming language used to invoke them.

Who should read this book

This book is useful to developers building applications for the Windows operating system. It teaches core WinRT API concepts and how to architect and design Windows Store apps, and it provides performance and debugging tips throughout. Much of the information presented in this book is also useful to developers building desktop apps for Windows.

Assumptions

This book expects that you have at least a minimal understanding of the Microsoft .NET Framework, the C# programming language, and the Visual Studio integrated development environment. For more information about C# and the .NET Framework, consider reading Jeffrey Richter's *CLR via C#, Fourth Edition* (Microsoft Press, 2012).

Who should not read this book

This book does not focus on user-interface concepts and how to design an app's user interface using technologies such as XAML or HTML. For information about using XAML to build user interfaces, consider reading Charles Petzold's *Programming Windows: Writing Windows 8 Apps with C# and XAML, Sixth Edition* (Microsoft Press, 2013).

Organization of this book

This book is divided into two sections. Part I, "Core concepts," focuses on concepts that all WinRT and Windows Store app developers must know.

- Chapter 1, "Windows runtime primer," defines the WinRT type system, its principles, and how to consume it from various programming languages. This chapter also addresses the importance of understanding asynchronous programming, which is pervasive throughout the WinRT API.

- Chapter 2, "App packaging and deployment," concentrates on the files that make up a Windows Store app, how those files get combined into a package file, and how the package file ultimately gets installed on users' PCs. Package files are a new core concept in Windows, and understanding them is critical to being successful when using WinRT APIs.

- Chapter 3, "Process model," explains the core concepts related to how Windows Store apps execute. The chapter focuses on app activation, threading models, main view and hosted view windows, XAML page navigation, efficient memory management, process lifetime management, and debugging. All Windows Store apps must adhere to the architecture described in this chapter.

Part II, "Core Windows facilities," contains chapters that explore various Windows facilities. The topics presented are key topics that almost all Windows Store app developers must know. Although the chapters can be read in any order, I recommend reading them in order because later chapters tend to reference topics presented in earlier chapters. Most of the chapters in Part II are about moving data around using settings, files, folders, streams, networking, and data sharing. However, there are also chapters explaining how apps can update tile content and display toasts. And there is a chapter explaining how apps can execute code when the user is not interacting with the app. The final chapter shows how to submit your app to the Windows Store and how to leverage the Windows Store commerce engine so that you can get paid for your development efforts.

Code samples

Most of the chapters in this book include code snippets showing how to leverage the various Windows features. Complete code samples demonstrating the features and allowing you to experiment with them can be downloaded from the following page:

http://Wintellect.com/Resource-WinRT-Via-CSharp

Follow the instructions to download the "WinRT via CS" .zip file.

> **Note** In addition to the code samples, your system must be running Windows 8.1 and must have Visual Studio 2013 installed.

The Visual Studio solution contains several projects. Each project starts with a two-digit number that corresponds to the book's chapter. For example, the "05a-Storage" project contains the code that accompanies Chapter 5, "Storage files and folders."

Acknowledgments

I couldn't have written this book without the help and technical assistance of many people. In particular, I'd like to thank my family. The amount of time and effort that goes into writing a book is hard to measure. All I know is that I could not have produced this book without the support of my wife, Kristin, and my two sons, Aidan and Grant. There were many times when we wanted to spend time together but were unable to due to book obligations. Now that the book project is completed, I really look forward to adventures we will all share together.

Of course, I also have to thank my coauthor, Maarten van de Bospoort. This book would not have existed at all if it were not for Maarten. Maarten started with my original course slides and demo code and turned that into the chapter text. Because books go into more technical depth and detail than courses, he had to research many areas in further depth and embellish the chapters quite a bit. Maarten would then hand the chapters over to me, and I would polish them by reorganizing a bit and add my own personal flair. It was a pleasure working with Maarten as he was always open to suggestions, and it was also really nice to have someone to discuss book organization and content with.

For technical content, there are many people on Microsoft's Windows team who had one-on-one meetings with me so that I could learn more about the features and their goals. In particular, I had two six-hour meetings with Howard Kapustein discussing packages, app containers, deployment, bundles, and so on. Talks with him changed my whole view of the system, and the chapters in this book reflect what I learned from these discussions. John Sheehan also spoke with me at length about package capabilities, declarations, and the resource system, which changed my whole view about app activation and contracts. Many others also had conversations with me about the WinRT type system, files, networking, background tasks, sharing, the Windows Store, tiles and toasts, and more. These people include Chris Anthony, Tyler Beam, Manoj Biswas, Arik Cohen, David Fields, Alain Gefflaut, Chris Guzak, Guanghui He, Scott Hoogerwerf, Suhail Khalid, Salahuddin Khan, Nathan Kuchta, Jon Lam, Nancy Perks, Hari Pulapaka, Brent Rector, Jamie Schwartz, Peter Smith, Ben Srour, Adam Stritzel, Henry Tappen, Pedro Teixeira, Dave Thaler, Marc Wautier, Sarah Waskom, and Terue Yoshihara.

As for editing and producing the book, I truly had some fantastic people helping me. Christophe Nasarre, who I've worked with on several book projects, has once again done just a phenomenal job ensuring that technical details are explained accurately. He has truly had a significant impact on the quality of this book. As always, the Microsoft Press team is a pleasure to work with. I'd like to extend a special thank you to Devon Musgrave and Carol Dillingham. Also, thanks to Curt Philips, Roger LeBlanc, and Andrea Fox for their editing and production support.

Errata & book support

We've made every effort to ensure the accuracy of this book and its companion content. Any errors that have been reported since this book was published are listed at:

http://aka.ms/WinRTviaCsharp/errata

If you find an error that is not already listed, you can report it to us through the same page.

If you need additional support, email Microsoft Press Book Support at:

mspinput@microsoft.com.

Please note that product support for Microsoft software is not offered through the addresses above.

We want to hear from you

At Microsoft Press, your satisfaction is our top priority, and your feedback our most valuable asset. Please tell us what you think of this book at:

http://aka.ms/tellpress

The survey is short, and we read every one of your comments and ideas. Thanks in advance for your input!

Stay in touch

Let's keep the conversation going! We're on Twitter: *http://twitter.com/MicrosoftPress*

Core concepts

CHAPTER 1

Windows Runtime primer

The Microsoft Windows operating system (OS) offers many features, which application developers use to simplify building applications. This book explains many of these Windows features and offers guidance and best practices when using them. Windows exposes its features via an application programming interface (API), called the *Windows Runtime* (*WinRT*). WinRT APIs are callable using many programming languages, including JavaScript, native C++, and .NET's C# and Visual Basic. However, in this book, I chose to demonstrate consuming the WinRT APIs via the C# programming language due to C#'s widespread adoption and the productivity gains it provides over the other languages.

The Windows OS supports many application models. For example, Windows supports several client-side application models, including console user interface (CUI) applications and graphical user interface (GUI) applications. It also supports server-side application models for building services, such as Internet Information Server (IIS), SQL Server, and Exchange. Collectively, all these application models are referred to as *desktop apps*. Admittedly, the term *desktop app* is not a great choice because some of these application models have no visible presence on the user's desktop. As of Windows 8, Windows now supports a new client-side GUI application model referred to as *Windows Store apps*. This term is also not ideal because Windows Store apps do not have to be installed by way of the Windows Store; they can be manually installed (side-loaded) via other means for development, testing, or employee usage.

Because the WinRT API is part of the OS, any app built using any of the application models can technically consume the API. However, due to time constraints, Microsoft was not able to test many of the WinRT APIs from desktop apps, so some are not yet sanctioned for use by non–Windows Store apps. Furthermore, Windows Store apps run in a different security context than desktop apps. This security context is called an *app container* (discussed in the appendix, "App containers"), and it restricts which resources a Windows Store app can access. For these reasons, this book focuses heavily on using the WinRT APIs from Windows Store apps. However, note that some of the WinRT APIs described in this book are consumable from desktop apps as well. You should also note that there are some WinRT APIs that are callable only from desktop apps, not Windows Store apps. The MSDN documentation for each WinRT type contains a Requirements section indicating whether the API is callable from desktop apps, Windows Store apps, or both.

While reading the various chapters in this book, keep in mind the principles Microsoft had in mind when designing the Windows Store app model. If you're wondering why a certain feature works the way it does or why a certain feature is missing, most likely it is because it didn't fit in with the principles. As you implement Windows Store apps yourself, you'll need to consider these principles. Here are the principles:

- **Secure**   Windows Store apps cannot access the user's data without the user's permission. This gives the user confidence that an app cannot delete, modify, or upload the user's data to an unknown Internet location. It also means that an app cannot acquire the user's location or record audio or video without the user's consent.

- **Power efficient**   For the most part, Windows Store apps can execute code only when the user is interacting with the app. The OS suspends all threads in the app when the app is in the background. This forbids an app from using system resources (like the CPU, network, and storage) that consume battery power while the app is in the background. Blocking the use of system resources also helps the foreground app remain fast and fluid. WinRT does provide some facilities that allow an app to *look like* is it running while it's in the background. Various chapters of this book explore these facilities.

- **The user is always in control**   Windows Store apps cannot overwrite a user's desires. For example, the user must grant permission for an app to add its tiles to the Start screen or to show a toast notification. The user decides if an app's data can sync between the user's PCs. The user decides which files or folders an app can access. The user decides whether an app can use the network when roaming or when doing so exceeds the user's monthly data limit. Apps cannot decide these things on behalf of the user. The OS itself actively enforces many of these limitations. However, some of them (such as using the network when roaming or going over the user's data limit) are enforced by Windows Store policy. That is, your app will not be certified and placed on the Windows Store if it violates this principle.

- **Isolation**   Windows Store apps are forbidden from affecting the OS or other apps the user has installed. For example, Windows Store apps cannot access data created and maintained by other apps (unless the user grants access via a file picker). Furthermore, apps cannot communicate with other installed apps; all interprocess communication is prohibited. However, Windows Store apps can communicate with other apps via well-defined mechanisms.

- **Confident install, upgrade, and uninstall**   Users can easily discover and install Windows Store apps via the Store app included with Windows. With Windows Store apps, users are confident the app adheres to all these principles. Installed apps remain up to date with the latest bug fixes and features. In addition, users can easily uninstall apps via the Start screen. When uninstalling an app, users are assured the app is fully uninstalled (no leftover directories, files, or registry settings). Moreover, due to app isolation, uninstalling an app cannot negatively affect the OS or other installed apps. Furthermore, unlike desktop apps, which can be installed only by an administrator, Windows Store apps are installable by a standard user.

- **Simplified app management**   Historically, desktop apps have many usability problems. These are largely because a user can run multiple instances of an app, each with its own window. For example, when a user is tapping on an app's icon, should the system launch a new instance of the app or bring the already running instance to the foreground? And, if the app has multiple instances running, which instance should come to the foreground? Exacerbating the problem, users sometimes forget that an app is running if its window is obscured by another app's window. On the other hand, Windows Store apps are always single instance, so selecting the app launches it if it's not running or brings it to the foreground if it is.

Another problem with desktop apps is that the user must decide which app to terminate if the system is running low on memory. But the user doesn't know which app is consuming the most amount of memory. To fix this problem, users never have to close a Windows Store app. The system can terminate the app automatically if memory is running low, and the system can automatically relaunch the app if the user switches back to it. Also, the system automatically terminates an app if the user upgrades the app to a new version or uninstalls the app. To help make this experience seamless for the user, you (the app developer) must do some additional work in your code. (See Chapter 3, "Process model.")

- **Fast and fluid**   Windows Store apps always respond immediately to user input so that the user always feels in control of the app and has a pleasant experience with it.

- **Content over chrome**   Windows Store apps tend to have a touch-optimized user interface that emphasizes its content over chrome (menus, toolbars, frames, and so on). This affords the user an immersive experience with the app and its data.

- **Device flexibility**   Windows and apps built for it get to enjoy a wide variety of hardware devices. This allows users to purchase PCs that work right for them. Windows supports three CPU architectures (ARM, x86, and x64), as well as PCs with varying amounts of RAM, storage, and display resolution. Windows PCs also support a large set of other peripherals, including local area network (LAN), wide area network (WAN), and mobile network adapters, cameras, scanners, printers, game controllers, and so on.

Note Any app that must violate one or more of these principles should not use the Windows Store application model. For example, apps that need to affect the OS and other apps—such as debuggers and other system tools and utilities—must be implemented as desktop apps.

Note When Windows is running on a PC with an ARM CPU, we call that PC a *Windows RT PC*. On a Windows RT PC, users can install only Windows Store apps or desktop apps signed by Microsoft's Windows division (like Task Manager, Microsoft Office apps, or Visual Studio's Remote Debugging tools[1]). Developers frequently ask me why they cannot install their own desktop apps on a Windows RT PC. The reason for this goes back to all the principles listed. Because desktop apps do not adhere to the principles, a desktop app could compromise the PC, thereby breaking user confidence, weakening security, hurting system responsiveness, and wasting battery power. By preventing the installation of arbitrary desktop apps on a Windows RT PC, Microsoft is assuring users that their Windows RT PC will be an excellent user experience over the lifetime of the PC.

---

[1] For more information about remote debugging, see *http://msdn.microsoft.com/en-us/library/vstudio/y7f5zaaa.aspx*.

To comply with many of the principles, Windows Store apps are created and deployed as self-contained package files (ZIP files), as discussed in Chapter 2, "App packaging and deployment." Everything an app needs to run has to be in this package. Because the package is a completely self-contained deployment unit, it includes all necessary dependencies. When a user installs an app, Windows automatically deploys its dependencies in the same directory. Hence, another app that needs the same component or dependency gets its own copy in its own directory.

Package files contain an XML manifest file describing how the app integrates into the system. This file specifies what capabilities (system resources)—such as storage locations, network access, location, webcam, and so on—the app desires. Before installing an app, the user is shown what capabilities the app desires and the user decides whether to install the app or not. The app also declares in the manifest file the various ways the system can activate the app. For example, an app declares that it can be activated to run code in the background, process certain file types or protocols, or accept shared data. Chapter 3 explains how an app supports these various activations.

When installing an app's package, the system parses the XML file and integrates the app into the system. When uninstalling the app, the system parses the XML file again and undoes the integration. By taking full control of app install and uninstall, Windows ensures that uninstall leaves no files, subdirectories, or registry keys behind and also ensures that no part of the system or another app depends on a component or setting that has been removed.

Microsoft's vision is that the Windows Runtime offers one unified programming model, allowing developers to write apps for any Windows device, including phones, tablets, notebook PCs, desktop PCs, server PCs, Xbox, and even large devices like Microsoft PixelSense. Unifying the programming model for all these devices takes time, and Microsoft fully admits that it has a long way to go. While this book does not focus on Windows Phone or Xbox directly, it is my hope that the content of this book will help you if you decide to target any of these other devices.

Windows Store app technology stacks

Figure 1-1 shows the three technology stacks you can use to create a Windows Store app. The bottom of the figure shows a large rectangle titled "Windows." This box indicates the various features that Windows exposes to developers. On the right, the "Win32 and COM" box represents APIs that have shipped with Windows for many versions now; these technologies continue to ship in order to support desktop apps. The Win32 and COM APIs are old and complicated. Furthermore, they were designed to be used by native C/C++ developers. The WinRT box on the left represents the new WinRT APIs. WinRT is a modern, simple, and object-oriented API designed for use by many programming languages. By the way, the boxes are not shown to scale: there are far more Win32 and COM APIs than there are WinRT APIs.

Technically speaking, all the Win32, COM, and WinRT APIs are callable from both desktop apps as well as Windows Store apps. However, the WinRT APIs are simpler and easier to use, so you should use them whenever possible. And although a Windows Store app can call any Win32 or COM API, many of them will fail due to the app container's security context. Other Win32 and COM APIs should not be called because their use violates the principles presented earlier. In fact, Microsoft created an approved list of Win32 and COM APIs that a Windows Store app is allowed to use. (See *http://msdn. microsoft.com/en-us/library/windows/apps/br205757.*) If your Windows Store app uses any Win32 or COM API not on the approved list, your app will fail Windows Store certification.

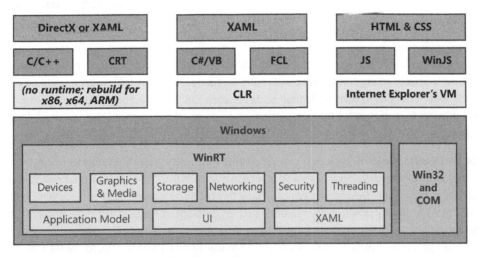

FIGURE 1-1 Window Store app technology stacks.

> **Note** I find it very useful to call some unapproved Win32 and COM APIs during app development. For example, I sometimes call the Win32 MessageBeep API during development so that I can hear when a particular location in my code executes. Then, before I submit my app to the Windows Store for certification, I remove the calls to these APIs.

The main purpose of an operating system is to abstract hardware devices to the application developer. For example, a PC can store files on a hard disk, an SSD drive, a USB drive, a DVD, a network share, and so on. The OS abstraction for this is a file, and an app developer can simply write code that opens a file and reads its contents. The app developer doesn't have to know what kind of hardware device contains the file and how to communicate with that device. If you look closely at the WinRT APIs, you'll see that many of them are about abstracting hardware devices—although there are a few APIs (like the Application Model APIs) related to managing your app within the system.

Microsoft supports three different technology stacks that developers can use to build Windows Store apps: native C/C++, .NET (C# and Visual Basic), and JavaScript. Each technology stack has its own programming language, supporting class libraries, presentation layer, and optionally an execution engine or virtual machine. Now, let me explain each technology stack (as shown in Figure 1-1):

- **Native C/C++** Developers can call WinRT APIs to leverage OS features using native C/C++. These developers also can leverage various C and C++ runtime libraries in their code.

However, not all C runtime (CRT) functions are available for Windows Store apps. See *http://msdn.microsoft.com/en-us/library/windows/apps/jj606124.aspx* for more information. For the app's presentation layer, C/C++ developers can use DirectX APIs (for high-performance graphics) or WinRT's XAML APIs (for forms-based) apps.[2] In fact, a single app can use DirectX and XAML together; see *http://msdn.microsoft.com/en-us/library/windows/apps/hh825871.aspx*. DirectX offers Direct2D and Direct3D libraries while XAML provides support for basic 2D primitives and effects.

Developers typically use this technology stack when they're concerned about conserving memory and improving performance. Probably the most common scenario in which native C/C++ is used is when developers build real-time games. Because C/C++ is compiled to native code, developers must recompile their code for each CPU architecture they want to support, create a package for each CPU architecture, and submit all packages to the Windows Store for certification.[3]

- **C# and Visual Basic**   Developers can call WinRT APIs to leverage OS features using C# or Visual Basic. These developers can also leverage a small subset of the .NET Framework Class Library in their code. Developers typically take this path to increase their productivity because .NET provides many productivity features, such as garbage collection, runtime-enforced type safety, reflection, Language Integrated Query (LINQ), regular expression parsing, and so on.[4] For the app's user interface, .NET developers can use WinRT's XAML APIs to create forms-based apps. .NET developers can also use P/Invoke to call DirectX APIs if they want more control over the UI with high performance.[5]

  If you have your project's Build Platform Target value set to *AnyCPU* (the default when you create a new project), the resulting EXE or DLL file is not tied to a specific CPU architecture (assuming you're not dependent on any CPU-specific libraries or SDKs). This allows you to create and submit to the Windows Store a single package capable of running on all CPU architectures.

- **JavaScript**   Developers can call WinRT APIs to leverage OS features using JavaScript and a Microsoft-provided JavaScript library called *WinJS*. This library encapsulates a lot of base functionality, such as application model, promises (for asynchronous function calls), data binding, and some UI controls. Developers also can leverage many existing JavaScript libraries (like jQuery) in their code. For the app's presentation layer, JavaScript developers can use HTML and CSS to create forms-based apps. Developers typically take this path if they are already familiar with JavaScript, HTML, and CSS, so they have only the WinRT APIs to learn in order to build a Windows Store app.

---

[2] Ultimately, all apps draw to their window via DirectX. WinRT's XAML APIs offer buttons, grid views, toggles, text boxes, and so on. All of these are just abstractions built on top of DirectX.

[3] Technically, you need to compile only for ARM and x86, because x86 can run as is on x64 CPUs.

[4] For a complete list of the .NET APIs usable within a Windows Store app, see *http://msdn.microsoft.com/en-us/library/windows/apps/br230232.aspx*.

[5] There are some .NET libraries available that wrap DirectX APIs, such as *http://SharpDX.org/* and *http://SlimDX.org/*.

JavaScript developers embed their source code into their package file when submitting it for Windows Store certification. Because the source code is just text, it is CPU agnostic; therefore, only one package file needs to be submitted. At runtime, Microsoft's Internet Explorer virtual machine parses the source code, allowing it to run on all the CPU architectures. The HTML and CSS are ultimately translated into DirectX, which is how the app's forms-based UI is shown to the user.[6]

Developers commonly ask which language or framework is the best one to use when building a Windows Store app. For the most part, Microsoft encourages developers to use what they already know. The WinRT API is equally exposed to the three technology stacks, but there are reasons you might prefer one stack over another:

- **Performance** Although .NET and JavaScript have a runtime with conveniences such as garbage collection and runtime compilers, C++ does not. For most situations, the performance penalty of these runtimes is negligible—especially if you understand how the runtime and the interoperability layer work. However, at times this can become a determining factor. For example, you can write simple canvas games in HTML and JavaScript; but, for real-time action games, C++ and DirectX is frequently a better choice.

- **Legacy and third-party code** You might choose a technology stack because you already have some existing code written in a particular language. You can deploy a library or component privately inside your Windows Store app's package, and that code will run inside your app's app container. This means it has to abide by the same principles and it won't be able to make any Win32 or .NET calls that are not on the approved list.

- **Sharing** You might choose a technology stack because you want to write code once and share it across different apps. For example, you might write code in C# because you want to use the same logic in a Windows Store app as well as in an a Windows Phone or ASP.NET app, or you might choose JavaScript to share code in a Windows Store app and on a webpage.

- **Framework support** Each technology stack has strengths in different areas. For example, if you need to process a lot of XML, .NET is a good choice because of its LINQ-to-XML support. Similarly, C++ allows the use of STL or BOOST libraries and JavaScript allows the use of jQuery libraries, simplifying HTML document manipulations.

- **IP protection** Windows Store apps written in JavaScript ship the actual source code (.js files) inside the package. This means that the source code files end up on the user's system where savvy users can find them and explore their contents, although Windows will not load the application if any of its files are modified. Similarly, .NET apps ship with assemblies whose Intermediate Language (IL) can easily be decompiled. This is nothing new for .NET apps. C++ code is compiled to machine language, which is the most difficult to reverse engineer.

---

[6] Windows Store apps written in JavaScript, HTML, and CSS run in an environment that is a superset of Internet Explorer's environment. So Windows Store apps have access to more features than a normal website. See *http://msdn.microsoft.com/en-us/library/windows/apps/hh465143.aspx* for more information.

The Windows Runtime type system

The WinRT APIs that ship as part of Windows are all written in native C/C++, which makes sense for platform code because it has to be fast and use as little memory as possible. However, these WinRT APIs are callable from C/C++, C#, Visual Basic, and JavaScript. To call WinRT APIs from all these languages, a small and simple type system had to be defined. This type system must use features available to all consuming programming languages. Here are the core concepts you need to know to consume the Windows Runtime type system from C#:

- **Common base type**   WinRT components do not share a common base class. When using a WinRT component from C#, the Common Language Runtime (CLR) makes the component look like it is derived from `System.Object`; therefore, you can pass it around throughout your code. In addition, all WinRT components inherit `System.Object`'s public methods like `ToString`, `GetHashCode`, `Equals`, and `GetType`; so all these methods are callable on WinRT objects. Because WinRT components are implemented as extended COM objects, internally, the CLR uses Runtime Callable Wrappers (RCWs) to access them. Invoking an RCW's members cause a managed-to-native code transition, which incurs some performance overhead.

- **Core data types**   The WinRT type system supports the core data types, such as Booleans; unsigned bytes;[7] 16-bit, 32-bit, and 64-bit signed and unsigned integer numbers; single-precision and double-precision floating-point numbers; 16-bit characters; strings;[8] and void. As in the CLR, all other data types are composed from these core data types. For a complete list, see *http://msdn.microsoft.com/en-us/library/br205768(v=vs.85).aspx*.

- **Classes**   WinRT is an object-oriented type system, meaning that WinRT components support data abstraction, inheritance, and polymorphism.[9] However, some languages (like JavaScript) do not support type inheritance. To cater to these languages, almost no WinRT components

---

[7] Signed byte is not supported.

[8] You cannot pass `null` to a WinRT component expecting a `String`. Attempting to do so throws an `ArgumentNullException`. However, you can pass `String.Empty`.

[9] Data abstraction is actually enforced because WinRT classes are not allowed to have public fields.

take advantage of inheritance. This means they also do not take advantage of polymorphism. In fact, only WinRT components consumable from non-JavaScript languages leverage inheritance and polymorphism. For the WinRT components that ship with Windows, only the XAML components (for building user interfaces) take advantage of inheritance and polymorphism. Applications written in JavaScript use HTML and CSS to produce their user interface instead.

- **Structures** WinRT supports structures (value types). Unlike CLR value types, WinRT structures can have only public fields of the core data types or of another WinRT structure.[10]

- **Enumerations** WinRT supports two kinds of enumerations. An enumeration can be a signed 32-bit integer with mutually exclusive values or an unsigned 32-bit integer with bit flags that can be OR'd together.

- **Interfaces** WinRT internally uses an extended version of COM, which requires interfaces to describe APIs. Then classes implement one or more interfaces. For this reason, C# developers interact with interfaces more when working with WinRT types than they usually do when working with .NET types.

In addition, the WinRT type system supports delegates, methods, properties (but not indexer properties), events, exceptions, and arrays (single-dimension, 0-based only). It also allows collections created in one language to be passed to and accessed from another language. For more information about the Windows Runtime type system, see my *CLR via C#, Fourth Edition* book (Microsoft Press, 2012). In Chapter 25, "Interoperating with WinRT Components," I explain how to define your own WinRT components in C# and consume them from other languages, such as C++ or JavaScript.

> **Note** The Windows Runtime type system is all about interoperating across programming languages. It has limitations required to perform this cross-language communication. Once across a language barrier, there are no restrictions. For example, although Windows Runtime classes cannot expose public fields, C# code consumed by other .NET code can certainly create classes with public fields.

Windows Runtime type-system projections

How is it possible for the various programming languages to know about and call WinRT APIs? There must be some description of the APIs consumable by all the languages. In the .NET Framework, code written in one language can interoperate with types written in a different language because of *metadata*. The metadata is programming-language-agnostic information that describes types and their members. Microsoft's WinRT team uses the same metadata format (ECMA-335) created by Microsoft's .NET team. That is, the Windows SDK ships with a DLL containing metadata describing all the WinRT components that ship with Windows itself. This DLL has a WinMD file extension (which stands for

---

[10] Enumerations are OK because they are really just 32-bit integers.

Windows MetaData), and Visual Studio automatically adds a reference to this WinMD file when you create a new Windows Store app project. The WinMD file is typically found here:

%WindowsSdkDir%\References\CommonConfiguration\Neutral\Windows.WinMD.

Because this file is just like a normal .NET assembly, you can use standard .NET utilities (such as ILDasm.exe or Reflector.exe) to open this file and explore its contents. Of course, because the WinRT APIs are written in native code, this WinMD file does not contain any IL code; it contains only metadata.

When compiling a native C/C++ app, the compiler itself parses the Windows.WinMD file, making the WinRT APIs callable to native C/C++ apps. Similarly, when developing a C# or Visual Basic app, the compiler parses the Windows.WinMD file, ensuring that our code calls the WinRT APIs correctly. At runtime, the CLR uses different WinMD files installed in the %WinDir%\System32\WinMetadata directory. Having separate, smaller WinMD files at runtime decreases the memory needed by apps because few apps (if any) will use all of Windows' WinRT components. When running a JavaScript app, Internet Explorer's virtual machine (VM) also parses the WinMD files, making the WinRT APIs callable to JavaScript code.

What's happening here is that the C++ compiler, the C# and Visual Basic compilers, the CLR, and Internet Explorer's VM are all parsing the same WinMD files and then they *project* the APIs using the Windows Runtime type system as if they were implemented using the C/C++ type system, the CLR's type system, or the JavaScript type system, respectively. This way, the developer consuming the WinRT APIs has a familiar and natural experience when working with the APIs. Let's look at an example. Here is some C# code that calls WinRT APIs to open a file and read its contents:

```
using System;          // .NET Framework Class Library
using Windows.Storage; // Most Windows.* namespaces are for WinRT APIs
using Windows.UI.Popups;

private async void ReadText() {
    var filename = "MyFile.txt";
    StorageFolder folder = ApplicationData.Current.LocalFolder;
    StorageFile file = await folder.GetFileAsync(filename);
    String text = await FileIO.ReadTextAsync(file);
    MessageDialog dialog = new MessageDialog(text, "File's Text");
    await dialog.ShowAsync();
}
```

You don't need to understand what this code actually does. What is important to understand is that this code uses lots of WinRT APIs (StorageFolder, StorageFile, ApplicationData, FileIO, and MessageDialog) but the code looks like you're just consuming ordinary .NET types.

Mario

ORDER # 785687

ate: 3/7/2018
me: 2:16:29 PM

----

22 SPECIAL BENTO A

Here's the same function written in native C++:

```
using namespace Windows::Storage;
using namespace Windows::UI::Popups;

void SimpleSampleCx::MainPage::ReadText() {
    auto filename = "MyFile.txt";
    create_task(ApplicationData::Current->LocalFolder->GetFileAsync(filename))
        .then([this](StorageFile^ file)             {
            create_task(FileIO::ReadTextAsync(file)).then([this](String^ txt) {
                MessageDialog^ dialog = ref new MessageDialog(txt, "File's Text");
                dialog->ShowAsync();
            });
        });
}
```

Readers familiar with C++/CLI might think this is actually managed code because it is using `ref new` and `^`. It is not. The syntax used is called *C++ Component eXtensions*, or C++/CX. It is a set of extensions to the C++ language, making it syntactically easy to invoke WinRT APIs.[11]

And here's the same function written in JavaScript:

```
function readText() {
    var filename = 'MyText.txt';
    var localFolder = Windows.Storage.ApplicationData.current.localFolder;
    localFolder.getFileAsync(filename).then( function(file){
        Windows.Storage.FileIO.readTextAsync(file).then( function(txt){
            var dialog = new Windows.UI.Popups.MessageDialog(txt, "File's Text");
            dialog.showAsync();
        })
    });
}
```

Notice that in JavaScript the first letter of the WinRT methods start with a lowercase letter (like `getFileAsync`). This is how the Internet Explorer VM projects the WinRT API methods to the JavaScript developer. This gives the developer a natural experience because initial lowercase letters is a standard convention in JavaScript. For .NET developers, there are two kinds of projections:

- **CLR projections**   CLR projections are mappings performed implicitly by the CLR, usually related to reinterpreting metadata. For example, the CLR makes all WinRT components look like they're derived from `System.Object` (as mentioned earlier). Other WinRT types already have well-known .NET types that .NET developers are familiar with. These types (some of which are listed in Table 1-1) are converted back and forth between .NET and WinRT and, frequently, the .NET projection of the type has more features (methods and properties) than the WinRT equivalent. For example, WinRT defines a `System.Foundation.Uri` type; but to .NET developers, this is exposed as the familiar `System.Uri` type.[12]

---

11   It's possible to invoke WinRT APIs without using C++/CX using the Windows Runtime C++ Template Library (WRL). For more information, see *http://msdn.microsoft.com/en-us/library/windows/apps/hh438466(v=vs.120).aspx*.

12   If you compare Windows.Foundation.winmd between IlDasm and ILDasm /project, you can see that the CLR projection hides `IClosable` by making it `private`. Also, `Windows.Storage.Streams.IInputStream` (Windows.Storage.winmd) inherits from `IClosable` before projection and from `IDisposable` after.

TABLE 1-1 WinRT types and their corresponding .NET type projection.

WinRT namespace	WinRT type	.NET namespace	.NET type	.NET assembly
Windows.Foundation.Metadata	AttributeUsageAttribute	System	AttributeUsageAttribute	System.Runtime.dll
Windows.Foundation.Metadata	AttributeTargets	System	AttributeTargets	System.Runtime.dll
Windows.UI	Color	Windows.UI	Color	System.Runtime.WindowsRuntime.dll
Windows.Foundation	DateTime	System	DateTimeOffset	System.Runtime.dll
Windows.Foundation	EventHandler<T>	System	EventHandler<T>	System.Runtime.dll
Windows.Foundation	EventRegistrationToken	System.Runtime.Interop-Services.WindowsRuntime	EventRegistrationToken	System.Runtime.Interop-Services.WindowsRuntime.dll
Windows.Foundation	Hresult	System	Exception	System.Runtime.dll
Windows.Foundation	IReference<T>	System	Nullable<T>	System.Runtime.dll
Windows.Foundation	Point	Windows.Foundation	Point	System.Runtime.WindowsRuntime.dll
Windows.Foundation	Rect	Windows.Foundation	Rect	System.Runtime.WindowsRuntime.dll
Windows.Foundation	Size	Windows.Foundation	Size	System.Runtime.WindowsRuntime.dll
Windows.Foundation	TimeSpan	System	TimeSpan	System.Runtime.dll
Windows.Foundation	Uri	System	Uri	System.Runtime.dll
Windows.Foundation	IClosable	System	IDisposable	System.Runtime.dll
Windows.Foundation.Collections	IIterable<T>	System.Collections.Generic	IEnumerable<T>	System.Runtime.dll
Windows.Foundation.Collections	IVector<T>	System.Collections.Generic	IList<T>	System.Runtime.dll
Windows.Foundation.Collections	IVectorView<T>	System.Collections.Generic	IReadOnlyList<T>	System.Runtime.dll
Windows.Foundation.Collections	IMap<K, V>	System.Collections.Generic	IDictionary<TKey, TValue>	System.Runtime.dll
Windows.Foundation.Collections	IMapView<K, V>	System.Collections.Generic	IReadOnlyDictionary<TKey, TValue>	System.Runtime.dll
Windows.Foundation.Collections	IKeyValuePair<K, V>	System.Collections.Generic	KeyValuePair<TKey, TValue>	System.Runtime.dll
Windows.UI.Xaml.Input	ICommand	Windows.UI.Xaml.Input	ICommand	System.ObjectModel.dll
Windows.UI.Xaml.Interop	IBindableIterable	System.Collections	IEnumerable	System.Runtime.dll
Windows.UI.Xaml.Interop	IBindableVector	System.Collections	IList	System.Runtime.dll

WinRT namespace	WinRT type	.NET namespace	.NET type	.NET assembly
Windows.UI.Xaml.Interop	INotifyCollectionChanged	System.Collections.Specialized	INotifyCollectionChanged	System.ObjectModel.dll
Windows.UI.Xaml.Interop	NotifyCollection-ChangedEventHandler	System.Collections.Specialized	NotifyCollection-ChangedEventHandler	System.ObjectModel.dll
Windows.UI.Xaml.Interop	NotifyCollection-ChangedEventArgs	System.Collections.Specialized	NotifyCollection-ChangedEventArgs	System.ObjectModel.dll
Windows.UI.Xaml.Interop	NotifyCollectionChangedAction	System.Collections.Specialized	NotifyCollection-ChangedAction	System.ObjectModel.dll
Windows.UI.Xaml.Data	INotifyPropertyChanged	System.ComponentModel	INotifyPropertyChanged	System.ObjectModel.dll
Windows.UI.Xaml.Data	PropertyChangedEventHandler	System.ComponentModel	PropertyChangedEventHandler	System.ObjectModel.dll
Windows.UI.Xaml.Data	PropertyChangedEventArgs	System.ComponentModel	PropertyChangedEventArgs	System.ObjectModel.dll
Windows.UI.Xaml	CornerRadius	Windows.UI.Xaml	CornerRadius	System.Runtime.WindowsRuntime.UI.Xaml.dll
Windows.UI.Xaml	Duration	Windows.UI.Xaml	Duration	System.Runtime.WindowsRuntime.UI.Xaml.dll
Windows.UI.Xaml	GridUnitType	Windows.UI.Xaml	DurationType	System.Runtime.WindowsRuntime.UI.Xaml.dll
Windows.UI.Xaml	GridLength	Windows.UI.Xaml	GridLength	System.Runtime.WindowsRuntime.UI.Xaml.dll
Windows.UI.Xaml	GridUnitType	Windows.UI.Xaml	GridUnitType	System.Runtime.WindowsRuntime.UI.Xaml.dll
Windows.UI.Xaml	Thickness	Windows.UI.Xaml	Thickness	System.Runtime.WindowsRuntime.UI.Xaml.dll
Windows.UI.Xaml.Interop	TypeName	System	Type	System.Runtime.dll
Windows.UI.Xaml.Controls.Primitives	GeneratorPosition	Windows.UI.Xaml.Controls.Primitives	GeneratorPosition	System.Runtime.WindowsRuntime.UI.Xaml.dll
Windows.UI.Xaml.Media	Matrix	Windows.UI.Xaml.Media	Matrix	System.Runtime.WindowsRuntime.UI.Xaml.dll
Windows.UI.Xaml.Media.Animation	KeyTime	Windows.UI.Xaml.Media.Animation	KeyTime	System.Runtime.WindowsRuntime.UI.Xaml.dll
Windows.UI.Xaml.Media.Animation	RepeatBehavior	Windows.UI.Xaml.Media.Animation	RepeatBehavior	System.Runtime.WindowsRuntime.UI.Xaml.dll
Windows.UI.Xaml.Media.Animation	RepeatBehaviorType	Windows.UI.Xaml.Media.Animation	RepeatBehaviorType	System.Runtime.WindowsRuntime.UI.Xaml.dll
Windows.UI.Xaml.Media.Media3D	Matrix3D	Windows.UI.Xaml.Media.3D	Matrix3D	System.Runtime.WindowsRuntime.UI.Xaml.dll

- **Framework projections**   Framework projections are mappings performed explicitly in your code by leveraging new APIs introduced in .NET Framework Class Library. Framework projections are required when the impedance mismatch between the WinRT type system and the CLR's type system is too great for the CLR to do it implicitly. Framework projections are used for asynchronous programming (discussed later in this chapter) and when working with streams and data buffers (discussed in Chapter 6, "Stream input and output").

Calling asynchronous WinRT APIs from .NET code

When a thread performs an I/O operation synchronously, the thread can block for an indefinite amount of time. When a GUI thread blocks for an I/O operation to complete, the application's user interface stops responding to user input—such as touch, mouse, and stylus events—causing the user to get frustrated with the application. To keep apps responsive, WinRT components that perform I/O operations expose the functionality via asynchronous APIs exclusively. In fact, WinRT components that perform compute operations also expose this functionality via asynchronous APIs exclusively if the CPU operation could take greater than 50 milliseconds. For more information about building responsive applications, see Part V, "Threading," of *CLR via C#, Fourth Edition* by Jeffrey Richter.

Because the WinRT APIs are mostly about abstracting hardware, many APIs perform I/O operations; therefore, many WinRT APIs are asynchronous. So, for you to be productive with them requires that you understand how to work with them from C#. To understand it, examine the following code:

```
public static void WinRTAsyncIntro() {
    IAsyncOperation<StorageFile> asyncOp = KnownFolders.MusicLibrary.GetFileAsync("Song.mp3");
    asyncOp.Completed = OpCompleted;
    // Optional: call asyncOp.Cancel() sometime later
}

// NOTE: Callback method executes via GUI or thread pool thread:
private static void OpCompleted(IAsyncOperation<StorageFile> asyncOp, AsyncStatus status) {
    if (status == AsyncStatus.Canceled) {
        // Process cancellation...
    } else {
        try {
            StorageFile file = asyncOp.GetResults();  // Throws if operation failed
            // Process result (do something with file)...
        }
        catch (Exception ex) {
            // Process exception...
        }
    }
    asyncOp.Close();
}
```

The WinRTAsyncIntro method invokes the WinRT GetFileAsync method to find a file in the user's music library. All WinRT APIs that perform asynchronous operations are named with the Async suffix, and they all return an object whose type implements a WinRT IAsyncXxx interface—in this example, an IAsyncOperation<TResult> interface where TResult is the WinRT StorageFile type. This object, whose reference I put in an asyncOp variable, represents the pending asynchronous operation. Your code must somehow receive notification when the pending operation completes. To do this, you must implement a callback method (OpCompleted in my example), create a delegate to it, and assign the delegate to the asyncOp's Completed property. Now, when the operation completes, the callback method is invoked via some thread (not necessarily the GUI thread). If the operation completed before assigning the delegate to the OnCompleted property, the system invokes the callback as soon as possible. In other words, there is a race condition here, but the object implementing the IAsyncXxx interface resolves the race for you, ensuring that your code works correctly.

As noted at the end of the WinRTAsyncIntro method, you can optionally call a Cancel method offered by all IAsyncXxx interfaces if you want to cancel the pending operation. All asynchronous operations complete for one of three possible reasons: the operation runs to completion successfully, the operation is explicitly canceled, or the operation results in a failure. When the operation completes due to any of these reasons, the system invokes the callback method, passing it a reference to the same object that the original XxxAsync method returned and an AsyncStatus. In my OnCompleted method, I examine the status parameter and either process the result due to the successful completion, handle the explicit cancellation, or handle the failure.[13] Also, note that after processing the operation's completion, the IAsyncXxx interface object should be cleaned up by calling its Close method.

Figure 1-2 shows the various WinRT IAsyncXxx interfaces. The four main interfaces all derive from the IAsyncInfo interface. The two IAsyncAction interfaces expose a GetResults method with a void return type. If the operation failed, this method throws an exception that you can catch, allowing your error-recovery code to execute. The two IAsyncOperation interfaces expose a GetResults method with a non-void return type. Calling this method returns the result of the operation or throws an exception if the operation failed.

The two IAsyncXxxWithProgress interfaces allow your code to receive periodic progress updates as the asynchronous operation is progressing through its work. Most asynchronous operations do not offer progress updates, but some do (like background downloading and uploading, which are discussed in Chapter 7, "Networking"). To receive periodic progress updates, you define another callback method in your code, create a delegate that refers to it, and assign the delegate to the IAsyncXxxWithProgress object's Progress property. When your callback method is invoked, it is passed an argument whose type matches the generic TProgress type. We'll show an example of this in the "Cancellation and progress" section.

---

[13] The IAsyncInfo interface offers a Status property that contains the same value that is passed into the callback method's status parameter. Because the parameter is passed by value, your application's performance is better if you access the parameter rather than querying IAsyncInfo's Status property. This is because querying the property invokes a WinRT API via an RCW.

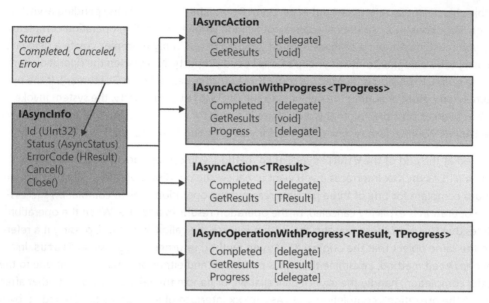

FIGURE 1-2 WinRT's interfaces related to performing asynchronous I/O and compute operations.

Simplifying the calling of asynchronous methods

In the .NET Framework, we use types in the `System.Threading.Tasks` namespace to perform asynchronous operations. In addition, C# offers the async and await keywords, allowing you to perform asynchronous operations by using a sequential programming model, thereby simplifying your code substantially. We'll now look at how C# developers work with asynchronous WinRT APIs.

The following code is a rewrite of the `WinRTAsyncIntro` method shown earlier. However, this version leverages some framework projections (extension methods) supplied with the .NET Framework Class Library. This code does not show progress reporting (because `GetFileAsync` doesn't offer it) and also ignores cancellation:

```
using System;    // Required for framework projection extension methods defined
                 // by the WindowsRuntimeSystemExtensions class
...
// NOTE: If invoked by a GUI thread, all code executes via that GUI thread:
public async static void WinRTAsyncIntro() {
   try {
      StorageFile file = await KnownFolders.MusicLibrary.GetFileAsync("Song.mp3");
      // TODO: Completed code
   }
   catch (SomeOtherException ex) {
      // Error code
   }
}
```

What's happening here is that the use of C#'s await operator causes the compiler to look for a `GetAwaiter` method on the `IAsyncOperation<StorageFile>` interface returned from the

GetFileAsync method. This interface doesn't provide a GetAwaiter method, so the compiler looks for an extension method. Fortunately, the .NET Framework team has provided a bunch of extension methods that are callable when you have one of WinRT's IAsyncXxx interfaces:

```
namespace System {
    public static class WindowsRuntimeSystemExtensions {
        public static TaskAwaiter GetAwaiter(
            this IAsyncAction source);
        public static TaskAwaiter GetAwaiter<TProgress>(
            this IAsyncActionWithProgress<TProgress> source);
        public static TaskAwaiter<TResult> GetAwaiter<TResult>(
            this IAsyncOperation<TResult> source);
        public static TaskAwaiter<TResult> GetAwaiter<TResult, TProgress>(
            this IAsyncOperationWithProgress<TResult, TProgress> source);
    }
}
```

Internally, all these methods construct a TaskCompletionSource and tell the IAsyncXxx object to invoke a callback that sets the TaskCompletionSource's final state when the asynchronous operation completes. The TaskAwaiter object returned from these extension methods is ultimately what C# awaits. When the asynchronous operation completes, the TaskAwaiter object ensures that the code continues executing via the SynchronizationContext that is associated with the original thread. If the calling thread is a GUI thread, this ensures that the code after the await executes via the same GUI thread, allowing the UI to be updated correctly; there's no need to deal with CoreDispatcher objects and writing code that marshals callback methods back to the GUI thread.

Then the thread executes the C# compiler–generated code, which queries the TaskCompletion-Source's Task's Result property, which returns the result (a StorageFile in my example) or throws some other exception if a failure occurred.

Cancellation and progress

What I've just shown is the common scenario of calling an asynchronous WinRT API and discovering its outcome. However, the preceding code ignored cancellation and progress updates. To properly handle cancellation and progress updates, instead of having the compiler implicitly call one of the GetAwaiter extension methods shown earlier, you instead explicitly call one of the AsTask extension methods that the WindowsRuntimeSystemExtensions class also defines:

```
namespace System {
    public static class WindowsRuntimeSystemExtensions {
        public static Task AsTask<TProgress>(this IAsyncActionWithProgress<TProgress> source,
            CancellationToken cancellationToken, IProgress<TProgress> progress);

        public static Task<TResult> AsTask<TResult, TProgress>(
            this IAsyncOperationWithProgress<TResult, TProgress> source,
            CancellationToken cancellationToken, IProgress<TProgress> progress);

        // Simpler overloads not shown here
    }
}
```

So now, we can add cancellation and progress. Here's how to call an asynchronous WinRT API and fully leverage cancellation and progress for those times when you need these enhancements:

```
using System;          // For WindowsRuntimeSystemExtensions's AsTask
using System.Threading;      // For CancellationTokenSource

internal sealed class MyClass {
    private CancellationTokenSource m_cts = new CancellationTokenSource();

    // NOTE: If invoked by a GUI thread, all code executes via that GUI thread:
    private async void MappingWinRTAsyncToDotNet(WinRTType someWinRTObj) {
        try {
            // Assume XxxAsync returns IAsyncOperationWithProgress<IBuffer, UInt32>
            IBuffer result = await someWinRTObj.XxxAsync(...)
                .AsTask(m_cts.Token, new Progress<UInt32>(ProgressReport));
            // TODO: Completed code
        }
        catch (TaskCanceledException) { // Derived from OperationCanceledException
            // TODO: Cancel code
        }
        catch (SomeOtherException) {
            // TODO: Error code
        }
    }

    private void ProgressReport(UInt32 progress) {
        // Update progress code
    }

    public void Cancel() { m_cts.Cancel(); } // Called sometime later to cancel
}
```

There are two additional points worth mentioning. First, if you don't care which thread executes the code after an await, you can improve your app's performance by calling Task's ConfigureAwait method, passing in false for the continueOnCapturedContext parameter. Second, there are a few scenarios where you might want to call an asynchronous method and then block the calling thread until the operation completes. These scenarios include calling asynchronous methods in a constructor (which you really should avoid to guarantee quick construction and reduce the chances of an exception), a property (which you also should avoid for the same reasons), or any method where the execution of code cannot continue until the operation is complete. For example, you will sometimes need to call an asynchronous method from inside a callback method, a method overriding a virtual method, or a method implementing an interface method. If you mark the method as async, the code that called your method can continue execution before the asynchronous method completes, and this is frequently undesirable. You'll see examples of this in Chapter 3, "Process model," and Chapter 9, "Background tasks." In addition, you can mark a method as async only if the method's return type is Task, Task<TResult>, or void. Because many delegate, virtual, and interface method signatures do not have one of these return types, you *must* block the thread if your method's implementation calls an asynchronous method.

Here is an example of the proper way to call a WinRT asynchronous method and then block the thread until the operation completes:

```
StorageFile file = KnownFolders.MusicLibrary.GetFileAsync("Song.mp3")
   .AsTask() GetAwaiter().GetResult();
```

The AsTask method converts the returned object into a .NET Task (or Task<TResult>) object. Then the GetAwaiter method returns a TaskAwaiter object that knows how to wait for the operation to complete. Its GetResult method blocks the calling thread until the operation completes, and then it either returns the result or throws an exception if the operation failed.

Although you could write the code like this, you should not:

```
StorageFile file = KnownFolders.MusicLibrary.GetFileAsync("Song.mp3").AsTask().Result;
```

The reason is that querying a Task's Result property throws an AggregateException if the operation fails instead of throwing the correct exception.

Be aware that blocking a GUI thread by calling GetAwaiter().GetResult() could potentially deadlock the thread, forcing the user or operating system to terminate your app. So you should really avoid blocking a thread issuing asynchronous operations whenever possible.

WinRT deferrals

Many WinRT components offer virtual or interface methods you can implement. Additionally, many WinRT classes expose events your app can register callback methods with. When your app returns from your methods, Windows believes your code has completed its operation and then Windows might take some next action. For example, when your app is about to be suspended (discussed in Chapter 3), Windows raises an event to notify your app. Upon receiving this notification, your app might want to persist some app state to the user's hard disk. When you perform this operation asynchronously, the thread returns to Windows before the asynchronous operation completes. However, when the thread returns to Windows, Windows believes your app has successfully suspended itself and then suspends all your app's threads, preventing them from executing any more code.

To deal with this, WinRT offers a mechanism known as a *deferral*. A deferral allows a method to return to Windows while indicating that the operation is not yet complete. This prevents Windows from performing the next action. Then later, after your app has completed its operation, it completes the deferral, telling Windows it can now perform the next action. Deferrals should be used only if your method performs some kind of asynchronous operation. Here is some code demonstrating the use of a deferral in an app's suspending event handler:

```
private async void OnSuspending(object sender, SuspendingEventArgs e) {

   // A deferral tells Windows the thread may return but the work is not done
   var deferral = e.SuspendingOperation.GetDeferral();
```

```
    // TODO: perform async operation(s) here...
    var result = await XxxAsync();  // Thread returns but app is NOT suspended

    deferral.Complete(); // Now, tell Windows we're done (app is suspended)
}
```

Remember that the deferral variable refers to a Runtime Callable Wrapper that internally refers to the WinRT component. So, if your code does not call the Complete method, the garbage collector will eventually run and clean up the object, which effectively calls Complete for you. Although, when suspending, the garbage collector (GC) cannot run if your app is terminated.

WinRT defines several deferral classes; the ones relevant to C# programmers are shown here:

```
Windows.ApplicationModel.SuspendingDeferral
Windows.ApplicationModel.Background.BackgroundTaskDeferral
Windows.ApplicationModel.Calls.LockScreenCallEndCallDeferral
Windows.ApplicationModel.DataTransfer.DataProviderDeferral
Windows.ApplicationModel.DataTransfer.DataRequestDeferral
Windows.ApplicationModel.Search.SearchPaneSuggestionsRequestDeferral
Windows.ApplicationModel.Search.SearchSuggestionsRequestDeferral

Windows.Devices.Printers.Extensions.PrintTaskConfigurationSaveRequestedDeferral
Windows.Devices.SmartCards.SmartCardPinResetDeferral

Windows.Graphics.Printing.PrintTaskRequestedDeferral
Windows.Graphics.Printing.PrintTaskSourceRequestedDeferral

Windows.Media.PlayTo.PlayToSourceDeferral

Windows.Storage.SetVersionDeferral
Windows.Storage.Pickers.Provider.PickerClosingDeferral
Windows.Storage.Pickers.Provider.TargetFileRequestDeferral
Windows.Storage.Provider.FileUpdateRequestDeferral

Windows.UI.StartScreen.VisualElementsRequestDeferral
```

The OnSuspending method I showed demonstrates what Microsoft considers best practices when you need to defer the execution of an OS action until your code can complete an asynchronous operation. However, you could rewrite the OnSuspending method as follows:

```
private void OnSuspending(object sender, SuspendingEventArgs e) {

    // TODO: perform blocking async operation(s) here...
    var result = XxxAsync().AsTask.GetAwaiter().GetResult();

}   // App is suspended
```

This code is simpler, and you have to ask yourself, what is the harm? This code does block the GUI thread, which means the UI could become unresponsive to the user. This would be bad in general; but, in this case, the user is not interacting with the app, which is why it is being suspended in the first place. In addition, the first version of this method used an async method, which makes the code bigger and can decrease app performance. This version does not use an async method and, in the case of suspending, your app has just a few seconds to complete its operation or Windows forcibly terminates your app. Therefore, making your code faster here could make a big difference. Background tasks have a similar time limit when they execute too, so you want to make background task code fast as well.

In addition, many deferral classes are used with operations that do not execute on GUI threads; therefore, app UI responsiveness is not even an issue. For example, background tasks never execute on GUI threads, so there is practically no reason to use the BackgroundTaskDeferral class.[14]

When writing code, always keep in mind the reason why the code is executing, what thread could be executing that code, and what will happen next after your code executes. Then, with this knowledge, decide how to best implement the code so that you are guaranteed to get the behavior you desire.

---

[14] In fact, WinRT has a design flaw with background tasks. If you use BackgroundTaskDeferral and your background task code throws an exception after an await, your app will not be able to determine that the background task failed. I discuss this more in the "Background task progress, completion, and cancelation" section of Chapter 9, "Background tasks."

CHAPTER 2

App packaging and deployment

In Chapter 1, "Windows Runtime primer," you learned that one of the design goals for Windows Store apps was that Windows should be able to cleanly install and uninstall the app so that users have confidence that an app will not irreparably affect their system. This means that everything your Windows Store app needs to run successfully must be combined together so that the system knows the complete footprint of your app. The resulting file is called an *app package*, and it contains binaries such as your executable, libraries, and Windows Runtime (WinRT) components. It also contains resource files your app uses such as images and media files. You use Microsoft Visual Studio to build your app and create your app's package file. This package file then can be uploaded to the Windows Store, enabling users to install it on their PCs, or you can manually distribute the package, enabling users to manually install (sideload) it on their PCs. Of course, Windows only installs packages that come from trusted sources, and it will make sure that the package's contents have not changed in transit.

In this chapter, I show how to build a package and what the package contains. You'll also see the different ways to deploy a package to users' PCs. I'll then go into more details on package installation, including staging and registration. Finally, I'll finish with some specifics regarding the use of Visual Studio and debugging. This is a very important chapter in helping you understand how to work with Windows Store apps. The concepts presented in this chapter are very useful and will help you understand the concepts presented throughout later chapters in this book.

A Windows Store app's project files

In this section, we look at the various files that make up a Windows Store app's package, with an emphasis on the manifest file. I'll also show how Visual Studio builds all the files and places them into a package file.

The first time you create a Windows Store app project in Visual Studio, Visual Studio prompts you with a dialog box telling you that you need to get a developer license, as you see in Figure 2-1. Developer licenses allows apps to run that have not been downloaded from the Windows Store. This is certainly useful when developing, testing, and debugging an app. Developer licenses expire every 30 days (90 days if you have registered an account with the Windows Store), but they are free to acquire. After your developer license expires, Visual Studio automatically prompts you to renew it. Windows provides PowerShell commands (shown in Table 2-1) to manage a PC's developer license.

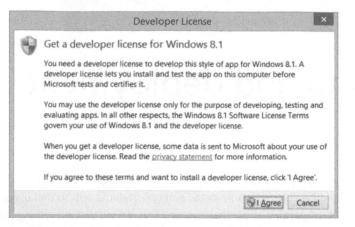

FIGURE 2-1 Visual Studio's Developer License dialog box prompting the user to install the license.

TABLE 2-1 PowerShell commands to manage a PC's developer license

PowerShell command	Description
Show-WindowsDeveloperLicenseRegistration	Renews the PC's developer license
Unregister-WindowsDeveloperLicense	Unregisters the developer license from the PC
Get-WindowsDeveloperLicense	Checks the validity and expiration date of the developer license on the PC

A Windows Store app project consists of many folders and files:

- In the **Properties** folder, you'll find the AssemblyInfo.cs file. This is the standard AssemblyInfo.cs file with assembly attributes for your project, such as AssemblyTitle, AssembyDescription, AssemblyVersion, and so on. This file is used in .NET assemblies and is not specific to Windows Store apps. For more information about them, see *CLR via C#, Fourth Edition* (Microsoft Press, 2012) by Jeffrey Richter.

- In the **References** folder, you'll find two entries. The first, ".NET for Windows Store apps," exposes the subset of the .NET Framework Class Library you can call from Windows Store apps (as discussed in Chapter 1). The second entry, "Windows," exposes the WinRT APIs provided by the Windows operating system that are callable by Windows Store apps.

- The **Assets** folder contains nonexecutable (resource) files, such as images and media files. These files are packaged and deployed with your app. By default, Visual Studio places image files in this folder that are for your app's store logo, splash screen, small app logo, and primary Start screen tile.

- **Package.appxmanifest** is an XML file that describes your Windows Store app. We'll explore the manifest in this chapter's next section and refer back to it frequently throughout this book. If you open the file in Visual Studio, you can see that the IDE provides a user-friendly editor for this manifest file. This user interface is called the *manifest designer*.

- A **{project}_TemporaryKey.pfx** file that contains a Software Publishing Certificate (SPC). Every Windows Store app must be signed with a certificate. Every time you create a new project, Visual Studio generates an untrusted, self-signed, code-signing certificate that expires in one year. Your app package file is signed with this certificate. Of course, Windows will not execute the contents of the package if the certificate is untrusted. To get your package to execute, the certificate must be added to the PC's trusted certificate store or the package will have to be signed with another certificate that is trusted. I'll talk about the certificates more in this chapter's "Deploying a Windows Store package" section. When you're debugging an app, a certificate is not required because you are not creating and deploying a package.

- The **App.xaml** and **App.xaml.cs** files contain XAML resources and the code behind for your app. The contents of this file and how your app are activated is discussed in Chapter 3, "Process model."

- Other **XxxPage.xaml** and **XxxPage.xaml.cs** files contain the XAML markup and code behind for your app's other pages. Because this book does not go into designing and building user interfaces, these other files are not discussed, although Chapter 3 does explore page navigation.

The app's package manifest file

The Package.appxmanifest file is referred to as the app's *package manifest file*, and you use it to describe the following:

- Your package's identity so that the Windows Store and Windows itself can uniquely identify your package. It is critically important to understand that Windows installs packages, not apps.

- The apps that ship inside the package and some UI-related features of each app. A single app package can contain multiple apps. However, Microsoft's user-experience team discovered a series of problems with this approach. For example, if a user uninstalled one of the package's apps, how could the user re-install it later? To simplify the user experience, the Windows Store has a policy that all packages must contain a single app. For this reason, Visual Studio's manifest designer supports only single app packages.[1] In addition, due to this simplification, the terms *package* and *app* are sometimes (unfortunately) used interchangeably.[2] For example, a more accurate term for *application data* is *package data* and a more accurate term for *app container* is *package container* because the data and the container are really owned by the package, which might consist of multiple apps. This is especially important to understand when working with background tasks because an app can have multiple background task processes all sharing the same data and container.

---

[1] The Windows Store has one exception to this policy. The "Mail, Calendar, and People" package contains the three apps that ship with Windows itself.

[2] You also can create packages that have no apps in them at all. These packages are called *framework packages*. Examples of framework packages are the Windows Library for JavaScript apps, Microsoft Visual C++ Runtime, and Microsoft PlayReady Content Protection Framework.

- The visual assets for your app. This includes the foreground text color and background color that make up your app's theme as well as the various logos (images) for your app's splash screen and static tiles.

- The device resources (*capabilities*) that each app in the package wants access to.

- The various ways the system can activate (open) each app in the package. In the manifest designer, these are called *declarations*, but in the XML schema, these are called *extensions*. Sometimes activations, declarations, and extensions are also referred to as *contracts*.

- Which pages in the web context have access to the system's geolocation devices and access to the clipboard. This is used for apps written in JavaScript, not for apps written in C#.

When you open the Package.appxmanifest file in Visual Studio, the manifest designer appears. The manifest designer exposes a graphical user interface for changing common manifest settings. For more advanced settings (like the Document Library capability or to declare support for the appointments or contacts activations), you must manually edit the XML file. The schema for the manifest's XML file can be found at *http://msdn.microsoft.com/en-us/library/windows/apps/br211473.aspx*.

The next three sections detail a package's identity as well as an app's capabilities and declarations. The manifest's Application UI information is discussed in other chapters.

Package identity

Figure 2-2 shows the manifest designer's Packaging tab.

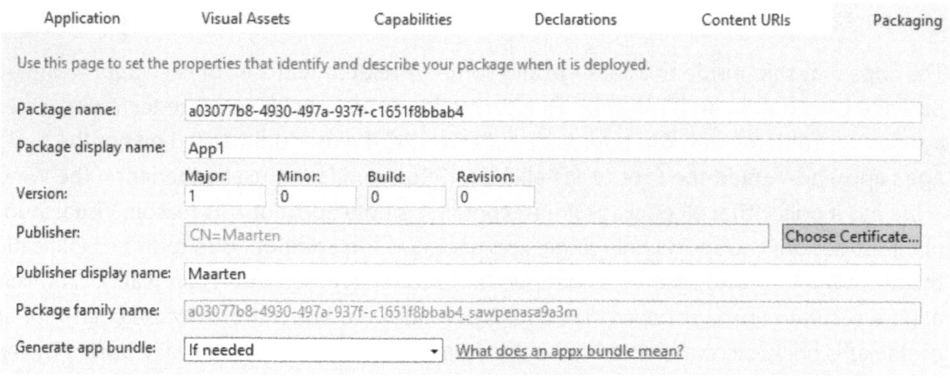

FIGURE 2-2 Visual Studio showing the manifest designer's Packaging tab.

You use this tab to establish your package's identity. Because these properties identify your package in the Windows Store and when it is installed, some of them are not completely under your control.

- **Package Name** identifies the name of your package. When you create a new project in Visual Studio, Visual Studio creates a GUID and uses it for your package's name. This should be changed to a more user-friendly name. Frequently, package names use a scheme such as *"CompanyName.AppName"*—for example: "Microsoft.Bing."

If you intend to distribute your package via the Windows Store, you should go to the Windows Store dashboard, reserve a name for your package, and then use Visual Studio's "Associate App with the Store" wizard to associate your package with your reserved package name. When you do this, Visual Studio automatically updates these manifest values: Package Name, Package Display Name, Publisher, Publisher Display Name, Version, and Application Display Name (shown on the designer's Application tab). If you do not intend to deploy your app via the Windows Store, you can change these manifest values manually to whatever you like.

- **Package Display Name** is the friendly name that users see in the Windows Store. The Windows Store requires that every package have a unique package display name. This was done to prevent a malicious person from producing a "Finance" app that has the same look and feel as a respectable company's "Finance" app, thereby spoofing the user to enter her personal financial data into the malicious app, where it can be stolen and abused.

- **Version** identifies the major, minor, build, and revision numbers you want to associate with your app. We'll talk about this more when we discuss creating an app's package.

- **Publisher** is the subject of the certificate that Visual Studio uses when signing the package file. This changes when the certificate changes. When you create a new project in Visual Studio, Visual Studio creates a certificate whose subject is the name of the user logging in to Windows. However, you can always generate a new certificate on your local machine, use a certificate obtained by your company, or obtain a certificate from the Windows Store by associating your app with the Windows Store.

- **Publisher Display Name** is the friendly name of the publisher. When you create a new project in Visual Studio, Visual Studio sets the Publisher Display Name to the name of the user logging in to Windows. When you associate an app with the Windows Store, the Publisher Display Name is set to the value you entered for the Publisher Name field in the Windows Store dashboard.

- **Package Family Name** is a computed read-only value that is generated by concatenating two values: the Package Name and the Publisher ID. The Publisher ID is produced by creating a hash value for the Publisher string and then base 32–encoding this hash value. The result is always a 13-character string that uniquely identifies the publisher (statistically). A package family name string uniquely identifies a package from a specific publisher. Here is an example for one of my apps, called Clips & Pieces: "JeffreyRichter.ClipsPieces_ape9s8gs6w87m".

- **Generate App Bundle** has nothing to do with your package's identity. It just tells Visual Studio how to generate a package file or files. I explain what an app bundle package is in the "Creating a bundle package file" section.

In addition to the package *family* name, there is also a string referred to as the package *full* name. The package full name is a concatenation of the package name, its version, its CPU architecture (x86, x64, ARM, or Neutral), a Resource ID (usually an empty string, ""), and the Publisher ID. Here is an example of my app's package full name: "JeffreyRichter.ClipsPieces_1.0.0.0_neutral__ape9s8gs6w87m". Most packages do not specify a Resource ID (in fact, Windows does not interpret this value), which is why my app's package full name doesn't show any resource ID information between the CPU architecture and the Publisher ID. There are just two underscores right next to each other.

When your Windows Store app is running, it can obtain information about its package by querying `Windows.ApplicationModel.Package`'s static `Current` property. This property returns a reference to a Package object that looks like this:

```
public sealed class Package {
    public static Package Current { get; }  // Gets calling app's package

    public PackageId Id { get; }  // See the PackageId class below

    // Members returning package attributes:
    public String DisplayName          { get; }
    public String PublisherDisplayName { get; }
    public String Description          { get; }
    public Uri    Logo                 { get; }

    // Package's files under %ProgramFiles%\WindowsApps
    public StorageFolder InstalledLocation { get; }

    // Returns framework packages this package requires to run
    public IReadOnlyList<Package> Dependencies { get; }

    // Properties indicating the type of package
    // If all return false, this is an .appx package containing 1 or more apps
    public Boolean IsFramework       { get; }
    public Boolean IsBundle          { get; }
    public Boolean IsResourcePackage { get; }

    // True when Visual Studio launches the app
    // If true, you can enable debugging/testing features in your app
    public Boolean IsDevelopmentMode { get; } // True if registered; not staged
}
```

The Id property returns a PackageId object that looks like this:

```
public sealed class PackageId {
    public String Name        { get; }  // Package name
    public String Publisher    { get; }  // Publisher name
    public String PublisherId { get; }  // Base-32 hash of Publisher
    public String FamilyName   { get; }  // Name_PublisherID

    public PackageVersion        Version      { get; } // Ex: "1.2.3.4"
    public ProcessorArchitecture Architecture { get; } // Neutral, x86, x64, ARM
    public String                ResourceId   { get; } // Usually ""

    // Name_Version_Architecture_ResourceId_PublisherID:
    public String                FullName     { get; }
}
```

Capabilities

When developing an app, you must indicate which secured system resources (or device capabilities) your app wants access to in the package manifest. Figure 2-3 shows the manifest designer's Capabilities tab. Some capabilities are so rarely used (or discouraged) that they do not appear in the manifest designer; to add these capabilities, you must manually edit the manifest XML file. Table 2-2 lists all the capabilities.

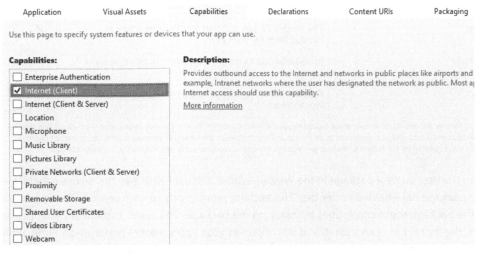

FIGURE 2-3 Visual Studio showing the manifest designer's Capabilities tab.

TABLE 2-2 Capabilities

Capability	Description	Additional confirmation
Documents Library1*	Provides programmatic access to the user's Documents library. You'll need to declare a file type association as well.	×
Music Library	Provides programmatic access to the user's Music library folders	×
Pictures Library	Provides programmatic access to the user's Pictures library	×
Videos Library	Provides programmatic access to the user's Videos library	×
Removable Storage	Provides programmatic access to the removable storage, such as USB drives	×
Internet (Client)	Provides outbound Internet access (on by default in the templates)	×
Internet (Client & Server)	Provides inbound as well as outbound Internet access. Superset of Internet (Client)	×
Private Networks (Client & Server)	Provides inbound and outbound connectivity over a home or work network	×

Capability	Description	Additional confirmation
Enterprise Authentication*	Enables your app to use your credentials to authenticate on the network	✕
Shared User Certificates*	Provides access to certificates, for example, on a smartcard	✕
Proximity	Provides access to the NFC sensor for bootstrapping connections with other devices and electronic wallet scenarios	✕
Location	The machine's geo-location provided by a GPS or derived from network info	✓
Microphone	Provides access to the machine's microphone audio stream	✓
Webcam	Provides access to the machine's camera audio and video stream	✓

* Three capabilities are referred to as special use capabilities and should be avoided. Enabling any of these capabilities will fail Windows Store certification if the package is submitted by an individual. Only companies (whose identity has been verified) can submit packages enabling these capabilities. For more information, see *http://msdn.microsoft.com/en-us/library/windows/apps/hh464936.aspx*.

When the user views a package in the Windows Store, the user is shown the device capabilities that the package has enabled under the "This app has permissions to use" section. The user implicitly grants the package these capabilities by installing the package. The fewer capabilities your package requires, the more users can trust it, and this improves your app's market penetration. Note, if the developer adds capabilities to a package in the future and uploads a new version of the package to the Windows Store, the new version of the package gets installed on all users' PCs automatically; the user is not informed that the new version can access additional resources. The user can always verify what capabilities an installed package has by running that package's app and then looking at its Settings charm > Permissions pane.

Some capabilities require additional approval from the user. The first time an app tries to access the user's location, microphone, or webcam, the system prompts the user for additional confirmation. To pass Windows Store certification requirements, your app must function reasonably well if the user fails to grant your app access to these resources. In addition, a user can always revoke access to any of these resources at any time by opening the Settings charm > Permissions pane.

App (not package) declarations (extensions/contracts)

When developing an app, you must indicate the various ways the system can activate your app in the manifest. Figure 2-4 shows the manifest designer's Declarations tab. Some declarations are so rarely used that they do not appear in the manifest designer; to add these declarations, you must manually edit the XML file. Also, note that some declarations can be specified multiple times for a single app. For example, a single app can support multiple file type associations, protocols, background tasks, AutoPlay contents, and AutoPlay devices. Table 2-3 lists all the declarations.

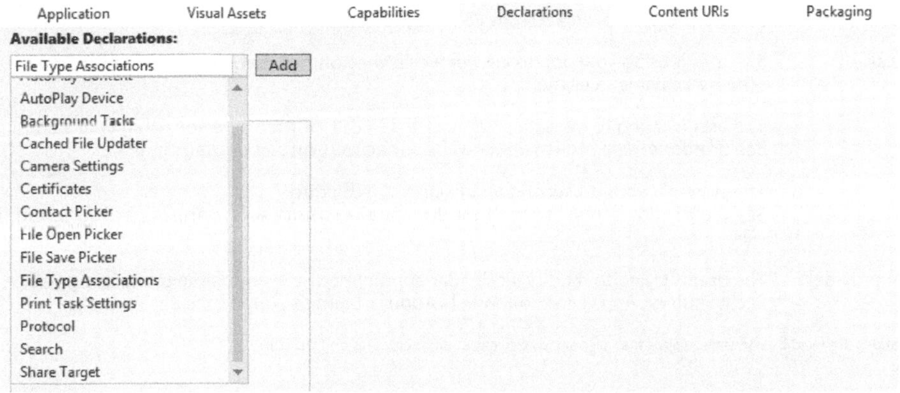

| Application | Visual Assets | Capabilities | Declarations | Content URIs | Packaging |

Available Declarations:

File Type Associations | Add

- AutoPlay Device
- Background Tasks
- Cached File Updater
- Camera Settings
- Certificates
- Contact Picker
- File Open Picker
- File Save Picker
- File Type Associations
- Print Task Settings
- Protocol
- Search
- Share Target

FIGURE 2-4 Visual Studio showing the manifest designer's Declarations tab.

TABLE 2-3 App declarations (extensions/contracts)

Declaration	Allows the system to activate your app when...
File Type Associations	The user or another app launches a file of a type your app supports (such as ".txt"). See the `Windows.System.Launcher` class.
Protocol	The user or another app launches a URI protocol your app supports (such as mailto:). See the `Windows.System.Launcher` class.
Background Tasks	A timer or system event triggers. See the `Windows.ApplicationModel.Background.BackgroundTaskBuilder` class.
Share Target	The user wants to share some data from another app to your app. See the `Windows.ApplicationModel.DataTransfer.DataTransferManager` class.
File Open Picker	The user wants to open a file from your app via the file open picker. See the `Windows.Storage.Pickers.FileOpenPicker` class.
File Save Picker	The user wants to save a file to your app via the file save picker. See the `Windows.Storage.Pickers.FileSavePicker` class.
Cached File Updater	Another app wants to read/write to a file your app returned via a picker. See the `Windows.Storage.Provider.CachedFileUpdater` class.
Search	Provides integration with the Search charm. See the `Windows.ApplicationModel.Search.SearchPane` class.
Contact Picker	Enables your app to provide contact data. See the `Windows.ApplicationModel.Contacts.ContactPicker` class.
AutoPlay Content	User inserts a removable storage device into the PC. See *http://msdn.microsoft.com/en-us/library/windows/apps/hh452741.aspx*.
AutoPlay Device*	User attaches a hardware device to the PC. See *http://msdn.microsoft.com/en-us/library/windows/apps/hh452741.aspx*.
Camera Settings*	Enables your app to provide a custom UI for a camera. See *http://msdn.microsoft.com/library/windows/hardware/hh454870*.
Print Task Settings*	Enables your app to provide a custom UI for its printer. See *http://msdn.microsoft.com/en-us/library/windows/hardware/br259129*.
Account Picture Provider	User wants to use your app to change his account picture. See the `Windows.System.UserProfile.UserInformation` class.

Declaration	Allows the system to activate your app when...
Lock screen call	The user is using your app to answer a call while on the lock screen. See the Toast XML schema's command element.
Contact	The user is trying to message, mail, call, video call, or map a person using your app. See `Windows.ApplicationModel.Contacts.ContactManager`.
Alarm	The system is within 1 second of an alarm coming due. See the `Windows.ApplicationModel.Background.AlarmApplicationManager` class.
Appointment provider	The user is trying to modify a calendar appointment or view a time frame using your app. See `Windows.ApplicationModel.Appointments.AppointmentManager`.

* These declarations are used by companion apps that accompany devices, such as cameras and printers.

> **Note** The terms *app declaration*, *app extension*, *app activation*, and *contract* all relate to the exact same thing. That is, in your package, you must *declare* an app *extension*, allowing the system to *activate* your app. We say that your app implements a *contract* when it responds to an activation.

In addition to the app declarations shown in Table 2-3, the package itself can have some declarations. Because package declarations are associated with a package, they have nothing to do with app activation. There are five package declarations: Certificates (the most useful), GameExplorer, InProcessServer, OutOfProcessServer, and ProxyStub. This declaration allows you to embed one or more certificates in your package, and this certificate will be part of your package's private certificate store, thereby making it available to the app in the package. The certificate is typically used to secure network communication between a package's app and an Internet service. (See Chapter 7, "Networking.")

Building a Windows Store app package

When you're developing and debugging your app, Visual Studio registers and runs your app from the project's build directories (discussed more in this chapter's "Debugging Windows Store apps" section). But, when you're ready to distribute an app, you must create a package file. From within Visual Studio, select Project Menu > Store > Create App Packages (or, with Visual Studio Express, select Store Menu > Create App Packages). Visual Studio presents you with the option to create either a package you can manually distribute or a package you can upload to the Windows Store. When you create a package to upload to the Windows Store, Visual Studio prompts you to associate your package with an app name that you must have previously reserved for yourself via the Windows Store dashboard. We'll look into the details of creating an app for the Windows Store in Chapter 11, "Windows Store."

The next step in the Create App Packages wizard (shown in Figure 2-5) is to specify your app's package version, supported CPU architecture or architectures, and solution configuration such as

Debug or Release. I'll talk about the Generate App Bundle setting in the "Creating a bundle package file" section.

For the CPU architecture, you can choose between Neutral, x86, x64, and ARM. C# Windows Store app projects default to Neutral (Any CPU) and packages built with this setting run on all three CPU architectures. However, your app can use other Windows Store components built in .NET or C++. If your app uses a component built for a specific CPU architecture (like Bing Maps), you must build one or more CPU-specific packages. Apps built for x86 will run on both x86 and x64 machines. The Windows Store uses the architecture information to filter out apps for the user's PC. Hence, if your app supports only x86, users with Windows RT machines (ARM processor machines) will not see your app when they are browsing in the Windows Store app.

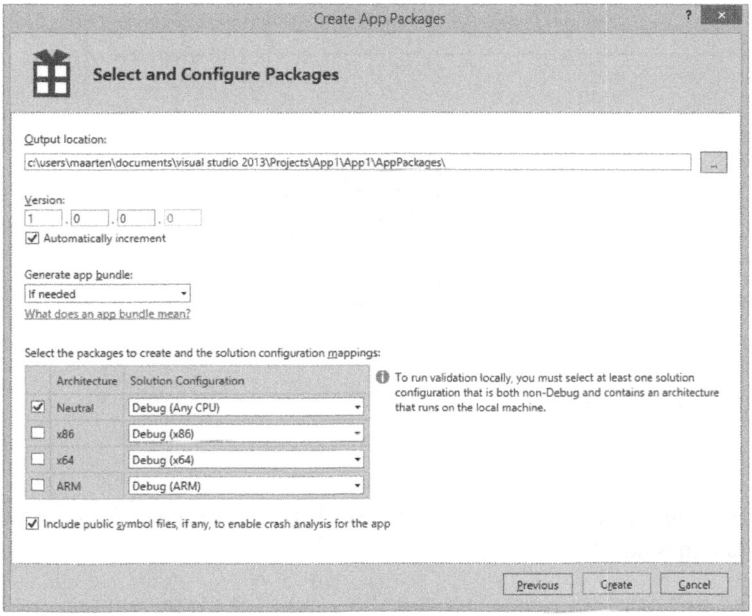

FIGURE 2-5 Visual Studio's Create App Packages wizard.

The Create App Packages wizard populates the version from the manifest file; changing the numbers updates the manifest file. If you select multiple architectures in the wizard, the build process creates multiple app package files. The check box asking for public symbol inclusion tells the wizard to create an additional file per chosen CPU architecture. These files contain public symbol information that allows Microsoft to provide you with better diagnostics in the Windows Store dashboard if your app crashes. (For more information, see Chapter 11.)

When you click the wizard's Create button, the build process starts as described by Figure 2-6.

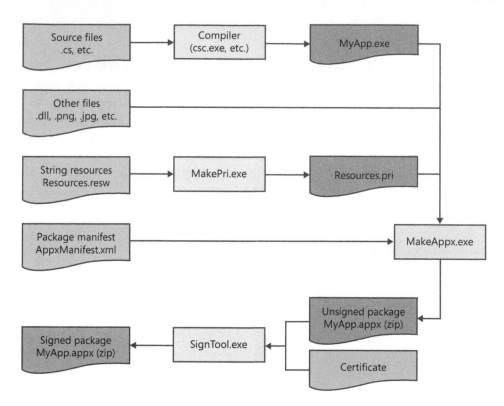

FIGURE 2-6 Process of building an app package file.

Here's what happens:

1. An MSBuild task generates source code files from the XAML markup, such as App.g.i.cs and MainPage.g.i.cs. This step is not shown in Figure 2-6.

2. The C# compiler (CSC.exe) compiles your source code files as well as the dynamically generated source code files, together producing a managed executable assembly (exe file). Producing a Windows Store app requires the /target:appcontainerexe compiler switch. By default, your executable will run on all CPU architectures, because Visual Studio adds the /platform:anycpu32bitpreferred compiler switch. Use the /platform:anycpu switch to use more address space when running on an x64 system.

3. Other files your app needs, such as referenced assembly files and other resource assets (such as images, music, videos), are also copied to the same directory as your .exe file. Your XAML files are compiled to a binary form and placed in this directory as files with an .xbf extension.

4. For string resources and other asset files, a utility called MakePRI.exe creates a Package Resource Index (.pri) file. (See *http://msdn.microsoft.com/en-us/library/windows/apps/jj552947.aspx* for details.) Windows Store apps use this .pri file at runtime to load resources

efficiently. The file contains your app's strings and an indexed set of file paths to other app resources. There is one .pri file for all the languages your app supports. The .pri file is also written to the same directory.

5. The final manifest file (AppxManifest.xml) is almost identical to your project's Package.appx-manifest file discussed earlier in this chapter. However, MSBuild does tweak some of the values inside the file for you.

6. MSBuild then spawns MakeAppx.exe to create an unsigned .appx package file consisting of all the produced files. An app package file is simply a ZIP file with an .appx file extension. It cannot have more than 100,000 files in it, and it can't be larger than 8 GB in size.

7. As a final step, MSBuild invokes SignTool.exe to sign the .appx file using the certificate that is part of your Visual Studio project.

You now have a single .appx package file containing your app and everything it needs in order to execute once this package gets installed on a user's PC. In the next section, we'll look at the contents of this .appx package file.

Contents of an .appx package file

If you look in a directory produced by the Create App Packages wizard, you'll see files similar to those listed in Table 2-4.

TABLE 2-4 Files created by the Create App Packages wizard for a single CPU architecture

File or folder name	Description
PackageSample_1.0.0.0_AnyCPU_Debug.appx	Signed package (ZIP) file containing all assemblies, resources, and so on.
PackageSample_1.0.0.0_AnyCPU_Debug.appxsym	ZIP file containing any symbols (.pdb files) for the assemblies embedded inside the .appx file. This file is produced if you select the Include Public Symbol Files check box (shown in Figure 2-5), and it allows you to get richer debugging information if your app experiences an unhandled exception when running on a user's PC.
PackageSample_1.0.0.0_AnyCPU_Debug.cer	Certificate file containing the public key corresponding to the private key used to sign the .appx file.
Add-AppDevPackage.ps1	PowerShell script you can use to install the package on a PC.
Add-AppDevPackage.resources	Subdirectory with localized strings used internally by the .ps1 file.

The .appx and .appxsym files are simply ZIP files. In fact, you can change the extension of these files to *.zip* to examine their contents. Table 2-5 shows the contents of an .appx file. Here, you can see the files resemble your project's folder structure, containing directories such as Assets and Common.

TABLE 2-5 Contents of an .appx file

File/directory	Contents
[Content_Types].xml	File listing the file types used in this package. See the Office Open XML file specification for more information.
AppxMetadata	Folder containing a CodeIntegrity.cat file used to validate the integrity of the .appx file's contents.
AppxBlockMap.xml	Contains hash values for blocks within the .appx file's files.
AppxManifest.xml	Generated XML manifest file.
AppxSignature.p7x	Contains the digital signature produced when signing the .appx file with your project's certificate (.pfx file).
PackageSample.exe	The app's executable.
App.xbf	Markup for the app.
MainPage.xbf	Markup for the app's main page.
Common	Folder containing common files, such as StandardStyles.xaml.
Assets	Folder containing the resources (images, and so on).
resources.pri	Package resource index file.

You can easily open any of the files in this .appx ZIP file because Visual Studio does not encrypt the file or any of its contents. If you open AppxBlockMap.xml, you'll see a list of files along with a hash value and size for each 64-KB compressed block of the file. The MakeAppx.exe utility created this AppxBlockMap.xml file. Windows uses the AppxBlockMap.xml file to verify the integrity of the package's files, ensuring that no modifications have been made to any of the file's contents after the .appx file was created.

Another cool feature provided by the AppxBlockMap.xml file is differential download. When creating a new version of your app, it is common to keep most of your existing asset files while modifying just a few of them or including some new asset files. When a user installs a new version of your package, Windows uses the AppBlockMap.xml file to see which files have changed and only downloads the portions (blocks) within files that have been updated. This greatly improves the speed of installing a newer version of an application and also decreases network usage, resulting in cheaper network charges for the user.

Furthermore, if multiple packages ship the same files (regardless of publisher), the system knows that the files are already installed (based on the hash values) and just creates NTFS hard links to the files. This greatly reduces download time and prevents the wasting of disk space by having the same file installed multiple times. For example, if multiple packages ship the same SQLite or Bing Maps files, the files will be downloaded just once and reside just once on the user's PC. For this reason, you should try to use the same files across multiple packages; avoid making special one-off builds that alter just a few bits here and there.

In Table 2-5, you see the AppxManifest.xml file that Visual Studio generated from the original Package.appxmanifest file. Most of the content of these two files is identical except for a few replacements and additions. For example, the <Resources> section now contains the languages your app supports. In addition, references to extension SDK packages get added to the <Extensions> node.

In addition to creating the files in Table 2-4, Visual Studio's Create App Packages wizard also generates an .appxupload file. This file is simply a ZIP file containing the .appx and .appxsym files. You can upload an .appxupload file to the Windows Store via the Windows Store dashboard.

Creating a bundle package file

The .appx package file described in the previous section is sometimes referred to as a *fat package* because it can become huge. It becomes huge if the package includes resources for many languages, many screen resolutions, or if it contains texture maps for various versions of DirectX. But when a user installs a package, that user may only ever need one set of language resources, one set of images for their monitor's resolution, and one set of texture maps for their video card. Installing a fat package installs all of its files whether the user needs them or not. Depending on the package, this can be a huge waste of bandwidth and a huge waste of disk space.

You can improve this situation for your users by creating a *bundle package file*. A bundle package file is a different kind of package file. Like an .appx package file, a bundle package file also has an identity composed of a package name, version, and publisher ID; the resource ID is always tilde (~), and the CPU architecture is always "neutral."

In Figures 2-2 and 2-5, you saw the Generate App Bundle option. If it's set to Never, a bundle package file will not be produced. However, if it's set to Always or Needed, the MakeAppx.exe tool is passed a "bundle" switch telling it to create an .appxbundle package file (if you have resources). This file is just another ZIP file containing its own XML manifest file as well as other .appx package files. The schema for the .appxbundle package file's XML manifest file can be found at *http://msdn.microsoft.com/en-us/library/windows/apps/dn263100.aspx*. There will be one .appx package for each CPU architecture you desire (x86, x64, or ARM), one .appx file for each set of language resources (en, es, fr, de, and so on), one .appx file for each resolution scale (80%, 100%, 140%, and 180%), and one .appx file for each version of DirectX you have texture maps for (dx9, dx10, and dx11).

What you upload to the Windows Store is this one .appxbundle package file. Then, when a user goes to install your package, the system detects the user's CPU and installs the .appx package containing the matching code. Then the system detects the user's installed languages, monitors, and video card and installs just the .appx package files the user requires. The remaining .appx package files are not downloaded and installed. This saves time and disk space.

At any time, you can modify a resource or your app and use the Create App Packages wizard to create a new version of the .appxbundle package file. You then upload the new version of the package file to the Windows Store. About once a day, each user's PC checks the Windows Store to see if a new version of the bundle package file exists and, if so, the PC downloads any of the blocks that have changed. (Remember the discussion of the block map in the previous section.) This keeps the parts of your package that are relevant to the user up to date on each user's PC.

Also, sometime in the future, a user might install another language, change the monitor, or upgrade a video card. Within a day of these changes, the system detects this and automatically installs any of the bundle package's embedded .appx resource packages that are now relevant to the user;

any now-irrelevant .appx packages are uninstalled. The user can force an update by going to the Store app's Settings charm > App Updates pane and then tapping the Check For Updates button.

> **Important** The primary .appx package containing code must have a complete set of resources embedded inside it. That is, you cannot have any resource in an .appx resource package that is not also in the primary package. The reason is obvious: if you have a resource in a German language package, a user who does not get the German language package installed cannot run the app successfully. The primary packages (one for each CPU architecture) must have one set of resources that act as a fallback should more specific resources not be available.

Deploying a Windows Store package

A Windows Store package can be deployed (installed) to a user's PC using three different techniques. The technique you use depends on the reach—that is, how many installs you anticipate. Here are the three reach categories and descriptions of when you use each one:

- **Restricted deployments** Use restricted deployments when you want to deploy a package to a small set of people. Typically, you use this technique for testing scenarios or when you want to give your package to some friends or family members for evaluation.

- **Enterprise deployments** Use this technique when you want to make a package installable by members of your company or enterprise but not to the public at large. This technique is typically used for packages containing an app that performs functions related to a company's way of doing business. This technique is frequently referred to as *sideloading*.

- **Windows Store deployments** Use this technique when you want to make your package available to the general public. Once your package is deployed to the Windows Store, anyone running Windows can install your package via the built-in Windows Store app. See Chapter 11 for more information about the Windows Store.

The next three sections examine these three techniques in detail.

Restricted deployments

Table 2-4 showed the files produced by Visual Studio's Create App Packages wizard. You can copy these files to another PC and install the package by running the Add-AppxDevPackage.ps1 PowerShell script. This script performs the following actions:

1. Prompts the user to acquire a developer license (if one is not already installed) by running the Show-WindowsDeveloperLicenseRegistration PowerShell script.

2. Installs the package's certificate (.cer file) in the PC's Trusted People store by running the CertUtil.exe utility.

3. Unzips the package's contents (and any dependent framework packages) to a directory on the user's PC by running the Add-AppxPackage PowerShell script.

Developer licenses are free, but to get one, the machine *must* have an Internet connection and the user must have a Microsoft account. Also, developer licenses do expire (approximately every 30 to 90 days), so they must periodically be renewed for the installed package to continue working. The prompt to acquire a developer license explicitly mentions that you can use the license only for developing, testing, and evaluating apps. When a developer license expires, packages that require it fail to execute. On the Start screen, a small cross sign is displayed in the lower-right corner of an app's tile.

In the second step, the package's certificate is installed in the PC's Trusted People certificate store. PowerShell warns you that this entails serious security risks because the system will now trust any package signed with this certificate. When this certificate expires, Windows also prevents the package from executing on the user's PC.

In the last step, the system unzips the .appx file's contents into a directory under %ProgramFiles%\ WindowsApps. The directory name matches the package full name, which includes the version number of the package. This means that different versions of the same package can be installed side-by-side on a single PC. This is useful if one user on the PC wants to run version 1.2.3.4 while another user is still using version 1.0.0.0.

The WindowsApps directory is a hidden directory, and its security settings prevent you from browsing it. However, the security settings are such that you can look inside one of WindowsApps' subdirectories. For example, you can navigate to %ProgramFiles%\WindowsApps\Microsoft. Bing_1.2.0.137_x64__8wekyb3d8bbwe and see this package's unzipped contents. Also, Wintellect's Package Explorer Desktop app (discussed later) can enumerate all packages installed by the current user.

At this point, the package is installed and integrated with the operating system. The user can go to the Start screen or App view screen and launch the package's app until either the developer license or the package's certificate expires.

Enterprise deployments

Many companies produce line-of-business (LOB) or enterprise (B2B) apps whose sole purpose is to be used by employees or partners of the company. For these kinds of apps, it would be too much of a burden to have all users install and periodically renew developer licenses. In addition, the developer license is for the purpose of app evaluation. For LOB apps, a company would not want to post its internal business apps in the Windows Store where anyone could install them. To install a package containing an enterprise app, Windows allows *sideloading*.

To sideload a package, the enterprise must obtain a Software Publisher Certificate (SPC) from a trusted certificate authority. Windows trusts many certificate authorities without any additional configuration. If your package's certificate is from one of these already trusted authorities, you don't need to deploy and manage additional certificates to the targeted Windows PCs. Alternatively, you can use a certificate from your company's internal Certificate Authority (CA) to sign your package. If you choose this option, your IT administrators need to deploy this CA certificate on the targeted Windows PCs. In Visual Studio's manifest designer, you can click the Packaging tab and then click the Choose Certificate button to select your company's SPC, ensuring that your .appx package file is signed with this SPC. Now the employees' PCs will trust packages signed with this certificate.

In addition to your package being signed with a trusted certificate, machines require the Allow-AllTrustedApps Group Policy setting be enabled. (See *http://technet.microsoft.com/en-us/library/hh852635.aspx*.)

Finally, the PC must be domain-joined and running Windows Enterprise edition or any of the Windows Server editions. Or, if the PC is not domain-joined or running another edition of Windows (such as Windows, Windows Pro, or Windows RT[3]), your company must acquire *Enterprise Sideloading keys* (part number: J7S-00005) from the Microsoft Volume Licensing Service Center (VLSC) website at (*https://www.microsoft.com/licensing/servicecenter/default.aspx*). These licenses never expire.

Customers with Software Assurance for Windows or Windows Virtual Desktop Access (VDA) subscriptions in the following Volume Licensing programs will be granted Enterprise Sideloading keys at no additional cost:

- Enterprise Agreement with Windows

- Enterprise Subscription Agreement with Windows

- Enrollment for Education Solutions with Windows

- Campus and School Agreement with Windows

- Select and Select Plus with Software Assurance for Windows

Other customers can purchase Enterprise Sideloading keys in packs of 100 through Volume Licensing. Enterprise Sideloading keys are available for purchase in the following programs:

- Select and Select Plus

- Open License

Unfortunately, you must purchase Enterprise Sideloading keys in packs of 100. This means that Microsoft provides no cost-effective way of unlocking just a few machines for family, friends, or small businesses. This is a pretty big change from how the Window ecosystem worked in the past with respect to deploying Windows applications. With Windows Store apps, Microsoft wants to enforce a managed environment where packages are verified by Microsoft before they can be installed on users' PCs. This gives Windows users confidence in their PCs and, more importantly, their data. So, while enterprise sideloading makes it possible to bypass the Windows Store, potentially opening up users' PCs and data to mischief, Microsoft is purposely making this difficult to do and hopes that enterprise sideloading is the exception to the rule.

---

[3] Windows RT PCs that run on ARM chips can't join a domain; these PCs require Enterprise Sideloading keys to sideload packages.

When you have the certificate, Group Policy, and Enterprise Sideloading key issues sorted out, actually deploying a package is easy: just run the PowerShell script. Additionally, IT administrators can provision Windows images with apps using Deployment Image Servicing and Management. (See *http://technet.microsoft.com/en-us/library/hh852134.aspx*.) Packages can also be sideloaded using Windows InTune and System Center Configuration Manager. These two Microsoft offerings have additional costs associated with them. However, a Microsoft employee has created a free Windows Store app (with source code) you can use; see *http://companystore.codeplex.com/*.

An additional benefit of deploying in an enterprise is that packages can be preconfigured with initial data such as configuration settings, database connection strings, and so on. For this, you will have to write a small desktop application that calls `Windows.Management.Core.Application-DataManager`'s `CreateForPackageFamily` method to gain access to the package's data directories. Wintellect's Package Explorer Desktop app uses this API.

Windows Store deployments

This method of deployment is by far the most important, and Chapter 11 is dedicated to covering the Windows Store in great detail. This section focuses on the mechanics of deploying an app via the Windows Store.

After reserving a name for your package via the Windows Store dashboard, you use Visual Studio's Associate Your App With The Store menu item to associate your package with the reserved package name. Once you've done this, Visual Studio creates a temporary untrusted signing certificate of which the subject is now a GUID (assigned by the Windows Store). This GUID is your Publisher ID, and it uniquely identifies you as the publisher when you registered your individual or business account with the Windows Store. In your package's manifest file, Visual Studio updates the Package Name, Package Display Name, Publisher, Publisher Display Name, and Application Display Name. Of course, the Package Family Name and Package Full Name are also updated to reflect the new Publisher ID value (GUID).

When you finish developing and testing your app, you upload your final .appxupload file to the Windows Store via the dashboard. Then Microsoft tests your app. After it passes certification, the Windows Store signs your package file with a Windows Store certificate where your Publisher ID GUID is the subject. The Windows Store certificate is already installed on all Windows PCs (which is why it is not necessary to have a developer license or Enterprise Sideloading key installed on users' PCs).

Now when a user downloads your package from the Windows Store, Windows unzips the package's contents into the %ProgramFiles%\WindowsApps directory, registers the package's app with the system for the current user, and the user can now launch the app.

Package staging and registration

The previous section explored the various ways of deploying a package to a user's PC. In this section, we explore how a package integrates itself with the system, allowing a user to activate the package's app. Specifically, we'll talk about staging and registration. Packages are staged once per PC and are registered once per user profile. Note that packages downloaded from the Windows Store are licensed to a user's Microsoft account but they are staged to the user's account on the PC. Usually, these are one and the same; that is, a user has linked her PC account with her Microsoft account. However, they do not have to be the same. In fact, a user can go to the Store app, display the Settings charm > Your Account pane, and change the Microsoft account she used to download packages from the WIndows Store. I do this when I want to install a package I have already purchased on another family member's PC (where that family member logs in as himself).

Staging occurs when Windows unzips the package file's contents into the %ProgramFiles%\ WindowsApps*PackageFullName* directory. You'll notice that Windows uses the package full name, which includes the package's version number. This allows the system to have different versions of the same app installed side by side on a single PC under the %ProgramFiles%\WindowsApps directory. Because the content of this folder is read-only, it can be shared by all users on a PC. The system keeps older versions of the package until all users have either uninstalled or upgraded away from the older version. When a particular version of a package is uninstalled, the subdirectory for the package is completely destroyed, ensuring that the package leaves no footprint behind.

Registration occurs when a user installs a package for himself. During registration, Windows adds entries in the registry for the package. For example, it adds the package under this key:

HKCU\Software\Classes\ActivatableClasses\Package*PackageFullName*

This key contains child nodes with information such as the full path to the package's app's executable and entry point. Additionally, Windows registers each app's declared activation types (contracts). All apps must implement the Launch activation, and Windows registers that here:

HKCU\Software\Classes\Extensions\ContractId\Windows.Launch

For those of you familiar with COM, you'll recognize some concepts.

During registration, Windows also creates a directory for the package's per-user state. This directory is created here:

%UserProfile%\AppData\Local\Packages*PackageFamilyName*

Package state and storage folders are discussed in Chapter 4, "Package data and roaming," and in "Chapter 5, "Storage files and folders." Unlike the %ProgramFiles%\WindowsApps*PackageFullName* directory created during staging, this directory uses the package's family name instead of the package's full name. The package family name does not include the version number. The system does not need the version number for the package's data, because a user can use only one version of a package at a time. Therefore, while a PC can have multiple versions of a package installed for different users at the same time, an individual user will have only one version of the package installed for himself. This also means that if a user upgrades to a new version of a package, the user's per-package data remains on the PC and is accessible by a newer version of the package. Of course, if the user uninstalls a package, the package gets unregistered for that user. This causes all the user's per-package data and registry settings to be completely destroyed, ensuring that the package leaves no footprint behind for that particular user.

If you are experiencing issues with deployment, registration, or staging, examine the following Windows event log locations:

- Application And Services Logs > Microsoft > Windows > AppXDeployment

- Application And Services Logs > Microsoft > Windows > AppXDeployment-Server

- Application And Services Logs > Microsoft > Windows > AppXPackagingOM

Wintellect's Package Explorer desktop app

From the accompanying source code (see *http://wintellect.com/Resource-WinRT-Via-CSharp*), you can download the Wintellect Package Explorer. (See Figure 2-7.) This app is a very useful utility for exploring all the packages installed by the current user. It also allows you to explore a package's data, navigate to its directories, launch its apps, and uninstall packages. It also shows the capabilities and declarations enabled by all the installed packages. The tool also shows the package's local and roaming settings in the bottom pane.

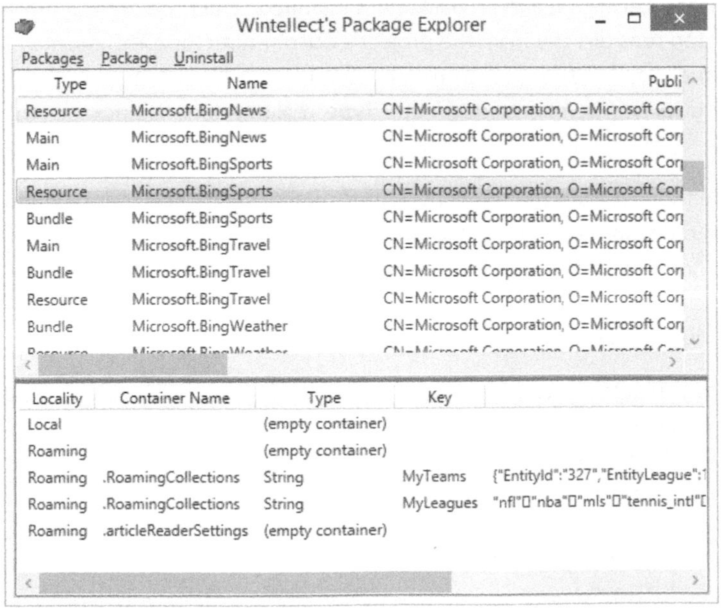

FIGURE 2-7 Wintellect's Package Explorer utility.

Without going into the details of Package Explorer's implementation, here are some of the methods it uses:

- It uses PackageManager's static FindPackagesForUser method to get all the installed packages. PackageManager also has methods to add and remove packages from the PC.

- It uses ApplicationDataManager's static CreateForPackageFamily method to access each package's data. You can see the package data displayed in the bottom pane of Figure 2-7.

- Package Explorer is able to launch apps by calling IApplicationActivationManager's ActivateApplication. This is a COM interface you can use from desktop apps to launch Windows Store apps given their AppUserModelID string.

Most of these methods are callable only from a Windows desktop app because these APIs require standard user privileges and Window Store apps don't have these within their app container. It is unlikely you would need any of these APIs for your Windows Store app development.

Debugging Windows Store apps

This last section presents some general information about debugging a Windows Store app with Visual Studio. Other chapters in this book give additional debugging tips and tricks.

When you use Visual Studio to build and debug your app, Visual Studio creates all your package's files under your project's build directory; the files are *not* zipped into an .appx package file; therefore, nothing is signed with a certificate and no package is installed under the %ProgramFiles%\ WindowsApps directory. The app runs directly from the project's output directory. This means that the app is registered for the user, but the app was never actually staged onto the machine. Wintellect's Package Explorer displays "Development" in the "Type" column for any packages that are registered and not staged.

Of course, if you just delete the files from the project's output directory, the app will no longer work but the app is still registered with the system. Attempting to launch the app via a Start tile immediately fails, returning you right back to the Start screen again. If you select the app and then tap Uninstall, the package will officially be unregistered, meaning that all the app's footprint for the user is destroyed but the package doesn't really get uninstalled because it was never actually staged.

When you make changes to your app in Visual Studio, rebuild it, and rerun it, any per-package data (discussed in Chapter 4) remains on your machine. This is usually desirable because you can run your app, create some state, fix a bug, and then test the fix against the old state. However, in some circumstances, Visual Studio will automatically unregister and reregister your app, thereby deleting any per-package data. Visual Studio does this if you run the app from a different disk location (for example, switching from a Debug build to a Release build), change the XML manifest file, or change certain files (such as Start screen logos). Sometimes, while debugging and testing, you might want to force Visual Studio to delete any per-package data each time you run your app. Visual Studio enables this via its Uninstall And Then Re-Install My Package check box, which is available to you when you look at your project's debug settings. (See Figure 2-8.)

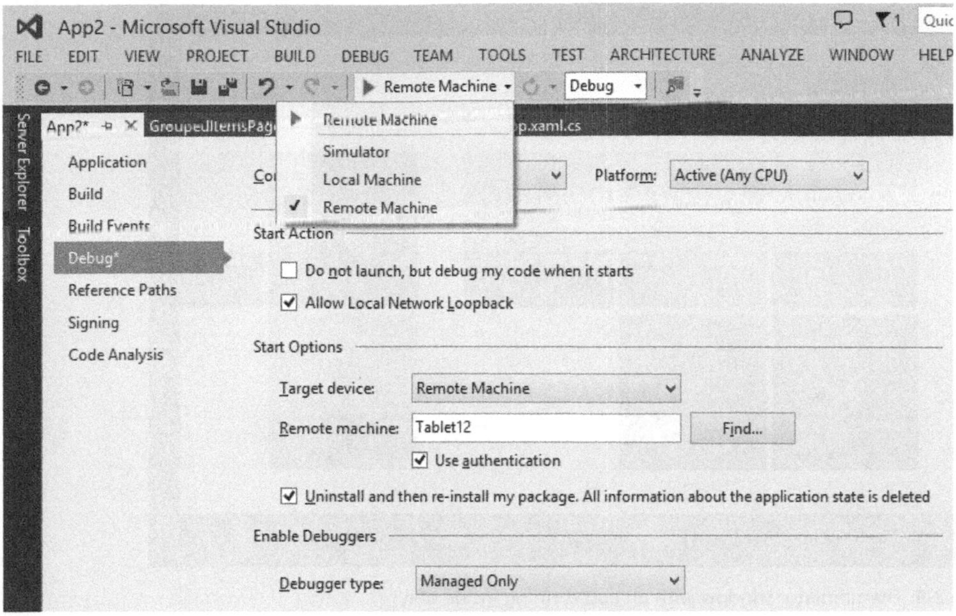

FIGURE 2-8 Visual Studio's Debug properties pane showing the various start options.

In Figure 2-8, you also see that there are different options for Target Device: Simulator, Local Machine, and Remote Machine. You can change the target in the Debug toolbar next to the Play button, or you can change it in the project's properties under the Debug tab. The default Target Device is Local Machine, and this will just register, run, and attach the debugger to your app in your local logon session. A second option is to use Simulator. Selecting this will result in a simulated tablet system, as you see in Figure 2-9.

The simulator provides a set of options in the border on the right. These allow you to simulate touch gestures such as tap, pinch and stretch, and rotate. You can also rotate the simulator's screen in 90-degree increments. An especially interesting feature of the simulator is that you can use it to check how your app would look on PCs with different screen sizes and dots per inch (DPI) settings. The remaining buttons allow you to simulate a change of geo-location, take screen shots of your app, and simulate different network conditions.[4]

You close the simulator by selecting Settings charm > Power > Disconnect or by displaying its context menu via its icon on the desktop taskbar and then selecting Close Window. But, to improve launching a debugging session, leave the simulator running between launches of your app.

---

[4] The simulator is implemented as a terminal services remote app. You can see in Task Manager's User tab that running the simulator results in an additional logon session. Because this additional session can lead to additional instances of apps running under the same user, some desktop apps might show unexpected behavior when the simulator is running. In addition, beware that deleting any files in the simulator actually deletes the files from your host system!

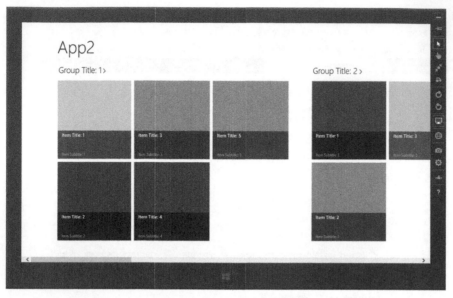

FIGURE 2-9 The simulator window with an app running inside of it.

In addition to debugging on the local PC and via the simulator, you can also debug your app when it is running remotely on another physical PC. On the remote PC, you will have to install the Remote Tools for Visual Studio, downloadable from here: *http://www.microsoft.com/visualstudio/eng/ downloads*. There is a version for x86, x64, and ARM, and this is the only way you can debug on ARM architectures because there is no ARM version of Visual Studio.

CHAPTER 3

Process model

In this chapter, we delve into a Windows Store app's process model. Specifically, we'll look at the various ways that an app gets activated as well as how it uses threads and windows. We'll also talk about how to best architect your app so that it uses memory efficiently as it navigates the user from page to page. We'll conclude with a discussion of process lifetime management (PLM) and how Microsoft Windows manages your app's lifetime to further conserve memory, reduce CPU usage, and simplify the end-user experience.

Understanding this topic is critical to building Windows Store apps. If you are familiar with the Windows desktop app process model, you know that it is relatively easy to understand because you can usually get away with using just one thread, a main window, and then lots of child windows. However, the Windows Store app process model is substantially different and more complex because it uses several threads, each having at most one window, and child controls are simply drawn on a window. And this is just the tip of the iceberg in terms of complexity. The additional complexity is the result of two main factors:

- Windows Store apps are single instance. Windows allows only one instance of a Windows Store app to run at a time on the system. This conserves memory because multi-instance apps would each have their own memory. Because most apps have a single window, switching between apps is simpler for end users. Instead of seeing many windows they can switch to, users now see fewer windows. However, this makes your app more complex because you must now write the code to manage multiple documents or tabs yourself.

- Windows Store app activations. Windows Store apps can be activated for myriad reasons. All activations re-activate the already-running app and some activations cause other threads and windows to be created that your code has to manage.

App activation

In this section, we talk about app activation. Specifically, we'll discuss how Windows creates a process for your app and allows your app to initialize itself, and then we'll look at how your app can start doing work on behalf of the user.

An app can be activated for several reasons. The most obvious is when the user taps your app's tile from the Start screen. This kind of activation is called a *launch activation*, and all Windows Store apps must support launch activation; there is no way for a Windows Store app to opt out of it. But your Windows Store app can also be activated by the user tapping one of your app's secondary tiles on the Start screen or if the user selects a toast notification that your app displays. (See Chapter 8, "Tiles and toast notifications," for more information.) Activating your app due to a secondary tile or toast notification is also known as a *launch activation*. In addition to supporting launch activations, your app can optionally support other activations. For example, you can allow your app to be activated by the user opening a file in File Explorer, attaching a device (like a camera) to the PC, attempting to share content from another app with your app, and so on. There is a WinRT-enumerated type called `Windows.ApplicationModel.Activation.ActivationKind` that indicates all the ways an app can be activated. Table 3-1 shows the values offered by this enumeration and briefly describes each. Some of these activations are discussed in other chapters in this book, and some are very rarely used, so we will not discuss them at all.

TABLE 3-1 ActivationKind values, their descriptions, and their view type.

ActivationKind value	Activates your app when	View activation
Launch	User taps app's primary tile, a secondary tile, or a toast notification.	Main
Search	User uses the Search charm to search within your app while it's in the foreground.	Main
File	Another app launches a file whose file type is supported by your app.	Main
Protocol	Another app launches a URI whose scheme is supported by your app.	Main
Device	User attaches a device to the PC that is supported by your app (AutoPlay).	Main
Contact	User wants your app to post, message, call, video call, or map a contact.	Main
LockScreenCall	User taps a toast that answers a call when the user has locked her PC.	Main
AppointmentsProvider	Another app wants your app to show a time frame.	Main
	Another app wants your app to add, replace, or remove an appointment.	Hosted
ShareTarget	User wants to share content from another app with your app.	Hosted
FileOpenPicker	Another app allows the user to open a file from a location your app has access to.	Hosted
FileSavePicker	Another app allows the user to save a file to a location your app has access to.	Hosted
CachedFileUpdater	Another app uses a file your app has cached.	Hosted
ContactPicker	Another app allows the user to access a contact maintained by your app.	Hosted
PrintTaskSettings	Your app is an app associated with a printer and exposes its settings.	Hosted
CameraSettings	Your app is an app associated with a camera and exposes its settings.	Hosted

Figure 3-1 shows the relationship between various WinRT types that make up a running app, and Figure 3-2 shows a flowchart explaining how these various WinRT objects get created at runtime during app activation. You'll want to periodically refer to these two figures as we continue the discussion.

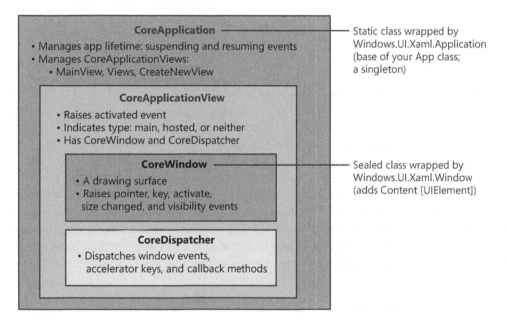

FIGURE 3-1 The relationship between various WinRT types that make up a running app.

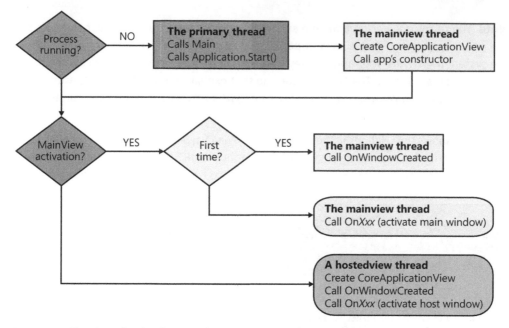

FIGURE 3-2 Flowchart showing how Windows activates an app.

When Windows needs to activate an app, it first displays a splash screen so that the user gets immediate feedback indicating that the app is starting. Windows gets the splash screen image and background color from the app's manifest; this allows Windows to display the splash screen while the app is initializing. At the same time, Windows creates a process and loads the app's code into it. After this, Windows creates the process' primary thread and invokes a Main method. When you build a Windows Store app, a Main method is created for you automatically in an App.g.i.cs file. The Main method looks like this:[1]

```
#if !DISABLE_XAML_GENERATED_MAIN
    public static class Program {
        static void Main(String[] args) {
            Windows.UI.Xaml.Application.Start((p) => new App());
        }
    }
#endif
```

As you can see, this method doesn't do very much. When the process' primary thread calls Main, it internally calls Windows.UI.Xaml.Application's static Start method, which creates another thread called the *main view thread*. This thread then creates a Windows.ApplicationModel.Core. CoreApplicationView object that is your app's main drawing surface. The CoreApplicationView object is associated with the main view thread and can be manipulated only by code executed by the main view thread. The main view thread then invokes the callback method passed as a parameter to Application's Start method, which constructs an instance of your app's App class. The

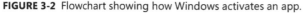

[1] If you want to implement your own Main method and not use the XAML-generated one, you can do so by adding the DISABLE_XAML_GENERATED_MAIN conditional compilation symbol to your project's build settings.

`Application` base class' constructor stores a reference to your App object in a private static field, ensuring that it never gets garbage collected for the entire lifetime of the process. You can always get a reference to your app's singleton App object by calling `Application`'s static `Current` property.

> **Important** This App object is a singleton object that lives throughout the entire lifetime of the process. Because this object is never destroyed, any other objects directly or indirectly referred to by any static or instance fields will prevent those other objects from being garbage collected. Be careful about this because this can be a source of memory leaks.

After the App object singleton is created, the primary thread checks the `ActivationKind` value to see why the app is being activated. All the activations fall into one of two categories: *main view activations* or *hosted view activations*. (See the last column in Table 3-1.) Main view activations are what most developers are familiar with. A main view activation causes your app's main window to become the foreground window and allows the user to interact with your app.

Hosted view activations are not as familiar to many people. In this case, an app wants to complete some operation leveraging some functionality provided by another app. The app the user is interacting with asks Windows to create a new window and then Windows activates the other app. This second app will create a small window that gets hosted inside Windows' big window. This is why the activation is called a hosted view activation: the app is being activated to have its window hosted for use by another app. An example of a hosted view activation is when the user wants to share a webpage with a friend via the Mail app. Figure 3-3 shows the Bing News app as the main app the user is interacting with. If the user taps the Share charm and selects the Mail app, Windows creates a narrow, full-height window on the edge of the user's screen. The header is displayed by Windows at the top of the window it created. The header contains the back arrow, app name (Mail), and logo. Underneath the header is a hosted view window created and managed by the Mail app itself.

Your App class is derived from the `Windows.UI.Xaml.Application` class, which defines some virtual methods as shown here:

```
public class Application {
   // Override to know when the main view thread's or
   // a hosted view thread's window has been created
   protected virtual void OnWindowCreated(WindowCreatedEventArgs args);

   // Override any of these main view activations:
   protected virtual void OnLaunched(LaunchActivatedEventArgs args);
   protected virtual void OnSearchActivated(SearchActivatedEventArgs args);
   protected virtual void OnFileActivated(FileActivatedEventArgs args);

   // Override any of these hosted view activations:
   protected virtual void OnShareTargetActivated(ShareTargetActivatedEventArgs args);
   protected virtual void OnFileOpenPickerActivated(FileOpenPickerActivatedEventArgs args);
   protected virtual void OnFileSavePickerActivated(FileSavePickerActivatedEventArgs args);
   protected virtual void OnCachedFileUpdaterActivated(
      CachedFileUpdaterActivatedEventArgs args);
```

```
// Override this for less-frequently used main view (Protocol, Device,
// AppointmentsProvider, Contact, LockScreenCall) and hosted view (ContactPicker,
// PrintTaskSettings, CameraSettings) activations:
protected virtual void OnActivated(IActivatedEventArgs args);
}
```

FIGURE 3-3 The Bing News app sharing a news story via the Mail app's hosted view window.

As soon as a main view or hosted view window is created, the thread creating the window calls the virtual OnWindowCreated method. If you override this method, the WindowsCreatedEventArgs object passed to it contains a reference to the thread's newly created window. In this method, you can register callback methods with any of the events (Activated, SizeChanged, VisibilityChanged, or Closed) it offers. After OnWindowCreated returns, one and only one of the other virtual methods is called, depending on why your app is being activated. The OnActivated method is called for the less-commonly used activation kinds.

Inside one of these virtual methods, you perform any initialization required for the specific kind of activation, create the desired user-interface element tree, set Window's Content property to the root of your user-interface element tree, and then activate the view's CoreApplicationView object, thereby bringing your app's window to the foreground so that the user can interact with it.

If your app is being activated due to a hosted view activation, your app's primary thread will create a hosted view thread. This thread then creates its own CoreApplicationView object that is your app's drawing surface while hosted. When the hosted view is no longer required by the hosting app, your host `CoreApplicationView` window and the hosted view thread are destroyed. Every time your app is activated with a hosted view activation, a new hosted view thread and `CoreApplicationView` window are created. In fact, multiple apps could host your app simultaneously. For example, several apps can host an app implementing the FileOpenPicker contract simultaneously. If this happens, your app's process will have one hosted view thread and `CoreApplicationView` window for each app that is currently hosting your app. On the other hand, your app's process will never have more than one main view thread and main `CoreApplicationView` window.

While your app is running, it could be activated with more main view activations. This typically happens if the user taps one of your app's secondary tiles or a toast notification. In this case, the app comes to the foreground but the act of tapping a tile or toast notification might direct the app to show something special when brought to the foreground. When an already-running app is activated with a new main view activation, the process' primary thread will not create the main view thread and its `CoreApplicationView` because these have already been created. Because the window has already been created, the virtual `OnWindowCreated` method will not be called, but the proper virtual method indicating why the main view is being re-activated will be called. This virtual method should respond accordingly by deciding what UI to show and then activating the main view window so that the user can interact with it.

> **Important** Avoid registering event handlers inside a main view activation's virtual method because these methods can be called multiple times and you do not want to register multiple callbacks with a single event over the lifetime of your process. It can be OK to register callback methods with events inside the `OnWindowCreated` method because this method is called only once per thread/window.

Note that your app might not be running at all, and then a user can activate your app for a hosted view. This causes your app's primary thread to be created, and then a hosted view thread and its window are created. But your app's main view thread and window are not created at this time. If the user now activates your app with a main view activation, Windows will now create your app's main view thread and window, call the `OnWindowCreated` method, and then call the virtual method indicating why your app is being activated with a main view activation.

Managing the process model

The previous section discussed how your app activates and initializes itself. In this section, we discuss some core WinRT classes you should be aware of and how you can use them now that your app is up and running. As you read this discussion, you might want to periodically refer back to Figure 3-1, which shows the relationship between these classes.

WinRT offers a `Windows.ApplicationModel.Core.CoreApplication` class that looks like this:

```
public static class CoreApplication {
    // Returns the CoreApplicationView associated with the calling thread
    public static CoreApplicationView GetCurrentView();

    // Returns all CoreApplicationViews existing within the process
    public static IReadOnlyList<CoreApplicationView> Views { get; }

    // Returns the main view thread's CoreApplicationView
    public static CoreApplicationView MainView { get; }

    // These events are discussed later in this chapter
    public static event EventHandler<Object> Resuming;
    public static event EventHandler<SuspendingEventArgs> Suspending;

    // These events are for debugging only
    public static event EventHandler<Object> Exiting;
    public static event EventHandler<UnhandledErrorDetectedEventArgs> UnhandledErrorDetected;

    // This method allows you to create multiple main view windows
    public static CoreApplicationView CreateNewView();

    // Some members not shown here...
}
```

As you can see, this class is a static class. This means that you cannot create instances of this class. So this static class manages your app as a whole. However, static classes don't lend themselves to nice object-oriented programming features like inheritance and virtual methods. So, for XAML developers, WinRT also offers the `Windows.UI.Xaml.Application` class that we discussed earlier; this is the class that has all the virtual methods in it, making it easier for you to implement your activation code. In effect, the `Application` singleton object we discussed wraps the static `CoreApplication` class. Now let me show you some of the other members of this `Application` class:

```
public class Application  {
    // Static members:
    public static void Start(ApplicationInitializationCallback callback);
    public static Application Current { get; }

    // The same Resuming & Suspending events offered by the CoreApplication class
    public event EventHandler<object> Resuming;
    public event SuspendingEventHandler Suspending;

    // XAML-specific properties and events:
    public DebugSettings DebugSettings { get; }
    public ApplicationTheme RequestedTheme { get; set; }
    public ResourceDictionary Resources { get; set; }
    public event UnhandledExceptionEventHandler UnhandledException;

    // The virtual methods shown earlier and some other members are not shown here...
}
```

Your App class derives from this Application class, inheriting all the instance members, and allows you to override the virtual methods.

Let's go back to the CoreApplication class. This class has many members that return Core-ApplicationView objects. Here is what the CoreApplicationView class looks like:

```
public sealed class CoreApplicationView {
    public CoreDispatcher Dispatcher { get; }
    public CoreWindow    CoreWindow { get; }
    public Boolean       IsMain     { get; }
    public Boolean       IsHosted   { get; }

    public event TypedEventHandler<CoreApplicationView, IActivatedEventArgs> Activated;
}
```

As you can see, a CoreApplicationView object refers to a CoreDispatcher (the message pump that dispatches window messages) and a CoreWindow (the actual drawing surface), and it has an additional field indicating whether the CoreWindow is the app's main window or one of the app's hosted windows. There is also an Activated event that is raised when the window is being activated; the IActivatedEventArgs interface includes a Kind property, which returns one of the Activation-Kind enumeration values (as shown in Table 3-1). Other members of this interface are described later in this chapter's "Process lifetime management" section.

A CoreWindow object is a drawing surface, and it has associated with it the standard things you'd expect with a window. It has state (fields) indicating the bounding rectangle, whether input is enabled, which cursor to display, and whether the window is visible or not. It also offers events such as Activated, Closed, SizeChanged, VisibilityChanged, as well as keyboard and pointer (mouse, touch, and stylus) input events. And there are methods such as Activate, Close, Get(Async)Key-State, Set/ReleasePointerCapture, and a static GetForCurrentThread method.

For XAML developers, there is a sealed Windows.UI.Xaml.Window class that puts a thin wrapper around a CoreWindow object:

```
public sealed class Window  {
    public static Window Current { get; }    // Returns calling thread's Window
    public CoreWindow CoreWindow { get; }
    public CoreDispatcher Dispatcher { get; } // Same as CoreApplicationView.Dispatcher

    // The Content property is how XAML integrates with the window's drawing surface:
    public UIElement Content { get; set; }

    // This class exposes some of the same properties (Bounds, Visible)
    // This class exposes some of the same events (Activated, Closed,
    // SizeChanged, VisibilityChanged)
    // This class exposes some of the same methods (Activate, Close)
}
```

The final WinRT class to discuss here is the `Windows.UI.Core.CoreDispatcher` class, which looks like this:

```
public sealed class CoreDispatcher {
    // Returns true if the calling thread is the same thread
    // that this CoreDispatcher object is associated with
    public Boolean HasThreadAccess { get; }

    // Call this to have the CoreDispatcher's thread execute the agileCallback
    // with a priority of Idle, Low, Normal, or High
    public IAsyncAction RunAsync(
        CoreDispatcherPriority priority, DispatchedHandler agileCallback);

    // Call this to get/set the priority of the code that dispatcher is currently executing
    public CoreDispatcherPriority CurrentPriority { get; set; }

    // Other members not shown...
}
```

Many .NET developers are already familiar with this `CoreDispatcher` class because it behaves quite similarly to the `Dispatcher` class found in Windows Presentation Foundation (WPF) and Silverlight. Because each `CoreApplicationView` has only one thread that manages it, its `CoreDispatcher` object lets you execute a method on that same thread, allowing the method to update that view's user interface. This is useful when some arbitrary thread calls one of your methods and you then need to update the user interface. I will talk more about the `CoreDispatcher` and show how to use it in other chapters.

A Windows Store app's main view can create additional views to show additional content. These views can be shown side by side on the same monitor and resized to the user's liking or shown on different monitors. For example, the Windows Mail app allows you to open new views, enabling you to refer to one mail message while composing another simultaneously. Apps can create new view threads and views by calling `CoreApplication`'s static `CreateNewView` method. This method creates a new thread along with its own `CoreDispatcher` and `CoreWindow`, ultimately returning a `CoreApplicationView`. For this `CoreApplicationView` object, the `IsMain` and `IsHosted` properties both return `false`. Of course, when you create a new view, your App's `OnWindowCreated` virtual method is called via the new thread. Then you can create the UI for this new view using code like this:

```
private async Task CreateNewViewWindow() {
    // Have Windows create a new thread, CoreDispatcher, CoreWindow, and CoreApplicationView
    CoreApplicationView cav = CoreApplication.CreateNewView();

    CoreWindow newAppViewWindow = null; // This will hold the new view's window

    // Have the new thread initialize the new view's content
    await cav.Dispatcher.RunAsync(CoreDispatcherPriority.Normal, () => {
        // Give the new thread's window back to the creating thread
        newAppViewWindow = Window.Current.CoreWindow;

        // Create the desired UI element tree and make it the content of the new window
        Window.Current.Content = new MyPage();
        Window.Current.Activate();
    });
```

```
    // After the new thread initializes its view, the creating thread makes it appear
    Int32 newAppViewId = ApplicationView.GetApplicationViewIdForWindow(newAppViewWindow);
    await ApplicationViewSwitcher.TryShowAsStandaloneAsync(newAppViewId,
        ViewSizePreference.UseLess);
    // The SDK documentation for Windows.UI.ViewManagement.ApplicationViewSwitcher explains
    // its other methods, allowing you to control switching between your app's views.
}
```

The previous code leverages the `Windows.UI.ViewManagement.ApplicationView` class. This class offers many dynamic properties related to a view. In other words, these properties' values change frequently. The class looks like this:

```
public sealed class ApplicationView {
    // Gets the view for the calling thread
    public static ApplicationView GetForCurrentView();

    // Gets the unique window ID corresponding to a specific CoreWindow
    public static Int32 GetApplicationViewIdForWindow(ICoreWindow window);

    // Gets a unique ID identifying this view. NOTE: This ID is passed to
    // an XxxActivatedEventArgs' CurrentlyShownApplicationViewId property
    public Int32 Id { get; }

    // Gets/sets the view's title (shown in task switchers) & if PrtScn can capture its content
    public String  Title { get; set; }
    public Boolean IsScreenCaptureEnabled { get; set; }

    // Read-only properties related to view's position & size
    public ApplicationViewOrientation Orientation { get; }  // Landscape or Portrait
    public Boolean AdjacentToLeftDisplayEdge { get; }
    public Boolean AdjacentToRightDisplayEdge { get; }
    public Boolean IsFullScreen { get; }
    public Boolean IsOnLockScreen { get; }
    // Raised when the view is removed from task switcher (if user closes the view)
    public event TypedEventHandler<ApplicationView, ApplicationViewConsolidatedEventArgs>
        Consolidated;

    // Indicates if app terminates when all views close (Default=false)
    public static Boolean TerminateAppOnFinalViewClose { get; set; }
}
```

XAML page navigation

Most XAML apps show the user a view with an initial page and then allow the user to navigate to other pages within the view. This is similar to a website paradigm where users start at a website's home page and then click on links to delve into specific sections of the website. Users are also quite familiar with navigating back to pages they've seen before and, occasionally, after navigating back, users navigate forward to a page they were just looking at. Windows Store apps typically offer this same user experience. Of course, some Windows Store apps might just show a single page and, in this case, navigation doesn't come into play at all.

In this section, I talk about the XAML support for page navigation and how to manage memory for this efficiently. Microsoft provides a WinRT class called `Windows.UI.Xaml.Controls.Frame`. An instance of this class manages a collection of UI pages allowing the user to navigate backward and forward through them. The class derives from `ContentControl`, which ultimately derives from `UIElement`, allowing you to assign a `Frame` object to `Window`'s `Content` property to place XAML content on a drawing surface. The `Frame` class looks like this:

```
public class Frame : ContentControl, INavigate {
    // Clears the stack from the next Page type to the end
    // and appends a new Page type to the stack
    public Boolean Navigate(Type sourcePageType, Object parameter);

    public Boolean CanGoBack { get; }      // True if positioned after the 1st Page type
    public void    GoBack();                // Navigates to the previous page type
    public Boolean CanGoForward { get; }   // True if a Page type exists after the current position
    public void    GoForward();             // Navigates to the next Page type

    // These members return the stack's content and size
    public IList<PageStackEntry> BackStack { get; }
    public Int23 BackStackDepth { get; }

    // Member to serialize/deserialize the stack's types/parameters to/from a string
    public String GetNavigationState();
    public void   SetNavigationState(String navigationState);

    // Some members not shown
}
```

Frame objects hold a collection of `Windows.UI.Xaml.Controls.Page`-derived types. Notice that they hold Page-derived *types*, not Page-derived *objects*. To have the `Frame` object navigate to a new Page-derived object, you call the `Navigate` method, passing in a reference to a `System.Type` object that identifies the page you want to navigate to. Internally, the `Navigate` method constructs an instance of the Page-derived type and makes this object be the content of the `Frame` object, allowing the user to interact with the page's user interface. Your Page-derived types must derive from `Windows.UI.Xaml.Controls.Page`, which looks like this:

```
public class Page : UserControl {
    // Returns the Frame that "owns" this page
    public Frame Frame { get; }

    // Invoked when the Page is loaded and becomes the current content of a parent Frame
    protected virtual void OnNavigatedTo(NavigationEventArgs e);

    // Invoked after the Page is no longer the current content of its parent Frame
    protected virtual void OnNavigatedFrom(NavigationEventArgs e);

    // Gets or sets the navigation mode that indicates whether this Page is cached,
    // and the period of time that the cache entry should persist.
    public NavigationCacheMode NavigationCacheMode { get; set; }

    // Other members not shown
}
```

After the `Frame` object constructs an instance of your `Page`-derived type, it calls the virtual `On-NavigatedTo` method. Your class should override this method and have it perform any initialization for the page. When you call `Frame`'s `Navigate` method, you get to pass an object reference as a parameter. Your `Page`-derived object can get the value of this parameter type by querying `NavigationEventArgs`'s read-only `Parameter` property. This gives you a way to pass some data from the code when navigating to a new page. For reasons that will be described later, in the "Process lifetime management" section, the value you pass should be serializable.

Page objects can be very expensive in terms of memory consumption because pages tend to have many controls and some of these controls are collection controls, which might manage many items. When the user navigates to a new `Page`, keeping all the previous `Page`s with all their child objects in memory can be quite inefficient. This is why the `Frame` object maintains `Page` types, not instances of `Page` objects. When the user navigates to another `Page`, the `Frame` removes all references to the previous page object, which allows the page object and all its child objects to be garbage collected, freeing up what can potentially be a lot of memory. Then, if the user navigates back to a previous page, the `Frame` constructs a new `Page` object and calls its `OnNavigatedTo` method so that the new `Page` object can initialize itself, reallocating whatever memory it needs.[2]

This is all fine and good but what if your `Page` needs to record some state in between being garbage collected and re-initialized? For example, the user might have entered some text in a `TextBox` control or scrolled to and selected a specific item in a `ListView` or `GridView` control. When the `Page` gets garbage collected, all of this state is destroyed by the garbage collector. So, when the user navigates away from a `Page`, in the `OnNavigatedFrom` method, you need to preserve the minimal amount of state necessary in order to restore the `Page` back to where it was before the user navigated away from it. And this state must be preserved in a place where it will not get garbage collected.

The recommended practice is to have your `App` singleton object maintain a collection of dictionaries; something like a `List<Dictionary<String, Object>>`. You have one dictionary for each page managed by the `Frame`, and each dictionary contains a set of key/value pairs; use one key/value pair for each piece of page state you need to persist. Now, because your `App` singleton object stays alive for the lifetime of your process, it keeps the collection alive and the collection keeps all the dictionaries alive.

When navigating to a new page, you add a new dictionary to the list. When navigating to a previous page, look up its dictionary in the list using `Frame`'s `BackStackDepth` property. Figure 3-4 shows what objects you should have in memory after the app navigates to Page_A. The `Frame` object has a single Page_A type in its collection along with its navigation parameter, and our list of dictionaries has just one dictionary in it. Notice that the Page_A object can reference the dictionary, but you must make sure that nothing in the `App` singleton object refers to any page object because this prevents the page object from being garbage collected. Also, avoid registering any of the page's instance methods with external events because this also prevents the page object from ever being garbage

---

[2] If you are less concerned about memory conservation, you can override this default behavior and have the `Frame` object keep your page objects in memory by setting your `Page` object's `NavigationCacheMode` property. See the SDK documentation for details.

collected. Or, if you do register any instance methods with events, make sure you unregister them in the OnNavigatedFrom method.

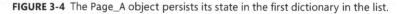

FIGURE 3-4 The Page_A object persists its state in the first dictionary in the list.

Now, if the user navigates to Page_B, the Frame constructs a Page_B object, makes it the current contents of the Frame, and calls its OnNavigatedTo method. In the OnNavigatedTo method, we add another dictionary to the list, and this is where the page instance persists its state. Figure 3-5 shows what objects you should have in memory after the user navigates from Page_A to Page_B.

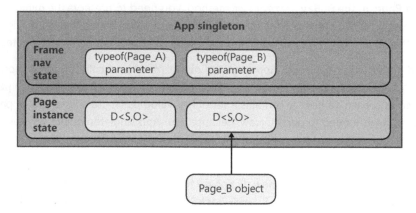

FIGURE 3-5 The Page_A object can be garbage collected, and the new Page_B object persists its state in the second dictionary in the list.

From here, the user might navigate from Page_B back to Page_A. Doing so would cause the Page_B object to be garbage collected, and a new Page_A object would be created, which would refer to the first dictionary in the list. Or, from Page_B, the user might navigate to a new Page_A object whose content is populated based on the navigation parameter passed to OnNavigatedTo and extracted via NavigationEventArgs's Parameter property. Figure 3-6 shows what objects you should have in memory after the user navigates forward from Page_B to a new Page_A.

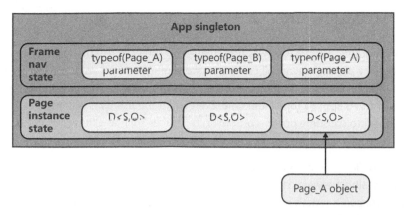

FIGURE 3-6 The second Page_A object persists its state in the third dictionary in the list.

Now, if the user navigates backward from the new Page_A to Page_B, the Frame object removes its reference to the Page_A object, allowing it to be garbage collected. But the dictionary maintains that instance of Page_A's state so that it can restore its state should the user later navigate forward again from Page_B to a new Page_A object. Similarly, the user can navigate back and forth throughout all the page types in Frame's collection. Navigating to a page constructs a new page, restoring its state from the dictionary. By the way, if the user is currently at the first Page_A and then, from this page, the app decides to navigate to Page_C, then the dictionaries beyond the current page must be removed from the list (allowing them to be garbage collected) because the user is navigating down a whole different branch of the app's user interface now.

With this model in place, memory is used very efficiently by your app. There is another benefit we get when using this model, which is described later in the "Process lifetime management" section of this chapter. By the way, some of the Visual Studio templates for creating Windows Store apps spit out source code for a SuspensionManager class that manages page instance state. This class is not a WinRT class, and it is not part of Windows; the source code for the class is injected into your Visual Studio project when you create it.

Personally, I do not use the SuspensionManager class in my own projects. Instead, I created my own FramePageStateManager class that, in my opinion, is better. It has a cleaner interface and also leverages some helper classes that put a type-safety wrapper around each dictionary, giving you support for IntelliSense, compile-time type safety, and data binding. These additional features greatly simplify the effort of coding your app and managing its state. The code to manage it all is part of the Process Model app that is available with the downloadable code that accompanies this book; see *http://Wintellect.com/Resource-WinRT-Via-CSharp.*

Process lifetime management

Back when the Windows operating system (OS) was first created (in the early 1980s), there were no computers that ran on battery power. Instead, all computers were plugged into an AC power source, which effectively meant that there was an infinite amount of power to draw on. Because power was in infinite supply, Windows allowed apps to run all the time. Even when the user was not interacting with the app, the app was allowed to consume power-consuming resources such as CPU time, disk I/O, and network I/O.

But today, users want mobile computer systems that do run on battery power and they want the battery to last as long as possible between charges. For Windows to meet user demands, Windows Store apps are allowed to consume system resources (and power) only when the user is interacting with the app; when the user switches away from a Windows Store app, the OS suspends all threads in the process, preventing the app from executing any more of its code, and this prevents consumption of power.

In addition, the original version of Windows was designed for keyboard and mouse input only. But nowadays, users demand systems that use more intuitive and natural touch-based input. When using a mouse as an input device, users are more likely to tolerate a lag. For example, when paging down in a document, the user can click the mouse on a scroll bar and then, after releasing the mouse button, the document scrolls. The user clicks *and then* the document scrolls. But, with touch input, the document needs to scroll *as* the user swipes his finger. With touch, users won't tolerate a lag between swiping and the document scrolling. When apps are allowed to run and consume resources when the user is not interacting with them, these apps can take resources away from the app the user is interacting with, negatively affecting the performance and introducing lag for the user. This is another reason why Windows Store apps have all their threads suspended when the user is not interacting with them.

Furthermore, Windows puts a lot of time restrictions on Windows Store apps. If your app does not meet a time restriction, the OS terminates your app, bringing the user back to the Start screen where he can relaunch your app or run another app that performs more satisfactorily.

Figure 3-7 shows the lifetime of a Windows Store app. When your app is activated, Windows immediately shows your app's splash screen (as specified in your app's manifest file). This gives the user immediate feedback that your app is initializing. While the splash screen is visible, Windows invokes your app's `Main` method and runs through all the activation steps as described at the beginning of this chapter. One of the last things your app does after initializing is activate its window (drawing surface) by calling `Windows.UI.Xaml.Window`'s `Activate` method. If your app does not call this method within 15 seconds, the OS terminates your app and returns the user to the Start screen.[3] While the OS gives your app 15 seconds to activate its window, your app must actually activate its window within 5 seconds in order to pass Windows Store certification. So you really should design your app to complete its initialization and activate its window within 5 seconds, not 15 seconds.

---

[3] Actually, Windows terminates your app only if the user navigates away from its splash screen. If the user leaves the splash screen in the foreground, the app is not terminated.

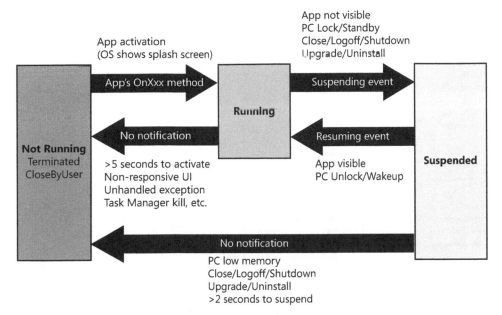

FIGURE 3-7 Lifetime of a Windows Store app.

If your app needs more than 5 seconds to initialize, you can implement an *extended splash screen* as shown in the Process Model app available with the downloadable code that accompanies this book. This means that your app is activating a window that looks similar to the splash screen during its initialization. But, because you activated a window, the OS believes that your app is alive and well and it will not terminate your app now. Because you are in control of this window, you can show the user a progress ring or use other UI affordances to indicate to the user that your app requires more time to initialize. For an example of an app that shows an extended splash screen, see the Skype app that comes with Windows.

If your app displays content such as news articles, your app can bring up an empty wireframe or grid that gets populated as data flows in from the network. In this scenario, your app does not require an extended splash screen; the user can start interacting with it immediately.

Windows Store app suspension

When the user switches away from your app, the OS suspends all the threads in your process. You can see this for yourself in Task Manager (shown in Figure 3-8). First, in Task Manager, select the View menu's Status Values option and make sure that Show Suspended Status is selected. Then launch multiple Windows Store apps. After a few seconds, Task Manager shows a status of Suspended for any apps whose threads are suspended. For suspended apps, you'll also notice that their CPU, Disk, and Network consumption all go to 0. Of course, memory is not impacted because these apps are still resident in memory.

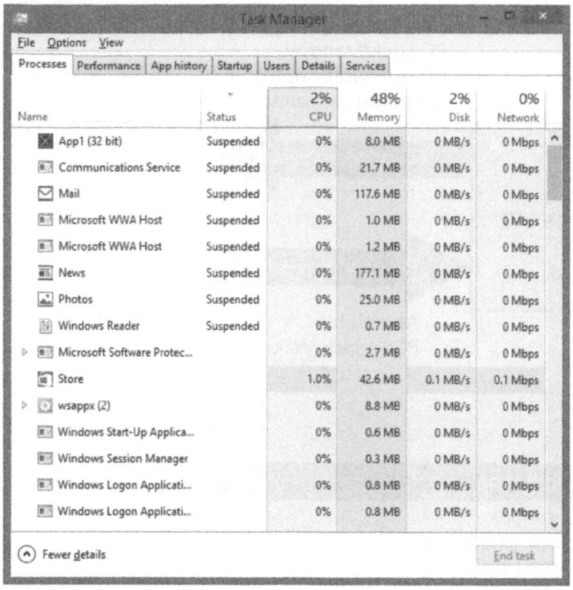

FIGURE 3-8 Task Manager showing some suspended Windows Store apps.

When the user switches back to a suspended app, the system simply resumes the app's threads and allows the app to interact with the user again. This is great, but what if your app shows real-time data like temperature, stock prices, or sports scores? Your app could have been suspended for weeks or maybe months. In this case, you wouldn't want your app to simply resume and show the user stale data. So WinRT's Application base class offers a Resuming event (which really just wraps CoreApplication's Resuming event). When an app is resumed, this event is raised and your app can refresh its data to show the user current information. To know how long your app was suspended, query the time in the Suspending event and subtract this value from the time obtained in the Resuming event; there might be no need to refresh data if only a small amount of time passed. There is no time restriction placed on your Resuming event's callback method. Many apps do not show real-time data, so many apps have no need to register with the Resuming event.

> **Important** If Windows suspends your app and subsequently activates it with a hosted view activation (such as Share), Windows does not resume all the threads in your app; the main view thread remains suspended. This can lead to blocking threads if you attempt to perform any kind of cross-thread communication.

Windows Store app termination

In this chapter, we've talked a lot about how to efficiently manage memory used by your app. This is critically important because many mobile PCs do not have the amount of memory that desktop computers traditionally have. But, even if all Windows Store apps manage their memory as described in this chapter, there is still a chance that the user could start many Windows Store apps and the system will still run out of memory. At this point, a user has to close some currently running app in order to run some new app. But which apps should the user close? A good choice is the one using the most amount of memory, but how does the user know which app this is? There is no good answer to this question, and even if there was, it puts a big burden on the user to figure this stuff out and to manage it.

So, for Windows Store apps, Microsoft has taken this problem away from the user and has instead solved the problem in the OS itself—although you, as a software developer, must also contribute effort to solving the problem. When available memory is running low, Windows automatically terminates a Windows Store app that the user is not currently interacting with. Of course, the user is not aware that this has happened because the user is not interacting with the app. The system remembers that the app was running and allows the user to switch back to the app via the Windows Store apps task list (Windows key+Tab). When the user switches back to the app, the OS automatically relaunches the app so that the user can interact with the app again.

> **Note** The less memory your app uses, the less likely the OS is to terminate it.

Of course, an app uses its memory to maintain state on behalf of the user. And, when the OS terminates an app, the memory is freed up and therefore the state is discarded. This is where you, as a developer, come in. Before your app is terminated, it must save its state to disk and, when your app is relaunched, it must restore its state. If your app does this correctly, it gives the illusion to the user that your app was never terminated and remained in memory the whole time (although your app's splash screen is shown while your app re-initializes). The result is that users do not have to manage an app's lifetime; instead, the OS works with your app to manage it, resulting in a better end-user experience. Again, this is especially useful with mobile PCs, which have limited amounts of memory.

Earlier, we talked about the Resuming event and how it is raised when the OS resumes your app's threads. Well, the WinRT Application base class also offers a Suspending event (which really just wraps CoreApplication's Suspending event). Just before an app's threads are suspended, this event is raised so that your app can persist its state out to a file on the user's disk.[4] Windows gives your app 5 seconds to complete its suspension; if you take longer than this, Windows just terminates your app. Although Windows gives you 5 seconds, your suspension must actually complete within 2 seconds to be certified for the Window Store.[5] If you follow the model described in the "XAML page navigation" section of this chapter, you are in great shape because all you have to do in your suspension code is create a file on disk and serialize the list of dictionaries into it. You'll also need to call your Frame object's GetNavigationState method, which returns a String that has encoded in it the

---

[4] When an app goes to the background, Windows waits a few seconds before raising the Suspending event. This gives the user a few seconds to switch back to the app in case the user switched away from it by accident.

[5] If you need more time than 2 seconds to complete your suspension, you could look at Window's VisibilityChanged event. This event is raised whenever a window becomes visible or invisible. A window always becomes invisible first before the app is suspending and its Suspending event is raised.

collection of pages the user built up while navigating through your app; serialize this string out to the file as well.[6]

While your app is suspended, the OS might terminate it to free up memory for other apps. If the OS chooses to terminate your app, your app is given no additional notification; it is simply killed. The reason is obvious: if the system allowed your app to execute code before termination, your app could allocate more memory, making the situation worse. The main point to take away from this is that your app must save its state when it receives the Suspending event because your app will not be given a chance to execute more code if the OS decides to terminate it.

Even if the OS terminates your app, it gives the illusion to the user that your app is still running and allows the user to switch back to your terminated app. Figure 3-9 shows the system's task list and Task Manager after the App1 app has been terminated. Notice that the task list shows the App1 app, allowing the user to switch to it.[7] However, Task Manager does not show any entry for the App1 app at all because it is no longer resident in memory.

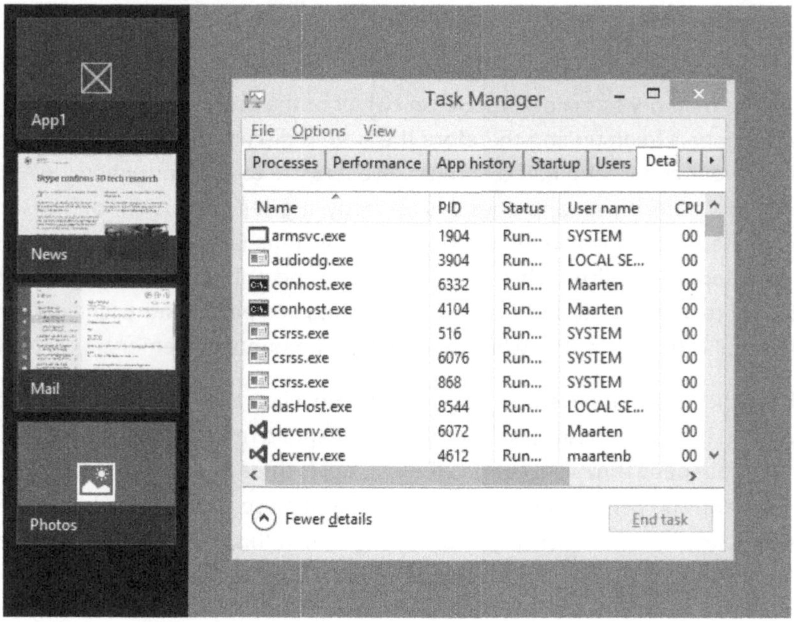

FIGURE 3-9 The Windows task list showing running, suspended, and terminated apps while Task Manager shows only running and suspended apps.

When the user switches back to a terminated app, the OS performs a main view activation of the app (showing its splash screen). The app must now initialize itself and restore its state back to what it

---

[6] GetNavigationState internally calls the page's OnNavigateFrom method so that it can store any state in its dictionary before GetNavigationState returns its encoded String. The format of the string is undocumented; do not write code that parses or interprets the string in any way.

[7] The task list shows the contents of the app's view if the app is still running and shows the default logo for the app if Windows terminated it.

was before the app was terminated.[8] The fact that the app got terminated should be transparent to the user. This is an important point. As far as the user is concerned, your app never stopped running: whether it is running, suspended, or even terminated, your app is available to the user.

When your app is activated, your app's `Main` method runs, the main view thread is created, your App's constructor executes, and then `Application`'s virtual `OnWindowCreated` method is called, followed by one of the other virtual `OnXxx` methods (depending on why your app is being re-activated). If your app is being activated with a hosted view activation, there is no need to restore your app's state to what it was when it was suspended. But, when your app starts due to a main view activation, you'll need to find out if your app is being re-activated because the OS terminated it.

All the virtual `OnXxx` methods are passed a parameter whose type implements the `IActivated-EventArgs` interface. This interface has a `PreviousExecutionState` property that returns an `ApplicationExecutionState` value. This type is an enumerated type, and if the `PreviousExecutionState` property returns `ApplicationExecutionState.Terminated`, your app knows that it's being relaunched because the OS terminated it. At this point, your code should open the file on the user's disk where you previously serialized the app's state, deserialize the list of dictionaries, and then grab the `String` with the encoded frame pages in it and pass it to your `Frame` object's `SetNavigationState` method. When you call `SetNavigationState`, it resets the state of the `Frame` object back to what it was when your app was suspended so that the user will be looking at the exact same thing she was looking at when the app got suspended.[9] To the user, it looks like your app never terminated.

Note that memory pressure is not the only reason your app can terminate. The user can close your app by typing Alt+F4, dragging your app's window from the top of the screen to the bottom and holding for a few seconds, or right-clicking your app in the task list and selecting Close. In addition, the OS closes all apps when the user logs off or shuts down the machine. In all the scenarios just given, the OS does raise the `Window`'s `VisibilityChanged` event, followed by the App's `Suspending` event, giving your app a chance to save its state. However, in the future, when your app is launched, you should not restore your app's state because the user has explicitly taken action to close your app as opposed to the OS implicitly terminating your app. If you check the `PreviousExecutionState` property, you'll see that in all these scenarios, it returns `ApplicationExecutionState.ClosedByUser`.

Users can also forcibly kill an app using the Task Manager and, of course, an app can kill itself by throwing an unhandled exception. In addition, Windows will automatically kill an app if it's running when the user uninstalls it or if the system updates the app to a newer version. In all these scenarios, when the app relaunches in the future, it should just initialize itself and not restore any previous state because state might have gotten corrupted, which is what might have caused the unhandled exception in the first place. If you check the `PreviousExecutionState` property, you'll see that in these scenarios, it returns `ApplicationExecutionState.NotRunning`.

---

[8] This does not always make senses for every app. For some apps, if they are suspended for a long time, the user might not remember or care about what she was last doing with the app. In this case, your app can just initialize itself and not restore any previous user state. You might take this approach for a newsreader app where the article might be stale or a weather app where the data is stale.

[9] `SetNavigationState` internally calls the page's `OnNavigatedTo` method so that the page can load state from its dictionary back into its UI.

How to best structure your app class' code

I know that all the information presented in this chapter can be difficult to take in, memorize, and turn into correctly implemented code. So, to simplify things, I've created an AppAid class that encapsulates a lot of this knowledge and makes building new Windows Store apps easier. Here is what this class looks like:

```
namespace Wintellect.WinRT.AppAids {
   public enum ViewType { None, Main, Hosted, Auxiliary }
   public enum LaunchReason { PrimaryTile, SecondaryTile, Toast, Proximity }

   public static class AppAid {
      private static ApplicationInitializationCallback m_appInitCallback;
      private static Func<Frame, IActivatedEventArgs, Task<Boolean>>
         s_deserializeFramePageStateAsync;

      /// <summary>Call this method from Main instead of calling Application.Start</summary>
      /// <param name="callback">The callback that constructs the App singleton object.</param>
      /// <param name="deserializeFramePageStateAsync">A callback that restores the user's
      /// session state. Called during 1st main view activation if the app was previously
      /// terminated.</param>
      public static void Start(ApplicationInitializationCallback callback,
         Func<Frame, IActivatedEventArgs, Task<Boolean>> deserializeFramePageStateAsync = null) {
         // Invoked via process' primary thread each time the process initializes
         s_deserializeFramePageStateAsync = deserializeFramePageStateAsync;
         m_appInitCallback = callback;
         Application.Start(AppInitialization);
      }

      private static void AppInitialization(ApplicationInitializationCallbackParams p) {
         // Invoked via main view thread
         // But the main view's CoreWindow & CoreDispatcher do NOT exist yet;
         // they are created by Application.Start after this method returns
         m_appInitCallback(p);  // Creates a singleton App object that never gets GC'd
         // because the base class (Application) holds a reference to it
         m_appInitCallback = null;   // Allow delegate to be GC'd
      }
```

```
/// <summary>Call this method from inside App's OnWindowCreated method to determine
/// what kind of window is being created.</summary>
/// <returns> The view type (main or hosted) for this kind of activation.</returns>
public static ViewType OnWindowCreated(this WindowCreatedEventArgs args) {
    // Invoked once via main view thread and once for each hosted view/auxiliary thread
    // NOTE: You can't tell what kind of activation (Share, Protocol, etc.) is occurring.
    return ViewType;
}


/// <summary>This method returns the kind of view for a given activation kind</summary>
/// <param name="args">Indicates what kind of activation is occurring.</param>
/// <returns>The view type (main or hosted) for this kind of activation.</returns>
public static ViewType GetViewType(this IActivatedEventArgs args) {
    switch (args.Kind) {
        case ActivationKind.AppointmentsProvider:
            String verb = ((IAppointmentsProviderActivatedEventArgs)args).Verb;
            if (verb == AppointmentsProviderLaunchActionVerbs.AddAppointment)
                return ViewType.Hosted;
            if (verb == AppointmentsProviderLaunchActionVerbs.ReplaceAppointment)
                return ViewType.Hosted;
            if (verb == AppointmentsProviderLaunchActionVerbs.RemoveAppointment)
                return ViewType.Hosted;
            if (verb == AppointmentsProviderLaunchActionVerbs.ShowTimeFrame)
                return ViewType.Main;
            break;

        case ActivationKind.Contact:
            verb = ((IContactsProviderActivatedEventArgs)args).Verb;
            if (verb == ContactLaunchActionVerbs.Call) return ViewType.Main;
            if (verb == ContactLaunchActionVerbs.Map) return ViewType.Main;
            if (verb == ContactLaunchActionVerbs.Message) return ViewType.Main;
            if (verb == ContactLaunchActionVerbs.Post) return ViewType.Main;
            if (verb == ContactLaunchActionVerbs.VideoCall) return ViewType.Main;
            break;

        case ActivationKind.Launch:
        case ActivationKind.Search:
        case ActivationKind.File:
        case ActivationKind.Protocol:
        case ActivationKind.Device:
        case ActivationKind.LockScreenCall:
            return ViewType.Main;

        case ActivationKind.ShareTarget:
        case ActivationKind.FileOpenPicker:
        case ActivationKind.FileSavePicker:
        case ActivationKind.CachedFileUpdater:
        case ActivationKind.ContactPicker:
        case ActivationKind.PrintTaskSettings:
        case ActivationKind.CameraSettings:
            return ViewType.Hosted;
    }
    throw new ArgumentException("Unrecognized activation kind");
}
```

```
            public static ViewType ViewType {
                get {
                    try {
                        CoreApplicationView cav = CoreApplication.GetCurrentView();
                        return cav.IsMain ? ViewType.Main :
                            (cav.IsHosted ? ViewType.Hosted : ViewType.Auxiliary);
                    }
                    catch { return ViewType.None; }
                }
            }


            /// <summary>Whenever you override one of App's virtual activation methods
            /// (eg: OnLaunched, OnFileActivated, OnShareTargetActivated), call this method.
            /// If called for the 1st Main view activation, sets Window's Frame,
            /// restores user session state (if app was previously terminated), and activates window.
            /// If called for a Hosted view activation, sets Window's Frame & activates window.
            /// </summary>
            /// <param name="args">The reason for app activation</param>
            /// <returns>True if previous state was restored; false if starting fresh.</returns>
            public static async Task<Boolean> ActivateViewAsync(this IActivatedEventArgs args) {
                Window currentWindow = Window.Current;
                Boolean previousStateRestored = false; // Assume previous state is not being restored
                if (args.GetViewType() == ViewType.Main) {
                    if (currentWindow.Content == null) {
                        currentWindow.Content = new Frame();
                    }

                    // The UI is set; this is the 1st main view activation or a secondary activation
                    // If not 1st activation,
                    // PreviousExecutionState == ApplicationExecutionState.Running
                    if (args.PreviousExecutionState == ApplicationExecutionState.Terminated
                        && s_deserializeFramePageStateAsync != null) {
                        // Restore user session state because app relaunched after OS termination
                        previousStateRestored =
                            await s_deserializeFramePageStateAsync(CurrentFrame, args);
                        s_deserializeFramePageStateAsync = null;    // Allow delegate to be GC'd
                    }
                } else {
                    currentWindow.Content = new Frame();
                }
                currentWindow.Activate();   // Activate the MainView window
                return previousStateRestored;
            }


            /// <summary>Returns the Frame in the calling thread's window.</summary>
            public static Frame CurrentFrame { get { return (Frame)Window.Current.Content; } }

            private const String ProximityLaunchArg = "Windows.Networking.Proximity:StreamSocket";
            public static LaunchReason GetLaunchReason(this LaunchActivatedEventArgs args) {
                if (args.Arguments == ProximityLaunchArg) return LaunchReason.Proximity;
                if (args.TileId == Windows.ApplicationModel.Core.CoreApplication.Id) {
                    return (args.Arguments == String.Empty)
                        ? LaunchReason.PrimaryTile : LaunchReason.Toast;
                }
                return LaunchReason.SecondaryTile;
            }
        }
    }
}
```

The code that accompanies this book has a souped-up version of the AppAid class. The souped-up version supports extended splash screens and thread logging, and it has some navigation helpers. Here is some code for a sample App class that uses my AppAid class. The code calls some additional methods that I provide in the code that accompanies this book to simplify saving and restoring user session state in case of app termination. The most important part of the following code is the comments.

```
// Our singleton App class; store all app-wide data in this class object
public sealed partial class App : Application {
    // Invoked because DISABLE_XAML_GENERATED_MAIN is defined:
    public static void Main(String[] args) {
        // Invoked via process' primary thread each time the process initializes
        AppAid.Start(AppInitialization,
            (f, a) => f.DeserializePageStateAsync(c_FramePageStateFileName, a));
    }

    private static void AppInitialization(ApplicationInitializationCallbackParams p) {
        // Invoked via main view thread
        // But the main view's CoreWindow & CoreDispatcher do NOT exist yet;
        // they are created by Application.Start after this method returns

        // Create a singleton App object. It never gets GC'd because the base class (Application)
        // holds a reference to it obtainable via Application.Current
        var app = new App();
    }

    private App() {
        // Invoked via main view thread; CoreWindow & CoreDispatcher do NOT exist yet
        this.InitializeComponent();
        this.Resuming += OnResuming;     // Raised when main view thread resumes from suspend
        this.Suspending += OnSuspending; // Raised when main view thread is being suspended
        // TODO: Add any additional app initialization
    }

    private void OnResuming(Object sender, Object e) {
        // Invoked via main view thread when it resumes from suspend
        // TODO: Update any stale state in the UI (news, weather, scores, etc.)
    }

    private void OnSuspending(Object sender, SuspendingEventArgs e) {
        // Invoked via main view thread when app is being suspended or closed by user

        // Windows gives 5 seconds for app to suspend or OS kills the app
        // Windows Store certification requires suspend to complete in 2 seconds

        // TODO: Save session state in case app is terminated
        // (see ApplicationData.Current.LocalFolder)
        // NOTE: I perform this operation synchronously instead of using a deferral
        this.GetCurrentFrame().SerializePageStateAsync(c_FramePageStateFileName)
            .GetAwaiter().GetResult();
    }
```

```
protected override void OnWindowCreated(WindowCreatedEventArgs args) {
    // Invoked once via the main view thread and once for each hosted view thread
    // NOTE: In here, you do not know the activation kind (Launch, Share, Protocol, etc.)
    switch (args.OnWindowCreated()) {
        case ViewType.Main:
            // TODO: Put code here you want to execute for the main view thread/window
            break;
        case ViewType.Hosted:
            // TODO: Put code here you want to execute for a hosted view thread/window
            break;
        case ViewType.Auxiliary:
            // TODO: Put code here you want to execute for an auxiliary view thread/window
            break;
    }

    // Optional: register handlers with these events
    Window w = args.Window; // Refers to the view's window (drawing surface)
    w.Activated += Window_Activated;
    w.VisibilityChanged += Window_VisibilityChanged;
}

private void Window_Activated(Object sender, WindowActivatedEventArgs e) {
    // Invoked via view thread each time its window changes activation state
    CoreWindowActivationState activateState = e.WindowActivationState;
}

private void Window_VisibilityChanged(Object sender, VisibilityChangedEventArgs e) {
    // Invoked via view thread each time its window changes visibility
    // A window becomes not-visible whenever the app is suspending or closing
    if (e.Visible) return;
}

protected override async void OnLaunched(LaunchActivatedEventArgs args) {
    Boolean previousStateRestored = await args.ActivateViewAsync();
    switch (args.GetLaunchReason()) {
        case LaunchReason.PrimaryTile:
            if (previousStateRestored) {
                // Previous state restored back to what it was
                // before app was terminated; nothing else to do
            } else {
                // Previous state not restored; navigate to app's first page
                // TODO: Navigate to desired page
            }
            break;

        case LaunchReason.SecondaryTile:
            // TODO: Navigate to desired page
            break;

        case LaunchReason.Toast:
            // TODO: Navigate to desired page
            break;
```

```
        case LaunchReason.Proximity:
            // TODO: Navigate to desired page
            break;
        }
    }
}
```

Debugging process lifetime management

When debugging, Windows will not suspend or terminate a Windows Store app because this would lead to a poor debugging experience. This makes it impossible for you to debug and step through your app's Resuming and Suspending event handlers. So, to allow you to debug these event handlers, Visual Studio offers a way to force suspending, resuming, and terminating your app. While your app is running, go to Visual Studio's Debug Location toolbar and select the operation you want to force, as shown in Figure 3-10. You might also want to use the PLMDebug tool, which you can download with the Debugging Tools for Windows. This tool allows you to turn off PLM for your app so that you can attach a debugger and debug the app without the OS suspending it.

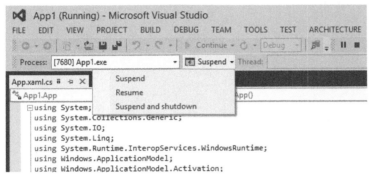

FIGURE 3-10 Forcing an app to suspend, resume, or terminate using Visual Studio's Debug Location toolbar.

PART II

Core Windows facilities

CHAPTER 4

Package data and roaming

Almost every app requires the ability to maintain some state on behalf of itself and the user. Typically, the Microsoft .NET Framework has offered a technology known as *isolated storage* to enable this. But now, Windows provides this technology built into the OS itself. When a package is registered (installed) for a user, Windows prepares storage that your package's app can write to and read from on behalf of the user. This storage is tied to the package. When the package is unregistered (uninstalled), Windows automatically destroys this storage. The storage is shared and accessible to all apps that run as part of the package (in the same app container [as discussed in the appendix]); this includes any background tasks (as discussed in Chapter 9, "Background tasks").

Using package data is quite simple. You just need to work with the `ApplicationData` class, which looks like this:[1]

```
public sealed class ApplicationData {
    // Call this first to get access to your package's ApplicationData object
    public static ApplicationData Current { get; }

    // Returns a folder to the package's temporary file store
    // NOTE: The files in this folder may be destroyed by the system at any time
    public StorageFolder TemporaryFolder { get; }

    // Members to access data that always resides on the user's PC
    public ApplicationDataContainer LocalSettings { get; }
    public StorageFolder LocalFolder { get; }

    // Members to access data that can roam across all of the user's PCs
    public ApplicationDataContainer RoamingSettings { get; }
    public StorageFolder RoamingFolder { get; }
    public UInt64 RoamingStorageQuota { get; }
    public void SignalDataChanged();
    public event TypedEventHandler<ApplicationData, Object> DataChanged;

    // Members related to versioning the package's data.
    // Typically used when the user upgrades to a new version of the package.
    public UInt32 Version { get; }
    public IAsyncAction SetVersionAsync(
        UInt32 desiredVersion, ApplicationDataSetVersionHandler handler);
```

---

[1] It's a shame this class isn't called `PackageData` to more accurately reflect that the data is associated with the package, not with an individual app.

```
// Members that clear out all (or some) of the package's per-user data
public IAsyncAction ClearAsync();
public IAsyncAction ClearAsync(ApplicationDataLocality locality);
}
```

For your app to access its per-user package data, it must first gain access to its own package data repositories by querying ApplicationData's Current property:

```
ApplicationData appData = ApplicationData.Current;
```

Once you have a reference to your package's ApplicationData object, you can access all the class' instance members. The next thing you must decide is the *locality* of the data. Here is a description of the three data localities:

- **Temporary**   Use this locality like a cache. That is, you typically store in here data that is costly or time consuming to acquire. Once you acquire the data, you store it in a file in the TemporaryFolder folder. Note that any files you store in this folder can be destroyed at any time, even while your app is still running. The system has a scheduled task that normally runs weekly to clear this data out. A user can modify the frequency of this using the Windows Task Scheduler. The scheduled task is Microsoft\Windows\ApplicationData\CleanupTemporaryState. In addition, the user could always run Windows' Disk Cleanup utility (CleanMgr.exe).

- **Local**   Use this locality for data you need to persist. The system will never destroy whatever data you put here unless the user uninstalls your package.

- **Roaming**   Use this locality for any data you want the system to automatically copy across the user's PCs. Windows Store apps are licensed to a user, and a user is allowed to install a single app on many PCs. This locality causes your package's data to be the same across all the user's PCs using an eventual consistency model. The "Roaming package data" section later in this chapter explores the details of using this locality.

Once you've decided the locality of the data, you then decide how to store and access it. There are two ways of storing data:

- **Settings**   Settings is a dictionary of key/value pairs. Each key is a string (up to 255 characters long) representing the name of a setting, and the value is some simple WinRT type or a single dimension array of these types that is no more than 8 KB in size. Settings is not just a collection of key/value pairs; it is a hierarchical collection of containers (up to 32 levels deep). That is, you can create a tree of containers to store key/value pair collections, allowing you to organize your package's data however you like.

- **Storage folder**   Storage folders are for items inappropriate for settings, such as items over 8 KB in size and items you want to treat as files (images, videos, music). You can create whatever files you want in these folders; you can also create subdirectories, allowing you to organize your data hierarchically. In the files, you can store whatever data you'd like. Files really contain arrays of bytes, but you can use rich .NET data types if you make them serializable and then use normal .NET mechanisms (like DataContractSerializer) to serialize the objects to byte arrays. See Chapter 5, "Storage files and folders," and Chapter 6, "Stream input and output," for more information about managing files and their contents.

Of course, the main purpose of package data is that it persists across invocations of your app. That is, if your app gets terminated, your package data continues to live. Also, package data continues to live even if the user upgrades from one version of your package to a newer version. But, when this happens, you might want to change the schema of the package data. To do this, the `Application-Data` class provides members allowing you to version the data; this will be discussed in this chapter's "Versioning package data" section.

Package data settings

Here is code demonstrating how to write and read a setting from local package data:

```
// Gain access to our package's data repositories
ApplicationData appData = ApplicationData.Current;

// Store an item in the collection: Key="DataUpdatedAt", Value=DateTimeOffset.Now
appData.LocalSettings.Values["DataUpdatedAt"] = DateTimeOffset.Now;

// Later, we can read it back:
DateTimeOffset dataUpdatedAt = (DateTimeOffset) appData.LocalSettings.Values["DataUpdatedAt"];
```

You can store only simple WinRT (not .NET) data types in settings. The valid WinRT data types are `Boolean`, `UInt8`, `Int16`, `UInt16`, `Int32`, `UInt32`, `Int64`, `UInt64`, `Single`, `Double`, `Char`, `String`, `DateTimeOffset`, `TimeSpan`, `Guid`, `Point`, `Size`, and `Rect`. You can also store single-dimension arrays of these data types, but the resulting value cannot be larger than 8 KB in size. However, there is no limit to the number of the key/value pairs you can add to the collection. The `Values` property returns an `ApplicationDataContainerSettings` object, which implements the `IObservableMap<String, Object>` interface, which offers a `MapChanged` event that is raised whenever an item in the collection changes.

In addition to the simple data types, there is one other special data type you can use: `Application-DataCompositeValue`. This type allows you to store multiple pieces of data atomically. For example, if you had this:

```
String videoName = ...;
appData.LocalSettings.Values["LastVideoWatched"] = videoName;

// Imagine an unhandled exception occurs here!

Int32 videoPosition = ...;
appData.LocalSettings.Values["LastVideoPosition"] = videoPosition;
```

Then it is possible that your app could store the last video the user was watching and then terminate before storing the user's position within the movie. If the user later restarts the app, it loads the last video the user was watching but positions it at the last place in the previous video the user was watching. This would result in a very poor user experience. You can rewrite the code using the `ApplicationDataCompositeValue` to fix this:

```
ApplicationDataCompositeValue compositeValue = new ApplicationDataCompositeValue {
   { "LastVideoWatched", videoName },
   { "LastVideoPosition", videoPosition }
};
appData.LocalSettings.Values["LastVideoInfo"] = compositeValue;

// This shows how to read the information back out:
compositeValue = (ApplicationDataCompositeValue) appData.LocalSettings.Values["LastVideoInfo"];
videoName = (String) compositeValue["LastVideoWatched"];
videoPosition = (Int32) compositeValue["LastVideoPosition"];
```

Now, the assignment of the `ApplicationDataCompositeValue` object into settings is an all-or-nothing transaction so that an unhandled exception means that the next time our app starts up it will either have the old video information or the latest video information; it cannot have some old and some new information. A single `ApplicationDataCompositeValue` object can contain up to 64 KB of data.

When building and debugging an app, it can be useful to know how Windows internally persists your package's data settings. The settings are stored in a registry hive file called Settings.dat. You can find this file in the following directory: %LocalAppData%\Packages*PackageFamilyName*\Settings. You can view and modify a package's data settings by loading this file into RegEdit.exe. To do this, start RegEdit.exe, select HKEY_LOCAL_MACHINE, and then select File, Load Hive. In the Load Hive dialog box, open the Settings.dat file, and give the hive a key name. Then expand the HKEY_LOCAL_MACHINE node, select the key name you just created, and explore. Although it is easy to see all the key values this way, unfortunately all the data is shown as byte arrays, which makes it a bit difficult to read and modify.

As an alternative, you can use Wintellect's Package Explorer desktop app (discussed in Chapter 2, "App packaging and deployment") to see all of a package's data settings. Package Explorer uses the publicly documented `Windows.Management.Core.ApplicationDataManager` class' `CreateForPackageFamily` method to access a package's data.

The ability for desktop applications to access a Windows Store package's data is quite powerful. For example, you could create a tool that exports and imports a package's data. This can be useful for repeatedly testing against a known set of initial data. Also, companies can produce desktop diagnostic tools that customers can use to capture information about their environment (including package data) to send back to the company to help diagnose customer issues. And, once package data is exported, it can be imported by many PCs, enabling a way to configure all these PCs identically. For example, an enterprise can use a desktop app or script to preset a Windows Store app's configuration settings, connection strings, and so on.

Package data storage folders

Here is code demonstrating how to write and read a file from a package's local storage folder:

```
// Gain access to our package's data repositories
ApplicationData appData = ApplicationData.Current;

// Store some text in a file:
StorageFile file = await appData.LocalFolder.CreateFileAsync("SomeAppData");
await FileIO.WriteTextAsync(file, "Here is some data to persist");

// Later, we can read it back:
file = await appData.LocalFolder.GetFileAsync("SomeAppData");
String persistedData = await FileIO.ReadTextAsync(file);
```

Files store only arrays of bytes, but there are many ways of converting richer data types into byte arrays. For example, `FileIO`'s `WriteTextAsync` and `ReadTextAsync` methods shown in the previous code convert strings to and from byte arrays by way of a UTF-8 encoding. For full details about manipulating files, see Chapters 5 and 6.

Windows does not impose limits on a package's data files. Files can be extremely large (2^{64} bytes), and there is no restriction on the number of package data files you can create. So package data files can fill all of the user's hard disk. To see how much disk space individual packages are using, go to Settings charm > Change PC Settings > Search And Apps, App Sizes. The indicated size is generally the sum of the package itself and its folders.

For debugging purposes, it is useful to know that all of a package's storage files can be found in the following three directories:

- Temporary files   %LocalAppData%\Packages*PackageFamilyName*\TempState
- Local files   %LocalAppData%\Packages*PackageFamilyName*\LocalState
- Roaming files   %LocalAppData%\Packages*PackageFamilyName*\RoamingState

Versioning package data

Over time, as you revise your app (creating new versions of its package), you'll likely want to change the kind or format of your package's data. Consequently, when a user upgrades your package to a newer version, you might want to execute a routine that updates your package's data. To help you manage your package's data, the system associates a version number (a 32-bit unsigned integer) with it. By default, your package's data is assigned a version number of 0. You query your package's data version number as follows:

```
var appDataVersion = ApplicationData.Current.Version;
```

Note that there does not have to be a relationship between versioning your package and versioning your package's data. That is, the first three versions of your package can all use version 0 of your package's data. And then, for version 4 of your package, you might decide to upgrade your package data to version 1. In this example, when the user first runs version 4 of your package's app, you'll want to upgrade your package's data.

When you do decide to upgrade your package data version, you'll need to write a method that transforms an earlier version of your package's data to the newest version. The method you write should look like this:

```
private async void AppDataSetVersion(SetVersionRequest setVersionRequest) {
    // To upgrade files, leave this method 'async', use the deferral & 'await' file I/O methods.
    // If you're only upgrading settings, delete 'async' and the deferral-related code
    var deferral = setVersionRequest.GetDeferral();
    switch (setVersionRequest.CurrentVersion) {
        case 0:
            // TODO: Code to convert from version 0 to latest version goes here
            break;
        case 1:
            // TODO: Code to convert from version 1 to latest version goes here
            break;
    }
    deferral.Complete();
}
```

You invoke this method by using code like this:

```
const UInt32 appDataLatestVersion = 2;
if (ApplicationData.Current.Version < appDataLatestVersion)
    ApplicationData.Current.SetVersionAsync(appDataLatestVersion, AppDataSetVersion);
        .AsTask().GetAwaiter().GetResult();
```

Note that when your AppDataSetVersion handler method returns, the system associates the latest version number with your package data so that future calls to ApplicationData's Version property return the latest version. Also, note that if your AppDataSetVersion handler method throws an unhandled exception, the system does not associate the latest version number with your package data; however, some of your package data might have successfully been upgraded to the new version. If an unexpected exception occurs while upgrading package data, you might want to consider destroying all of it (by calling ApplicationData's ClearAsync method) and reconstruct all of your package's data from scratch.

Now, the question is where should you put this code? The best place to put this code is inside a background task triggered by a servicing complete system trigger. (See Chapter 9.) This way, when the user installs the latest version of your package, the background task will execute and update your package's data at that time. However, if you do not have or want to create a background task, you can put this code inside your app itself. If you do this, you will probably want to call SetVersion-Async synchronously (as shown in the previous example). This blocks the thread from making further progress, preventing any other parts of your app code from accessing package data until you're sure the upgrade is complete. And, if you execute this code synchronously, you can call it from your app's Main method or inside your App class' constructor, ensuring that your package data upgrades when your app is activated no matter how it gets activated.[2] The only problem with upgrading the version of your package's data here is that this executes while your app's splash screen is displayed, and this delays the user's ability to interact with your app. So, if upgrading your package's data can take a long time, you might want to consider upgrading the data while showing an extended splash screen. If you do this, you can avoid upgrading the data synchronously. But be careful not to access the data from other threads until the upgrade is complete.

> **Note** To help test your `AppDataSetVersion` handler method, you can clear your package's data and reset its version number by opening your project's Properties, selecting the Debugging pane, and then selecting the Uninstall And Then Re-Install My Package check box.

Roaming package data

Increasingly, users have multiple PCs that they use on a regular basis. For example, they might have a PC at home, a PC at work, and a tablet that they travel with. It is a pain for users to configure all these PCs similarly for each app they use. For this reason Windows provides the ability for Windows Store apps to roam any package settings and storage files. Now, a user can configure your app once, and the configuration will automatically roam across all the user's PCs where the user has installed your package. In addition, your app can offer the user a continuous experience where the user starts an operation with your app on one PC and then continues the operation on a different PC. For example, imagine a user is using your app to watch a video on her desktop PC and then she grabs her tablet and opens your app, and the video continues from where it left off. In fact, the main way for users to force the current PC's settings to sync with their other PCs is by locking their PC.

Many settings in Windows itself roam across the user's PCs automatically as well, such as desktop background images, Internet favorites, and language settings. To have settings roam, users must log in to their Windows PC using their Microsoft account or link their local or domain account with their Microsoft account. Users associate their Microsoft account with Windows by opening the Settings charm > Change PC Settings > Accounts > Your Account > Connect To A Microsoft Account.

As with everything in Windows, the user always maintains control of her data and experience. To this end, the user controls what data can and cannot roam using the Settings charm > Change PC Settings > SkyDrive > Sync Settings pane as shown in Figure 4-1. Most of these settings control operating system settings, but App Settings controls the roaming of package data. Users can also specify whether they want to use potentially expensive network connections for roaming. (See Chapter 7, "Networking.") Note that in an enterprise, administrators can adjust or block roaming with Group Policy for domain-joined machines.

---

[2] C# doesn't allow you to mark your `Main` method or a constructor with the `async` keyword; therefore, you cannot use the `await` operator in these kinds of methods. But, if you invoke `SetVersionAsync` synchronously, this is not a problem.

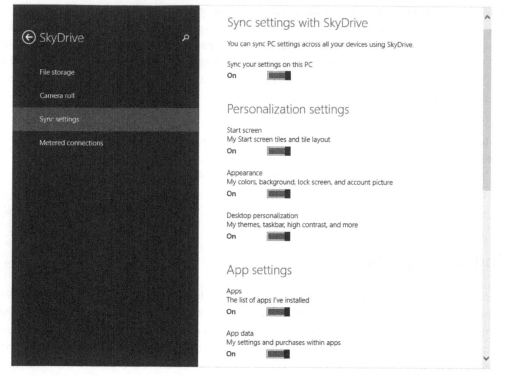

FIGURE 4-1 Users control the roaming of their data via the Sync Settings pane.

Having your app support roaming settings is free, and it couldn't be easier to implement. All you have to do is add settings to `ApplicationData`'s `RoamingSettings` or add files to `Application-Data`'s `RoamingFolder`. Windows takes care of everything else. For example, Windows will automatically roam the data when an Internet connection is available, Windows will keep the user's data secure, and Microsoft provides and maintains the storage servers that persist the user's data.[3] Note that Microsoft's servers limit how much storage a package can roam. An app can determine this amount by querying `ApplicationData`'s `RoamingStorageQuota` property. Currently, this property returns a value of 100 KB. If your package goes over its quota, Windows stops roaming any of your package's data.[4] It is up to you to capacity plan how you use your package's roaming storage. This means that you should roam small pieces of data. For example, instead of roaming content, roam links to the content instead. If you need more than the allowed quota, you will have to build your own roaming infrastructure (servers, authentication and communication mechanisms, and so forth).[5] The purpose of the Windows-provided roaming is to allow any developer, college student, or enthusiast to roam data without having to deal with all these infrastructure details.

[3] Your package's data is actually in the user's SkyDrive account, but the storage is not part of the user's quota and the user has no direct access to the package data maintained by SkyDrive.

[4] Remember, Windows does not limit the amount of data that can be stored in roaming settings or roaming folders, but there is a limit to how much of that can be sync'd with the cloud.

[5] One option is to have your app use SkyDrive APIs to explicitly sync your package's data with the user's SkyDrive account. This will require the user's permission.

Note Certain files types do not roam. For example, if you put a file with a .zip or .cab extension in the roaming folder, it will not roam. This is particularly troublesome because many developers want to compress the data they roam to get more data in the 100-KB quota. Microsoft does not document the list of file types that do not roam. If you're not seeing a file you put in the roaming folder roam, try changing the file's extension.

Important Do not store passwords in package data. Instead, create a `Windows.Security.Credentials.PasswordCredential` object with the desired password. Then add the `PasswordCredential` object to a `Windows.Security.Credentials.PasswordVault` object. This causes the `PasswordCredential` object to roam securely across the user's PCs. Note: When a `PasswordCredential` object is inserted into a `PasswordVault` on a domain-joined PC, the `PasswordCredential` will not roam, to prevent domain credentials from going out over the Internet. Use the Windows' Credential Manager applet to view the persisted credentials for all apps.

Windows typically syncs a package's roaming settings and files within a few minutes, but there is no guarantee of this because there could be network-connectivity issues. Because of this, the roaming feature is not designed to enable scenarios where two or more PCs are being used side by side, and the feature is also not designed to be used as a cross-PC communication technology. Also, if the user changes her roaming data on two or more PCs and then Internet connectivity is restored, data that has been written last will be synced across the user's PCs; older data will be overwritten. As discussed in this chapter's "Versioning package data" section, package data is versioned independently of the package itself. Windows will not roam a newer version of package data to a PC whose package data is an older version, because this would most likely cause the older version of the app to malfunction the next time it was activated.

Windows does not sync data when the user logs out or when the PC hibernates or sleeps because this would hurt performance. However, if you are running on a PC that supports connected standby, sync'ing does eventually occur even if the PC is "off." If a package is installed on just one of a user's PCs, Windows still syncs the data approximately once per day. This means a user can destroy (or lose) that PC, purchase a new PC, install the package, and the sync'd data will come onto the new PC. If a package is uninstalled from all of a user's PCs, the package's roaming data remains in the cloud for about one month before it gets destroyed. During that month, if the user installs the package onto a PC, the persisted data will come onto the PC.

If the user wants to purge all the data (perhaps for privacy reasons) after uninstalling a package, the user can go to *https://SkyDrive.Live.com/Win8PersonalSettingsPrivacy/* and click the Remove button. This actually removes all of the user's roaming data from the cloud, but for packages the user still has installed, Windows will simply copy their roaming data back up to the cloud. Deleting storage from the cloud can be a useful technique when developing an app because it allows you to clear out any bad roaming data created during development. You can also clear out roaming data programmatically by calling `ApplicationData`'s `ClearAsync` method, passing in the `ApplicationDataLocality.Roaming` flag.

In some scenarios, you might want a setting to roam very quickly from one PC to all the others. The video example comes to mind where the user might switch from her desktop PC to her tablet and want to pick up watching the video immediately. In this case, having the video info sync in a few minutes is too slow. To address this scenario, Windows allows a package to consider one setting to be high priority and Windows will do what it can to sync this setting quickly (usually within one minute). You roam one setting very quickly if you give it a key name of `"HighPriority"` (with this exact casing), and you must store this key in the root `ApplicationDataContainer`:

```
// NOTE: Use an ApplicationDataCompositeValue object to roam multiple values quickly
ApplicationDataCompositeValue compositeValue = new ApplicationDataCompositeValue {
    { "LastVideoWatched", videoName },
    { "LastVideoPosition", videoPosition }
};
appData.LocalSettings.Values["HighPriority"] = compositeValue;
```

You must avoid continuously updating the `"HighPriority"` setting; instead, update it at specific times, such as when the user pauses or stops a video, when your app gets suspended, or perhaps once every minute. Similarly, you'll want to read the value when your app is launched, when it gets resumed, or when `ApplicationData`'s `DataChanged` event is raised. (See the "Package data change notifications" section later in this chapter.) If the value of the `"HighPriority"` setting is an `ApplicationDataCompositeValue` (as shown in the previous example), it must contain no more than 8 KB of data to have it roam quickly. If it contains more than 8 KB of data, it will roam as quickly as any other normal setting.

To help developers test their package's roaming data, Microsoft makes a Roaming Monitor Tool that integrates with Visual Studio. You can download it via the Visual Studio Gallery from *http:// VisualStudioGallery.MSDN.Microsoft.com/3ccf8c24-5e72-4ba0-b3e9-d822ca345fd0*. With this tool, you can monitor, view, and manipulate your package's roaming settings. In addition, you can force the data to roam on demand. Similarly, you can force the system to sync roaming package data to the cloud by executing the following:

```
SchTasks.exe /run /i /tn Microsoft\Windows\SettingSync\BackgroundUploadTask
```

After the PC uploads its package data to SkyDrive, a Windows push notification (discussed in Chapter 8, "Tiles and toast notifications") is sent to the user's other PCs causing them to download the latest package data from SkyDrive.

Finally, to help you with troubleshooting, the system logs roaming-related events in the following system event logs:

- Applications And Services Logs > Microsoft > Windows > SettingSync

- Applications And Services Logs> Microsoft > Windows > PackageStateRoaming

Package data change notifications

When Windows copies a package's roaming data from the cloud onto a user's PC, Windows raises ApplicationData's DataChanged event. If your app registers with this event, it can refresh its new roaming settings and modify its behavior on the fly while the user is interacting with your app. Note that Windows raises this event on a thread pool thread, so you'll have to use a CoreDispatcher if you want to update your app's user interface.

Windows raises the DataChanged event automatically whenever the PC downloads new roaming package data. But your app can raise this event itself by calling ApplicationData's Signal-DataChanged method. Calling this method is useful if a setting changes in one part of your app and you need to let another part of your app know that settings have changed so that it can query its new value. This is also useful if you need your app to signal a setting change to one of its background tasks (as discussed in Chapter 9) or vice versa.

CHAPTER 5

Storage files and folders

I n this chapter, you'll learn how Windows Store apps access storage files and folders. We'll start by exploring how apps can access read-only resources such as images, music, and videos embedded in their package files. Then we'll show how your app can access its own private, per-user data folders to store package-specific data. Of course, apps can access files in many other storage locations, such as the user's documents and pictures libraries, removable media, and network-shared folders. For security reasons, accessing some of these locations requires either user interaction or that you, as a developer, enable settings in your app package's manifest file.

This chapter focuses on navigating through files and folders, obtaining their properties and thumbnail images, and performing rich file queries. But this chapter does not address how to read and write a file's contents; this is discussed in Chapter 6, "Stream input and output."

The WinRT storage object model

Figure 5-1 shows the relationship between the main WinRT interfaces and classes you need to understand to work effectively with storage files and folders. This object model scares many developers when they first see it because it is much more complex than what is available in other developer platforms. However, I personally love this object model because it is well segmented and compartmentalized; all members were carefully placed, and new features not available on other platforms are prominently exposed. Note that I am excluding some less important interfaces from Figure 5-1 to simplify the discussion.

Let's now walk through the object model to understand it. The `IStorageItem` interface is the core of the model. This interface exposes members that operate on both files and folders. For example, you can rename and delete both files and folders. They also share several properties, such as `Name`, `Path`, `DateCreated`, and `Attributes`.

`IStorageFolder` inherits from `IStorageItem` and adds members that are specific to folders; `StorageFolder` is the concrete class implementing these two interfaces' members. Similarly, `IStorageFile` also inherits from `IStorageItem` and adds members that are specific to files; `StorageFile` is the concrete class implementing these two interfaces' members.

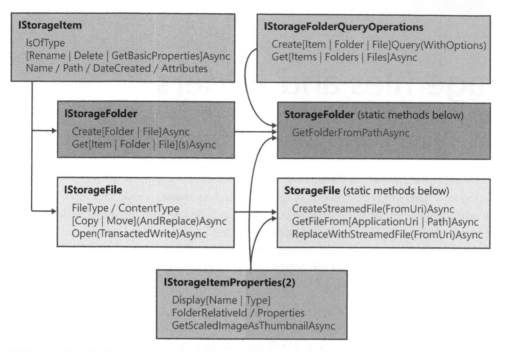

IStorageItem

IsOfType
[Rename | Delete | GetBasicProperties]Async
Name / Path / DateCreated / Attributes

IStorageFolderQueryOperations

Create[Item | Folder | File]Query(WithOptions)
Get[Items | Folders | Files]Async

IStorageFolder

Create[Folder | File]Async
Get[Item | Folder | File](s)Async

StorageFolder (static methods below)

GetFolderFromPathAsync

IStorageFile

FileType / ContentType
[Copy | Move](AndReplace)Async
Open(TransactedWrite)Async

StorageFile (static methods below)

CreateStreamedFile(FromUri)Async
GetFileFrom[ApplicationUri | Path]Async
ReplaceWithStreamedFile(FromUri)Async

IStorageItemProperties(2)

Display[Name | Type]
FolderRelativeId / Properties
GetScaledImageAsThumbnailAsync

FIGURE 5-1 The WinRT object model for working with storage files and folders.

The IStorageItemProperties interface defines members that expose a storage item's properties, such as thumbnail image, display name, and display type. Because files and folders both have properties, both the StorageFolder and StorageFile concrete types implement this interface. We'll discuss how your app can work with properties in this chapter's "Storage item properties" section.

Finally, as we mentioned in the introduction, WinRT exposes a rich set of operations for querying files and folders. The IStorageFolderQueryOperations interface exposes this functionality. Because you'll initiate a query via some root folder, only the StorageFolder class implements this interface; StorageFile does not.

A StorageFile object represents an actual file on disk. However, a StorageFolder object does not necessarily represent a folder on a disk. A StorageFolder object can also refer to a virtual folder, such as the user's pictures library. A library is a virtual folder, and its contents come from many subdirectories spread across fixed disks or disks attached to different machines on the network. When a StorageFolder object refers to a virtual folder, its Path property will be an empty string (""). In WinRT, virtual folders are first-class citizens in the storage object model. This enables some very rich and powerful scenarios, such as querying and filtering, as shown in this chapter's "Performing file and folder queries" section.

As you saw in Chapter 1, "Windows Runtime primer," all WinRT APIs that perform I/O operations are exposed as XxxAsync methods. Making I/O APIs asynchronous ensures that they don't block your app's UI thread, allowing the thread to continue processing user input so that it remains responsive to the user.

To simplify Figure 5-1, all the static methods defined by the StorageFolder and Storage-File concrete classes are not shown. However, you should be aware that these methods do exist and they are all factory methods that simply return IAsyncOperation<StorageFile> or IAsyncOperation<StorageFolder> objects.

Package and user files

As your app runs, it can access various files that are classified as follows:

- **Read-only package files** are static, read-only files that you include inside your app's package. Package files are installed once per machine and shared by all users. By default, Windows installs package files under the %ProgramFiles%\WindowsApps*PackageFullName* directory.[1] Your package's binary files, WinRT components, and other asset files are all staged (installed) in this directory. When all users on the system uninstall this version of your package, this directory and its contents are permanently removed.

- **Read-write package files** are for per-user data created by your app (or background tasks) at runtime. Windows manages the per-user package files under the %UserProfile%\AppData\Local\Packages*PackageFamilyName* directory. This directory has several subdirectories to support local, roaming, and temporary package files that were discussed in Chapter 4, "Package data and roaming." The system itself creates some additional subdirectories to manage system services (such as the background transfer service and Internet cache discussed in Chapter 7, "Networking") on your package's behalf. Your app can create whatever files it so desires under the LocalState, RoamingState, and TempState directories. The files are for your package and remain on the user's machine when the user upgrades to newer versions of your package. The package files are permanently destroyed if the user uninstalls your package.

- **User files** are considered to be owned and managed by the user, not an app or a package. They typically contain documents, pictures, music, or videos. The user decides where these files are stored, but they usually reside in one of the user's Documents, Pictures, Music, or Videos libraries. However, they can also reside on network shares or in cloud storage (such as SkyDrive). Your app can access user files but only with user consent. Users *explicitly* consent via a folder or file picker or *implicitly* consent by choosing to install your package after being notified that your package has specified a user file capability in its manifest. More details related to consent are presented later in this chapter. Because user files are managed by the user, the files can be accessed by multiple apps and can also be accessed by multiple users. Upgrading

---

[1] The %ProgramFiles%\WindowsApps directory is a hidden, system directory, so you will not be able to see it in File Explorer unless you choose to show hidden items. Once you've found the directory and subsequently try to open it, you'll get an "access denied" error. However, you can open any of this directory's subdirectories. Windows actually determines the package directory via the PackageRoot value, which can be found in the registry in the HKEY_LOCAL_MACHINE\SOFTWARE\Microsoft\Windows\CurrentVersion\Appx key.

or uninstalling a package has no impact on user files. Table 5-1 summarizes the differences between the three different file classifications.

TABLE 5-1 File-classification differences.

Feature	Read-only package files	Read-write package files	User files
File accessibility	Read-only	Read/write	Read/write
Location decided by	Windows	Windows	User
Stored per-user	No	Yes	User decides
Accessible by other apps	No	No	Yes
Destroyed on package uninstall	Yes	Yes	No
Destroyed on package upgrade	Yes	No	No
App requires user consent to access	No	No	Picker/capability

Accessing read-only package files

When a user installs a package, the system unzips the entire contents of the package file into a %ProgramFiles%\WindowsApps*PackageFullName* directory. Of course, you can include any kinds of files you desire in the package. At runtime, your app has read-only access to the contents of this subdirectory.

> **Note** When debugging an app using Visual Studio, the package directory is under the project's directory (usually in a bin\debug subdirectory). This subdirectory is writable; how-ever, your app should not write to this subdirectory because it will succeed during devel-opment and fail when properly installed (staged and registered).

There are two ways you can access a read-only package file: by storage folder or by URI. The fol-lowing code shows how to obtain a `StorageFolder` object representing your package's directory and then how to get a file in this directory:

```
// Get StorageFolder object that represents our package's install directory:
StorageFolder folder = Windows.ApplicationModel.Package.Current.InstalledLocation;

// In our package's directory go to the Assets subdirectory and find the Image.png file:
StorageFile file = await folder.GetFileAsync(@"Assets\Image.png");
```

Once you have a `StorageFile` object, you can open it and read its contents. I discuss how to do this in Chapter 6.

Alternatively, you can access the same file using a special URI:

```
StorageFile file = await StorageFile.GetFileFromApplicationUriAsync(
   new Uri("ms-appx:///Assets/Image.png"));
```

This Microsoft-specific URI scheme (ms-appx) tells Windows you want to access a file that is included in your app's package. Note the three slashes after the colon. The third slash indicates the omission of the package's name. Therefore, "ms-appx:///Assets/Image.png" is equivalent to

```
"ms-appx://" + Windows.ApplicationModel.Package.Current.Id.Name + "/Assets/Image.png"
```

Using the URI technique is very useful because there are occasions when a URI is mandatory—for example, setting the source attribute of a XAML Image control. In addition, when you use a URI, you are tapping into the Windows resource system. This means that Windows will search directories looking for the file based on the user's culture, contrast settings, and display DPI information.

Let's briefly take DPI as an example. When you have a file Image.png, you can provide scaled versions of this asset for 100, 140, and 180% DPI, by tagging it with .scale followed by the percentage—for example, Image.scale-140.png. If you don't provide these explicit versions, Windows will scale the 100% version up, which will inevitably lead to blurry or jagged images. By providing explicit files for each DPI setting, you can make sure that the image looks good on all devices. Similar schemes exist for contrast (for example, contrast-high), language (for example, lang-nl-NL), layout direction (for example, layoutdir-RTL), and so on. You can concatenate those resource qualifiers on the specific resources like this: Image.scale-140_contrast-high.png. See *http://msdn.microsoft.com/en-us/library/windows/apps/xaml/Hh965324(v=win.10).aspx* for more information.

Accessing read-write package files

When a user installs a package, the system creates a subdirectory where the app can create and manage some per-user files. The directory can be found here: %UserProfile%\AppData\Local\Packages\ *PackageFamilyName*. Because the *PackageFamilyName* does not include a version number, this directory is used by all versions of a particular package.[2] This directory contains three subdirectories: LocalState, RoamingState, and TempState; these are described in Chapter 4. In these subdirectories, your app can create additional subdirectories, up to 32 levels deep if desired.

> **Important** The contents of the TempState subdirectory can be destroyed by the system *at any time*. By default, the system cleans it out once per week by using a scheduled task. A user can modify the frequency of this using the Windows Task Scheduler.[3] The scheduled task is called CleanupTemporaryState, and it can be found under Microsoft > Windows > ApplicationData.

There are two ways you can access per-user package files: by storage folder or by URI. To get a StorageFolder, you first get your package's current ApplicationData object and then you query

---

[2] For details about how to handle schema changes in your package's data on upgrade, refer back to Chapter 4.

[3] To update it, you must export it to an XML file, edit the XML file, and then import it back in.

its LocalFolder, RoamingFolder, or TemporaryFolder property. You can use the URI technique (with a URI scheme of ms-appdata) to get a StorageFile object for a file that was previously created using the StorageFolder technique. The following code demonstrates how to create a file in each folder and subsequently get a reference to the file using the URI technique. The code also shows the various flags exposed by CreationCollisionOption to handle potential file-name conflicts.

```
StorageFolder folder;
StorageFile file;

// Create and then access a local package file:
folder = ApplicationData.Current.LocalFolder;
file = await folder.CreateFileAsync("LocalFile.txt",
   CreationCollisionOption.ReplaceExisting);
file = await StorageFile.GetFileFromApplicationUriAsync(
   new Uri("ms-appdata:///local/LocalFile.txt"));

// Create and then access a roaming package file:
folder = ApplicationData.Current.RoamingFolder;
file = await folder.CreateFileAsync("RoamingFile.txt",
   CreationCollisionOption.GenerateUniqueName);
file = await StorageFile.GetFileFromApplicationUriAsync(
   new Uri("ms-appdata:///roaming/RoamingFile.txt"));

// Create and then access a temporary package file:
folder = ApplicationData.Current.TemporaryFolder;
file = await folder.CreateFileAsync("TemporaryFile.txt",
   CreationCollisionOption.OpenIfExists);
file = await StorageFile.GetFileFromApplicationUriAsync(
   new Uri("ms-appdata:///temp/TemporaryFile.txt"));

// The line below deletes all read-write package files:
await ApplicationData.Current.ClearAsync();
```

In this chapter's "Performing file and folder queries" section, we'll show how to execute queries over files and folders. However, for this to work, Windows must know which folders contain files to index. Windows Search does not index the contents of your package's folders; see *http://msdn.micro-soft.com/en-us/library/windows/desktop/bb266513.aspx* for details. However, if you create a folder called "Indexed" in your package's local folder, Windows Search will index the contents of this folder.[4] Searches the user performs using File Explorer will not show results that include the contents of the folder unless the File Explorer is positioned at the root of this folder: %UserProfile%\AppData\Local\Packages*PackageFamilyName*\LocalState\Indexed. Also, you can check whether the contents of this folder have been indexed by Windows Search by opening the Windows desktop Control Panel and then opening the Indexing Options dialog box. If it says "Indexing complete" at the top, you know the contents of this directory have all been indexed.

---

[4] The subdirectory must be named "Indexed"; this will not work if you use any other name.

Of course, the reason to do this is so that your app can perform programmatic queries against the indexed files. The following code demonstrates how to create the "Indexed" folder, add some text files to it, and then perform a query against the folder:

```
// Create the local package folder's "Indexed" subdirectory:
StorageFolder localFolder = ApplicationData.Current.LocalFolder;
StorageFolder indexedSubdir = await localFolder.CreateFolderAsync("Indexed");

// Create two text files in the "Indexed" subdirectory:
await FileIO.WriteTextAsync(await indexedSubdir.CreateFileAsync("File1.txt"), "abc");
await FileIO.WriteTextAsync(await indexedSubdir.CreateFileAsync("File2.txt"), "abcd");

// Create a query that looks for .txt files containing "abcd"
var qo = new QueryOptions(CommonFileQuery.DefaultQuery, new[] { ".txt" }) {
   ApplicationSearchFilter = "abcd",
      IndexerOption = IndexerOption.OnlyUseIndexer,   // Indexed files only!
   FolderDepth = FolderDepth.Deep   // Search subdirectories too
};
StorageFileQueryResult searchResults = localFolder.CreateFileQueryWithOptions(qo);

// Perform the query and get the results
IReadOnlyList<StorageFile> result = await searchResults.GetFilesAsync();
// 'result' contains a single StorageFile object referring to File2.txt
```

Accessing user files via explicit user consent

Users typically have files they care deeply about in various folders, such as the Documents, Pictures, Music, and Videos libraries, network shares, and so on. Windows desktop apps have always been able to access the user's files and folders arbitrarily. This allows desktop apps to traverse the user's folders and modify any files it finds there. Or, a desktop app might upload those files to a web server somewhere on the Internet. Clearly, this is not an ideal situation and it has caused users to be scared to use Windows desktop applications. To address users' valid concerns, a Windows Store app can access only its own package files without user consent.

If your app wishes to manipulate a user file, your app can present the user with a folder or file picker. (See Figure 5-2.) The picker allows the user to navigate over her own folders and files securely. The user can then select a single folder, single file, or set of files, thereby granting your app access to the selected item or items only. In addition, the user can cancel the picker, thereby granting your app no access to anything. The key point here is that the user is in control of her files, not your app.

> **Note** In reality, the user is granting your *package* access to the folder or files. So your app can prompt the user for consent to allow a background task (that is part of the same package) access to the folder or files.

FIGURE 5-2 File-open picker in multiple-select mode with basket shown at bottom.

Let's examine the UI for the file-open picker shown in Figure 5-2. This file-open picker dialog has a single-select mode and a multiple-select mode. Figure 5-2 shows the picker in multiple-select mode. As the user selects files from the UI, the files are placed in what's called the *basket*, which appears at the bottom of the screen. As soon as any file is in the basket, the file-open picker enables the Open button at the lower-right corner. The user can remove files from the basket by tapping the items in the basket or deselecting items in the folder's list. Some apps implement the FileOpenPicker, FileSave-Picker, and CachedFileUpdater declarations in their manifest to provide the user a custom file open/save UI experience. For example, Microsoft's SkyDrive Windows Store app does this, allowing users to download files from cloud storage. The resulting file is then returned back to the hosting Windows Store app. A hosted view (as discussed in Chapter 3, "Process model") is not allowed to show a picker; attempting to do so throws an exception. The reason why Windows forces this limitation is because pickers are hosted themselves and it would be confusing to end users to have hosted views nest other hosted views.

The picker classes are defined in the `Windows.Storage.Pickers` namespace. Here is code prompting the user to select a folder via the `FolderPicker`:

```
var fop = new FolderPicker { FileTypeFilter = {"*"} };
var folder = await fop.PickSingleFolderAsync();
if (folder == null) return; // User canceled the picker
// folder refers to the user-selected StorageFolder object
```

There are three types of pickers: `FolderPicker`, `FileOpenPicker`, and `FileSavePicker`. Table 5-2 lists them with their properties.

TABLE 5-2 Pickers and their properties.

Property	FolderPicker	FileOpenPicker	FileSavePicker
CommitButtonText	String (example: "Choose this folder")	String (example: "Choose this file")	String (example: "Choose this file")
SuggestedStartLocation (PickerLocationId)	Documents, Computer, Desktop, Downloads, HomeGroup, Music, Pictures, Videos	Documents, Computer, Desktop, Downloads, HomeGroup, Music, Pictures, Videos	Documents, Computer, Desktop, Downloads, HomeGroup, Music, Pictures, Videos
SettingsIdentifier	String (for separate user state: location and file type)	String (for separate user state: location and file type)	String (for separate user state: location and file type)
FileTypeFilter	".jpg", ".bmp", and so on	".jpg", ".bmp", and so on	—
ViewMode	List/thumbnail	List/thumbnail	—
DefaultFileExtension	—	—	".jpg"
FileTypeChoices	—	—	"Images": ".jpg", ".png"
SuggestedFileName	—	—	"MyPicture"
SuggestedSaveFile	—	—	StorageFile
Method to Show	PickSingleFolderAsync	PickSingleFileAsync PickMultipleFilesAsync	PickSaveFileAsync

For the folder and file-open picker, only the `FileTypeFilter` property is mandatory. This property is a collection of strings telling the picker which file types to show. Your app can use the wildcard ("*") string to show all files to the user. All the other properties are self-explanatory except for one, `SettingsIdentifier`. Your app can set the `SettingsIdentifier` property to any string value. When your app shows a picker for the first time, the picker will navigate to the folder specified by the `SuggestedStartLocation`. However, the user can use the picker to navigate to a different folder. When the user subsequently picks a location or file and closes the picker, the system saves this last-selected location. If, in the future, your app brings up a picker with the same `SettingsIdentifier` value, the picker remembers the user's last location and navigates to it directly, thereby overriding the `SuggestedStartLocation`. This is the reason why the name of the property is SuggestedStart-Location; it is a suggested location and not a demand.[5]

A `FolderPicker` returns a `StorageFolder` object representing a folder that the user is allowing your app to use. With this `StorageFolder` object, your app can access any files in this folder **and any child items such as subfolders and files in any subfolders**. This grants your app a lot of power; use it wisely. The folder picker UI does not give any indication to the user that your app gets access to the folder and its complete contents.

---

[5] Windows persists `SettingsIdentifier` info in the registry here: HKEY_CLASSES_ROOT\Local Settings\Software\Microsoft\Windows\CurrentVersion\AppModel\SystemAppData*PackageFamilyName*\PersistedPickerData. It is really a package-specific value; not an app-specific value.

When the user selects a file via a picker, the system returns a StorageFile object, allowing your app access to the file. But the user could switch away from your app, causing the system to suspend it and possibly even terminate it. (See Chapter 3 for reasons why.) When the user switches back to your app, the system launches it again and your app is supposed to act as if it were running the whole time. However, when Windows terminated your app, the StorageFile object got destroyed and, now, your app can no longer access the user-selected file. Your app could present the user with another picker and have her grant consent to your app again, but this would be a horrible user experience. What we need is a mechanism that allows your package to remember the StorageFile and StorageFolder objects that the user granted your app's package access to.

Fortunately, this mechanism does exist, and it's called the FutureAccessList. Each package has a single FutureAccessList property exposed by the static type StorageApplicationPermissions, and it's a simple dictionary of key/value pairs. The keys are Strings, and we call them *tokens*. The values contain an IStorageItem and a String, which we call *metadata*. The metadata string is optional; if you don't specify it, the empty string ("") is used. When adding an IStorageItem object to the FutureAccessList, you can specify a specific key string, but you don't have to. If you omit a key (token), a GUID will be generated and used as the key.

The following line adds an entry to the FutureAccessList. The key is "FileWeWereUsing", and the value is some StorageFile object as well as some metadata String:[6]

```
StorageApplicationPermissions.FutureAccessList.AddOrReplace(
    "FileWeWereUsing", storageFile, "SomeMetadata");
```

If your app terminates and launches again, you regain access to the file by doing this:

```
StorageFile file = await
StorageApplicationPermissions.FutureAccessList.GetFileAsync("FileWeWereUsing");
```

Getting the metadata string back (if you need it) is a bit trickier:

```
String metadata = StorageApplicationPermissions.FutureAccessList.Entries
    .First(e => e.Token == "FileWeWereUsing").Metadata;
```

The FutureAccessList can hold up to 1,000 storage items, and your code controls addition and removal. The StorageApplicationPermissions static class also offers a MostRecentlyUsedList property. The MostRecentlyUsedList works exactly like the FutureAccessList, except it holds up to 25 storage items and Windows manages them automatically for you. That is, when you add a new storage item and the list has reached its limit of 25, the oldest item is automatically removed. Moreover, the system sorts the items in the MostRecentlyUsedList; thus, if you enumerate the storage items, the items are returned in most-recently-used order. Finally, because both lists implement the IStorageItemAccessList interface, their APIs are identical. The interface looks like this:

---

[6] Windows persists access list info in the registry here: HKEY_CLASSES_ROOT\Local Settings\Software\Microsoft\ Windows\CurrentVersion\AppModel\SystemAppData*PackageFamilyName*\PersistedStorageItemTable.

```
public interface IStorageItemAccessList {
    UInt32 MaximumItemsAllowed { get; }         // Returns 1000 or 25
    void Clear();                               // Erases all entries in the collection

    String Add(IStorageItem file, string metadata);  // Returns token (GUID)
    void AddOrReplace(String token, IStorageItem file, String metadata);
    void Remove(String token);

    Boolean ContainsItem(String token);
    IAsyncOperation<IStorageItem>  GetItemAsync(String token);
    IAsyncOperation<StorageFolder> GetFolderAsync(String token);
    IAsyncOperation<StorageFile>   GetFileAsync(String token);

    AccessListEntryView Entries { get; }        // Returns collection of token/metadata pairs
    // Some members not shown here
}
```

One of the really cool features of these lists is that they automatically track changes to the storage item. Specifically, if the user uses another application (for example, File Explorer or cmd.exe) to rename or move the item to another subdirectory on the same disk volume, your app will still be able to access the item with its new name or location after extracting it from a list.[7]

> **Note** When your app accesses files or folders with the pickers or one of the `IStorageItemAccessList` classes, WinRT forwards the storage APIs your app calls to another process called a *Broker* (RuntimeBroker.exe). The broker process is a very important part of the Windows security model because it ensures that your app is allowed to access only the files and folders that the user consents to. Because the WinRT file APIs now have to make an additional cross-process call through the broker instead of going directly to the file system, you need to be aware that performance might suffer in order to provide users with the additional security of restricting apps' access to the file system.

File-type associations

When a user double-clicks a text file in File Explorer or opens a text file from within an email application, typically Notepad.exe starts up and opens the document. This happens because Windows has associated Notepad.exe with the file extension .txt. Similarly, you can associate file extensions with your own Windows Store app. Your app can define its own file extension, or it can use an already-existing extension such as .txt. When a user opens a file, Windows checks to see how many apps have registered for the file's file extension. If multiple apps have registered for the file extension, Windows presents the user with a list of these apps. The user can then decide which app to use and indicate if this app should be the default in the future. (See the dialog box shown in Figure 5-3.)

---

[7] For the curious, Windows assigns a unique file Id to all files on an NTFS volume and this is how it can track these changes. For more information about this, check out the Win32 `OpenFileById` function and its `FILE_ID_DESCRIPTOR` parameter on MSDN.

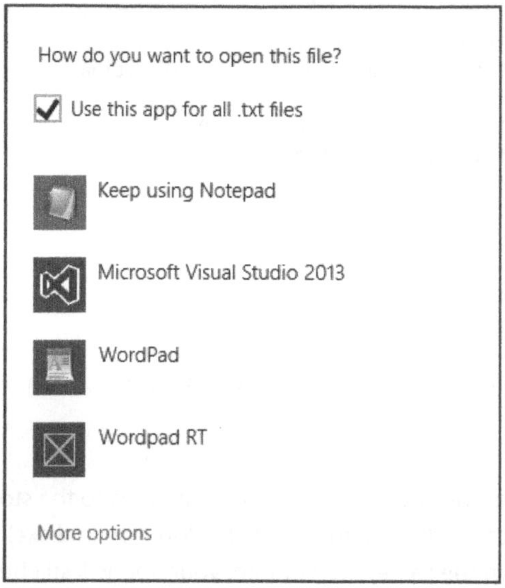

How do you want to open this file?

☑ Use this app for all .txt files

▢ Keep using Notepad

▢ Microsoft Visual Studio 2013

▢ WordPad

▢ Wordpad RT

More options

FIGURE 5-3 Dialog box prompting the user to choose the app for a given file extension.

The user can also view and edit all the file-type associations in the system by selecting Settings charm > Change PC Settings > Search & Apps > Defaults > Choose Default Apps By File Type. This displays the pane shown in Figure 5-4.

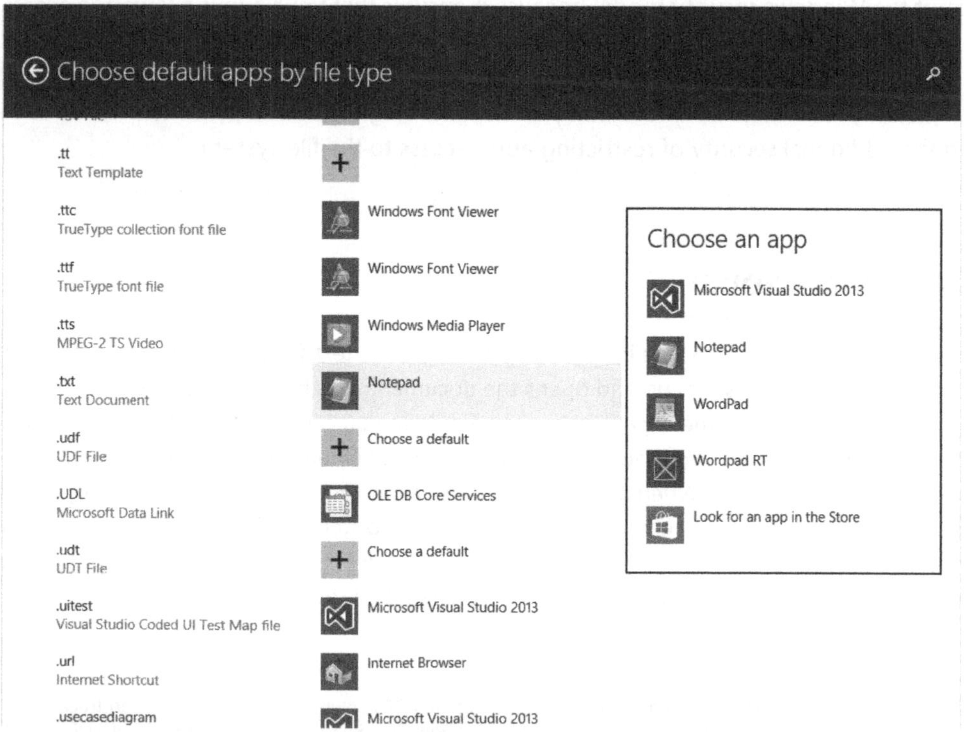

← Choose default apps by file type

.tt Text Template	✛
.ttc TrueType collection font file	Windows Font Viewer
.ttf TrueType font file	Windows Font Viewer
.tts MPEG-2 TS Video	Windows Media Player
.txt Text Document	Notepad
.udf UDF File	✛ Choose a default
.UDL Microsoft Data Link	OLE DB Core Services
.udt UDT File	✛ Choose a default
.uitest Visual Studio Coded UI Test Map file	Microsoft Visual Studio 2013
.url Internet Shortcut	Internet Browser
.usecasediagram	Microsoft Visual Studio 2013

Choose an app

Microsoft Visual Studio 2013

Notepad

WordPad

Wordpad RT

Look for an app in the Store

FIGURE 5-4 The Choose Default Apps By File Type pane.

For a Windows Store app, launching a file is similar to using a file-open picker because the user is trying to open a file and the user is in control of which app should be used to open the file. When an app is installed, Windows needs to know which file types your app supports so that it can activate your app when the user opens a supported file type. You declare file-type associations for each file type you want your app to support in your package's manifest. (See Figure 5-5.)

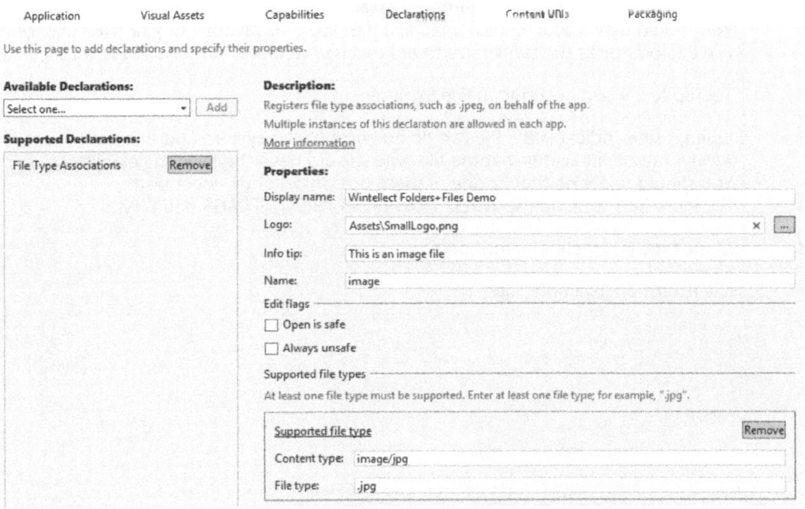

FIGURE 5-5 Declaring a file-type association in an app's manifest.

> **Note** When declaring support for file-type associations, there are many file types that are forbidden, including .accountpicture-ms, .appx, .application, .appref-ms, .bat, .cer, .chm, .cmd, .com, .cpl, .crt, .dll, .drv, .exe, .fon, .gadget, .hlp, .hta, .inf, .ins, .jse, .lnk, .msi, .msp, .ocx, .pif, .ps1, .reg, .scf, .scr, .shb, .shs, .sys, .ttf, .url, .vbe, .vbs, .ws, .wsc, .wsf, and .wsh. The most current list can be found at *http://msdn.microsoft.com/en-us/library/windows/apps/hh779669.aspx*.

Table 5-3 describes the various properties

Once you've built your package and deployed it on a machine, Windows will know about its file-type associations. You can verify this using File Explorer to see your manifest values appear as in Figure 5-6.

TABLE 5-3 File-type association properties and their descriptions.

Property	Required	Description
Name	✓	Unique name (lowercase) for all associations (Content type/File type) sharing DisplayName, Logo, Info Tip, and Edit Flags
Display name	✗	String shown in File Explorer's Type column
Logo	✗	Icon shown in File Explorer (example: "Assets\Icon.png") You should define four icons named like this: Icon.targetsize-[16 | 32 | 48 | 256].png File Explorer picks the target size based on List, Medium, Large, and Extra Large views
Info tip	✗	Tooltip text when hovering in File Explorer
Edit flags	✗	Open is safe: indicates the file can do no harm to the system (.txt file; not an .exe file). Always unsafe: indicates that the file type should never be trusted (.exe file). You should select neither or one of these options; do not select both. For more info, look up the Win32 FILETYPEATTRIBUTEFLAGS enum type.
Content type	✗	Mime type (example: "Image/jpeg")
File type	✓	File extension (example: ".jpg")

FIGURE 5-6 File Explorer showing file-type information for a .jeff file obtained from the app's manifest.

When the user launches your Windows Store app via a file-type association, Windows calls your app's `OnFileActivated` override instead of your app's `OnLaunched` method. In this `OnFile-Activated` method, Windows passes a `FileActivatedEventArgs` object:

```
public sealed class FileActivatedEventArgs : IActivatedEventArgs,
IApplicationViewActivatedEventArgs {
   // Members specific to FileActivatedEventArgs objects:
   public String Verb { get; }
   public IReadOnlyList<IStorageItem> Files { get; }
   public StorageFileQueryResult NeighboringFilesQuery { get; }

   // IActivatedEventArgs members:
   public ActivationKind Kind { get; }
   public ApplicationExecutionState PreviousExecutionState { get; }
   public SplashScreen SplashScreen { get; }

   // IApplicationViewActivatedEventArgs member:
   public Int32 CurrentlyShownApplicationViewId { get; }
}
```

The Verb property enables your app to handle different operations on the file, such as Open and Edit. The Files property contains the set of files the user selected when she launched your app. The following code shows the verb and the first file the system passes to your app:

```
protected override async void OnFileActivated(FileActivatedEventArgs args) {
    IStorageItem firstFile = args.Files[0];
    await new MessageDialog(
        String.Format("Activated to '{0}' the '{1}' file.\n\rPath='{2}'",
            args.Verb, firstFile.Name, firstFile.Path)).ShowAsync();
}
```

Sometimes, when launching a file, the launched app would like to process the neighboring files too. For example, the Windows Mail app allows the user to tap on a picture attachment, which launches a photo viewer app. If the mail message has multiple photos in it, the user could go back to the message and tap on each photo attachment individually to look at them all. But this is rather inconvenient. It would be better if the user could tap on one of the photo attachments, launch a photo viewer app, and then navigate through all the attachment's photos. To enable this kind of scenario, the Mail app would first download all of a message's attachments into a folder and then launch one of the files, thereby activating the photo viewer app. The photo viewer app would query File-ActivatedEventArgs's NeighboringFilesQuery property. If this property is not null, it refers to a StorageFileQueryResult object that is scoped to the folder containing the file that launched it. The photo viewer app can now call StorageFileQueryResult's GetFilesAsync method to access the other files in the same folder.

A StorageFileQueryResult object is scoped to whatever launched it. For example, if the user launches a file from her desktop, the StorageFileQueryResult object is scoped to the user's desktop. If the user was in File Explorer and did some complex search query and then launched a file, the StorageFileQueryResult object is scoped to File Explorer's search results. Furthermore, the StorageFileQueryResult object is scoped to the same kinds of files, which must be pictures, music, or videos. That is, if the user launches a .jpg file, the StorageFileQueryResult object will return only other image files (like .gif, .png, .tif, and so on). Your app does not need to declare file-type associations for all these file types. One last thing, if the user launches an app, passing it multiple storage items, then FileActivatedEventArgs's NeighboringFilesQuery property will always return null.

So far, we've been talking about how your app gets activated because of a file-type association. Now, we'll discuss how an app can activate another app's file-type association. Here is code allowing the user to select a file and then open the file by launching its corresponding app:

```
StorageFile file = new FileOpenPicker { FileTypeFilter = { ".txt" } }.PickSingleFileAsync();
Boolean launched = await Launcher.LaunchFileAsync(file);
```

Note For Windows desktop apps, the ability to launch a file has created many security-related issues for Windows. For example, mail attachments that run .exe files can install viruses or do other harm to the user's PC. To greatly improve the security of a user's PC, Windows Store apps are greatly restricted as to what files they can launch. For example, Launcher's methods prevent launching a desktop app (which runs less restricted than a Windows Store app) with files that could execute code, such as .asp, .aspx, .bat, .cmd, .com, .dll, .exe, .inf, .jar, .js, .mdb, ,msi, .pl, .vb, .vbs, .wsf, .vsi, and so forth.

In addition, you'll notice that LaunchFileAsync returns a Boolean (true if the launch is successful, and false if the launch failed). If the launch fails, the system exposes no way to find out the reason why. No additional information is given because Microsoft doesn't want malicious apps to learn more about the failure in order to attempt to work around it. Also, calling LaunchFileAsync throws an exception if it's not called from a UI thread or if it's called from a UI thread whose window is not active. This prevents apps from popping up and activating themselves at arbitrary times, disturbing the user's workflow, and from capturing user input (like passwords). And finally, there is an overload of the LaunchFileAsync method that accepts a LauncherOptions object. Your app can create one of these and set options that force the user to select the app to be launched for a certain file type or always display a warning to the user that the file being launched is potentially unsafe.

It's also possible to launch an app to access a file via a URI. This is useful for apps that can access files directly from an Internet location. This feature is called *direct invoke*, and it requires that you associate a content type with your file-type association. For more about content types, see the IANA website here: *http://www.iana.org/assignments/media-types*. Because our file-type association declared a content type of "application/jeff", another app can launch our app via a URI as follows:

```
Uri uri = new Uri("http://Wintellect.com/SomeFile");    // URI to file on Internet
LauncherOptions options = new LauncherOptions { ContentType = "application/jeff" };
Boolean ok = await Launcher.LaunchUriAsync(uri, options);
```

Launching an app this way also causes its OnFileActivated method to be called; the URI can be found in the StorageFile's FolderRelativeId property.

Developers frequently ask how their Windows Store app can launch another app. Because of security concerns, there is no direct way for one app to launch another. However, Windows Store apps can be activated if they declare file-type associations (as just discussed) or if they declare URI protocols. Both of these techniques are indirect; that is, an app launches a file or a URI protocol, but the user controls which app actually starts running in response to this. The user views and edits all the

URI protocol associations in the system by selecting Settings charm > Change PC Settings > Search & Apps > Defaults > Default Apps By Protocol. There is no way for a Windows Store app to directly launch another app. Again, this is by design for security reasons.

Like file-type associations, URI protocols are declared via the app's manifest and then the app should override `Windows.UI.Xaml.Application`'s `OnActivated` method to handle the activation.

For example, the Bing maps app has declared support for the "bingmaps" URI protocol, and this allows another app to launch the Bing maps app with the following code:

```
// See http://msdn.microsoft.com/en-us/library/windows/apps/jj635237.aspx for Maps URI scheme
var uri = new Uri("bingmaps:?where=1600%20Pennsylvania%20Ave,%20Washington,%20DC");
await Launcher.LaunchUriAsync(uri);
```

Storage item properties

The `IStorageItem` interface offers properties applicable to both files and folders. These properties are Name, Path, DateCreated, and Attributes (Normal, ReadOnly, Directory, Archive, Temporary, and LocallyIncomplete[8]). In addition, both the StorageFile and StorageFolder classes implement the `IStorageItemProperties` interface, which defines the DisplayName, DisplayType, and FolderRelativeId properties. And the `IStorageFile` interface offers some file-specific properties: FileType and ContentType. Table 5-4 shows all these properties and an example of what they look like.

TABLE 5-4 Various properties available on a `StorageFile` object.

Interface/class	Property	Example value
`IStorageItem`	Name	"photo.JPG"
	Path	"E:\Pictures\2013\photo.JPG"
	DateCreated	{5/22/2013 11:59:00 AM -07:00}
	Attributes	`FileAttributes.Archive`
`IStorageItemProperties`	DisplayName	"photo"
	DisplayType	"JPEG image"
	FolderRelativeId	"5EF38814DAD2922E\\photo.JPG"
`StorageFile`	FileType	".JPG"
	ContentType	"image/jpeg"

---

[8] Other classic attributes like Hidden, System, Device, SparseFile, ReparsePoint, Compressed, Offline, NotContentIndexed, Encrypted, IntegrityStream, and NoScrubData are not exposed.

The IStorageItem interface also defines a GetBasicPropertiesAsync method that ultimately returns a BasicProperties object exposing some other properties common to both files and folders:

```
public sealed class BasicProperties : IStorageItemExtraProperties {
   // Gets the timestamp of the last time the file was modified.
   public DateTimeOffset DateModified { get; }

   // Gets the most relevant date for the item.
   // For a photo, date taken. For a song, date released.
   public DateTimeOffset ItemDate { get; }

   // Gets the size of the file.
   public UInt64 Size { get; }
}
```

You can also think of a thumbnail image as being a property, and your app can obtain this property by querying IStorageItemProperties' GetThumbnailAsync method. However, this method should no longer be used; instead, both StorageFile and StorageFolder implement the new IStorageItemProperties2 interface, which defines a GetScaledImageAsThumbnailAsync method. This method can return thumbnail images of any size or cropped to meet your app's needs. The method scans for the thumbnail you desire from the PC's local cache first. If the thumbnail is not found, the method checks the file itself for an embedded thumbnail. Finally, if the file is available only in the user's SkyDrive, the method makes a request to the SkyDrive service to have the service produce and download a thumbnail image. The great thing here is that the file itself (which could be huge in the case of a 20-MB image) does not get downloaded in order to get and show the user a thumbnail for it; this reduces bandwidth usage, reduces local disk consumption, and improves performance. Of course, if the SkyDrive service can't be reached, GetScaledImageAsThumbnailAsync returns null.

However, we have just discussed the very tip of the property-system iceberg. The Windows property system is enormous and incredibly rich. Windows actually captures many properties related to specific data files and stores them in a database on your hard disk. This database is called the *content indexer*, and I discuss some other features it offers in the "Searching over a stream's content" section in Chapter 6. This allows your app to query (and modify) a phenomenal set of properties. The IStorageItemProperties interface offers a Properties property that returns a StorageItem-ContentProperties object. The class looks like this:

```
public sealed class StorageItemContentProperties : IStorageItemExtraProperties {
   public IAsyncOperation<IDictionary<String, Object>> RetrievePropertiesAsync(
      IEnumerable<String> propertiesToRetrieve);

   public IAsyncAction SavePropertiesAsync();
   public IAsyncAction SavePropertiesAsync(
      IEnumerable<KeyValuePair<String, Object>> propertiesToSave);

   // Convenience methods that internally call RetrievePropertiesAsync to
   // get commonly used properties for commonly used file types
   public IAsyncOperation<DocumentProperties> GetDocumentPropertiesAsync();
```

```
    public IAsyncOperation<ImageProperties> GetImagePropertiesAsync();
    public IAsyncOperation<MusicProperties> GetMusicPropertiesAsync();
    public IAsyncOperation<VideoProperties> GetVideoPropertiesAsync();
}
```

When calling RetrievePropertiesAsync, you must pass it a collection of strings identifying the properties you wish to obtain. Go to *http://msdn.microsoft.com/en-us/library/dd561977(VS.85).aspx* to see the enormous list of all possible strings. To get strings for some common properties, see the static Windows.Storage.SystemProperties class. The following code shows an example calling this method:

```
IDictionary<String, Object> props = await storageFile.Properties.RetrievePropertiesAsync(
    new String[] {
        "System.FileAttributes", "System.DateModified",
        "System.Size", SystemProperties.ItemNameDisplay
    });
```

You can retrieve literally hundreds of predefined properties, ranging from the straightforward FileOwner to the more esoteric System.ComputerName or even System.FreeSpace (free space on the system disk).

To simplify your code when obtaining commonly used properties for common file types, the StorageItemContentProperties class offers the four GetXxxPropertiesAsync methods to easily obtain properties commonly used when apps work with documents, images, music, or videos. Table 5-5 shows the properties returned for a specific file type.

TABLE 5-5 Commonly used properties for document, image, music, and video files.

File type	Properties
Document	Author, Comments, Keywords, Title
Image	CameraManufacturer, CameraModel, DateTaken, Height, Keywords, Latitude, Longitude, Orientation, PeopleNames, Rating, Title, Width
Music	Album, AlbumArtist, Artist, Bitrate, Composers, Conductors, Duration, Genre, Producers, Publisher, Rating, Subtitle, Title, TrackNumber, Writers, Year
Video	Bitrate, Directors, Duration, Height, Keywords, Latitude, Longitude, Orientation, Producers, Publisher, Rating, Subtitle, Title, Width, Writers, Year

Accessing user files with implicit user consent

So far, we've discussed accessing user data through file pickers and file-type associations. In both scenarios, the end user explicitly gives your app access to a file or folder. But what about a photo viewer app that allows the user to browse all his pictures? Or a music player that shows the user's songs organized by artists or albums? Or an app that indexes all the user's documents, allowing him to search through them? Your app could certainly use pickers for these scenarios. However, that would force the user to choose the folders containing his pictures or music files before he could use the app. Moreover, the user already has a dedicated virtual location for media files and documents in libraries that we could use. (See the side note if you're unfamiliar with libraries.)

Libraries

In Windows, a *library* is a virtual folder that provides a consolidated view of files contained in multiple physical directories. Users can add and remove physical directory paths from a library; the physical directories can reside on the local system, a network share, or even on removable media. For example, the Music library typically contains the %UserProfile%\Music subdirectory, but the user can add a network share on a home server. Windows creates a database of files and their properties contained within the libraries, which allows for rich content searching, filtering, and ordering.

By default, the system has libraries for Music, Pictures, Videos, and Documents. Users can create new libraries but the WinRT API provides APIs to access only these four.[9] Using the `Windows.Storage.StorageLibrary` class, a Windows Store app can allow the user to add storage folders to and remove storage folders from a library. An instance of this class can also raise an event when the user changes the folders that make up a library, allowing an app to rescan the library's contents.

Windows Store apps are forbidden from accessing a user's files unless the user allows the app to do it. For an app to traverse the contents of a library, the app's package manifest must first specify in the Capabilities section which libraries the package wants access to. Figure 5-7 shows the capabilities related to accessing a user's files. Selecting a library capability in the manifest grants your package bulk access to a large set of the user's files. Your package's app must be diligent here and not abuse this privilege. In fact, packages that use library capabilities are scrutinized much more stringently than packages that use pickers when submitted for Windows Store certification. If you can implement your app using pickers instead of library capabilities, you should. You should specify library capabilities only when your package absolutely requires programmatic access to the user's files.

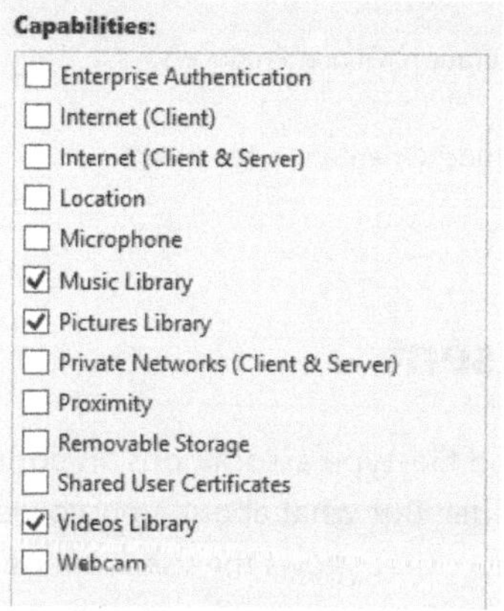

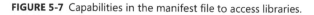

Capabilities:

- ☐ Enterprise Authentication
- ☐ Internet (Client)
- ☐ Internet (Client & Server)
- ☐ Location
- ☐ Microphone
- ☑ Music Library
- ☑ Pictures Library
- ☐ Private Networks (Client & Server)
- ☐ Proximity
- ☐ Removable Storage
- ☐ Shared User Certificates
- ☑ Videos Library
- ☐ Webcam

FIGURE 5-7 Capabilities in the manifest file to access libraries.

---

[9] Libraries aren't actual physical folders, and when you programmatically browse the file system, you will not find them. They are stored as XML files in %UserProfile%\AppData\Roaming\Microsoft\Windows\Libraries.

Important Whereas the Pictures library contains pictures, the Music library contains music, and the Videos library contains videos, the Documents library contains all kinds of files on behalf of the user. My personal Documents library contains Microsoft Excel files, PowerPoint files, Word files, PDF files, Microsoft Money files, C# source code files, and the list goes on and on. Having access to all these files opens up security issues where private user files could too easily be accessed and even uploaded to servers somewhere on the Internet. For this reason, packages are strongly discouraged from enabling the Documents Library capability in the manifest. In fact, as you can see in Figure 5-7, Visual Studio doesn't even show "Documents Library" in the list of Capabilities. If you really want to use this capability, you must manually add it to the manifest's XML file.

In addition, packages that specify the Documents Library capability will not pass Windows Store certification if submitted using an individual account. Only company accounts (which are verified) can submit packages that specify the Documents Library capability. Furthermore, a package that specifies the Documents Library capability **must** also specify one or more file-type associations. This gives the app access to only the specified file types within the library. From a security perspective, having apps declare a file-type association is the equivalent of having a virtual documents library like "My Excel Files," which the user can feel more comfortable granting access to.

Then, when the user goes to the Store app to install the package, the Store app shows the user what capabilities the package requires. By installing the package, the user is implicitly granting the package access to the specified capabilities. Figure 5-8 shows how the Store app shows a package's required capabilities to a user before the user installs the package.

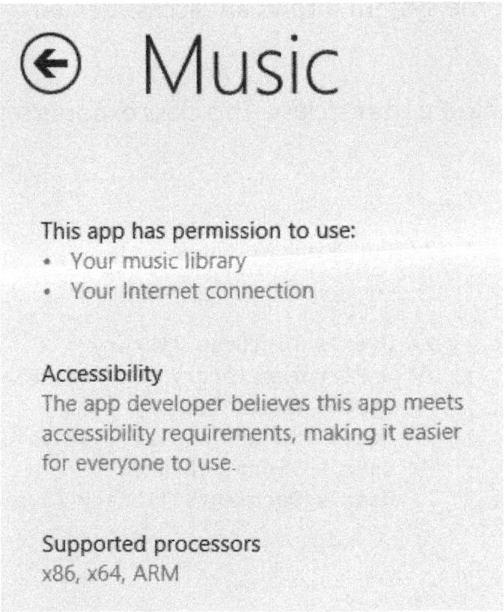

FIGURE 5-8 The Music app requires access to the user's Music library.

After a user installs a package, she can always see what capabilities the package needs by running the package's app, opening the Settings charm, and then selecting Permissions, as you can see in Figure 5-9.

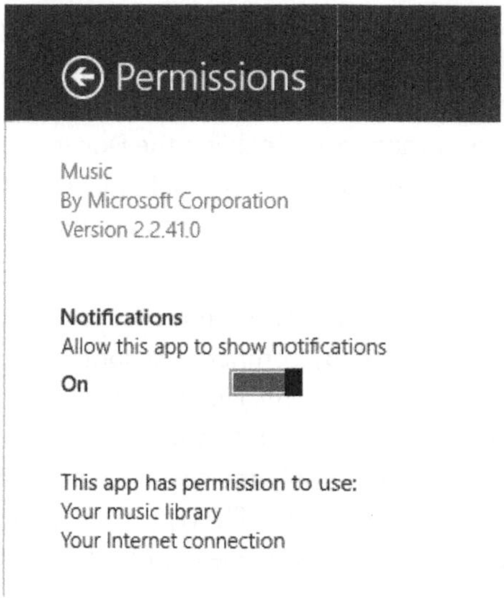

Permissions

Music
By Microsoft Corporation
Version 2.2.41.0

Notifications
Allow this app to show notifications
On

This app has permission to use:
Your music library
Your Internet connection

FIGURE 5-9 The Music app has permission to access your Music library and to the Internet.

If a package specifies the Music Library capability, its app can easily access all the folders in this library with a single line of code:

```
IReadOnlyList<StorageFolder> folders = await KnownFolders.MusicLibrary.GetFoldersAsync();
```

If your package does not have the required capability, the system throws an "access denied" exception.

In the line just shown, you'll notice that we use the KnownFolders class. This class exposes several StorageFolder objects:

```
public static class KnownFolders {
    public static StorageFolder CameraRoll        { get; }  // For Windows Phone only

    // The main library folders:
    public static StorageFolder PicturesLibrary  { get; }  // User's Pictures library
    public static StorageFolder SavedPictures     { get; }  // = PicturesLibrary (for Phone)
    public static StorageFolder MusicLibrary      { get; }  // User's Music library
    public static StorageFolder Playlists         { get; }  // Music library's play list folder
    public static StorageFolder VideosLibrary     { get; }  // User's Video library
    public static StorageFolder DocumentsLibrary { get; }  // User's Documents library (avoid)
```

```
    // Allows Picture, Music, Video library access on user's Home Group
    public static StorageFolder HomeGroup        { get; }

    // Allows Picture, Music, Video library access on removable devices:
    public static StorageFolder RemovableDevices { get; }

    // The folder of media server (Digital Living Network Alliance [DLNA]) devices.
    public static StorageFolder MediaServerDevices { get; }
}
```

Windows has a feature called HomeGroup that grants a user easy access to multiple machines in a home environment. Figure 5-10 shows under my name that I have two machines in my HomeGroup: BOSBOX8 and VIRTBOS.

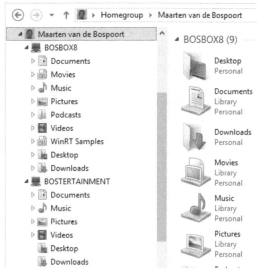

FIGURE 5-10 Libraries available on multiple machines in a HomeGroup.

You've seen that libraries can include physical directories on other systems to get a consolidated view of media files or documents. But what if a user wants to browse, for example, his wife's pictures either on the home system or even on her computer? That is what a HomeGroup is for. The Known-Folders class exposes this too as a virtual folder. When a user first joins a machine to a HomeGroup, the system asks if the machine's library should be shared. Your app can access these shared Home-Group libraries by using KnownFolders's HomeGroup property.

A package specifying the HomeGroup capability must also specify one or more of the Pictures Library, Music Library, or Videos Library capabilities. The package will also need the Home Or Work Networking capability, which is not on by default. (See Chapter 7.) For security reasons, it is not possible to get access to a HomeGroup machine's Documents library.

The following code shows how to enumerate the contents of the virtual HomeGroup folder:

```
StorageFolder folder = KnownFolders.HomeGroup;

foreach (var user in await folder.GetFoldersAsync()) {          // Users
    foreach (var machine in await user.GetFoldersAsync()) {       // Machines
        foreach (var library in await machine.GetFoldersAsync()) {  // Libraries
            // Process a library folder...
        }
    }
}
```

The KnownFolders class also has a MediaServerDevices property. Like the virtual HomeGroup storage folder, use of this property also requires that one or more of the media library capabilities be specified as well as the Home Or Work Networking capability.

The KnownFolders.RemovableDevices property is used for removable storage such as USB drives. Accessing the contents on removable media has similar security concerns to that of accessing the contents of the Documents library. That is, the app must also specify at least one file-type association as well as the package's Removable Storage capability. Just as when you use the Documents library, the system exposes only files on the removable storage device that meet the specified file-type association or associations. The following code shows how to enumerate the contents of the virtual removable devices storage folder:

```
StorageFolder devices = KnownFolders.RemovableDevices;

foreach (var device in await devices.GetFoldersAsync()) { // Drives
    foreach (var folder in await device.GetItemsAsync()) { // Files or folders
        //  Process a storage item...
    }
}
```

Windows Store apps can access files on the network through UNC paths too, for example:

```
StorageFile file = StorageFile.GetFileFromPathAsync(@"\\SomeMachine\SomeShare\SomeFile.txt");
```

Windows treats shares on the network the same way as it treats KnownFolders.Removable-Devices; you will need to specify file-type associations to indicate the file types your app works with. Instead of specifying the Removable Storage capability in the manifest, the package must specify the Private Networks and Enterprise Authentication capabilities. The Enterprise Authentication capability allows the app to use the user's credentials to authenticate on the remote system. Be aware that Enterprise Authentication is a special-use capability requiring that the package be submitted by a company account instead of an individual account.

One final folder to discuss is the user's Downloads folder. On a PC, each user gets his or her own Downloads folder. When an app first puts something in the user's Downloads folder, Windows creates a subfolder within the Downloads folder for the app. This subfolder name matches the app's package family name, followed by an exclamation mark and the application ID (usually "App" as specified in the manifest's Application element). This keeps one app's downloaded files separate from another app's downloaded files. Figure 5-11 shows this subfolder name as viewed from cmd.exe.

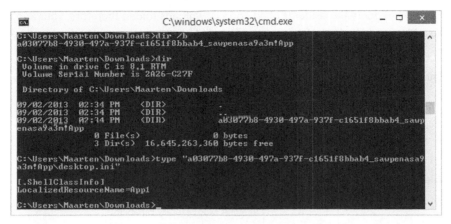

FIGURE 5-11 The app's Downloads subfolder and its Desktop.ini file as viewed with cmd.exe.

In the app's subfolder, Windows also creates a hidden (and system) Desktop.ini file whose contents are shown in Figure 5-11. The existence of this file causes Windows File Explorer to show the subfolder with a different name (as indicated by the *LocalizedResourceName* value). So, when the user looks at his Downloads folder with File Explorer, he sees what's shown in Figure 5-12.

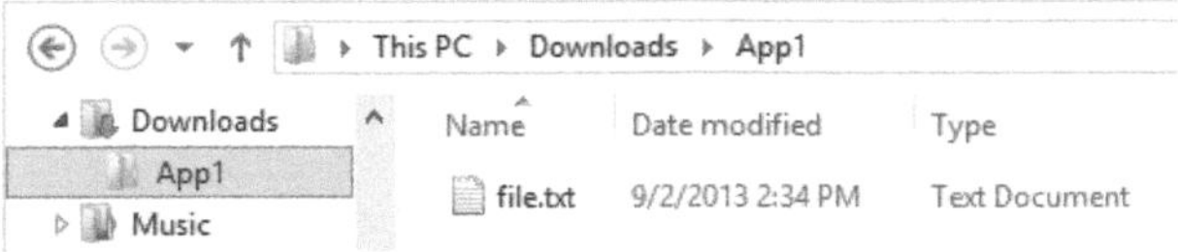

FIGURE 5-12 The Downloads folder shows a subfolder matching the app's name due to the Desktop.ini file placed in the subfolder.

Note that Downloads subfolders are not destroyed when packages are uninstalled because the files in these subfolders are considered to be user files, not package or app files. An app creates files and subfolders in its Downloads subfolder by calling methods defined by the DownloadsFolder class:

```
public static class DownloadsFolder {
    public static IAsyncOperation<StorageFile> CreateFileAsync(String desiredName);
    public static IAsyncOperation<StorageFile> CreateFileAsync(String desiredName,
        CreationCollisionOption option);

    public static IAsyncOperation<StorageFolder> CreateFolderAsync(String desiredName);
    public static IAsyncOperation<StorageFolder> CreateFolderAsync(String desiredName,
        CreationCollisionOption option);
}
```

The following code creates a text file for the user in the app's Downloads subfolder:

```
IStorageFile file = await DownloadsFolder.CreateFileAsync("file.txt");
await FileIO.AppendLinesAsync(file, new [] { "Hello there"});
```

WinRT offers no API to query the contents of an app's Downloads folder; therefore, your app must keep track of the folders and files it creates using the `FutureAccessList` property discussed earlier in this chapter.

Table 5-6 summarizes the capability and file-type association requirements of the various virtual storage folders.

TABLE 5-6 Capability and file-type association requirements for virtual storage folders.

Virtual folder	Requires capability	Requires file type assoc.	Notes
Music/Pictures/Videos Library	✓	✗	1+ required for HomeGroup.
Playlists	✓	✗	Requires Music Library capability.
HomeGroup	(special)	✗	Requires Music, Pictures, or Videos Library capability.
DocumentsLibrary	✓	✓	HomeGroup can't access this.
RemovableStorage	✓	✓	Children are drives.
MediaServerDevices	(special)	✗	Children are media servers.
DownloadsFolder	✗	✗	Creates subfolders and files only.

Performing file and folder queries

This chapter has discussed how to work with folders, files, properties, thumbnail images, and libraries. In this section, I show how to quickly search for items within a folder using a query that can filter on multiple properties, such as date, size, rating, or even user-defined strings. You can also specify how you want the query results sorted. Additionally, you can receive notifications when storage items are added or removed.

The following code demonstrates how to perform a query over the user's Pictures library. The query returns a set of virtual folders, with each folder representing a year.[10] Then, within each folder, pictures taken that year are returned. Let me make something perfectly clear: this works regardless of how the user organizes his pictures in his Pictures library. That is, all the pictures could be at the root of the user's Pictures library, or they could be in subdirectories organized by person or location. None of this matters; the following code returns the pictures grouped by year:

```
// Create QueryOptions to filter/sort results; this example groups the results by year
QueryOptions qo = new QueryOptions(CommonFolderQuery.GroupByYear)
   { FolderDepth = FolderDepth.Deep };
```

---

[10] You can easily tell that the folders do not physically exist by looking at each `StorageFolder`'s `Path` property. For virtual folders, the property will show the empty string ("") because there is no actual path to a disk location that can be shown.

```
// From the user's Pictures library, create a query that returns virtual folders
StorageFolderQueryResult folders = KnownFolders.PicturesLibrary
   .CreateFolderQueryWithOptions(qo);

// Process each year's files
foreach (StorageFolder folder in await folders.GetFoldersAsync()) {
   Debug.WriteLine(folder.Name);  // Folder name is year, e.g. "2014"

   foreach (StorageFile file in await folder.GetFilesAsync()) {
      Debug.WriteLine("   " + file.Name);  // Pictures taken in 2014
   }
}
```

Wow, this is all there is to it. Let's talk a little more about the QueryOptions class. You create and initialize an instance of this class to fully describe the kind of query you wish to perform. Table 5-7 summarizes the various options.

TABLE 5-7 QueryOptions constructor parameter and other property options.

Kind	QueryOptions member	Description
Constructor flags	CommonFolderQuery	DefaultQuery or GroupByType/Author/Tag/Year/Month Artist/Album(Artist)/Composer/Genre/PublishedYear/Rating
	CommonFileQuery	DefaultQuery or OrderByName/Title/SearchRank/Date/MusicInfo
Configurable properties	FileTypeFilter	File extension list (empty for all).
	FolderDepth	Shallow (folder only) or Deep (folder and subfolders)
	Language	Language ID string (example: "en-US")
	IndexerOption	UseIndexerWhenAvailable, OnlyUseIndexer, DoNotUseIndexer
	ApplicationSearchFilter UserSearchFilter	Advanced Query Syntax (AQS) strings combined together. See *http://msdn.microsoft.com/en-us/library/windows/desktop/ bb266512.aspx*.
	SortOrder	Set of PropertyName/AscendingOrder pairs See *http://msdn.microsoft.com/en-us/library/windows/apps/ windows.storage.search.queryoptions.aspx#properties*.
Read-only properties	DateStackOption	Indicates how results are grouped (None, Month, or Year).
	GroupPropertyName	Indicates the property being used to group the CommonFolderQuery.

When you construct a QueryOptions object, you pass to its constructor a CommonFolder-Query enumeration value or a CommonFileQuery enumeration value indicating whether you want results grouped by folder or an ordered flat set of results. The remaining properties are pretty self-explanatory; you can look them up in the SDK documentation if you need more information about them. When filtering on storage item properties, you have access to the complete set of properties as described in the "Storage item properties" section in this chapter. And you can create rich filter strings using the Windows Advanced Query Syntax (AQS) along with the ApplicationSearchFilter and UserSearchFilter properties.

For example, the following code creates a query that returns music files in the rock genre that are older than November 5, 2004 and whose album title contains the word "Sky":

```
QueryOptions qo = new QueryOptions(CommonFolderQuery.GroupByPublishedYear) {
    FolderDepth = FolderDepth.Deep,
    ApplicationSearchFilter = "date:>11/05/04 AND genre:rock AND System.Music.AlbumTitle:~~Sky"
};

StorageFolderQueryResult folders = KnownFolders.MusicLibrary.CreateFolderQueryWithOptions(qo);
```

By the way, your app doesn't have to process all of a query's results. The `StorageFolderQuery-Result` class offers an overload of the `GetFoldersAsync` method that takes a starting index and a max number of items. Similarly, the `StorageFileQueryResult` class offers an overload of the `GetFilesAsync` method that also takes a starting index and a max number of items.

Here is another example that creates a query resulting in a flat set of pictures ordered by date taken:

```
QueryOptions qo = new QueryOptions(CommonFileQuery.OrderByDate, new[] { "*" });

StorageFileQueryResult files = KnownFolders.PicturesLibrary.CreateFileQueryWithOptions(qo);
files.OptionsChanged += OnOptionsChanged;
files.ContentsChanged += OnContentsChanged;
```

This creates a flat, ordered list of all files by using a wild card ("*"). In addition, the `Options-Changed` event handler will invoke our `OnOptionsChanged` method whenever one of our `QueryOptions` object's properties gets changed. Also, the `ContentsChanged` event handler will invoke our `OnContentsChanged` method if any storage items change that affect the results of our query. An app can dynamically update its user interface in response to this event.

It is common for apps to process the resulting folders and files, getting thumbnail images and properties for each storage item. However, iterating over all the items individually to get this data would be quite time consuming, and it is also highly unlikely that all the information could fit on the user's screen anyway. To acquire thumbnail images more efficiently, call `QueryOptions`' `Set-ThumbnailPrefetch` method. This causes the system to start loading thumbnail images immediately; this approach uses more resources but makes thumbnail retrieval on query results much faster. The `QueryOptions` class also offers a `SetPropertyPrefetch` method to get storage item properties more efficiently.

The following code demonstrates using these methods to improve the performance of fetching properties and thumbnail images:

```
// Create QueryOptions to filter/sort results
QueryOptions qo = new QueryOptions(CommonFileQuery.OrderByDate, new[] { "*" });

// Improve performance of fetching properties and/or thumbnails
String[] propertiesToRetrieve = new String[] { "System.Size" };
qo.SetPropertyPrefetch(PropertyPrefetchOptions.ImageProperties, propertiesToRetrieve);
qo.SetThumbnailPrefetch(ThumbnailMode.PicturesView, 190, ThumbnailOptions.None);

// From virtual folder call Create[File|Folder|Item]QueryWithOptions
StorageFileQueryResult files = KnownFolders.PicturesLibrary.CreateFileQueryWithOptions(qo);
```

CHAPTER 6

Stream input and output

In Chapter 5, "Storage files and folders," I explained how your app could navigate various storage folders to manipulate files. However, I did not explain how to access the contents of the files. In this chapter, you'll learn how to transfer data to and from files using stream input and output. However, streams are not just for files; you can use them as a general-access mechanism to transfer data. For example, you also use streams to transfer data over sockets. (See Chapter 7, "Networking.") Streams are also used to manipulate in-memory data, as I'll show later in this chapter's "Compressing and decompressing data" and "Encrypting and decrypting data" sections.

Simple file I/O

Before diving into streams, I want to show some WinRT APIs that simplify reading and writing the contents of a file for common scenarios. Internally, these simple APIs wrap the slightly more complex stream APIs. The `FileIO` class looks like this:

```
public static class FileIO {
    public static IAsyncAction WriteBytesAsync(IStorageFile file, Byte[] buffer);

    public static IAsyncAction WriteBufferAsync(IStorageFile file, IBuffer buffer);
    public static IAsyncOperation<IBuffer> ReadBufferAsync(IStorageFile file);

    public static IAsyncAction WriteLinesAsync(IStorageFile file, IEnumerable<String> lines);
    public static IAsyncAction AppendLinesAsync(IStorageFile file, IEnumerable<String> lines);
    public static IAsyncOperation<IList<String>> ReadLinesAsync(IStorageFile file);

    public static IAsyncAction WriteTextAsync(IStorageFile file, String contents);
    public static IAsyncAction AppendTextAsync(IStorageFile file, String contents);
    public static IAsyncOperation<String> ReadTextAsync(IStorageFile file);
}
```

Files always contain arrays of bytes, and the first three methods shown transfer byte arrays or buffers (which are also byte arrays). The `IBuffer` interface is explained in this chapter's "Transferring byte buffers" section. The remaining methods simplify working with text files. Text (characters) are always converted to byte arrays via an encoding. The remaining six methods all convert the specified string to a byte array using a UTF-8 encoding. There are overloads of these six methods (not shown) that allow you to pass a `UnicodeEncoding` parameter. UTF-8 and UTF-16 (big-endian and little-endian) are supported.

The following code creates a file in our package's temporary folder, writes strings to that file, and then reads the strings back:

```
// Create a file:
StorageFile file = await ApplicationData.Current.TemporaryFolder.CreateFileAsync("MyFile.txt");

// Write 2 lines of text to the file (encoded with UTF-8):
String[] output = new[] { "This is line 1", "This is line 2" };
await FileIO.WriteLinesAsync(file, output);

// Read the lines of text from the file (decoded with UTF-8):
IList<String> input = await FileIO.ReadLinesAsync(file);
```

WinRT also provides a static `PathIO` class whose methods are identical to those of the `FileIO` class except that the methods accept an absolute path string instead of an `IStorageFile`. In addition, `PathIO`'s methods require that the file already exist. Here is the previous code modified to use the `PathIO` class:

```
// NOTE: You MUST create the file before writing to it:
StorageFile file = await ApplicationData.Current.TemporaryFolder.CreateFileAsync("MyFile.txt");

// Write 2 lines of text to the file (encoded with UTF-8):
String[] output = new[] { "This is line 1", "This is line 2" };
await PathIO.WriteLinesAsync(file.Path, output);

// Read the lines of text from the file (decoded with UTF-8):
IList<String> input = await PathIO.ReadLinesAsync(file.Path);
```

As you can see, `FileIO`'s and `PathIO`'s methods are straightforward to use. All their methods open the file, transfer the data, and subsequently close the file. These methods are great for some common scenarios, but they provide little control and are certainly not suitable for working with large files because they read the whole file into memory all at once. When you need more control over the stream, you'll use the WinRT interfaces and classes defined in the `Windows.Storage.Streams` namespace. These types make up the streams object model.

The streams object model

Figure 6-1 shows WinRT's streams object model. Both `IInputStream` and `IOutputStream` inherit from `IClosable`. This indicates that classes implementing either of these interfaces require special cleanup because they wrap a native resource like a file or socket handle. In Chapter 1, "Windows Runtime primer," I discussed how the CLR projects WinRT's `Windows.Foundation.IClosable` interface (which has only a `Close` method) as the .NET Framework's `System.IDisposable` interface (with its `Dispose` method). This allows you to use C#'s `using` statement with WinRT `IClosable` types so that their `Close` method is called within a `finally` block, causing cleanup to occur immediately after the `try` block executes or if an exception is thrown as opposed to waiting for a future garbage collection.

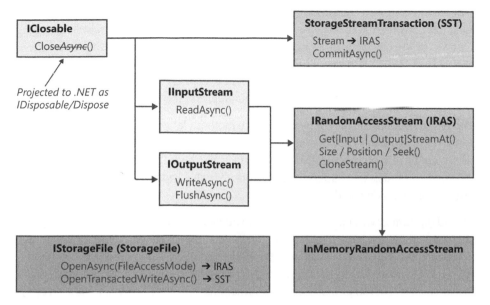

FIGURE 6-1 WinRT's streams object model.

> ⚠ **Important** One thing to take note of here is that *all* WinRT APIs that perform I/O operations are implemented asynchronously. Because the name for IClosable's method is Close and not CloseAsync, the Close method cannot perform any I/O operations. This is semantically different from how Dispose works in the Microsoft .NET Framework. For .NET Framework–implemented types, calling Dispose can do I/O and, in fact, it frequently causes buffered data to be flushed before actually closing a device. When C# code calls Dispose on a WinRT type, however, I/O (like flushing) will not be performed and a loss of data is possible. You must be aware of this and, in some cases, you might have to flush data in your code explicitly. I will explicitly point out in this chapter when it is necessary to do this.

IInputStream and IOutputStream are the basic interfaces that read buffers (byte arrays) from and write buffers to a stream. IInputStream's ReadAsync method reads bytes from a stream into a buffer and IOutputStream's WriteAsync method writes bytes from a buffer to a stream.

IOutputStream has an additional method: FlushAsync. Most apps will never call this method. Let me explain its purpose. When writing to a stream, Windows internally buffers (caches) the data in memory and writes the data to the stream when the memory buffer fills or if the buffer sits idle for a while. Windows does this to improve performance for apps that frequently issue small write operations because accessing the hardware (which is slower than RAM) incurs a performance hit. Because of this, an app could "write data to a stream" and, if the power fails on the machine before the data is flushed to the stream, the data would be lost.

Apps that are working with critically important data can call `FlushAsync` to reduce the chance of data being lost. Beware that calling `FlushAsync` does not guarantee that data will not be lost because a power failure could still occur between calling `WriteAsync` and `FlushAsync`. Internally, WinRT's `FlushAsync` method does the same thing as Win32's `FlushFileBuffers` function. (See *http://msdn.microsoft.com/en-us/library/windows/desktop/aa364439.aspx*.) Note that calling `FlushAsync` frequently hurts the performance of your app, and this is why most apps will not call it.[1]

The `IInputStream` and `IOutputStream` interface methods let you access a stream sequentially and are useful when you don't know the number of bytes in the stream (as is the case with network streams). However, the `IRandomAccessStream` interface allows you to access the underlying stream randomly. Because `IRandomAccessStream` inherits from both `IInputStream` and `IOutputStream`, it can be used for both reading and writing.

To start reading from or writing to a specific byte within a stream, call `IRandomAccessStream`'s Seek method to position the stream to the desired byte and then call `ReadAsync` or `WriteAsync` to start accessing the stream sequentially from the desired position. Alternatively, you can call `GetInputStreamAt` or `GetOutputStreamAt` to get a stream starting at a byte offset within the stream. The stream's `Position` property advances whenever you call `ReadAsync` or `WriteAsync`.

> **Important** Make sure you issue read and write operations sequentially against a single stream to maintain the integrity of the stream's current position. Issuing multiple requests concurrently produces non-deterministic results.

The `IRandomAccessStream` interface offers a `Size` property you can use to query or set the size of the stream. Under normal circumstances, you would not set the size because the system automatically grows it when appending to a random-access stream. But, if you know what size you want the stream to be before writing to it, you might want to set the size first because this tends to improve performance when writing to the stream.

Therefore, to read from or write to a file, you would simply call `IStorageFile`'s `OpenAsync` method to obtain an `IRandomAccessStream` and then start calling its `ReadAsync` or `WriteAsync` methods. When done, you can call `Dispose` or let the garbage collector take care of it for you. You'll see code demonstrating this shortly. `IStorageFile` offers an `OpenTransactedWriteAsync` method that returns a reference to a `StorageStreamTransaction` object that implements the `IClosable` interface. The `StorageStreamTransaction` class is discussed in this chapter's "Performing transacted write operations" section.

Understanding the streams object model is critically important when building Windows Store apps because many WinRT components use streams. For example,

- The `IRandomAccessStream` interface is used by storage files, images, bitmaps, thumbnails, media, and the `InMemoryRandomAccessStream` class.

---

[1] For more information, read *http://blogs.msdn.com/b/oldnewthing/archive/2010/09/09/10059575.aspx*.

- The `IInputStream` interface is used by the background transfer manager and the `DataReader`, `DataProtectionProvider`, `Decompressor`, and `AtomPubClient` classes.

- The `IOutputStream` interface is used by networking, as well as the `DataWriter`, `DataProtectionProvider`, `Compressor`, and `InkManager` classes.

Interoperating between WinRT streams and .NET streams

The .NET Framework has its `System.IO.Stream` class (and many types derived from it), and there are many useful classes in the .NET Framework designed to take input and output from these `Stream`-derived classes. LINQ to XML and the serialization technologies are two that immediately come to mind. So, if you want to use these .NET technologies with WinRT storage files, you're going to have to use the framework projection methods (as discussed in Chapter 1) defined in the `System.IO.WindowsRuntimeStorageExtensions` class to help you:

```
namespace System.IO {   // Defined in System.Runtime.WindowsRuntime.dll
   public static class WindowsRuntimeStorageExtensions {
      public static Task<Stream> OpenStreamForReadAsync(this IStorageFile file);
      public static Task<Stream> OpenStreamForWriteAsync(this IStorageFile file);

      public static Task<Stream> OpenStreamForReadAsync(this IStorageFolder rootDirectory,
         String relativePath);
      public static Task<Stream> OpenStreamForWriteAsync(this IStorageFolder rootDirectory,
         String relativePath, CreationCollisionOption creationCollisionOption);
   }
}
```

Here is an example that opens a WinRT `StorageFile` and reads its contents into a .NET Framework `System.Xml.Linq.XDocument` object:

```
StorageFile winRTfile = await Package.Current.InstalledLocation
   .GetFileAsync("AppxManifest.xml");
using (Stream netStream = await winRTfile.OpenStreamForReadAsync()) {
   XDocument xml = XDocument.Load(netStream);
   // Use the xml here...
}
```

The `System.IO.WindowsRuntimeStreamExtensions` class also offers extension methods, which "cast" WinRT stream interfaces (such as `IRandomAccessStream`, `IInputStream`, or `IOutputStream`) to the .NET Framework's `Stream` type and vice versa:

```
namespace System.IO {   // Defined in System.Runtime.WindowsRuntime.dll
   public static class WindowsRuntimeStreamExtensions {
      public static Stream AsStream(this IRandomAccessStream winRTStream);
      public static Stream AsStream(this IRandomAccessStream winRTStream, Int32 bufferSize);

      public static Stream AsStreamForRead(this IInputStream winRTStream);
      public static Stream AsStreamForRead(this IInputStream winRTStream, Int32 bufferSize);
```

```
   public static Stream AsStreamForWrite(this IOutputStream winRTStream);
   public static Stream AsStreamForWrite(this IOutputStream winRTStream, Int32 bufferSize);

   public static IInputStream          AsInputStream (this Stream netStream);
   public static IOutputStream         AsOutputStream(this Stream netStream);
   public static IRandomAccessStream AsRandomAccessStream(this Stream netStream);
   }
}
```

Transferring byte buffers

Now that you have the basic concepts around working with streams, let's take a closer look at the specifics. The `IInputStream` and `IOutputStream` interfaces are shown here:

```
public interface IInputStream : IDisposable {
   IAsyncOperationWithProgress<IBuffer, UInt32> ReadAsync(
      IBuffer buffer, UInt32 count, InputStreamOptions options);
}

public interface IOutputStream : IDisposable {
   IAsyncOperationWithProgress<UInt32, UInt32> WriteAsync(IBuffer buffer);
   IAsyncOperation<Boolean> FlushAsync();
}
```

As you can see, the `ReadAsync` and `WriteAsync` methods both operate on `IBuffer` objects. So, what is an `IBuffer`? Well, an `IBuffer` object represents a byte array and the interface looks like this:

```
public interface IBuffer {
   UInt32 Capacity { get; }        // Maximum size of the buffer (in bytes)
   UInt32 Length   { get; set; }   // Number of bytes currently in use by the buffer
}
```

As you can see, the `IBuffer` interface has length and maximum capacity properties. Oddly enough, this interface offers no way to access the buffer's bytes. The reason for this is that WinRT types cannot express pointers in their metadata because pointers do not map well to some languages (like JavaScript or safe C# code). The interface could offer a method to access individual bytes in the buffer, but calling a method to get each byte would hurt performance too much. Therefore, an `IBuffer` object lets you pass buffers around, but you can't access their contents.

However, all is not lost because all WinRT `IBuffer` objects implement an internal COM interface known as `IBufferByteAccess`. Note that this interface is a COM interface (because it returns a pointer) and it is not a WinRT interface. The CLR defines an internal (not public) Runtime Callable Wrapper (RCW) for this COM interface that looks like this:

```
namespace System.Runtime.InteropServices.WindowsRuntime {
   [ComImport]
   [InterfaceType(ComInterfaceType.InterfaceIsIUnknown)]
   [Guid("905a0fef-bc53-11df-8c49-001e4fc686da")]
   internal interface IBufferByteAccess {
      unsafe Byte* Buffer { get; }
   }
}
```

Internally, the CLR can take an `IBuffer` object, query for its `IBufferByteAccess` interface, and then query the `Buffer` property to get an unsafe pointer to the bytes contained within the buffer. With the pointer, the bytes can be accessed directly.

To avoid having developers write unsafe code that manipulates pointers, the .NET Framework Class Library includes a `WindowsRuntimeBufferExtensions` class that defines a bunch of extension methods that .NET Framework developers explicitly call to convert between .NET byte arrays and streams to WinRT `IBuffer` objects. The methods are shown here:

```
// Defined in System.Runtime.WindowsRuntime.dll
namespace System.Runtime.InteropServices.WindowsRuntime {
  public static class WindowsRuntimeBufferExtensions {
     public static IBuffer AsBuffer(this Byte[] source);
     public static IBuffer GetWindowsRuntimeBuffer(this MemoryStream stream);

     public static Byte[]  ToArray(this IBuffer source);
     public static Stream  AsStream(this IBuffer source);

     // Not shown: other overloads, CopyTo, GetByte, & IsSameData
  }
}
```

> **Note** In general, methods that start with As (like AsBuffer and AsStream) are like casts; that is, they make one type *look like* another type. These methods are fast and efficient. On the other hand, methods that start with To (like ToArray) *convert* one type to another type by copying data and are therefore not as efficient as the As methods.

Here is code demonstrating how to use many of `WindowsRuntimeBufferExtension`'s framework projection methods:

```
private async void SimpleWriteAndRead(StorageFile file) {
   using (IRandomAccessStream raStream = await file.OpenAsync(FileAccessMode.ReadWrite)) {
      Byte[] bytes = new Byte[] { 1, 2, 3, 4, 5 };
      UInt32 bytesWritten = await raStream.WriteAsync(bytes.AsBuffer()); // Byte[] -> IBuffer

      using (var ms = new MemoryStream())
      using (var sw = new StreamWriter(ms)) {
         sw.Write("A string in a stream");
            sw.Flush(); // Required: Flushes StreamWriter's contents to underlying MemoryStream
         bytesWritten =
            await raStream.WriteAsync(ms.GetWindowsRuntimeBuffer()); // Stream -> IBuffer
      }
   } // Close the stream
```

```
    using (IRandomAccessStream raStream = await file.OpenAsync(FileAccessMode.Read)) {
        // NOTE: This is the most efficient way to allocate, populate, & access data:
        Byte[] data = new Byte[5];  // Allocate the Byte[]
        IBuffer proposedBuffer = data.AsBuffer(); // Wrap it in an object that implements IBuffer
        IBuffer returnedBuffer = await raStream.ReadAsync(proposedBuffer,
            proposedBuffer.Capacity, InputStreamOptions.None);
        if (returnedBuffer != proposedBuffer) {
            // The proposed & returned IBuffers are not the same.
            // Copy the returned bytes into the original Byte[]
            returnedBuffer.CopyTo(data);
        } else {
            // The proposed & returned IBuffers are the same.
            // The returned bytes are already in the original Byte[]
        }
        // TODO: Put code here to access the read bytes from the data array...

        data = new Byte[raStream.Size - 5]; // Allocate Byte[] for remainder
        proposedBuffer = data.AsBuffer();   // Wrap it in an object that implements IBuffer
        returnedBuffer = await raStream.ReadAsync(proposedBuffer,
            proposedBuffer.Capacity, InputStreamOptions.None);

        // We just use the returned IBuffer here
        using (var sr = new StreamReader(returnedBuffer.AsStream())) {
            String str = sr.ReadToEnd();
        }
    } // Close the stream
}
```

When you call AsBuffer, it internally constructs a System.Runtime.InteropServices .WindowsRuntimeBuffer object around your byte array. The WindowsRuntimeBuffer class also offers a static Create method that can allocate the array and wrap it with a WindowsRuntimeBuffer object.

Similarly, WinRT offers a Windows.Storage.Streams.Buffer class that creates an IBuffer object whose bytes are in the native heap. For most .NET Framework developers, there should be less need to use this class because memory in the managed heap can be pinned and accessed from native code without copying.

When calling ReadAsync, you pass it a proposed IBuffer where the code implementing the IInputStream interface can put the read bytes. However, the code can ignore the proposed IBuffer and instead use another IBuffer that it creates internally (which may have a different Capacity). An implementation might do this if it has prefetched data that is already residing in one of its buffers, for example. So, when calling ReadAsync, you must always access the read bytes using the IBuffer it returns. If ReadAsync returns the same buffer that was proposed, you can optimize the code (as shown in the preceding code). ReadAsync's InputStreamOptions parameter is discussed in Chapter 7's "StreamSocket: Client-side TCP communication" section.

Writing and reading primitive data types

Streams contain bytes. But, in our apps, we frequently have other primitive data types like Int32s, Strings, DateTimeOffsets, and so on. To write any of these to a stream, we'd have to decompose each one into its constituent bytes. And, to read these from a stream, we'd have to read the right number of bytes and then compose them into an object of the right type. In the .NET Framework, you use the System.IO.BinaryWriter and System.IO.BinaryReader classes to store and retrieve primitive data types from a stream. The equivalent WinRT classes are the Windows.Storage .Streams.DataWriter and Windows.Storage.Streams.DataReader classes. In essence, these classes provide an abstraction over a byte buffer and a stream.

Here is what the DataWriter class looks like (personally, I think my comments explain how the class works better than the MSDN documentation):

```
public sealed class DataWriter : IDataWriter, IDisposable {
   // Constructs a DataWriter over a growable buffer (see DetachBuffer below)
   public DataWriter();

   // Constructs a DataWriter over an output stream and a growable buffer
   public DataWriter(IOutputStream outputStream);

   // All WriteXxx methods append data to the buffer (growing it if necessary)
   public void WriteBoolean(Boolean value);
   public void WriteByte(Byte value);
   public void WriteBytes(Byte[] value);
   public void WriteBuffer(IBuffer buffer);
   public void WriteBuffer(IBuffer buffer, UInt32 start, UInt32 count);
   public void WriteInt16(Int16 value);
   public void WriteUInt16(UInt16 value);
   public void WriteInt32(Int32 value);
   public void WriteUInt32(UInt32 value);
   public void WriteInt64(Int64 value);
   public void WriteUInt64(UInt64 value);
   public void WriteSingle(Single value);
   public void WriteDouble(Double value);
   public void WriteGuid(Guid value);
   public void WriteDateTime(DateTimeOffset value);
   public void WriteTimeSpan(TimeSpan value);

   // For WriteXxx methods, indicates how bytes append to buffer (big/little endian)
   public ByteOrder ByteOrder { get; set; } // Default=BigEndian

   // Strings are encoded via UnicodeEncoding (Utf8, Utf16LE, or Utf16BE) instead of ByteOrder
   public UnicodeEncoding UnicodeEncoding { get; set; }  // Default=Utf8
   // Returns how many bytes a string requires when encoded via UnicodeEncoding
   public UInt32 MeasureString(String value);
   // Appends the encoded string's bytes to the buffer
   public UInt32 WriteString(String value);

   // Returns the current size of the buffer
   public UInt32 UnstoredBufferLength { get; }
```

```
    // Writes the buffer to the underlying stream & clears the internal buffer
    public DataWriterStoreOperation StoreAsync();

    // Returns the buffer the DataWriter was using and associates a new empty buffer with it
    public IBuffer DetachBuffer();

    // Disassociates stream; stream will NOT be closed when Dispose is called
    public IOutputStream DetachStream();

    // Closes stream (if not detached); does NOT call StoreAsync
    public void Dispose();

    // Calls FlushAsync on underlying stream
    public IAsyncOperation<Boolean> FlushAsync();
}
```

> ⚠️ **Important** To work effectively with the DataWriter class, you must really appreciate that only *Xxx*Async methods perform I/O operations and all the other methods cannot perform I/O operations. Therefore, all the WriteXxx methods cannot do I/O; they all append bytes to an in-memory buffer. You must periodically call StoreAsync to have the in-memory buffer's contents written to the underlying stream. And, if you do not call StoreAsync and later call Dispose, the contents of the in-memory buffer will *not* be written to the underlying stream and the contents of it will be thrown away. Because Dispose is not an asynchronous method, it cannot perform I/O operations, and therefore it cannot internally call StoreAsync for you.

The following code shows how to use a DataWriter to store a byte array and a string into a stream:

```
private async void DataWriterSample(StorageFile file) {
    using (var dw = new DataWriter(await file.OpenAsync(FileAccessMode.ReadWrite))) {
        dw.WriteBytes(new Byte[] { 1, 2, 3, 4, 5 });
        const String text = "Some text";
        // Store the string length first followed by the string so we can read it back later
        UInt32 encodedStringLength = dw.MeasureString(text);
        dw.WriteUInt32(encodedStringLength);
        dw.WriteString(text);
        UInt32 bytesStored = await dw.StoreAsync();  // Commit buffer to stream
    } // Close DataWriter & underlying stream
}
```

Here is what the DataReader class looks like:

```
public sealed class DataReader : IDataReader, IDisposable {
    // Constructs a DataReader over an existing buffer instead of loading a buffer from a stream
    public static DataReader FromBuffer(IBuffer buffer);

    // Constructs a DataReader over an input stream and a growable buffer
    public DataReader(IInputStream inputStream);

    // Reads count bytes from stream appending them to buffer
    public DataReaderLoadOperation LoadAsync(UInt32 count);
```

```
    // Indicates whether LoadAsync can prefetch more bytes than requested to by 'count'
    public InputStreamOptions InputStreamOptions { get; set; }

    // Returns number of bytes in buffer yet to be read
    public UInt32 UnconsumedBufferLength { get; }

    // All ReadXxx methods read data from buffer (throwing Exception if buffer is empty)
    public Boolean        ReadBoolean();
    public Byte           ReadByte();
    public void           ReadBytes(Byte[] value);
    public IBuffer        ReadBuffer(UInt32 length);
    public Int16          ReadInt16();
    public UInt16         ReadUInt16();
    public Int32          ReadInt32();
    public UInt32         ReadUInt32();
    public Int64          ReadInt64();
    public UInt64         ReadUInt64();
    public Single         ReadSingle();
    public Double         ReadDouble();
    public Guid           ReadGuid();
    public DateTimeOffset ReadDateTime();
    public TimeSpan       ReadTimeSpan();

    // For ReadXxx methods, indicates how bytes get read from the buffer (big/little endian)
    public ByteOrder ByteOrder { get; set; } // Default=BigEndian

    // Strings are decoded via UnicodeEncoding (Utf8, Utf16LE, or Utf16BE) instead of ByteOrder
    public UnicodeEncoding UnicodeEncoding { get; set; }  // Default=Utf8
    // Decodes codeUnitCount bytes from the buffer to a string via UnicodeEncoding
    public String ReadString(UInt32 codeUnitCount);

    // Returns the buffer the DataReader was using and associates a new empty buffer with it
    public IBuffer DetachBuffer();

    // Disassociates stream; stream will NOT be closed when Dispose is called
    public IInputStream DetachStream();

    // Closes stream (if not detached)
    public void Dispose();
}
```

The following code shows how to use a DataReader to read back the data stored in the file by the DataWriterSample method shown earlier:

```
private async void DataReaderSample(StorageFile file) {
    using (var dr = new DataReader(await file.OpenAsync(FileAccessMode.Read))) {
        Byte[] bytes = new Byte[5];
        UInt32 bytesRead = await dr.LoadAsync((UInt32) bytes.Length);
        dr.ReadBytes(bytes);

        // Get length of string & read the rest of it in:
        bytesRead = await dr.LoadAsync(sizeof(UInt32));
        var encodedStringLength = dr.ReadUInt32();
        bytesRead = await dr.LoadAsync(encodedStringLength);
        String text = dr.ReadString(encodedStringLength);
    } // Close DataReader & underlying stream
}
```

If you have objects more complex than the primitive types supported by `DataWriter` and `DataReader`, you're probably best off using a .NET serialization technology (such as the `Data-ContractSerializer` or the `DataContractJsonSerializer`) to convert the objects to a byte array or JSON string first, and then you can write this to a stream. Later, you can read it back from the stream and deserialize the byte array or string back to an object graph.

Performing transacted write operations

Imagine you're writing an app that allows the user to enter some data and then you write the data to a file. If, while saving the user's data, your app crashes or the power goes out, the file's contents are incomplete and your app might not be able to read the file back successfully. To make matters worse, what if the user was saving the new data in an existing file. Now the old data is destroyed and the new data is corrupt.

To address this problem, WinRT allows you to perform file write operations in a transacted fashion. That is, either the entire write occurs or none of it occurs. When writing data to a file, you should use the technique shown in this section to guarantee the consistency of file data. The reason not to use this technique is that it temporarily requires some additional disk space and, if you are making changes to a large existing file, there is a performance impact.

To start, you must first open a file with transacted write access by calling `IStorageFile`'s `Open-TransactedWriteAsync` method. This method returns a `StorageStreamTransaction` object:

```
public sealed class StorageStreamTransaction : IDisposable {
    public IRandomAccessStream Stream { get; }
    public IAsyncAction CommitAsync();
    public void Dispose();
}
```

Once you have this object, all you need to do is query its `Stream` property, which returns an `IRandomAccessStream`. You get this same interface back when you call `IStorageFile`'s `OpenAsync` method. With the `IRandomAccessStream`, you can use all the techniques already discussed in this chapter. For example, you can pass the `IRandomAccessStream` when constructing `DataWriter` and `DataReader` objects.

The first time you actually write data to the stream, WinRT creates a hidden file in the same directory as the original file and your writes actually go into this hidden file. For example, if the original file is called "MyFile.txt", the hidden file is called "MyFile.txt.~tmp". This temporary file is filled with a copy of the original file's bytes up to the offset where you start writing new data. Depending on what offset within the stream you start writing, there could be a performance impact on your app while bytes are being copied. After copying the bytes, any new data is written to the temporary file. If your app crashes or if a power failure occurs, the original file is left untouched and the user still has access to the original file.

Once your app has finished writing to the temporary file's stream, you call `StorageStreamTransaction`'s `CommitAsync` method. This method copies any unchanged bytes from the original file to the temporary file, and then it atomically deletes the original file and renames the temporary file with the original file's name (calls the `StorageFile.RenameAsync` method, passing `NameCollision-Option.ReplaceExisting`).

The following code demonstrates how to perform an atomic write operation to a file:

```
private async void TransactedWriter(StorageFile file) {
    // Populate the file with some original data
    const String header = "Data: ";
    using (var dw = new DataWriter(await file.OpenAsync(FileAccessMode.ReadWrite))) {
        dw.WriteString(header + "The original data.");
        await dw.StoreAsync();
    }

    // Now, perform a transacted write to the file. The 1st time we won't commit the new data.
    for (Int32 commit = 0; commit <= 1; commit++) {
        // Perform transacted write without & with commit
        using (StorageStreamTransaction txStream = await file.OpenTransactedWriteAsync())
        using (var dw = new DataWriter(txStream.Stream.GetOutputStreamAt((UInt32)header.Length))) {
            dw.WriteString("The new & improved data.");
            await dw.StoreAsync();
            if (commit == 1) await txStream.CommitAsync();
        }
        String text = await FileIO.ReadTextAsync(file);
    }
}
```

When this code executes, the first time through the loop `CommitAsync` is not called and `text` will contain "Data: The original data." But the second time through the loop, `CommitAsync` is called and therefore text will contain "Data: The new & improved data."

Polite reader data access

Long-time users of Windows might be familiar with a problem that has plagued Windows for quite some time. Sometimes, when using an app to save a file, the save operation fails with an error indicating that the file is in use by another app. If you wait a few seconds and try to save the file again, the save operation succeeds. This problem occurs when an app (like the Windows Content Indexing service) opens the file for reading with exclusive access, preventing other apps from opening the same file at the same time.

Many users have complained about this situation and, with the WinRT API, Microsoft took steps to solve it. When an app calls `IStorageFile`'s `OpenAsync` method passing `FileAccessMode.Read`, the app opens the file in such a way that allows other apps to also open the file for reading. In addition, the file is opened with a feature of the file system called an *opportunistic lock* (or *oplock* for short). With the oplock applied to the file, if another app attempts to open the file by calling the `IStorageFile`'s `OpenAsync` method passing `FileAccessMode.ReadWrite`, the app gets access to the file, and any app that had the file opened for reading will get an exception thrown the next time it attempts to read from the file.

The behavior I just described is referred to as *polite reader* behavior because the app reading from the file is being polite to the app that wants to write to the file. The idea is based on the notion that writes to a file are based on explicit end-user actions. On the other hand, reads from a file can be app initiated (like content indexing or backup apps) and app-initiated operations should not interfere with explicit user actions; the user should always be in control, and the system should behave predictably to them.

Although this WinRT API behavior is great for end users, it does make more work for the app developer. There are three approaches for how to handle the polite reader issue in an app:

- Wrap your code that reads from a file in a loop containing a `try`/`catch` block. If a read fails, catch the exception, close the file, and loop around to try again. Writing the code this way is annoying, but this is really the best approach to follow.

- Do not catch the exception, and let your app terminate. Then the user will relaunch your app, which will try to access the file again. Most likely, your app will be successful. Or, if the code is executed by a recurring background task, the OS will automatically re-execute it in the future. As much as it pains me to suggest this option, many developers take this route because it is very unlikely that another app will try to write to a file while your app is reading from it. The other reason why many developers take this route is simply that they are not aware of WinRT's polite reader behavior. Because the exception almost never occurs, most developers have never seen it, so they don't even know that this is something they should be taking into consideration when implementing their code.[2]

- Always open the file for writing, even if you just intend to read from the file. WinRT allows only one app to open a file for writing. If other apps use WinRT APIs in an attempt to open the file for reading or writing, the open operation fails. So, if an app has a file open for writing, it never loses its access to the file. I can't really recommend this approach, though, because it is not in keeping with the philosophy that the user should always be in control. If you go this route, users might get errors when they are actively interacting with an app that tries to write to the same file.

Here is a method that demonstrates how to implement polite reader logic:

```
private async void PoliteReader(StorageFile file) {
    await FileIO.WriteTextAsync(file, "Here is some data I wrote to the file");

    Int32 injectWriteForTesting = 0; // Demos polite reader recovery
    while (true) {
        injectWriteForTesting++;
        try {
            // Open the file for read access
            using (IRandomAccessStream readOnly = await file.OpenAsync(FileAccessMode.Read)) {
```

---

[2] You can detect how your app crashes in the field by using the Windows Store developer dashboard. (See Chapter 11, "The Windows Store.")

```
                    if (injectWriteForTesting == 1) {
                        // NOTE: another app can write to file while this app has file open for reading:
                        await FileIO.WriteTextAsync(file, "Write NEW data to the file");
                    }

                    // This app tries to read from the file it already opened:
                    Byte[] bytes = new Byte[readOnly.Size]; // NOTE: Size returns 0 if file written to
                    IBuffer buffer = bytes.AsBuffer();

                    if (injectWriteForTesting == 2) {
                        // NOTE: another app can write to file while this app has file open for reading:
                        await FileIO.WriteTextAsync(file, "Write NEWER data to the file");
                    }

                    // NOTE: If Size is 0, this throws IndexOutOfRangeException; otherwise this throws
                    // Exception (HResult=0x80070323) if file is written to; else no exception
                    await readOnly.ReadAsync(buffer, buffer.Capacity, InputStreamOptions.ReadAhead);
                    // TODO: Process the data read here...
                }
                break;    // Success, don't retry
            }


            catch (IndexOutOfRangeException) {
                // NOTE: Thrown from ReadAsync if Size is 0
                // If we get here, we'll loop around and retry the read operation
            }
            catch (Exception ex) {
                const Int32 ERROR_OPLOCK_HANDLE_CLOSED = unchecked((Int32)0x80070323);
                if (ex.HResult != ERROR_OPLOCK_HANDLE_CLOSED) throw;
                // If we get here, we'll loop around and retry the read operation
            }
        }
    }
}
```

This code is a little depressing to look at because of the unobvious and undocumented behaviors it exhibits. The code tries to open a file for reading, reads the file's contents, and then closes the file. But, after the file is open for reading, another app could successfully write to the file. The first time through the loop, I inject a write operation after opening the file for reading and before querying the stream's Size property. The write operation causes the Size property to return zero, which causes my code to create a 0-byte array/buffer, and then I call ReadAsync. When 0 is passed to ReadAsync's second parameter, it throws an IndexOutOfRangeException. I catch this and retry the read operation.

The second time through the loop, the Size property does not return zero. Therefore, my code allocates an actual array/buffer and attempts to read from the stream. This time, I inject a write operation just before the call to ReadAsync, causing ReadAsync to throw a System.Exception object whose HResult property contains the value 0x80070323 corresponding to the Windows error ERROR_OPLOCK_HANDLE_CLOSED.[3] If you look at the exception object's Message property, you'll see

---

[3] If you're interested, you can read more about opportunistic lock at *http://msdn.microsoft.com/en-us/library/windows/desktop/aa365433(v=vs.85).aspx*.

the following: "The handle with which this oplock was associated has been closed. The oplock is now broken. (Exception from HRESULT: 0x80070323)." The code shows the best way to detect this failure. On the third retry, no writes are injected and the read operation completes successfully.

> **Important** For Windows Store apps, it is just a good practice to avoid keeping files open for long periods of time. It is much better to open a file, access its contents, and then close the file. Not keeping files open makes it easier to implement code that deals with this polite reader issue because the longer a file is open, the greater chance there is another app could open it for writing, making recovery much harder. And it also makes it easier to deal with Process Lifetime Management (discussed in Chapter 3, "Process model") issues where the OS can terminate your app at any time, requiring you to architect your app to launch back to where the user was when last using your app. Figuring out where in your code you'd have to re-open files can be very complicated. This complication goes away if, at every place in your code where you need to access the file's contents, you open and close the file.

Compressing and decompressing data

When writing data to a stream, you can compress the data thereby minimizing the amount of data you're sending over a network or persisting in a file. To do this, you'll use the Windows.Storage. Compression.Compressor class:

```
public sealed class Compressor : IOutputStream, IDisposable {
    // Bytes are compressed in a buffer of 'blocksize' bytes and written to underlying stream
    public Compressor(IOutputStream stream, CompressAlgorithm algorithm, UInt32 blockSize);

    // Compresses a buffer's bytes; the first write includes a header indicating the algorithm
    public IAsyncOperationWithProgress<UInt32, UInt32> WriteAsync(IBuffer buffer);

    // Called after last WriteAsync; stores internal buffer's remaining bytes to stream
    public IAsyncOperation<Boolean> FinishAsync();

    // Disassociates stream; stream will NOT be closed when Dispose is called
    public IOutputStream DetachStream();

    // Closes stream (if not detached); does NOT call FinishAsync
    public void Dispose();

    // Calls FlushAsync on underlying stream
    public IAsyncOperation<Boolean> FlushAsync();
}
```

This is the currently supported set of compression algorithms:

```
public enum CompressAlgorithm {
    InvalidAlgorithm = 0, // Invalid; used for error checking
    NullAlgorithm    = 1, // No compression; typically used for testing
    Mszip            = 2, // MSZIP algorithm
    Xpress           = 3, // XPRESS algorithm
    XpressHuff       = 4, // XPRESS algorithm with Huffman encoding
    Lzms             = 5, // LZMS algorithm
}
```

So now you could trivially write a method that compresses a file:

```
async Task CompressFileAsync(IStorageFile originalFile, IStorageFile compressedFile) {
    using (var input = await originalFile.OpenAsync(FileAccessMode.Read))
    using (var output = await compressedFile.OpenAsync(FileAccessMode.ReadWrite))
    using (var compressor = new Compressor(output, CompressAlgorithm.Mszip, 0)) {
        // NOTE: Compressor implements the IOutputStream interface
        await RandomAccessStream.CopyAsync(input, compressor);
        await compressor.FinishAsync();
    }
}
```

When reading data from a stream, you can decompress the data using the Windows.Storage.
Compression.Decompressor class:

```
public sealed class Decompressor : IInputStream, IDisposable {
    // Bytes are decompressed as they are read from the underlying stream
    public Decompressor(IInputStream underlyingStream);

    // Decompresses a stream's bytes; the first read includes a header indicating the algorithm
    public IAsyncOperationWithProgress<IBuffer, UInt32> ReadAsync(
        IBuffer buffer, UInt32 count, InputStreamOptions options);

    // Disassociates stream; stream will NOT be closed when Dispose is called
    public IInputStream DetachStream();

    // Closes stream (if not detached)
    public void Dispose();
}
```

The method to decompress a file is even simpler:

```
async Task DecompressFileAsync(IStorageFile compressedFile, IStorageFile decompressedFile) {
    using (var decompressor = new Decompressor(
        await compressedFile.OpenAsync(FileAccessMode.Read)))
    using (var output = await decompressedFile.OpenAsync(FileAccessMode.ReadWrite)) {
        // NOTE: Decompressor implements the IInputStream interface
        await RandomAccessStream.CopyAsync(decompressor, output);
    }
}
```

So this is all there is to it; pretty easy. Note that Compressor's WriteAsync method and Decompressor's ReadAsync method both return an IAsyncOperationWithProgress. With this, your app can give progress updates to the user if the buffer/stream is large. Finally, note that these classes compress/decompress a stream. They do not compress multiple files into a library like common ZIP utilities. Although WinRT does not offer classes to accomplish this, the .NET Framework does; see the System.IO.Compression.ZipArchive class.

Encrypting and decrypting data

When writing data to a stream, you can encrypt the data thereby making it difficult for others to interpret it when sending it over a network or persisting it to a file. To do this, you'll use the Windows.Security.Cryptography.DataProtection.DataProtectionProvider class:

```
public sealed class DataProtectionProvider {
    // When encrypting a buffer or stream, use these three members
    public DataProtectionProvider(String protectionDescriptor);
    public IAsyncOperation<IBuffer> ProtectAsync(IBuffer data);
    public IAsyncAction ProtectStreamAsync(IInputStream src, IOutputStream dest);

    // When decrypting a buffer or stream, use these three members
    public DataProtectionProvider();
    public IAsyncOperation<IBuffer> UnprotectAsync(IBuffer data);
    public IAsyncAction UnprotectStreamAsync(IInputStream src, IOutputStream dest);
}
```

The following code shows how to encrypt the contents of a file:

```
async Task EncryptFileAsync(IStorageFile originalFile, IStorageFile encryptedFile,
    String protectionDescriptor) {
    using (var input = await originalFile.OpenAsync(FileAccessMode.Read))
    using (var output = await encryptedFile.OpenAsync(FileAccessMode.ReadWrite)) {
        var dpp = new DataProtectionProvider(protectionDescriptor);
        await dpp.ProtectStreamAsync(input, output);
    }
}
```

When encrypting data, you must create a DataProtectionProvider, passing a string to its constructor. This string indicates the encryption method you want to use. The method is written to the encrypted stream and is read back when decrypting. This is why you create a DataProtection-Provider object for decrypting by invoking its parameterless constructor.

Here are some sample protection-descriptor strings:

- "LOCAL=logon" encrypts for the current logon session only on the local computer.

- "LOCAL=user" encrypts for the logged-in user on the local computer.

- "LOCAL=machine" encrypts for any user on the local computer.

- "WEBCREDENTIALS=Jeffrey,wintellect.com" encrypts for Jeffrey on Wintellect.com.

- "SID=S-1-5-21-4392301 AND SID=S-1-5-21-3101812" encrypts for the domain account.

- "SDDL=O:S-1-5-5-0-290724G:SYD:(A;;CCDC;;;S-1-5-5-0-290724)(A;;DC;;;WD)" encrypts for the domain account.

When using SID or SDDL, the machine must be domain joined. In addition, your app must specify the Enterprise Authentication capability in its manifest and will pass Windows Store certification only if submitted by a company (not an individual account). For more information about protection descriptors, look up "CNG DPAPI Protection Providers" and "CNG DPAPI Constants" on MSDN.

Many of these protection descriptors are self-explanatory, but the one related to web credentials could benefit from some additional discussion. If you want your app to retain web credentials for a user, you store them securely in a Windows.Security.Credentials.PasswordCredential object and then add this object to the user's PasswordVault:

```
// Create a web credential (resource/username/password tuple) & add it to the password vault
String webSite = "Wintellect.com", username="Jeffrey", password="P@ssw0rd";
var pc = new PasswordCredential(new HostName(webSite).CanonicalName, username, password);
new PasswordVault().Add(pc);
```

Once the credential is added to the password vault, the user can view it via the Control Panel's Credential Manager applet. Then, to encrypt data using these web credentials, you construct the protection-descriptor string like this:

```
String webSite = "Wintellect.com", username="Jeffrey";
PasswordCredential pc = new PasswordVault()
   .Retrieve(new HostName(webSite).CanonicalName, username);
String protectionDescriptor = "WEBCREDENTIALS=" + pc.UserName + "," + pc.Resource;
// Now, pass protectionDescriptor to DataProtectionProvider's constructor
```

When reading data from a stream, you can decrypt it using the same DataProtectionProvider class. The following code shows how to decrypt the contents of a file:

```
async Task DecryptFileAsync(IStorageFile encryptedFile, IStorageFile decryptedFile) {
   using (var input = await encryptedFile.OpenAsync(FileAccessMode.Read))
   using (var output = await decryptedFile.OpenAsync(FileAccessMode.ReadWrite)) {
      var dpp = new DataProtectionProvider();
      await dpp.UnprotectStreamAsync(input, output);
   }
}
```

Populating a stream on demand

Frequently, we use `StorageFile` objects to transfer data from one app to another. For example, Windows allows you to launch an app via a file-type association (discussed in Chapter 5) or to transfer a file via the clipboard or the Share charm (discussed in Chapter 10, "Sharing data between apps"), and there are also FileOpenPicker and FileSavePicker activations.

Windows provides a mechanism allowing you to create and pass a `StorageFile` object to other apps before the file's contents are available. In addition, the app creating the `StorageFile` object can populate its contents while the consuming app is reading it. You leverage this mechanism by calling `StorageFile`'s static `CreateStreamedFileAsync` method:

```
public static IAsyncOperation<StorageFile> CreateStreamedFileAsync(
    String displayNameWithExtension,
    StreamedFileDataRequestedHandler dataRequested,
    IRandomAccessStreamReference thumbnail);
```

The first parameter identifies the name of the `StorageFile`. The second parameter identifies a callback method that is invoked only when the contents of the stream are required; this method populates the file's stream with contents at this time. The third parameter identifies a thumbnail image that a receiving app can display to the user if it desires; the app calling `CreateStreamedFileAsync` can pass `null` for this parameter if it does not wish to provide a thumbnail image.

The following method creates a thumbnail image and then creates a `StorageFile` object whose stream will be populated on demand:

```
private async void StreamOnDemand(Object sender, RoutedEventArgs e) {
    // Get a generic thumbnail image for PNG files
    StorageItemThumbnail thumbnail =
        await GetTypeThumbnailAsync(".png", ThumbnailMode.SingleItem);
    RandomAccessStreamReference thumbnailSource =
        RandomAccessStreamReference.CreateFromStream(thumbnail);

    // Create a StorageFile object whose stream will be populated by OnDataRequested
    Uri uri = new Uri("http://WintellectNOW.com/assets/img/winnow-logo.png");
    StorageFile file = await StorageFile.CreateStreamedFileAsync(
        "MyImage.png",
        outputStream => OnDataRequested(outputStream, uri),
        thumbnailSource);

    // Show it works by passing the StorageFile to another app
    var noWarning = Launcher.LaunchFileAsync(file);
}
```

The StreamOnDemand method obtains a generic thumbnail image based on a file extension by calling GetTypeThumbnailAsync:

```
private async static Task<StorageItemThumbnail> GetTypeThumbnailAsync(
    String fileType, ThumbnailMode mode) {

    // Gets a thumbnail for a specific file type
    StorageFile file = await ApplicationData.Current.TemporaryFolder.CreateFileAsync(
        "~" + fileType, CreationCollisionOption.GenerateUniqueName);
    StorageItemThumbnail sitn = await file.GetThumbnailAsync(mode);
    await file.DeleteAsync();
    return sitn;
}
```

The method that populates the stream on demand is OnDataRequested, and it looks like this:

```
private async void OnDataRequested(StreamedFileDataRequest outputStream, Uri uri) {
    // Have the background downloader transfer the image
    DownloadOperation download = new BackgroundDownloader().CreateDownload(uri, null);
    var noWarning = download.StartAsync();

    // Copy the downloaded image's bytes to the storage stream
    // NOTE: The consuming app can read the stream's contents while it is downloading;
    //       it does not have to wait until the download is complete
    using (IInputStream inputStream = download.GetResultStreamAt(0)) {
        // NOTE: StreamedFileDataRequest implements IOutputStream
        await RandomAccessStream.CopyAndCloseAsync(inputStream, outputStream);
        // We get here when the download and copy is complete.
    }
}
```

It is interesting to think about how all of this works. You see, if your app creates a StorageFile and then passes it to another app, the other app comes to the foreground and your app goes to the background. This means that Windows suspends your app's threads (as discussed in Chapter 3) and might even terminate your app. Therefore, when launching a StorageFile, Windows invokes the OnDataRequested callback method as soon as LaunchFileAsync is called, regardless of whether the app receiving the StorageFile actually wants the file's contents. Therefore, in this scenario, you might think that rendering the stream's contents on demand is not that useful. However, it does allow you to launch an app immediately while the callback method renders the stream's contents as opposed to rendering the contents first and then launching the app; this can improve the end-user experience.

When passing a StorageFile via a share source app, OnDataRequested is called only when the target app requests the stream's contents. This is allowed because the source app must remain active to complete the share operation. However, for the share operation, there is another way to defer rendering of a StorageFile by using DataPackage's SetDataProvider method. If an app copies a StorageFile object to the clipboard and then the app is suspended, Windows resumes the app for up to 30 seconds so that it can render the stream's contents. If the app terminated, an exception is raised in the consuming app because the stream's contents cannot be rendered. CreateStreamed-FileAsync is most useful by an app that declares the FileOpenPicker activation. It allows the user to add a `StorageFile` to her basket and subsequently remove it or cancel the picker without rendering the stream's contents at all.

`CreateStreamedFileAsync` creates a temporary and read-only `StorageFile` object. Conceptually, this `StorageFile` object is in memory, and querying its `Path` property returns an empty string. However, the `StorageFile` is implicitly backed by a file that Windows creates. The data written to the stream by the `OnDataRequested` method is persisted in this file. This way, if the receiving app opens the `StorageFile` object again (or passes it to another app), the callback method is not invoked again; the data is simply returned from the file Windows created. If a `StorageFile` object is passed to a desktop app, the system creates a read-only copy of the file in the user's Temporary Internet Files directory (similar to what Outlook does when the user opens an email attachment).

In my code example, I populated the file's stream by downloading data from the Internet; but, of course, you can populate a stream any way you'd like. However, because populating a stream from the Internet is so common, the `StorageFile` class offers a static `CreateStreamedFileFromUriAsync` method. I can use this method to simplify my example by removing the need for a callback method:

```
StorageFile file = await StorageFile.CreateStreamedFileFromUriAsync(
    "MyImage.png", uri, thumbnailSource);
```

Finally, the `StorageFile` class offers two other static methods that, instead of creating a file, will replace the contents of an existing `StorageFile` on demand:

```
public static IAsyncOperation<StorageFile> ReplaceWithStreamedFileAsync(
    IStorageFile fileToReplace,
    StreamedFileDataRequestedHandler dataRequested,
    IRandomAccessStreamReference thumbnail);

public static IAsyncOperation<StorageFile> ReplaceWithStreamedFileFromUriAsync(
    IStorageFile fileToReplace,
    Uri uri,
    IRandomAccessStreamReference thumbnail);
```

The `StorageFile` object returned from these methods can refer to a file that is both readable and writable. These methods are most useful when implementing the CachedFileUpdater activation. They allow an app to replace the contents of a local file that is caching a remote file. For example, the SkyDrive app uses these methods to replace a local file's contents with a new version of the file residing in the cloud.

Searching over a stream's content

The last stream-related technology I'd like to bring to your attention is the content indexer. The content indexer gives you a way to quickly perform rich search queries over your app's data. The content indexer is the same one that Windows uses when users search for documents on their PCs. With it, a user can perform a rich search query looking for documents containing desired text, modified after a certain date, and authored by a particular person. However, when used by your app, you are creating a private content index whose content is not accessible to other apps or to Windows itself.

You use the content indexer to index files that the built-in Windows indexer would not normally index or to index streams of data that do not reside in files.[4] Typically, an app allows the user to search its content by showing the user a `Windows.UI.Xaml.Controls.SearchBox` control. The content indexer returns results very fast; therefore, it's a good technology choice when you want to return search results as the user types characters into a `SearchBox` control incrementally refining his search. Of course, you do not have to use the content indexer only with the `SearchBox` control; you can use it in any way you wish.

Using the content indexer is extremely easy. First, you call `ContentIndexer`'s static `GetIndexer` method to create or get a reference to your package's default index or to a named index. Named indexes allow your package to have multiple indexes separate from one another. Here is what the `ContentIndexer` class looks like:

```
public sealed class ContentIndexer {
   // Static members to create/get a reference to your package's default or named index:
   public static ContentIndexer GetIndexer();
   public static ContentIndexer GetIndexer(String indexName);

   // Instance members to add/update an item and delete item(s) from an index:
   public IAsyncAction AddAsync(IIndexableContent indexableContent);
   public IAsyncAction UpdateAsync(IIndexableContent indexableContent);
   public IAsyncAction DeleteAsync(String contentId);
   public IAsyncAction DeleteMultipleAsync(IEnumerable<String> contentIds);
   public IAsyncAction DeleteAllAsync();

   // Every method (above) that modifies the index increments the index's Revision
   public UInt64 Revision { get; }

   // Get the properties for a specific item:
   // For valid properties, see http://msdn.microsoft.com/en-us/library/dd561977(VS.100).aspx
   public IAsyncOperation<IReadOnlyDictionary<String, Object>> RetrievePropertiesAsync(
      String contentId, IEnumerable<String> propertiesToRetrieve);

   // Query the index passing an Advanced Query Syntax (AQS) filter,
   // properties to retrieve, sort order, and language
   // For AQS, http://msdn.microsoft.com/en-us/library/windows/desktop/bb266512(v=vs.85).aspx
   public ContentIndexerQuery CreateQuery(
      String searchFilter, IEnumerable<String> propertiesToRetrieve);
   public ContentIndexerQuery CreateQuery(
      String searchFilter, IEnumerable<String> propertiesToRetrieve,
      IEnumerable<SortEntry> sortOrder, String searchFilterLanguage);
}
```

---

[4] In Chapter 5's "Accessing read-write package files" section, I explained how Windows automatically indexes any files in the "Indexed" subdirectory of your package's local folder.

To add an item to a content index, you construct an `IndexableContent` object, which looks like this:

```
public sealed class IndexableContent : IIndexableContent {
    public IndexableContent();
    public String Id { get; set; }                        // Uniquely identifies item in index
    public IRandomAccessStream Stream { get; set; }       // Stream with content to index
    public String StreamContentType   { get; set; }       // Mime type of stream's content
    public IDictionary<String, Object> Properties { get; } // Pre-defined Windows properties
}
```

After constructing an `IndexableContent` object, set its `Id` property (which uniquely identifies the item in the index). Then you set its `Stream` property to refer to the content you wish to have indexed and its `StreamContentType` property to the mime type that describes the format of the stream's contents. The indexer does not save the original stream because this would be too memory intensive; if you need to get back to the original stream contents, you must manage this yourself. Then you can also add any of the standard predefined Windows properties documented at *http://msdn.microsoft. com/en-us/library/dd561977(VS.100).aspx* and also described in Chapter 5's "Storage item properties" section. Although you must use the Windows predefined properties, you can interpret them however you'd like. For example, I show later how I use the `System.Media.Duration` property to indicate how long it takes to create a recipe, and I use the `System.Keywords` property to reflect a recipe's ingredients. By the way, you can construct an item without a stream; the item could have only properties. Then you could retrieve the properties for an item. Property values can have a language associated with them too.

After you populate an index with items, you call `ContentIndexer`'s `CreateQuery` method, passing in an AQS string, what properties you want returned, the sort order of the results, and optionally a language. The `CreateQuery` method returns a `ContentIndexerQuery` object:

```
public sealed class ContentIndexerQuery {
    public IAsyncOperation<UInt32> GetCountAsync();    // Returns the count of resulting items

    // Returns resulting items' Id and requested properties (not Stream & StreamContentType)
    public IAsyncOperation<IReadOnlyList<IIndexableContent>> GetAsync();

    // Returns just the properties for each resulting item:
    public IAsyncOperation<IReadOnlyList<IReadOnlyDictionary<String, Object>>>
        GetPropertiesAsync();

    // Some members not shown here...
}
```

To help put all this together, imagine a recipe app where users can search for recipes by ingredients or by the time it takes to cook. First, let's define a Recipe data type:

```
internal sealed class Recipe {
   private readonly List<String> m_ingredients = new List<String>();
   public String Title { get; set; }   // Stream content
   public List<String> Ingredients { get { return m_ingredients; } } // System.Keywords property
   public UInt64 MinutesToCreate { get; set; ] // SystemProperties.Media.Duration property
}
```

Now, let's define a few recipes:

```
private static readonly Recipe[] s_recipes = new Recipe[] {
   new Recipe { Title = "Chicken Parmesan", MinutesToCreate = 45,
      Ingredients = { "chicken", "cheese", "tomatoes" } },
   new Recipe { Title = "Chicken Teriyaki", MinutesToCreate = 30,
      Ingredients = { "chicken", "teriyaki", "sauce", "rice" } },
   new Recipe { Title = "Macaroni and Cheese", MinutesToCreate = 20,
      Ingredients = { "Macaroni", "pasta", "cheese" } },
   new Recipe { Title = "Chicken Alfredo", MinutesToCreate = 45,
      Ingredients = { "chicken", "Pasta", "alfredo", "sauce" } }
};
```

When our app runs, we'll have to add these recipes to a content index. Here's a method that does that:

```
private async Task PopulateRecipeContentIndexAsync() {
   // Create or get a reference to a "Recipes" content index:
   ContentIndexer indexer = ContentIndexer.GetIndexer("Recipes");
   await indexer.DeleteAllAsync();  // Clear contents to start fresh

   // Add all the recipes to the index:
   for (Int32 r = 0; r < s_recipes.Length; r++) {
      IndexableContent content = new IndexableContent {
         Id = r.ToString(),       // ID = index into s_recipes array

         // Index words in the recipe's title by converting the string to a UTF-8 byte stream
         StreamContentType = "text/plain",
         Stream = CryptographicBuffer.ConvertStringToBinary(
            s_recipes[r].Title, BinaryStringEncoding.Utf8).AsStream().AsRandomAccessStream(),

         // For each recipe, Duration is how long it takes to cook & Keywords is ingredient list
         Properties = { // http://msdn.microsoft.com/en-us/library/dd561977(VS.100).aspx
            { SystemProperties.Media.Duration, s_recipes[r].MinutesToCreate },
            { SystemProperties.Keywords, String.Join(";", s_recipes[r].Ingredients) },
         }
      };
      await indexer.AddAsync(content);
   }
}
```

And now, after all this is done, we can perform rich queries against the index. The following code demonstrates many of the content indexer's features:

```
// Search for all recipes with "Chicken" in their title, sauce as an ingredient and that take
// 30 minutes or less to make. The results come back sorted in duration order with the Duration
property.
ContentIndexer indexer = ContentIndexer.GetIndexer("Recipes");
ContentIndexerQuery query = indexer.CreateQuery(
    "chicken System.Keywords:\"sauce\" System.Media.Duration:<=30",
    new[] { SystemProperties.Media.Duration },
    new[] {
        new SortEntry { PropertyName = SystemProperties.Media.Duration, AscendingOrder = true }
    });

UInt32 resultCount = await query.GetCountAsync();            // 1
IReadOnlyList<IIndexableContent> resultItems = await query.GetAsync();
foreach (var r in resultItems) {
    Int32 recipeIndex = Int32.Parse(r.Id);                  // 1
    String recipeTitle = s_recipes[recipeIndex].Title;   // "Chicken Teriyaki"
}


// Here's how to update an item's properties (make "Chicken Alfredo" take 20 minutes to cook):
IndexableContent contentItem = new IndexableContent {
    Id = 3.ToString(),
    Properties = { { SystemProperties.Media.Duration, 20 } }
};
await indexer.UpdateAsync(contentItem);

// Now if we perform the same query, we get back 2 results:
query = indexer.CreateQuery(
    "chicken System.Keywords:\"sauce\" System.Media.Duration:<=30",
    new[] { SystemProperties.Media.Duration },
    new[] {
        new SortEntry { PropertyName = SystemProperties.Media.Duration, AscendingOrder = true }
    });
resultCount = await query.GetCountAsync();                  // 2
resultItems = await query.GetAsync();
foreach (var r in resultItems) {
    Int32 recipeIndex = Int32.Parse(r.Id);                  // 3, 1
    String recipeTitle =
        s_recipes[recipeIndex].Title;   // "Chicken Alfredo", "Chicken teriyaki"
}


// Here's how to get just the properties (no Ids) for a query's items:
IReadOnlyList<IReadOnlyDictionary<String, Object>> itemsProperties =
    await query.GetPropertiesAsync();
foreach (IReadOnlyDictionary<String, Object> item in itemsProperties) {
    foreach (var property in item) {
        String propertyInfo =
            String.Format("Property: Name={0}, Value={1}", property.Key, property.Value);
    }
}
```

CHAPTER 7

Networking

Today, almost all apps transfer data over a network to other PCs and servers. In this chapter, I present the WinRT APIs available for you to use in your Windows Store apps.[1] However, before you roll up your sleeves and start coding against these APIs, you should see if there is some simpler system-provided functionality you can leverage.

For example, Windows can automatically sync a package's settings and files across a user's PCs. (See Chapter 4, "Package data and roaming.") Or your app might want to post some data to a social networking site or share some data through a messaging app. Instead of writing code that works with a specific service, you could use the Windows Share charm. (See Chapter 10, "Sharing data between apps.") For updating tiles or badges, or for displaying a toast notification, your own service could use the Windows Push Notification Service (WNS) to send an update to your app. (See Chapter 8, "Tiles and toast notifications.") You can also send a raw WNS notifications to execute code in response to an input message coming in over the network. (See Chapter 9, "Background tasks.")

Your app can also rely on one of the file pickers to let the user open files from network-accessible locations. (See Chapter 5, "Storage files and folders.") And, for those apps that process Atom Publishing Protocol, ATOM, and RSS feeds, you can use the APIs in the `Windows.Web.AtomPub` and `Windows.Web.Syndication` namespaces.

It's recommend that, when possible, you use the highest networking abstraction you can because this simplifies your code. But, if your app needs more traditional networking (HTTP, TCP, WebSockets, and UDP), WinRT does have APIs for you, and using these APIs is the focus of this chapter.

Network information

Windows supports different kinds of networks, such as LAN, Wi-Fi, and mobile (GSM, 3G/4G, and so on). Each of these networks has its own characteristics (such as bandwidth) that might affect your app's responsiveness. Additionally, these networks might have different costs associated with their usage. LAN and Wi-Fi at home or work are usually considered unlimited. Connections in hotel rooms or hotspots might be capped, and mobile networks could have additional restrictions such as roaming costs. When connecting to a network, Windows prioritizes a user's available networks. It prefers lower cost and better performance networks such as LAN and Wi-Fi to mobile networks. Additionally,

---

[1] Note that many of the WinRT APIs described in this chapter are also usable by Windows desktop apps.

when connecting to a Wi-Fi network, the system prefers the most recently-connected-to and available access point.

The Windows Runtime provides APIs so that you can get information about the network's speed and cost, allowing your app to make informed decisions about whether and how to use the connection. However, the system does not always have all the necessary information to decide if a connection should be metered (for example, when it is being used in hotel rooms). Therefore, Windows allows users to change a connection to Set As A Metered Connection as shown in Figure 7-1 by going to PC Settings > Network > Connections > *network name*. Changing a connection like this is also useful for developers so that they can test how their app behaves with different connection types. Additionally, the simulator allows you to modify these network settings.

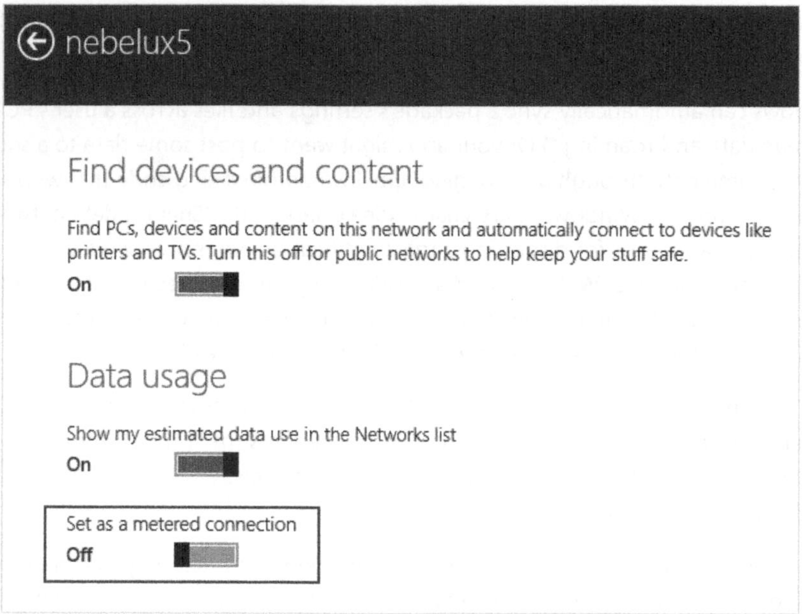

FIGURE 7-1 Setting a connection as metered using the PC Settings > Network > Connections settings.

Windows surfaces this information to your app, as you'll see in this chapter's "Network connection profile information" section. The system itself also changes its behavior when on a metered network. For example, open PC Settings and look at SkyDrive > Files, SkyDrive > Sync Settings, and PC & Devices > Devices. All of these provide a Metered Connections section, allowing a user to control network costs.

Users can use Task Manager's App History tab (shown in Figure 7-2) to see how much bandwidth individual apps have consumed. Task Manager shows Network usage, Metered Network usage, and also Tile Updates. If a user gets a large bill at the end of a month, he can easily find out which app or apps are using the most bandwidth. The user can then alter how he works with that app or uninstall it entirely.

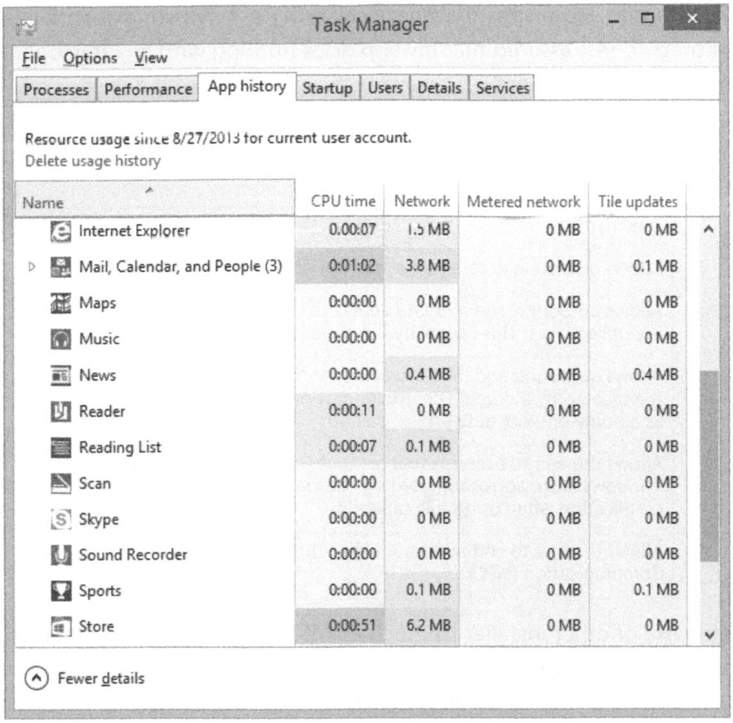

FIGURE 7-2 Task Manager's App History tab showing each app's network usage.

Network isolation

When Visual Studio creates a Windows Store app, it sets one capability in the app's manifest file: Internet (Client). With this, Microsoft is assuming that all Windows Store apps will make outgoing connections over the Internet. However, if your app performs all its networking using other features (like roaming settings, sharing, or WNS), your app does not need this capability and you should turn it off.

> **Important** Packages that enable any network capability *must* have a privacy policy when they are submitted to the Windows Store for certification. The reason is because each network request includes the user's IP address, and this is considered personal information. The privacy policy must be part of the package's description and must also be available via the app's settings as displayed in the Windows Settings charm. The setting can open a webpage displaying the privacy policy. The privacy policy simply states what you intend do to with the user's personal information. Of course, the policy can say that you discard any personal information; you just have to make it clear to users what you intend to do with *their* information.

In fact, I have written a few Windows Store apps that specifically do not have any network capabilities turned on because I want users to rest assured that my app does nothing with any personal data they enter into it. Without these capabilities, there is no way for an app to transmit a user's personal data. Table 7-1 shows the various capabilities related to networking:

TABLE 7-1 Manifest capabilities related to networking.

Capability	Description
Internet (Client)	Allows outbound access to the Internet and networks in public places.
Internet (Client & Server)	Allows outbound and inbound access to/from the Internet and networks in public places. This capability is a superset of Internet (Client).
Private Networks (Client & Server)	Allows outbound and inbound access to/from an intranet network authenticated by a domain controller or a network the user has designated as a home or work network.
Enterprise Authentication	Allows the app to access resources that require domain credentials. Only Windows Store apps submitted by companies (not individuals) can pass certification when using this capability.
Proximity	Allows the app to communicate with other PCs via Near Field Communication (NFC)

If you've ever written a Setup.exe or other installer file, such as MSI, for an application that needed access to the network, you probably had to write some code or a script to open up the firewall for your application (and, of course, close the firewall when your app is uninstalled). As you learned in Chapter 2, "App packaging and deployment," Windows Store apps are always installed by the system; there is no separate installer app. When Windows installs a Windows Store package, the system looks at the manifest file, sees the capabilities, and automatically opens up the firewall for the package's app. You can verify this by going to the firewall settings and looking for your package. (See Figure 7-3.)

As explained in Chapter 1, "Windows Runtime primer," Windows Store apps are isolated from one another. That is, they cannot communicate with each other, any desktop app, or even a service running on the same PC. However, when debugging client/server communications, it is convenient to run the client and server applications on the same PC. To help developers and testers, Visual Studio exposes a Debug setting called "Allow Local Network Loopback." (See Figure 7-4.) This setting is for development purposes only, and you won't find this anywhere in the manifest file.

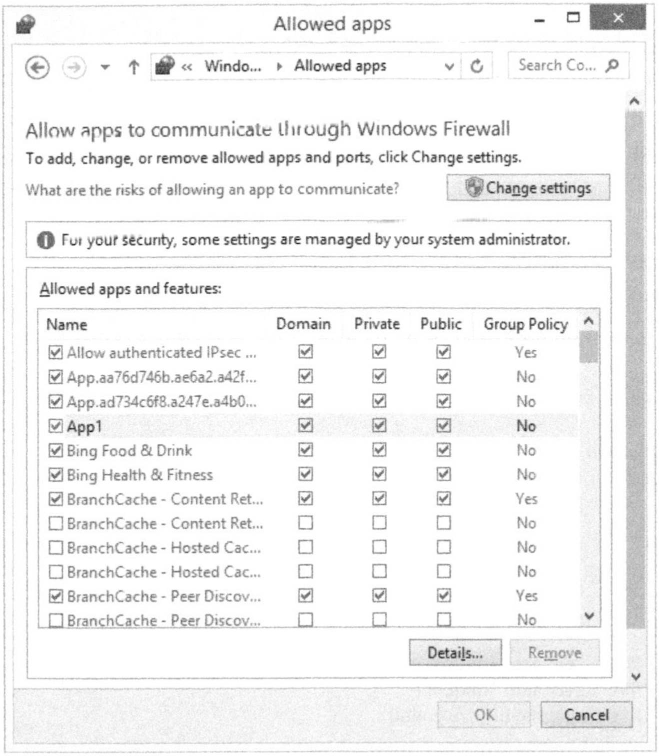

FIGURE 7-3 Windows automatically configures a package's firewall settings based on the package's manifest capabilities.

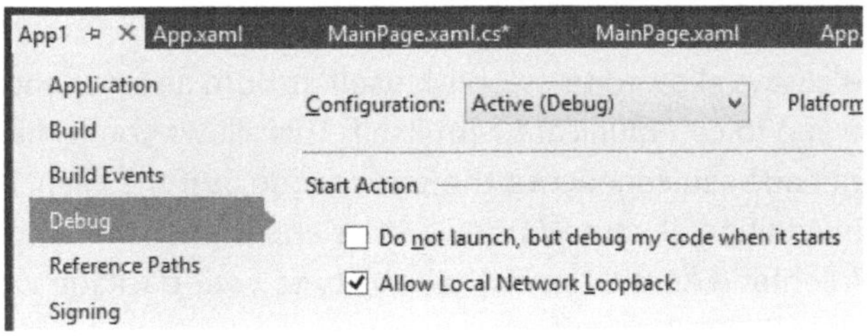

FIGURE 7-4 Visual Studio's Allow Local Network Loopback Debug setting.

Internally, toggling this check box from selected to not selected executes a command-line tool called CheckNetIsolation.exe. This tool can add and remove packages to the loopback exempt list. (For more information, see *http://msdn.microsoft.com/en-us/library/windows/apps/hh780593.aspx*.)

> **Important** Many developers debug their client/server app on their machine successfully because Visual Studio, by default, selects the Allow Local Network Loopback option. But then, when the app and server are deployed for testing on another machine, the communication fails. On the test machine, you must run CheckNetIsolation.exe to enable loopback or, better yet, set up the client and server on different machines because this tests the apps in a more true-to-life environment.

You can also run the CheckNetIsolation.exe tool (as an Administrator) to see what networking capabilities your app actually used when running. Here is an example:

```
C:\>CheckNetIsolation.exe debug -n=JeffreyRichter.AzureSASGenerator_ape9s8gs6w87m

Network Isolation Debug Session started.
Reproduce your scenario, then press Ctrl-C when done.
    Collecting Logs.....

Summary Report

Network Capabilities Status
-------------------------------------------------------------------
    InternetClient              Not Used and Insecure
    InternetClientServer        Not Used and Insecure
    PrivateNetworkClientServer  Missing, maybe intended
```

CheckNetIsolation.exe is monitoring the firewall, and if it finds that your app is trying to reach an address the firewall has blocked, it flags it. As you can see from the preceding example, it has noticed that the app was trying to reach an address on the intranet and flagged the capability as missing.

> **Important** A Windows Store app is always allowed to establish itself as both a server and client, and Windows does allow the app to communicate with itself. This allows you to have a clean architecture where the client code can connect to the server code as if the client were connecting via the network. In addition, if your Windows Store app is just talking to itself, you do not need to add the Internet (Client & Server) capability to your package's manifest.

Network connection profile information

Network connections are tenuous, especially Wi-Fi and mobile connections. This means you must code your app to be resilient against dynamic network changes, bandwidth changes, and cost changes. Your app learns about the current state of the network by calling the `NetworkInformation` class' static `GetInternetConnectionProfile` method:

```
ConnectionProfile cp = NetworkInformation.GetInternetConnectionProfile();
```

This method returns a `ConnectionProfile` that has a lot of information packed into it:

```
public sealed class ConnectionProfile {
    // Enum indicating access: None, LocalAccess, ConstrainedInternetAccess, InternetAccess
    public NetworkConnectivityLevel GetNetworkConnectivityLevel();

    // Returns network adapter info including bandwidth speeds:
    public NetworkAdapter NetworkAdapter { get; }

    // Returns the cost associated with accessing this network:
    public ConnectionCost GetConnectionCost();

    // Returns info about the connection's data plan
    public DataPlanStatus GetDataPlanStatus();

    // Less useful members not shown here...
}
```

The `GetNetworkConnectivityLevel` method returns an enumerated type indicating what the app can access: nothing, local intranet resources, constrained Internet resources,[2] or Internet resources. The `NetworkAdapter` property tells you what network interface card (NIC), Wi-Fi card, or mobile broadband radio the current connection is using, its bandwidth characteristics, and so on. Other members reveal the connection's authentication and encryption—for example, Wired Equivalent Privacy (WEP) or Wi-Fi Protected Access (WPA) in the case of wireless networks—the name of the network (such as the SSID for wireless), and more.

The `GetConnectionCost` method returns a `ConnectionCost` object indicating the costs associated with a network connection:

```
public sealed class ConnectionCost {
    // Enum: Unknown, Unrestricted (LAN & Wi-Fi),
    //       Fixed (free to a limit), Variable (has a cost per byte)
    public NetworkCostType NetworkCostType { get; }

    public Boolean ApproachingDataLimit { get; } // Applies when NetworkCostType is Fixed
    public Boolean OverDataLimit        { get; } // Applies when NetworkCostType is Fixed
    public Boolean Roaming              { get; }
}
```

`NetworkCostType` has four different values: `Unknown`, `Unrestricted`, `Fixed`, and `Variable`. `Unknown` is a transient network state that quickly changes to one of the other three categories. LAN and Wi-Fi connections will almost always fall in the `Unrestricted` category. Typically, these connection types have either no cap or one that is very high. Mobile broadband networks typically indicate `Fixed` or `Variable`. `Fixed` indicates that the bandwidth is free up to a certain amount (for example, 5 GB per month) and then additional costs kick in. The `ApproachingDataLimit` and `OverDataLimit` properties apply to this `Fixed` network cost type. `ApproachingDataLimit` returns true once the connection has reached a threshold close to the data usage allowance.[3] `Variable` indicates that

---

[2] Constrained access is an indication that the user needs to provide credentials to get full Internet access (such as when connecting via a web portal from a hotel room). This is also known as *captive portal*.

[3] The `ApproachingDataLimit` value is defined by the network provider.

the bandwidth has a cost per byte associated with it. The Roaming property indicates that the network access is expensive because the user is roaming away from her usual network.

The GetDataPlanStatus method returns a DataPlanStatus object containing information (populated by the network provider) about the user's data plan:

```
public sealed class DataPlanStatus {
    // Your app uses this when on a metered network:
    public UInt32? MaxTransferSizeInMegabytes { get; }

    // Indicates speed of connection (most apps ignore these):
    public UInt64? InboundBitsPerSecond { get; }
    public UInt64? OutboundBitsPerSecond { get; }

    // Billing cycle information (most apps ignore these):
    public DateTimeOffset? NextBillingCycle { get; }
    public UInt32? DataLimitInMegabytes { get; }
    public DataPlanUsage DataPlanUsage { get; }
}
```

How your app must use connectivity profile information

For your app to pass Windows Store certification,[4] it *must* have code that leverages the connection profile just discussed. The goal here is to prevent users from getting unexpected carrier fees by using an app that internally performs networking operations. When on a nonmetered network, your app can use network bandwidth to its heart's content. But, when on a metered network, your app should dynamically adjust its bandwidth usage based on network connectivity. For example, Windows itself does not download normal system updates when connected via a metered network. However, it does download critical security updates when on a metered network.

Specifically, when on a metered network, your app should

- Stream audio no more than 64 Kbps

- Stream video no more than 256 Kbps

- Not perform any single transfer larger than the number of bytes returned from Data-PlanStatus' MaxTransferSizeInMegabytes property without requesting user permission.[5]

- Not transfer any data when the connection is over its data limit or when the PC is roaming because this can be quite expensive for the user. If a transfer is in progress when a connection goes over its data limit or is roaming, the policy allows an app to transfer up to 1 MB of additional data before stopping.

---

[4] See section 4.5 of Microsoft's "Windows 8 app certification requirements" document (*http://msdn.microsoft.com/en-us/library/windows/apps/hh694083.aspx*).

[5] This limitation complies with mobile operator requirements. It helps prevent devices from clogging mobile networks. An app can make multiple transfers smaller than MaxTransferSizeInMegabytes, but this is not in keeping with the spirit of the Windows Store policy.

The Windows Store cannot easily verify that your app adheres to these policies. However, if users of your app complain about your app's network consumption because it is not adhering to these policies, your app will be removed from the Windows Store.

That being said, your app can offer the user a setting that allows your app to violate these restrictions, but the important thing here is the user must be in control. Here is an example of an extension method you can use in your app before initiating a transfer operation. This method returns the maximum size of the transfer in megabytes allowed given the current network connection and the user's preference:

```
public static UInt64 GetMaxTransferSizeInMegabytes(this ConnectionProfile cp,
    Boolean userOptIn = false,
    NetworkConnectivityLevel requiredLevel = NetworkConnectivityLevel.InternetAccess) {

    // If no physical connection or less than required, transfer 0 bytes
    if ((cp == null) || (cp.GetNetworkConnectivityLevel() < requiredLevel)) return 0;

    // If the user opts in to full network usage, there is no limit
    if (userOptIn) return UInt64.MaxValue;

    ConnectionCost cc = cp.GetConnectionCost();

    // If expensive, don't transfer anything (your app can really use 1MB more)
    if (cc.Roaming || cc.OverDataLimit) return 0;

    // No limit if not metered
    Boolean isMetered = cc.NetworkCostType == NetworkCostType.Fixed
        || cc.NetworkCostType == NetworkCostType.Variable;
    if (!isMetered) return UInt64.MaxValue;

    // Return MaxTransferSizeinMegabytes (if exist) or no limit
    return cp.GetDataPlanStatus().MaxTransferSizeInMegabytes ?? UInt64.MaxValue;
}
```

When your app is about to transfer data, it should call this method to see how large a transfer it can do to keep your users happy with your app's network consumption and also to pass Windows Store certification.

In addition to costs, there are other issues worth keeping in mind when building a networking app—for example, power conservation. Apps should use as little bandwidth as possible to decrease power consumption. Also, it is best to avoid frequent periodic requests because this prevents the network hardware from entering an idle state. Instead, batch requests together and perform them all simultaneously less frequently. Also, consider caching data offline to avoid unnecessary network requests and also to give your users a good experience with your app when a network is unavailable.

Network connectivity change notifications

Your app can receive a notification whenever network connectivity changes by having it register a callback method with the NetworkInformation class' static NetworkStatusChanged event. Apps typically use this to re-establish connections whenever network connectivity is restored.

Unfortunately, there is no way to easily find out what exactly changed. Also, this event is raised whenever any connection changes. For example, if your system has both wired and Wi-Fi connections, the event is raised when either of these changes. This means your app might have to walk through all the connections (by calling NetworkInformation's static GetConnectionProfiles method) to see if the one it is currently using has changed; some changed events might not affect your app at all.

Situations might arise where the system or even your app is using multiple connections simultaneously. For example, if your app opened a socket to connect with a server over a mobile broadband connection, your app will continue to use that connection even if other better networks become available later. For these scenarios, you can certainly use the NetworkStatusChanged event to find out if a better connection has become available and re-establish the connection within your app's code. Finally, if your app is suspended when a network status change occurs, the system will raise the event once when your app resumes.

Although the NetworkStatusChanged event does not indicate what has changed, you can get more information if you create a background task triggered by a SystemTrigger with a System-TriggerType of NetworkStateChange. Then, whenever this task executes, its IBackground-TaskInstance's TriggerDetails property will refer to a NetworkStateChangeEventDetails object that exposes what has changed:

```
public sealed class NetworkStateChangeEventDetails {
    public Boolean HasNewConnectionCost { get; }
    public Boolean HasNewDomainConnectivityLevel { get; }
    public Boolean HasNewHostNameList { get; }
    public Boolean HasNewInternetConnectionProfile { get; }
    public Boolean HasNewNetworkConnectivityLevel { get; }
    public Boolean HasNewWwanRegistrationState { get; }
}
```

Background transfer

Many Windows Store apps transfer files (documents, pictures, audio, and video) over the network. Typically, users use an app to initiate a transfer and then the user works with other apps while the transfer takes place. However, as discussed in Chapter 3, "Process model," Windows Store apps are suspended while not in the foreground, and therefore, the file transfer stops. This is clearly not an ideal user experience.

Fortunately, Windows provides a background transfer feature allowing an app to initiate a transfer, and then the system continues the transfer while the app is running or suspended (but not if the app is terminated). The WinRT background transfer APIs are simple to use and have the following capabilities:

- Support small and large transfers (although they are most commonly used for large transfers)

- Automatically take connection profile and cost into account so that you don't have to worry about this

- Can resume downloads and restart uploads even if network connectivity issues arise during the transfer

- Support HTTP(S) with custom headers (typically used for authentication) and FTP (download only) protocols

- Support progress reporting, pause/resume (downloads only), and cancel operations

- Support normal and high-priority transfer operations

- Support transfer groups, allowing you to perform a set of transfers serially or in parallel

- Can update a tile or display a toast notification when a transfer or transfer group completes or fails

- Allow your app to read the data while downloading; your app does not have to wait for the download to complete

Performing a background transfer starts with two classes in the `Windows.Networking.Back-groundTransfer` namespace: `BackgroundDownloader` and `BackgroundUploader`. Because it is more common for apps to download data, I'll focus the discussion on downloading. However, because these two classes are practically identical, the discussion applies to uploading as well. Where appropriate, I will point out differences. The `BackgroundDownloader` class looks like this:

```
public sealed class BackgroundDownloader : IBackgroundTransferBase {
    public BackgroundDownloader();

    // These members set properties/headers you want applied to 1 or more download operations
    public BackgroundTransferCostPolicy CostPolicy {get; set; }
    public String Method { get; set; }                      // HTTP method: "GET", "POST", "PUT"
    public BackgroundTransferGroup TransferGroup { get; set; }
    public PasswordCredential ProxyCredential  { get; set; }        // For HTTP requests
    public PasswordCredential ServerCredential { get; set; }
    public void SetRequestHeader(String headerName, String headerValue); // For HTTP requests
    public TileNotification SuccessTileNotification { get; set; }   // Used if ALL succeed
    public TileNotification FailureTileNotification { get; set; }   // Used if ANY fail
    public ToastNotification SuccessToastNotification { get; set; } // Used if ALL succeed
    public ToastNotification FailureToastNotification { get; set; } // Used if ANY fail

    // This method creates a download operation using the specified properties & headers
    public DownloadOperation CreateDownload(Uri uri, IStorageFile resultFile);

    // This method asks the user if the downloads can proceed if the PC is on battery power
    public static IAsyncOperation<UnconstrainedTransferRequestResult>
        RequestUnconstrainedDownloadsAsync(IEnumerable<DownloadOperation> operations);

    // These static methods (discussed later) resume transferring when
    // a terminated process relaunches
    public static IAsyncOperation<IReadOnlyList<DownloadOperation>> GetCurrentDownloadsAsync();
    public static IAsyncOperation<IReadOnlyList<DownloadOperation>>
        GetCurrentDownloadsForTransferGroupAsync(BackgroundTransferGroup group);
}
```

After you construct a `BackgroundDownloader` object, you set any desired properties and optionally add any request headers. Let's discuss a few of these properties.

The `CostPolicy` property controls the cost of the transfer. Here are the possible values and what each means:

- **Default**   The transfer occurs on unrestricted networks or on metered networks if not roaming or over the data limit. Note that a download operation won't even start if the file size is known and would take the connection over its data limit.

- **UnrestrictedOnly**   The transfer occurs on unrestricted networks if not roaming.

- **Always**   The transfer occurs regardless of network costs. Your app should specify this value only if the user opts into this behavior. To do this, you could call `BackgroundDownloader`'s `RequestUnconstrainedDownloadsAsync` method.

The `Method` property is for HTTP(S) requests; it defaults to an empty string, which means GET for a download operation and POST for an upload operation. The `TransferGroup` property allows you to assign a bunch of operations to a group (identified by a string [typically a GUID]) and whether you want the operations to transfer sequentially or in parallel (the default). The operations that are part of this group can be obtained when calling the static `GetCurrentDownloadsForTransfer-GroupAsync` method (discussed later). Transfer groups allow an app to use a third-party component to initiate several transfers using a group name string that is unknown to the app. Because the app doesn't know the group name string, it can't discover and manipulate the component's transfers. The `ProxyCredential` and `ServerCredential` properties allow you to specify any username/passwords required.

After you initialize a `BackgroundDownloader` object, you use it to create one or more transfers. You create a transfer by calling its `CreateDownload` method. A download operation downloads data from the specified `Uri` to the specified `IStorageFile`. For an FTP download, the URI must include credentials and must look something like this:

```
ftp://username:password@server.com/FolderName/FileName.ext
```

If you want to process the data as it downloads without persisting it into your own file, pass `null` for the `resultFile` parameter and then call `DownloadOperation`'s `GetResultStreamAt` method, which returns an `IInputStream` you can use to read the data as it is downloading. Note that a background download operation always stores the downloaded data to a system-created temporary file; the `GetResultStreamAt` method really returns an `IInputStream` to this temporary file.[6] Downloading to a temporary file allows your app to be suspended while the download continues and then process the data when your app resumes. I show an example using this technique in the "Populating a stream on demand" section of Chapter 6, "Stream input and output."

---

[6] The temporary files is created in the %UserProfile%\AppData\Local\Packages*PackageFamilyName*\AC\BackgroundTransferApi directory.

You create a background upload operation by calling BackgroundUploader's CreateUpload method:

```
public UploadOperation CreateUpload(Uri uri, IStorageFile sourceFile);
```

The upload operation uploads data from the specified IStorageFile to the specified Uri. If you want to upload from memory instead of using a file, you cannot pass null for the sourceFile parameter because that throws a NullReferenceException. Instead, call BackgroundUploader's CreateUploadFromStream method:

```
public IAsyncOperation<UploadOperation> CreateUploadFromStreamAsync(
   Uri uri, IInputStream sourceStream);
```

The BackgroundUploader class also offers a CreateUploadAsync method that allows you to upload data as a MIME multipart message.

The DownloadOperation and UploadOperation objects are practically identical. Here's what these classes look like:

```
public sealed class XxxOperation : IBackgroundTransferOperation {
   // Members initialized when you called CreateDownload or CreateUpload:
   public BackgroundTransferCostPolicy CostPolicy { get; set; }
   public BackgroundTransferGroup TransferGroup { get; }
   public String Method         { get; }
   public Uri RequestedUri      { get; }
   public IStorageFile ResultFile { get; }  // Called "SourceFile" for UploadOperation
   public Guid Guid             { get; }  // Uniquely identifies this transfer operation
   public BackgroundTransferPriority Priority { get; set; } // Default or High

   // Members to control the transfer; cancel via IAsyncOperationWithProgress' Cancel method
   public IAsyncOperationWithProgress<XxxOperation, XxxOperation> StartAsync();
   public IAsyncOperationWithProgress<XxxOperation, XxxOperation> AttachAsync();
   public BackgroundXxxProgress Progress { get; }
   public void Pause();                        // Offered by DownloadOperation only
   public void Resume();                       // Offered by DownloadOperation only

   public ResponseInformation GetResponseInformation();
   public IInputStream GetResultStreamAt(UInt64 position);
}
```

Once you have one of these objects, you can alter some of its properties (if desired) and then tell Windows to start transferring the data by calling the StartAsync method. This method returns an IAsyncOperationWithProcess object, which you can use to register for periodic progress notifications and transfer completion. You can also use it to cancel the operation. When you get a progress notification, you can query *Xxx*Operation's Progress property to get detailed progress information:

```
public struct BackgroundXxxProgress {
   public Boolean HasRestarted;
   public Boolean HasResponseChanged;

   // Idle, Running, Paused[ByApplication|CostedNetwork|NoNetwork], Completed, Canceled, Error
   public BackgroundTransferStatus Status;

   public UInt64 BytesReceived;
   public UInt64 TotalBytesToReceive;

   public UInt64 BytesSent;        // Offered by BackgroundUploadProgress only
   public UInt64 TotalBytesToSend; // Offered by BackgroundUploadProgress only
}
```

So now, let me show you an example that downloads a file:

```
void StartDownload(Uri uri, IStorageFile file, CancellationToken ct) {
   BackgroundDownloader bd = new BackgroundDownloader();
   DownloadOperation dop = bd.CreateDownload(uri, file);
   var p = new Progress<DownloadOperation>(DownloadProgress);

   // NOTE: It is common NOT to use await here as you DO want the
   // next line of code to execute before the transfer completes.
   // Instead, when transfer completes, TransferDone is called.
   dop.StartAsync().AsTask(ct, p).ContinueWith(TransferDone);
}


void DownloadProgress(DownloadOperation dop) {
   // Windows calls this method approximately once every 500 milliseconds
   // NOTE: This method is called by the GUI thread
   // TODO: Update UI with dop.Progress properties...
}

async void TransferDone(Task<DownloadOperation> task) {
   // NOTE: This method could be called by any thread; to update UI use a CoreDispatcher
   DownloadOperation dop = null;
   try {
      dop = await task;   // Get DownloadOperation; throws if transfer canceled/failed
      // TODO: Update UI/show toast...
   }
   catch (Exception ex) {
      if (ex is OperationCanceledException) {
         // TODO: Code to handle cancellation...
      } else {
         // Converts HResult to HTTP response code
         WebErrorStatus webErrorStatus = BackgroundTransferError.GetStatus(ex.HResult);
      }
   }
}
```

The preceding code initiates a transfer, which Windows performs while your app is running or suspended. If progress or completion notifications come in, your app receives them if it is running. If your app is suspended, Windows remembers the most recent events only and raises them when your app resumes. But what if your app is terminated? In this case, Windows stops the transfer operation. Then, when the user switches back to your app, Windows automatically relaunches your app. But, at this point, any callback methods you've registered for progress reporting and completion have been destroyed. Furthermore, Windows doesn't automatically detect that your app relaunched, so it will not resume your app's transfers.

So, when your app relaunches, it must call the BackgroundDownloader.GetCurrentDownloadsAsync and BackgroundUploader.GetCurrentUploadsAsync methods. These methods return a collection of *Xxx*Operation objects—one object for each transfer your app initiated by calling StartAsync. Just calling these methods is enough to have Windows resume the transfers; you do not actually have to iterate through the returned collections. Note that uploads using the HTTP PUT method restart, while uploads using the HTTP POST method do not.

If you want, you can iterate through these collections and register any progress, cancellation, and completion notifications you'd like:

```
// NOTE: This code assumes one CancellationToken for all transfer operations.
// It also assumes one progress and completion callback for all downloads & for all uploads
// You must modify this code if you desire different behavior
private async void AttachToBackgroundTransfers(CancellationToken ct, String group,
   Progress<DownloadOperation>      downloadProgress,
   Action<Task<DownloadOperation>> downloadComplete,
   Progress<UploadOperation>        uploadProgress,
   Action<Task<UploadOperation>>   uploadComplete) {

   foreach (DownloadOperation dop in
      await BackgroundDownloader.GetCurrentDownloadsAsync(group)) {

      var noWarning = dop.AttachAsync().AsTask(ct, downloadProgress)
         .ContinueWith(downloadComplete);
   }

   foreach (UploadOperation uop in
      await BackgroundUploader.GetCurrentUploadsAsync(group)) {

      var noWarning = uop.AttachAsync().AsTask(ct, uploadProgress)
         .ContinueWith(uploadComplete);
   }
}
```

When you start a transfer operation, the system remembers it. If your app closes or terminates, it must reattach to the previously started transfer operations or they will remain dormant in the system, wasting resources. Your app has to complete or cancel each operation to release its resources. Don't forget about this when debugging your app. When you stop a debugging session, the system still remembers any initiated operations. If you debug and stop a lot, your app can accumulate a lot of transfer operations. The easy way to destroy all of the operations is to go to your app's properties in Visual Studio and, on the Debug pane, select the "Uninstall and then re-install my package. All information about the application state is deleted." option and then start your app again.

Debugging background transfers

Because your app can be suspended, background transfers execute in a separate process. You can see this in Task Manager. Figure 7-5 shows the App1 app suspended, but there is also an App1 Download/Upload Host process that is not suspended. If you tap and hold this process and choose Go To Detail, Task Manager takes you to the Details tab, selecting a process called BackgroundTransferHost.exe. (This process ships with Windows itself.)

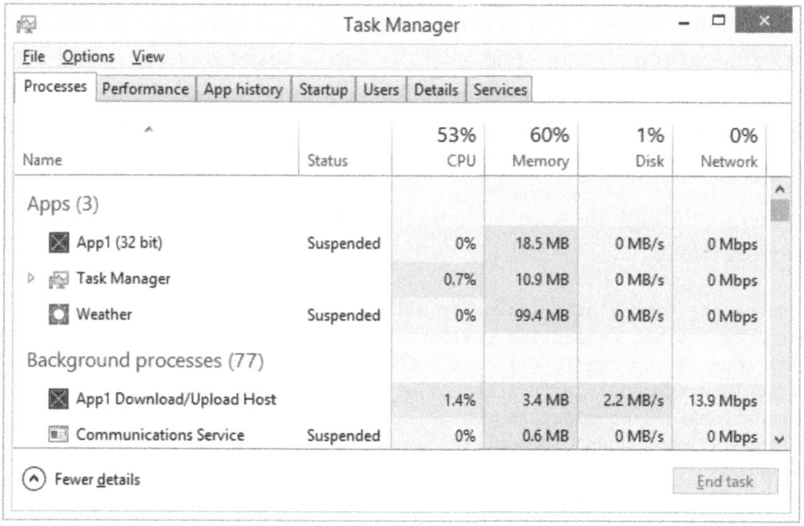

FIGURE 7-5 Task Manager showing the separate process Windows uses to perform background transfers.

Each app using WinRT's background transfer API gets its own instance of the BackgroundTransfer-Host.exe process, and each instance runs in the package's app container. If your app uses the background transfer API, you must turn on the Internet (Client) capability in your package's manifest so that the host process gets this capability too.

As always, you can use the Windows Event Viewer (EventVwr.exe) to see system logs related to background transfer. Here's where to look for the log entries: Applications And Service Logs > Microsoft > Windows > Runtime-Networking-BackgroundTransfer.[7]

---

[7] Show Analytic And Debug Logs has to be enabled from the Event Viewer View menu. This log is disabled by default.

HttpClient: Client-side HTTP(S) communication

Probably the most common form of network communication is client-side HTTP(S) communication. To accomplish this with WinRT, you use the `Windows.Web.Http.HttpClient` class, which looks like this:[8]

```
public sealed class HttpClient : IDisposable, IStringable {
    public HttpClient();                    // Construct using HttpBaseProtocolFilter
    public HttpClient(IHttpFilter filter); // Construct with a specific IHttpFilter

    // Use this property to set request headers sent with each request.
    public HttpRequestHeaderCollection DefaultRequestHeaders { get; }

    // This method sends a request. The operation is considered complete
    // after reading response headers or the entire response.
    public IAsyncOperationWithProgress<HttpResponseMessage, HttpProgress>
        SendRequestAsync(HttpRequestMessage request);
    public IAsyncOperationWithProgress<HttpResponseMessage, HttpProgress>
        SendRequestAsync(HttpRequestMessage request, HttpCompletionOption completionOption);

    // These methods simplify calling SendRequestAsync for common operations:
    public IAsyncOperationWithProgress<HttpResponseMessage, HttpProgress>
        PostAsync(Uri uri, IHttpContent content);
    public IAsyncOperationWithProgress<HttpResponseMessage, HttpProgress>
        PutAsync(Uri uri, IHttpContent content);
    public IAsyncOperationWithProgress<HttpResponseMessage, HttpProgress> DeleteAsync(Uri uri);
    public IAsyncOperationWithProgress<HttpResponseMessage, HttpProgress> GetAsync(Uri uri);
    public IAsyncOperationWithProgress<HttpResponseMessage, HttpProgress>
        GetAsync(Uri uri, HttpCompletionOption completionOption);

    // These methods simplify calling GetAsync for common HTTP GET operations:
    public IAsyncOperationWithProgress<String, HttpProgress> GetStringAsync(Uri uri);
    public IAsyncOperationWithProgress<IBuffer, HttpProgress> GetBufferAsync(Uri uri);
    public IAsyncOperationWithProgress<IInputStream, HttpProgress> GetInputStreamAsync(Uri uri);

    public String ToString(); // Returns filter and default header information
    public void Dispose();     // Releases unmanaged resources associated with the HttpClient
}
```

Once you've constructed an `HttpClient` object, you can easily download a string like this:

```
using (HttpClient client = new HttpClient()) {
    String html = await client.GetStringAsync(new Uri("http://WintellectNOW.com/"));
}
```

This is very simple, but sometimes you need to have more control over the communication. All of the simple *Xxx*Async methods are really just wrappers around `HttpClient`'s more capable

---

[8] WinRT's `Windows.Web.Http.HttpClient` class is the latest and greatest class from Microsoft that allows developers to perform HTTP(S) requests. You should use this class instead of using the .NET Framework's `System.Net.Http.HttpClient` class.

SendRequestAsync method. To have more control over the request, you must construct an Http-RequestMessage object that looks like this (some members not shown):

```
public sealed class HttpRequestMessage : IDisposable, IStringable {
   // Set the HTTP method (GET, POST, PUT, DELETE, etc.) and server URI
   public HttpRequestMessage(HttpMethod method, Uri uri);

   // Set this request's headers (HttpClient's DefaultRequestHeaders are merged with these)
   public HttpRequestHeaderCollection Headers { get; }

   // Set any content to send to the server (not used for some methods, like GET)
   public IHttpContent Content { get; set; }

   // Optional: When using HTTPS, examine information about the server's certificate
   public HttpTransportInformation TransportInformation { get; }

   public void Dispose();     // Releases HttpRequestMessage's unmanaged resources
}
```

Here is an example of how to make an HTTPS POST request to the *http://httpbin.org* service:

```
using (HttpClient client = new HttpClient()) {
   HttpRequestMessage request =
      new HttpRequestMessage(HttpMethod.Post, new Uri("https://httpbin.org/post")) {
         Content = new HttpStringContent("Some test data", UnicodeEncoding.Utf8, "text/plain")
      };

   HttpResponseMessage response = await client.SendRequestAsync(request);
   String json = await response.Content.ReadAsStringAsync();
}
```

When I look at the returned JSON string, I get this:

```
{
  "headers": {
    "Content-Length": "14",
    "Content-Type": "text/plain; charset=UTF-8",
    "Accept-Encoding": "gzip, deflate",
    "Cache-Control": "no-cache",
    "Connection": "close",
    "Host": "httpbin.org"
  },
  "args": {},
  "data": "Some test data",
  "files": {},
  "url": "http://httpbin.org/post",
  "json": null,
  "form": {},
  "origin": "50.135.158.248"
}
```

In the preceding code, I set the content by constructing an `HttpStringContent` object, passing in an encoding and mime type. This class is just one of many that implement the `IHttpContent` interface:

```
public interface IHttpContent : IDisposable {
    HttpContentHeaderCollection Headers { get; }  // Use this to set/get content headers
    Boolean TryComputeLength(out UInt64 length);  // Gets content length in bytes

    // Sends content to an output stream
    IAsyncOperationWithProgress<UInt64, UInt64> WriteToStreamAsync(IOutputStream outputStream);

    // Serializes content into memory
    IAsyncOperationWithProgress<UInt64, UInt64> BufferAllAsync();

    // Read response content as an IInputStream, IBuffer, or a String
    IAsyncOperationWithProgress<IInputStream, UInt64> ReadAsInputStreamAsync();
    IAsyncOperationWithProgress<IBuffer, UInt64> ReadAsBufferAsync();
    IAsyncOperationWithProgress<String, UInt64> ReadAsStringAsync();
}
```

All the classes that implement this interface convert rich content into a stream whose data can be sent over the network. Here are all the WinRT classes that implement this interface:

```
HttpStringContent
HttpBufferContent
HttpStreamContent
HttpFormUrlEncodedContent
HttpMultipartContent
HttpMultipartFormDataContent
```

The `SendRequestAsync` method returns an `HttpResponseMessage`:

```
public sealed class HttpResponseMessage : IDisposable, IStringable {
    // Members that return request's response status
    public HttpStatusCode StatusCode { get; set; }        // Gets response status code
    public Boolean IsSuccessStatusCode { get; }           // True for codes between 200-299
    public HttpResponseMessage EnsureSuccessStatusCode(); // Throws if !IsSuccessStatusCode
    public String ReasonPhrase { get; set; }              // Gets status reason (eg: "OK")

    public HttpResponseMessageSource Source { get; set; } // Network or Cache
    public HttpResponseHeaderCollection Headers { get; }  // Returns this response's headers
    public IHttpContent Content { get; set; }             // Returns content sent from server

    public void Dispose();    // Releases HttpResponseMessage's unmanaged resources
    // Some members not shown here...
}
```

Again the `Content` property returns an object whose type implements the `IHttpContent` interface. You would then call `IHttpContent`'s `ReadAsInputStreamAsync`, `ReadAsBufferAsync`, or `ReadAsStringAsync` method to read the data returned from the server. At this point, I have covered the core features of the `HttpClient` class. However, it offers some additional features that make it very powerful and flexible. I'll cover these next.

HttpBaseProtocolFilter

WinRT defines a `Windows.Web.Http.Filters.HttpBaseProtocolFilter` class. When you construct an `HttpClient` object using its default constructor, the object uses an instance of the `HttpBaseProtocolFilter` class internally. It is the `HttpBaseProtocolFilter` object that establishes the TCP socket connection with the server, sends the bytes to it, and receives the response bytes back. In addition, this filter manages caching, cookies, credentials, and a slew of other communication parameters. The class looks like this:

```
public sealed class HttpBaseProtocolFilter : IHttpFilter, IDisposable {
   public HttpBaseProtocolFilter();

   // Gets an object allowing you to set cache read and write behavior
   public HttpCacheControl CacheControl { get; }

   // Returns the cookie manager allowing you to get and set cookies
   public HttpCookieManager CookieManager { get; }

   // Allows you to set the maximum connections from filter to an HTTP server
   public UInt32 MaxConnectionsPerServer { get; set; }

   // Can filter follow a redirect response (default = true)
   public Boolean AllowAutoRedirect { get; set; }

   // Can filter automatically decompress response data (default = true)
   public Boolean AutomaticDecompression { get; set; }

   // Ignorable SSL errors
   public IList<ChainValidationResult> IgnorableServerCertificateErrors { get; }

   // Can filter use a proxy to send request
   public Boolean UseProxy { get; set; }

   // Sets HTTP proxy credentials
   public PasswordCredential ProxyCredential { get; set; }

   // Sets client certificate to send to server (if requested)
   public Certificate ClientCertificate { get; set; }

   // Sets HTTP server credentials
   public PasswordCredential ServerCredential { get; set; }

   // Can filter prompt for user credentials at server's request (default = true)
   public Boolean AllowUI { get; set; }

   // Sends HTTP request over the wire (SendRequestAsync is IHttpFilter's only member)
   public IAsyncOperationWithProgress<HttpResponseMessage, HttpProgress>
      SendRequestAsync(HttpRequestMessage request);

   // Releases unmanaged resources associated with the HttpBaseProtocolFilter
   public void Dispose();
}
```

Each package has a per-user cache that can hold downloaded HTTP content.[9] This prevents one package's downloaded content from being visible to another package's app, and it also prevents content downloaded by one user from being visible to another user who happens to be using the same package. Using HttpBaseProtocolFilter's CacheControl property, your app can control how HTTP responses are cached on the user's local machine and use this to alter your app's performance.

Before making an HTTP request, you can set CacheControl's ReadBehavior to Default (as described in RFC 2616), MostRecent (if the server has more recent data, get it; otherwise, use cached data),[10] or OnlyFromCache (get data from cache [useful when a PC is offline or at app startup time to show what's cached quickly]). You can also set CacheControl's WriteBehavior to control how the read data gets put into the user's local cache. The possible values are Default (save the response in the local cache) and NoCache (do not save the response in the local cache [useful when streaming media]). When your app gets a response back, HttpResponseMessage's Source property indicates whether the response came from the server or from the user's local cache.

Here is an example that reads the most recent data from the server (or cache if it exists there); if read from the server, the data is not cached locally:

```
using (HttpBaseProtocolFilter filter = new HttpBaseProtocolFilter())
using (HttpClient client = new HttpClient(filter)) {
   // Try to get most recent data from server (or cache)
   filter.CacheControl.ReadBehavior = HttpCacheReadBehavior.MostRecent;

   // If we get it from server, don't store it in cache
   filter.CacheControl.WriteBehavior = HttpCacheWriteBehavior.NoCache;

   HttpRequestMessage request =
      new HttpRequestMessage(HttpMethod.Get, new Uri("http://Wintellect.com/"));
   HttpResponseMessage response = await client.SendRequestAsync(request);
   switch (response.Source) {
      case HttpResponseMessageSource.Cache:      // Data came from cache
         break;
      case HttpResponseMessageSource.Network:    // Data came from server
         break;
   }
}
```

---

[9] The cache is stored under %LocalAppData%\Packages*PackageFamilyName*\AC\INetCache. The INetCache directory is hidden, so you won't normally see it when using File Explorer or a CMD prompt.

[10] This option causes the HttpBaseProtocolFilter to add an If-Modified-Since header to the request. If the server returns a 200 (OK) or 304 (Not modified) status code, the cache version is returned, thus conserving bandwidth and improving performance.

To improve application performance, WinRT offers a simple `Windows.Networking.Back-groundTransfer.ContentPrefetcher` class:

```
public static class ContentPrefetcher {
    // Set of URIs to content the system periodically downloads and caches for your app
    // Use this when URIs don't change between runs of the app (Ex: a URI to weather in a city)
    public static IList<Uri> ContentUris { get; }

    // A URI to an XML file the system periodically downloads. The XML file contains prioritized
    // URIs to other content the system will also download and cache. Use this when URIs to
    // content do change between runs of the app.
    // Example: a URI to an XML file with URIs to the latest news stories
    public static Uri IndirectContentUri { get; set; }

    // NOTE: The system can prefetch data for up to 40 URIs. ContentUris takes precedence
    // over URIs in the XML file referred to by IndirectContentUri
}
```

After populating the `ContentPrefetcher` with some URIs, the system uses heuristics to determine when to periodically download the content on your app's behalf. The goal is that, when your app runs, the data it needs has already been downloaded and stored in the package's cache so that the app can simply make an HTTP request, get the data from the cache, and show the user relevant data without incurring a network performance hit. The exact heuristics are not documented and are subject to change, but they take into account power and network conditions as well as how often the app actually consumed the prefetched data and how often the app is used. The `ContentPrefetcher` is best for data an app shows at startup time, frequently used data, and data whose usefulness is long-lived.

In addition to a cache, each package also has a per-user set of cookies.[11] Using `HttpBaseProto-colFilter`'s `CookieManager` property, your app can examine cookies returned from HTTP servers. It can also create cookies to send to a server. The following code demonstrates how to examine the cookies returned in an HTTP response from a server:

```
using (HttpBaseProtocolFilter filter = new HttpBaseProtocolFilter())
using (HttpClient client = new HttpClient(filter)) {
    HttpRequestMessage request =
        new HttpRequestMessage(HttpMethod.Get, new Uri("http://Bing.com/"));
    HttpResponseMessage response = await client.SendRequestAsync(request);

    // See the returned cookies (HttpCookieManager also has SetCookie and DeleteCookie methods)
    foreach (HttpCookie cookie in filter.CookieManager.GetCookies(request.RequestUri)) {
        String cookieInfo = String.Format(
            "Domain={0}, Expires={1}, HttpOnly={2}, Name={3}, Path={4}, Secure={5}, Value={6}",
            cookie.Domain, cookie.Expires, cookie.HttpOnly, cookie.Name, cookie.Path,
            cookie.Secure, cookie.Value);
    }
}
```

---

[11] Cookies are stored under %LocalAppData%\Packages*PackageFamilyName*\AC\INetCookies. The INetCookies directory is hidden, so you won't normally see it when using File Explorer or a CMD prompt.

The last thing I want to say about filters is that you can chain them together. That is, you can create your own classes that implement the IHttpFilter interface with its SendRequestAsync method. Then you can create instances of your class and pass them into HttpClient's constructor. Your filter class' constructor should accept another filter object in order to maintain the chain of filters. Here is an example of a filter that calculates how much time it takes for the server to respond to each request:

```
internal sealed class RequestDurationFilter : IHttpFilter {
    private readonly IHttpFilter m_nextFilter;

    public RequestDurationFilter(IHttpFilter nextFilter) {
        if (nextFilter == null) throw new ArgumentNullException("nextFilter");
        m_nextFilter = nextFilter;
    }

    public void Dispose() { m_nextFilter.Dispose(); }

    public TimeSpan RequestDuration { get; private set; }

    public IAsyncOperationWithProgress<HttpResponseMessage, HttpProgress>
        SendRequestAsync(HttpRequestMessage request) {
        return AsyncInfo.Run<HttpResponseMessage, HttpProgress>(
          async (cancellationToken, progress) => {
            RequestDuration = TimeSpan.Zero;
            Stopwatch time = Stopwatch.StartNew(); // Get the current time

            HttpResponseMessage response =
                await m_nextFilter.SendRequestAsync(request).AsTask(cancellationToken, progress);

            RequestDuration = time.Elapsed;         // Set the request's duration
            cancellationToken.ThrowIfCancellationRequested();
            return response;
        });
    }
}
```

Using this filter is extremely simple:

```
using (RequestDurationFilter filter = new RequestDurationFilter(new HttpBaseProtocolFilter()))
using (HttpClient client = new HttpClient(filter)) {
    HttpRequestMessage request = new HttpRequestMessage(HttpMethod.Get,
                                    new Uri("http://WintellectNOW.com/"));
    HttpResponseMessage response = await client.SendRequestAsync(request);
    String s = String.Format("Request took {0}ms", filter.RequestDuration.TotalMilliseconds);
}
```

Custom filters open up all kinds of possibilities. You could create a filter that

- Automatically retries sending a request when a server responds with an HTTP 503 (service unavailable)

- Checks if the user's PC is on a metered network, and produces an error instead of attempting the network access

- Automatically authenticates against the server it wants to communicate with

- Logs requests to assist with diagnostics and debugging

- Takes advantage of your own custom cache implementation

- Injects simulated network failures to help test the resiliency of your app's code

Really, you're only limited by your imagination. Microsoft has already implemented some of these filters for you. You can download the source code for them from the MSDN website. For sample filters showing retry and metered networks, see *http://code.msdn.microsoft.com/windowsapps/HttpClient-sample-55700664*. For a sample showing authentication, see *http://code.msdn.microsoft.com/windowsapps/Web-Authentication-d0485122* and look at its AuthFilters folder.

Windows Runtime sockets

Windows provides sockets that allow apps to communicate using special protocols like SMTP, MAPI, Telnet, and so on. Table 7-2 shows the different kinds of sockets you can use in your Windows Store app.

TABLE 7-2   Windows Runtime sockets.

Class	Protocol	Side
StreamSocket	TCP	Client
StreamSocketListener	TCP	Server
StreamWebSocket	WebSocket	Client
MessageWebSocket	WebSocket	Client
DatagramSocket	UDP	Peer

Once a connection is established, all sockets offer objects implementing the `IInputStream` and `IOutputStream` interfaces as discussed in Chapter 6. By implementing these interfaces, you transfer data through sockets the same way you transfer data to files and you get to leverage all the helper classes, such as `DataReader`, `DataWriter`, `DataProtectionProvider`, `Compressor`, and so on.

When performing I/O operations, your app can be suspended. In general, this is not a problem and your app should not abort connections before being suspended and re-establish connections when resumed. When an app initiates any I/O operation, that operation is sent to a Windows device driver and the driver performs the actual operation. The driver is capable of accessing the app's data buffers even when the app's threads are suspended, so the I/O operation continues. Of course, if the app is terminated, the app's buffers are destroyed and the device driver cancels any of the app's outstanding I/O operations. Connections will have to be re-established when the app is relaunched.

Socket addressing

Before showing examples working with sockets, I need to explain how your app identifies a remote system to WinRT. WinRT offers a `Windows.Networking.HostName` class that abstracts the name or address of a remote system:

```
public sealed class HostName : IStringable {
   // Constructor
   public HostName(String hostName);              // e.g. "server", "192.168.1.125", etc.

   // Read-only information about the host name:
   public HostNameType Type { get; }              // DomainName, Ipv4, Ipv6, Bluetooth
   public String RawName { get; }                 // Same value passed to constructor
   public String DisplayName { get; }             // String that can be shown to a user
   public String CanonicalName { get; }           // String that can be used by the app's code
   public IPInformation IPInformation { get; }    // NetworkAdapter info for an Ipv4/Ipv6 address

   // Methods to compare canonical hostnames with one another:
   public Boolean IsEqual(HostName hostName);
   public static Int32 Compare(String value1, String value2);
}
```

You can construct a `HostName` object, passing in an IPv4 or IPv6 literal, an actual host name ("Wintellect.com"), or a Bluetooth address. The constructor then sets the Type property to indicate what kind of string you passed in, determines the `DisplayName` version of the host name (which you can show to a user), and also determines the `CanonicalName` version (which you can use programmatically within your code).

The `HostName` class also offers `IsEqual` and `Compare` methods, which compare the canonical versions of two host names. Here is an example demonstrating how to compare host names:

```
// The top-level domain for the Russian Federation is "xn--p1ai" (in ASCII) and "рф" (in
// Cyrillic). For more information, see http://en.wikipedia.org/wiki/.%D1%80%D1%84
String kremlinAscii = "президент.xn--p1ai";
HostName kremlin = new HostName(kremlinAscii);
String display = kremlin.DisplayName;        // "президент.рф"
String canonical = kremlin.CanonicalName;    // "президент.рф"

// Compares canonical names:
Boolean same = kremlin.IsEqual(new HostName("президент.рф")); // true
Int32 order = HostName.Compare(kremlinAscii, "президент.рф"); // 0

// Compare IPv6 addresses
HostName hostname = new HostName("0::1");
same = hostname.IsEqual(new HostName("0:0::1"));             // true

// Compare host names
hostname = new HostName("WINTELLECT.COM");
same = hostname.IsEqual(new HostName("Wintellect.com"));      // true
```

In addition to needing a `HostName`, your app also needs the name of a service that it wants to communicate with on the remote system. The service name is represented by a string. You can use a numeric literal for a port number (like "80" for HTTP) or a service name. Service names are similar to DNS names. DNS names are strings passed to a DNS server that then returns the IP address. Likewise, service names can be passed to a DNS server whose SRV records return a port number.[12] Instead of querying DNS servers, Windows can map a host name to an IP address by looking up the host name in the %WinDir%\System32\Drivers\Etc\Hosts text file. Similarly, Windows can map a service name to a port number by looking up the service name in the %WinDir%\System32\Drivers\Etc\Services text file.

The combination of a host name and a service name results in an endpoint. When your app's local socket connects to a remote socket, you have a pair of endpoints. WinRT defines an `EndpointPair` class that encapsulates connection information:

```
public sealed class EndpointPair {
    public EndpointPair(
        HostName localHostName,  String localServiceName,
        HostName remoteHostName, String remoteServiceName);

    public HostName LocalHostName    { get; set; }
    public String   LocalServiceName { get; set; }
    public HostName RemoteHostName   { get; set; }
    public String   RemoteServiceName { get; set; }
}
```

As you'll see, some WinRT APIs accept an `EndpointPair` argument.

StreamSocket: Client-side TCP communication

To accomplish client-side TCP communication with WinRT, you use the `StreamSocket` class, which looks like this:

```
public sealed class StreamSocket : IDisposable {
    public StreamSocket();

    // OPTIONAL: Modify connection (keep alive, outbound buffer size, QoS)
    // before calling ConnectAsync
    public StreamSocketControl Control { get; }

    // Returns connection read-only information (bandwidth, host/service names, timings)
    public StreamSocketInformation Information { get; }

    // Connect to a service on a remote machine (other overloads not shown here)
    public IAsyncAction ConnectAsync(HostName remoteHostName, String remoteServiceName,
        SocketProtectionLevel protectionLevel);
```

---

[12] For more information about DNS SRV records, see *http://tools.ietf.org/html/rfc2782*. For a list of well-known service-to-port mappings, see *http://www.iana.org/assignments/service-names-port-numbers/service-names-port-numbers.xml*.

```
    // After calling ConnectAsync, the app uses these to read & write data
    public IInputStream  InputStream  { get; }
    public IOutputStream OutputStream { get; }

    // Upgrade a connected socket to use SSL
    public IAsyncAction UpgradeToSslAsync(
        SocketProtectionLevel protectionLevel, HostName validationHostName);

    public void Dispose();  // Close the socket
}
```

Here is an example that uses a StreamSocket to establish a connection with a server sending it a 32-bit integer length header followed by a set of bytes. The server sums the bytes and returns a 32-bit integer:

```
private async Task TcpClientAsync() {
    using (StreamSocket socket = new StreamSocket())
    using (DataWriter dw = new DataWriter(socket.OutputStream))
    using (DataReader dr = new DataReader(socket.InputStream)) {
        // Connect to the remote server:
        await socket.ConnectAsync(new HostName("localhost"), "8080");

        // Send message header (UInt32) and message bytes to server:
        Byte[] messageData = new Byte[] { 1, 2 };
        dw.WriteUInt32((UInt32)messageData.Length);
        dw.WriteBytes(messageData);
        await dw.StoreAsync();

        // Read UInt32 response from server:
        await dr.LoadAsync(sizeof(Int32));
        Int32 sum = dr.ReadInt32();
    }
}
```

When calling IInputStream's ReadAsync method or when using a DataReader (which calls ReadAsync internally), think about the InputStreamOptions bit flags. Here is what the flags mean:

- **None (0)**   The ReadAsync or LoadAsync operation will not complete until the number of bytes requested has come in over the socket. None is useful when you're expecting a specific number of bytes.

- **Partial (1)**   The ReadAsync or LoadAsync operation completes when one or more bytes is available; all the bytes you requested might not be available yet. Partial is useful when you're expecting a stream of data and your app must parse it to know exactly how many additional bytes your app expects. I show an example using this technique in the StreamWeb-SocketClientAsync method later in this chapter.

- **ReadAhead (2)**   The ReadAsync or LoadAsync operation might complete with more bytes than actually requested. ReadAhead is useful to reduce latency and improve performance.

When any member of a StreamSocket, StreamSocketListener, or DatagramSocket fails, an Exception object is thrown. The Exception object's HResult property indicates the reason for failure. You can easily convert the HResult value to a more meaningful value by passing it to the Windows.Networking.Sockets.SocketError class' static GetStatus method. This returns a value from the SocketErrorStatus enumeration.

StreamSocketListener: Server-side TCP communication

Although it's not nearly as common as client-side-initiated communication, your Windows Store app can listen for TCP connections coming into it. This is useful for peer-to-peer scenarios where your app wants to let multiple users collaborate with each user on his or her own PC. A game might use this to allow two users to play against each other. Setting your app as a TCP listener requires the use of the StreamSocketListener class, which looks like this:

```
public sealed class StreamSocketListener : IDisposable {
    public StreamSocketListener();

    // OPTIONAL: Modify connection (QoS) before calling BindXxxAsync
    public StreamSocketListenerControl Control { get; }

    // Returns read-only information about the connection (local port)
    public StreamSocketListenerInformation Information { get; }

    // This event is raised whenever a client connects to this socket listener
    public event TypedEventHandler<StreamSocketListener,
        StreamSocketListenerConnectionReceivedEventArgs> ConnectionReceived;

    // Start listening on local IP addresses of all NICs
    // If localServiceName is "", system picks port
    public IAsyncAction BindServiceNameAsync(String localServiceName);

    // Start listening on the hostname/IP address and service name specified.
    // If localHostName is 'null', local IP is used; if localServiceName is "", OS picks port.
    public IAsyncAction BindEndpointAsync(HostName localHostName, String localServiceName);

    public void Dispose();    // Close the socket
}
```

When another machine connects to this StreamSocketListener, the ConnectionReceived event is raised. Any registered callback method receives a reference to the StreamSocketListener and, more importantly, a reference to a StreamSocketListenerConnectionReceivedEventArgs object, which looks like this:

```
public sealed class StreamSocketListenerConnectionReceivedEventArgs {
    // Returns a StreamSocket created by the client connection
    // Use its IInputStream and IOutputStream to talk to the client
    public StreamSocket Socket { get; }
}
```

Here is an example that uses a `StreamSocketListener` to process requests when clients connect. Each client sends the service a set of bytes. The service sums the bytes together and returns the sum back to the client:

```
// NOTE: Don't let the returned StreamSocketListener be garbage collected
//       until you no longer want to accept connections
private async Task<StreamSocketListener> StartTcpServiceAsync(String localServiceName) {
   var tcpService = new StreamSocketListener();

   // You must register handlers before calling BindXxxAsync
   tcpService.ConnectionReceived += OnConnectionReceived;
   await tcpService.BindServiceNameAsync(localServiceName); // Listen on desired port
   return tcpService;
}

private async void OnClientConnectionReceivedAsync(StreamSocketListener listener,
   StreamSocketListenerConnectionReceivedEventArgs e) {

   using (StreamSocket client = e.Socket)
   using (DataReader dr = new DataReader(e.Socket.InputStream))
   using (DataWriter dw = new DataWriter(e.Socket.OutputStream)) {
      // Read request header from client:
      await dr.LoadAsync(sizeof(Int32));
      UInt32 messageLength = dr.ReadUInt32();

      // Read request data from client:
      await dr.LoadAsync(messageLength);
      Byte[] bytes = new Byte[messageLength];
      dr.ReadBytes(bytes);

      Int32 sum = bytes.Sum(number => number);   // Calculate response

      // Send response to client:
      dw.WriteInt32(sum);
      await dw.StoreAsync();   // Required to send the response back to the client
   }
}
```

StreamWebSocket: Streaming client-side WebSocket communication

Many organizations configure their firewalls to disallow traditional socket communication to better secure their resources. However, many organizations do allow their firewalls to flow HTTP and HTTPS traffic over ports 80 and 443, respectively. This allows standard Internet access to the World Wide Web. But HTTP(S) traffic has its own shortcomings. For example, it is a request/response protocol that has a lot of overheard associated with it, making it less efficient than using the TCP protocol that HTTP(S) is built upon.

To address the HTTP(S) protocol's strengths and weaknesses, the WebSocket protocol was created. (See *http://www.w3.org/TR/websockets/*.) The WebSocket protocol allows asynchronous, bidirectional, high-performance communication through firewalls using ports 80 and 443. It works by having a client initiate an HTTP(S) communication with a server. And then, once communication is established, the client and server continue using the same TCP socket. This establishes the connection successfully through the firewall (and proxy servers) and then allows for high-performance, bidirectional communication thereafter.[13] The bidirectional aspect allows a server to send data to the client when it wants to; there's no need for clients to periodically poll the server, use long-polling, or establish the client as a server, too, so that it can accept requests.[14]

Of course, the client and the server must both support the WebSocket protocol, and today, not many servers support this protocol. A WebSocket client connects to a server by specifying a URL with a "ws://" or "wss://" schema. The former imitates the conversation using HTTP and transfers data in the clear over the network, while the latter initiates the conversation using HTTPS and encrypts the data as it goes over the network. In most cases, you'll want to use a secure WebSocket connection because this sets up a secure end-to-end tunnel that intermediate proxy servers allow, dramatically increasing the chance your connection succeeds.

WinRT offers two classes that allow a Windows Store app to initiate the client-side communication to a WebSocket server: StreamWebSocket and MessageWebSocket.[15] I'll talk about the StreamWeb-Socket class in this section and the MessageWebSocket class in the next section. The StreamWeb-Socket class is very similar to the StreamSocket class; here is what it looks like:

```
public sealed class StreamWebSocket : IWebSocket, IDisposable {
   public StreamWebSocket();

   // OPTIONAL: Modify connection (output buffer size, NoDelay, credentials)
   //           before calling ConnectAsync
   public StreamWebSocketControl Control { get; }

   // Returns connection read-only information (local address, protocol, bandwidth stats)
   public StreamWebSocketInformation Information { get; }

   // This event is raised when the server closes the connection
   public event TypedEventHandler<IWebSocket, WebSocketClosedEventArgs> Closed;

   // Adds an HTTP request header sent when ConnectAsync is called
   public void SetRequestHeader(String headerName, String headerValue);

   // Connect to a remote machine ("ws://" or "wss://")
   public IAsyncAction ConnectAsync(Uri uri);

   // After calling ConnectAsync, the app uses these to read & write data
   public IInputStream  InputStream  { get; }
   public IOutputStream OutputStream { get; }
```

---

[13] Beware that some proxy servers and routers do not support the WebSocket protocol properly, thus preventing its use in some environments.

[14] Internally, the WebSocket protocol specification defines Ping and Pong frames that are used for keep-alive, heartbeats, network status probing, latency instrumentation, and so forth. So, for some situations where real-time response is not necessary, polling might still be preferred because it doesn't keep the connection open, thereby freeing up resources.

[15] WinRT does not offer any class that allows an app to be a WebSocket server. However, Windows itself does support this, and the .NET Framework offers a System.Net.WebSockets namespace containing classes usable by desktop apps.

```
    // Closes the socket, indicating a reason and optional UTF-8 string with additional info
    public void Close(UInt16 code, String reason);

    public void Dispose();  // Close the socket
}
```

The WebSocket protocol defines a closing handshake. If the server closes the connection, the Closed event is raised. If you want to close the connection, just call the Dispose method or the Close method that takes a status code and reason.[16] For troubleshooting issues related to WebSockets, see the system event logs under the following: Applications And Services Logs > Microsoft > Windows > Websocket-Protocol-Component.

And here is code demonstrating how to use the StreamWebSocket class to send data to the publicly accessible WebSocket Echo service (which you can learn more about at *http://www.websocket.org/echo.html*):

```
private async Task StreamWebSocketClientAsync() {
    using (StreamWebSocket ws = new StreamWebSocket()) {
        // Connect to the remote service (use "wss" for secure WebSocket [TLS])
        await ws.ConnectAsync(new Uri("wss://echo.websocket.org/"));

        // Write a UInt32 (string length) & a UTF-8 string to the service:
        using (DataWriter dw = new DataWriter(ws.OutputStream)) {
            String s = "Jeffrey";
            dw.WriteUInt32(dw.MeasureString(s));
            dw.WriteString(s);
            await dw.StoreAsync();
        }

        // The WebSocket Echo service just returns back whatever you send it.
        // Read a UInt32 (string length) & a UTF-8 string response from the service:
        using (DataReader dr = new DataReader(ws.InputStream)
            { InputStreamOptions = InputStreamOptions.Partial }) {

            while (dr.UnconsumedBufferLength < sizeof(UInt32)) {
                await dr.LoadAsync(1024);
            }
            UInt32 stringLen = dr.ReadUInt32();
            while (dr.UnconsumedBufferLength < stringLen) {
                await dr.LoadAsync(1024);
            }
            String s = dr.ReadString(stringLen);
        }
    }
}
```

---

[16] You can and should think of the Dispose and Close methods as being overloads of each other. Remember the WinRT type system has an IClosable interface with a Close method, but the CLR projects this interface as IDisposable with its Dispose method.

MessageWebSocket: Messaging client-side WebSocket communication

Sometimes, it can be difficult to work with streaming protocols (as required by StreamSocket, StreamSocketListener, and StreamWebSocket). Instead, it's frequently useful to send messages back and forth. To simplify these scenarios, WinRT offers a MessageWebSocket class that sends and receives data as messages consisting of UTF-8 text or binary data. The MessageWebSocket class looks like this:

```
public sealed class MessageWebSocket : IWebSocket, IDisposable {
   public MessageWebSocket();

   // OPTIONAL: Modify connection (max msg size, msg type (binary/UTF8), output buffer size,
   //           credentials) before calling ConnectAsync
   public MessageWebSocketControl Control { get; }

   // Returns connection read-only information (local address, protocol, bandwidth stats)
   public MessageWebSocketInformation Information { get; }

   // This event is raised when a message is received
   public event TypedEventHandler<MessageWebSocket, MessageWebSocketMessageReceivedEventArgs>
      MessageReceived;

   // This event is raised when the server closes the connection
   public event TypedEventHandler<IWebSocket, WebSocketClosedEventArgs> Closed;

   // Adds an HTTP request header sent when ConnectAsync is called
   public void SetRequestHeader(string headerName, string headerValue);

   // Connect to a remote machine ("ws://" or "wss://")
   public IAsyncAction ConnectAsync(Uri uri);

   // After calling ConnectAsync, the app uses this to write a message
   public IOutputStream OutputStream { get; }

   // Closes the socket, indicating a reason and optional UTF-8 string with additional info
   public void Close(UInt16 code, String reason);

   public void Dispose();  // Close the socket
}
```

Here is a rewrite of the StreamWebSocketClientAsync method shown at the end of the previous section. This new version uses the MessageWebSocket class, greatly simplifying the code that processes the server's response:

```
private async void MessageWebSocketClientAsync() {
  using (MessageWebSocket socket = new MessageWebSocket()) {
    // You must register handlers before calling ConnectAsync
    socket.MessageReceived += OnWebSocketMessageReceived;
    await socket.ConnectAsync(new Uri("wss://echo.websocket.org/"));

    using (DataWriter dw = new DataWriter(socket.OutputStream)) {
      dw.WriteString("Jeffrey");
      await dw.StoreAsync();  // Send a "message" to the service
    }
  }
}

private void OnWebSocketMessageReceived(MessageWebSocket sender,
  MessageWebSocketMessageReceivedEventArgs args) {

  // The service responded with a "message"; read all of it as a string
  using (DataReader dr = args.GetDataReader()) {
    String s = dr.ReadString(dr.UnconsumedBufferLength);
  }
}
```

DatagramSocket: Peer-to-peer UDP communication

For peer-to-peer communication using the UDP protocol, WinRT offers the DatagramSocket class. The DatagramSocket class allows you to

- Send messages to another machine (act as a client).

- Receive messages from another machine (act as a server).

- Broadcast messages to multiple machines (multicast). This will be discussed in the next section.

The class itself looks like this:

```
public sealed class DatagramSocket : IDisposable {
  public DatagramSocket();

  // OPTIONAL: Modify connection (outbound unicast hop limit, QoS, don't fragment, inbound
  //           buffer size) before calling BindXxxAsync, ConnectAsync, or GetOutputStreamAsync
  public DatagramSocketControl Control { get; }

  // Returns connection read-only information (local & remote hostname/port)
  public DatagramSocketInformation Information { get; }

  // This event is raised whenever this socket receives a message
  public event TypedEventHandler<DatagramSocket, DatagramSocketMessageReceivedEventArgs>
    MessageReceived;

  // Call these methods to listen for incoming data (OS picks port if localServicename is "0").
  public IAsyncAction BindServiceNameAsync(String localServiceName);
  public IAsyncAction BindEndpointAsync(HostName localHostName, String localServiceName);

  // After calling BindXxxAsync, a listener can call this to listen for multicast data packets.
  public void JoinMulticastGroup(HostName host);
```

```
    // Call this method to send data to a single remote machine
    public IAsyncAction ConnectAsync(HostName remoteHostName, String remoteServiceName);
    public IAsyncAction ConnectAsync(EndpointPair endpointPair);

    // After calling ConnectAsync, the app uses this to send data to the remote machine
    public IOutputStream OutputStream { get; }

    // Call this method (instead of ConnectAsync) to make a single request to a remote machine
    public IAsyncOperation<IOutputStream>
        GetOutputStreamAsync(HostName remoteHostName, String remoteServiceName);
    public IAsyncOperation<IOutputStream> GetOutputStreamAsync(EndpointPair endpointPair);

    public void Dispose();   // Close the socket

    // Static methods returning all endpoints based on remote hostname/service name.
    // You can connect to one of the returned endpoints
    public static IAsyncOperation< IReadOnlyList<EndpointPair>> GetEndpointPairsAsync(
        HostName remoteHostName, String remoteServiceName);
    public static IAsyncOperation< IReadOnlyList<EndpointPair>> GetEndpointPairsAsync(
        HostName remoteHostName, String remoteServiceName, HostNameSortOptions sortOptions);
}
```

Here is an example that uses a DatagramSocket to establish a listening server. The server accepts a set of bytes, sums them together, and returns the sum back to the client:

```
// NOTE: Don't let the returned DatagramSocket be garbage collected
//       until you no longer want to accept messages
private async Task<DatagramSocket> StartDatagramServiceAsync(String localServiceName) {
    var datagramService = new DatagramSocket();

    // You must register handlers before calling BindXxxAsync
    datagramService.MessageReceived += OnDatagramServiceMessageReceived;
    await datagramService.BindServiceNameAsync(localServiceName); // Listen on desired port
    return datagramService;
}

private async void OnDatagramServiceMessageReceived(DatagramSocket sender,
    DatagramSocketMessageReceivedEventArgs e) {
    // NOTE: This method could be called by any thread; to update UI use a CoreDispatcher

    // Read request from client:
    DataReader dr = e.GetDataReader();
    Byte[] bytes = new Byte[dr.UnconsumedBufferLength];
    dr.ReadBytes(bytes);

    // Process client's request:
    Int32 sum = bytes.Sum(number => number);

    // Send response to client:
    IOutputStream outputStream =
        await sender.GetOutputStreamAsync(e.RemoteAddress, e.RemotePort);
    using (var dw = new DataWriter(outputStream)) {
        dw.WriteInt32(sum);
        await dw.StoreAsync();
    }
}
```

Here is the client-side code that demonstrates how to make multiple requests to the same server:

```
private async Task DatagramClientAsync() {
   HostName localhost = new HostName("localhost");

   // This pattern makes multiple requests to a single server:
   using (var socket = new DatagramSocket()) {
      // You must register handlers before calling ConnectAsync
      socket.MessageReceived += OnDatagramClientMessageReceived;

      // ConnectAsync implicitly binds to a port so the server can respond
      await socket.ConnectAsync(localhost, c_datagramServiceName);

      // Send the 1st request:
      await socket.OutputStream.WriteAsync(new Byte[] { 1, 2 }.AsBuffer());

      // Send the 2nd request:
      await socket.OutputStream.WriteAsync(new Byte[] { 2, 3 }.AsBuffer());
   }
}

private void OnDatagramClientMessageReceived(
   DatagramSocket sender, DatagramSocketMessageReceivedEventArgs e) {
   // NOTE: This method could be called by any thread; to update UI use a CoreDispatcher
   using (DataReader dr = e.GetDataReader()) {
      Int32 sum = dr.ReadInt32();
   }
}
```

You can use a different pattern to perform client requests to multiple servers. The following code demonstrates this pattern:

```
private async Task DatagramClientAsync() {
   HostName host1 = new HostName("server1.com");
   HostName host2 = new HostName("server2.com");

   // This pattern makes multiple requests to different servers:
   using (var socket = new DatagramSocket()) {
      // Register handler before calling GetOutputStreamAsync
      socket.MessageReceived += OnDatagramClientMessageReceived;

      // Send 1st request (GetOutputStreamAsync implicitly binds to a port
      // so the server can respond):
      IOutputStream output = await socket.GetOutputStreamAsync(host1, c_datagramServiceName);
      await output.WriteAsync(new Byte[] { 1, 2 }.AsBuffer());

      // Send  2nd request (GetOutputStreamAsync implicitly binds to a port
      // so the server can respond):
      output = await socket.GetOutputStreamAsync(host2, c_datagramServiceName);
      await output.WriteAsync(new Byte[] { 2, 3 }.AsBuffer());
   }
}
```

There is a crucial difference between ConnectAsync and GetOutputStreamAsync. When you use ConnectAsync, the local socket will accept response data only from the remote host/service name passed to `ConnectAsync`. You can verify this by creating a new `DatagramSocket` on the server and then use it to send a response. If you do this, you see that the client does not get the response. On the other hand, `GetOutputStreamAsync` accepts response data from any other host/service name.

ConnectAsync and `GetOutputStreamAsync` both have overloads that take an `EndpointPair` as a parameter. Because the definition of an `EndpointPair` is the two endpoints between a local and remote host, you can imagine there are multiple `EndpointPairs` from one machine to another. The static `GetOutputStreamAsync` method returns the endpoints. On my PC, I get three `EndpointPair` objects: one pair over IPv6 (Ethernet), and two pairs over IPv4 (Ethernet and Wi-Fi). By default, the system sorts these endpoint pairs in order of quickest connection. But this means that Windows might connect quickly to an unreliable connection. In your app, you can get the list sorted with the most-reliable connection first by calling `GetEndpointPairsAsync` and passing in the `HostNameSort-Options.OptimizeForLongConnections` flag.

DatagramSocket: Multicast UDP communication

With `DatagramSocket`, you can also send and receive UDP multicast packets. Multicast allows one machine to broadcast a data packet to a number of other machines simultaneously. The sender sends the packet once, and the network infrastructure (like routers) replicates the data as it gets forwarded to the receivers. Multicast is typically used to stream audio and video to a large number of clients.

You set up a PC as a multicast listener the exact same way you set up a `DatagramSocket` listener. But then you must join the socket to a multicast group by specifying a multicast IP address (which you can learn more about at *http://en.wikipedia.org/wiki/Multicast_address*):

```
// NOTE: Don't let the returned DatagramSocket be garbage collected
//       until you no longer want to accept messages
private async Task<DatagramSocket> StartMulticastListenerAsync(String localServiceName) {
   DatagramSocket multicastListener = new DatagramSocket();

   // You must register handlers before calling BindXxxAsync
   multicastListener.MessageReceived += OnMulticastListenerMessageReceived;
   await multicastListener.BindServiceNameAsync(localServiceName); // Listen on desired port

   // IPv4 multicast IP addresses: 224.0.0.0 to 239.255.255.255
   HostName hostname = new HostName("224.168.100.2"); // Pick a multicast IP address
   multicastListener.JoinMulticastGroup(hostname);    // Join socket to the multicast IP address
   return multicastListener;
}
```

When the socket receives a message, you process it as you normally would in the `OnMulticast-ListenerMessageReceived` event handler. In the handler, you can examine the `DatagramSocket-MessageReceivedEventArgs` object's `RemoteAddress` and `RemotePort` properties to determine which remote machine sent the data packet.

You can check how the multicast address is bound to the network cards with `netsh interface ipv4 show joins`. The output will be similar to what's shown next. Note how `224.168.100.2` is bound to all network interfaces.

```
C:\>netsh interface ipv4 show joins
Interface 1: Loopback Pseudo-Interface 1

Scope      References Last  Address
---------- ---------- ----  --------------------------------
0                   1 Yes   224.168.100.2
0                   4 Yes   239.255.255.250


Interface 13: Wi-Fi

Scope      References Last  Address
---------- ---------- ----  --------------------------------
0                   0 No    224.0.0.1
0                   1 Yes   224.0.0.252
0                   1 No    224.168.100.2
0                   4 No    239.255.255.250


Interface 12: Ethernet

Scope      References Last  Address
---------- ---------- ----  --------------------------------
0                   0 No    224.0.0.1
0                   1 No    224.0.0.252
0                   1 Yes   224.0.0.253
0                   1 No    224.168.100.2
0                   4 No    239.255.255.250


Interface 18: Bluetooth Network Connection

Scope      References Last  Address
---------- ---------- ----  --------------------------------
0                   0 Yes   224.0.0.1
0                   1 Yes   224.168.100.2
```

Sending data to a multicast group is identical to how you normally send data using a Data-gramSocket; you just need to use the multicast IP address and service name (port).

Encrypting data traversing the network with certificates

Frequently, when sending data over a network, you want to encrypt it so that other people cannot intercept the data you're sending. There are many ways to encrypt data as it traverses a network, but the most common way is using certificates. There are two ways a client app can encrypt data it wants to send to a server. The first way is by using a URI scheme. When using the BackgroundDownloader, BackgroundUploader, or HttpClient class, simply use "*https://*" instead of "*http://*". When using the MessageWebSocket or DatagramWebSocket class, use "*wss://*" instead of "*ws://*".

When using StreamSocket, you can specify a SocketProtectionLevel enumeration when calling ConnectAsync, or you can make a call to UpgradeToSslAsync once you establish a connection. The StreamSocketListener class does not have a mechanism of setting up Secure Sockets Layer (SSL) on the server side. Thus, your Windows Store app can participate only in an SSL connection to a server that exposes SSL, not to another Windows Store app.

You should also know that securing network traffic from a Windows Store app to your own web service is pretty easy. Here are the steps:

1. Create a certificate (it can be self-signed), and install it in the certificate store on your web server.

2. Export the certificate's public key into a .cer file.

3. In Visual Studio, open your Windows Store app's package manifest and go to the Declarations tab.

4. Under Available Declarations, select Certificates and click Add.

5. In the Trust Flags section, select Exclusive Trust if you want your Windows Store app to use only your certificate, ignoring any other certificates installed on the user's PC. If your app will communicate securely with multiple servers, do not select Exclusive Trust.

6. In the Store Name field, enter the name of the certificate store (such as Root) where you want the public key stored. Each package has its own private certificate store. In the Content field, navigate to the .cer file you exported in step 2.

Executing the preceding steps embeds the public key of your certificate in your package file and allows it to be used when communicating via SSL.

CHAPTER 8

Tile and toast notifications

The Start screen is the users' personal dashboard, containing information they care about. It consists of tiles, all nicely ordered with animating content. One glance shows you new email, the latest price of your favorite stocks, when and what your next appointment is, the latest weather information for locations you care about, and so on.

For developers, these tiles provide tremendous advantages compared to other platforms. Showing useful information in a tile compels the user to open your app more often. And the more time spent in your app, the better it is for you as an app developer if your app offers in-app advertising or in-app purchases. In addition to updating tile content, your app can place a badge over a tile drawing the user's attention to important information such as new emails or missed calls. The Start screen is designed to show information the *user* cares about. So users control whether your app's tile can reside on their Start screen, the size of the tile, and whether your app can update the tile's contents. Your app cannot control these things. In addition to containing tiles and badges, your app can also pop up toast notifications that inform the user of time-critical information, such as an incoming call or meeting reminders. Again, the user is in control and can silence toast notifications produced by your app.

In Chapter 3, "Process model," you saw that the system gives CPU time only to Windows Store apps in the foreground. So you might wonder how an app can update its tile's contents or pop up a toast notification when the app is in the background or not running at all. Tiles, badges, and toast notifications are updated using four techniques, summarized in Table 8-1. All of these techniques are explained in this chapter.

TABLE 8-1 Four techniques to update tiles, badges, and toast notifications.

Update technique	Applies to	Description and examples
Foreground	Tile Badge Toast	App's code updates the notification while the app is running in the foreground. Examples: Music app shows the current song; Game app shows the high score; Clear the badge when the app activates to reset an "unseen" notification (described later).
Scheduled	Tile Toast	App's code schedules the notification update for a future time. Examples: Calendar reminders, countdowns to something
Periodic	Tile Badge	App's code instructs Windows to periodically poll an HTTP(S) server. This is great for distributing the same content to a wide audience. You specify the URI, start time, and frequency of recurrence (such as a ½ hour, 1 hour, 6 hours, 12 hours, or 24 hours). Examples: Weather update, "daily deals" site
Push (WNS)	Tile Badge Toast	App's companion server pushes the notification to Windows on demand. This is great for personalized data, real-time data, or both. Examples: Breaking news, sports updates, social updates, incoming messages

Tiles and badges

Your app can use its tile for a variety of purposes. Of course, users can always tap or click a tile to launch an app. If the app is in the suspended state when the user taps its tile, the system brings the app back to the foreground, thereby using the tile as a mechanism to switch tasks. Users select one or more tiles by right-clicking and pressing the spacebar, or with a tap and hold gesture. The Start screen's app bar offers options to control the selected tiles. Specifically, the user can unpin an app's tile from the Start screen, uninstall the app, change the tile's size, and disable tile updates by tapping Turn Live Tile Off. (See Figure 8-1.)

FIGURE 8-1 App bar on the Start screen for a selected tile.

A user can remove personal information from all tiles (for example, when giving a presentation) via Settings pane > Tiles > Clear. Also, users can rearrange their tiles, group their tiles, and assign names to groups. In addition, users can zoom out to see more tiles using semantic zoom.[1] Desktop apps can also have tiles; however, the tiles are always square and their content cannot be updated. In addition, Internet Explorer can pin a website to the Start screen; this tile can update its contents periodically. For more information, see *http://www.buildmypinnedsite.com/*.

The Start screen supports four tile sizes (as shown in Figure 8-2). An app must provide static logos (images) for tile sizes that Windows requires and can optionally provide logos for tile sizes the app wishes to support. An app must also provide a logo used for the app's branding. The app must provide some additional logos if it supports certain background tasks that allow the app to be placed on the user's lock screen. (See Chapter 9, "Background tasks," for more information.) Table 8-2 lists the logos related to Start screen tiles, branding, and the lock screen.

FIGURE 8-2 The Start screen showing four small tiles (top left), one medium tile (with "Mail" as the branding name and "1" as the badge), one wide tile (bottom left, with a branding logo), and one large tile (with "Weather" as the branding name).

---

[1] Enter semantic zoom mode by pinching your fingers together, using Ctrl+Mouse wheel, or using Ctrl+Plus Sign or Ctrl+Minus Sign.

TABLE 8-2 App logos.

End-user term	Developer term	Manifest file name	Mandatory	Where shown
Small	Square 70x70	Square70x70Logo.png	✕	Start screen. This tile is always static; you cannot dynamically change its contents.
Medium	Square 150x150	Logo.png	✓	Start screen
Wide	Wide 310x150	WideLogo.png	✕	Start screen
Large	Square 310x310	Square310x310Logo.png	✕	Start screen
(N/A)	Square 30x30	SmallLogo.png	✓	Bottom/left portion of the tile, bottom/right portion of the toast, Start screen semantic zoom, App list, Search/Share panes, Open With dialog box
(N/A)	Badge 24x24	BadgeLogo.png	For some background tasks	Lock screen. The "badge logo" identifies the app on the user's lock screen. It is the app's badge. This logo is not related to the badge placed on a tile.

In Microsoft Visual Studio, you specify settings for your app's tile using the Visual Assets tab of the manifest designer as shown in Figure 8-3. The tile background color shows through the logo's transparent pixels. The file names you specify in the manifest are for your app's static tiles. These are the tiles the user sees unless your app executes some code that updates the tiles' contents or unless you set a URI template via the manifest's Tile Update settings. (See the "Updating a tile periodically" section for more information.)

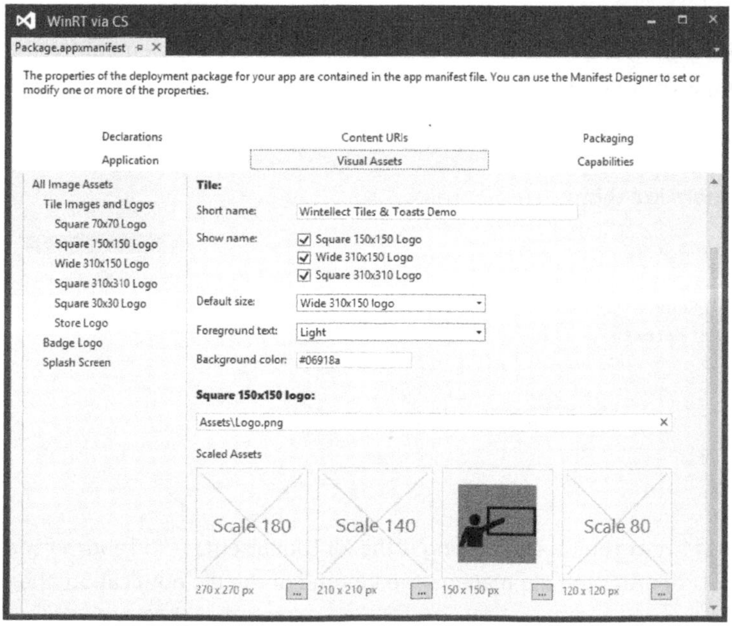

FIGURE 8-3 Tile settings in the manifest.

To accommodate users with screens of varying dots-per-inch (DPI), you should provide four DPI scalings for each tile logo: 80%, 100%, 140%, and 180%. So, when creating your app's medium logo, you should create four files: Logo.scale-80.png, Logo.scale-100.png, Logo.scale-140.png, and Logo.scale-180.png. For more information, see the "Accessing read-only package files" section in Chapter 5, "Storage files and folders."

Updating a tile when your app is in the foreground

Your app describes its tile's content to Windows declaratively. That is, your app creates an XML document describing the desired contents of the tile and then your app passes this XML document to Windows. Windows predefines several XML tile templates; each offers a different way to lay out text and images on the tile.[2] Windows then parses the document, builds the tile's image, and displays that image on the user's Start screen. So, in your code, you first start by creating an XML document that matches one of the predefined templates. The XML schema for tiles is documented at *http://msdn.microsoft.com/en-us/library/windows/apps/br212859.aspx*. The catalog of tile templates, along with examples of what each template produces, is documented at *http://msdn.microsoft.com/en-us/library/windows/apps/hh761491.aspx*.

Let's look at some code that updates your app's tile. Here we'll update a square 150-pixel by 150-pixel tile. You start by creating an XML document matching one of the predefined templates. To simplify this, WinRT provides an API that returns a predefined template. Here is an example of how to get an empty, predefined XML template:

```
XmlDocument tileXml =
    TileUpdateManager.GetTemplateContent(TileTemplateType.TileSquare150x150Text01);
```

Once you have this template, you modify the tile's text by retrieving the text element from the XmlDocument and appending a text node to it:

```
tileXml.GetElementsByTagName("text")[0].AppendChild(tileXml.CreateTextNode("New text"));
```

The XML document now looks like this:

```
<tile>
    <visual version="2">
        <binding template="TileSquare150x150Text01" fallback="TileSquareText01">
            <text id="1">New text</text>
            <text id="2"></text>
            <text id="3"></text>
            <text id="4"></text>
        </binding>
    </visual>
</tile>
```

Now you create a TileNotification object, passing it the XmlDocument. A TileNotification object offers some additional properties to help manage the lifetime of the tile notification; these

---

[2] If you need more control over your tile's content, create an image file containing any content you want and then have your tile show this image file.

will be described later. Then, to update your app's tile, you use the `TileUpdateManager` to create a `TileUpdater` object and then use this object to update your tile:

```
TileNotification tileNotification = new TileNotification(tileXml);
TileUpdater updater = TileUpdateManager.CreateTileUpdaterForApplication();
updater.Update(tileNotification);
```

If your app supports multiple tile sizes, you must prepare an XML template for each size, package all the templates together into a single XML document, create one `TileNotification` object from the XML document, and then update the tile. Remember, the user can change a tile's size whenever he wants. This is why you must include XML templates for all tile sizes; the system remembers the last `TileNotification` object you sent to it and will update the tile's content automatically if the user later changes its size.

This code demonstrates how to create an XML template for a square 150-by-150 tile and another XML template for a wide 310-by-150 tile, merge them together, and update the tile's content:

```
// Create square 150x150 tile template
XmlDocument tileXml =
    TileUpdateManager.GetTemplateContent(TileTemplateType.TileSquare150x150Text01);
tileXml.GetElementsByTagName("text")[0].AppendChild(tileXml.CreateTextNode("New text"));

// Create wide 310x150 tile template
XmlDocument wide310x150Xml =
    TileUpdateManager.GetTemplateContent(TileTemplateType.TileWide310x150ImageAndText01);
wide310x150Xml.GetElementsByTagName("text")[0]
    .AppendChild(wide310x150Xml.CreateTextNode("New text"));
wide310x150Xml.GetElementsByTagName("image")[0].Attributes.GetNamedItem("src")
    .NodeValue = "ms-appx:///Assets/snowday.jpg";

// Merge the two tile templates into a single XML document:
IXmlNode node =
    tileXml.ImportNode(wide310x150Xml.GetElementsByTagName("binding").Item(0), true);
tileXml.GetElementsByTagName("visual").Item(0).AppendChild(node);
```

The resulting XML document looks like this:

```
<tile>
    <visual version="2">
        <binding template="TileSquare150x150Text01" fallback="TileSquareText01">
            <text id="1">New text</text>
            <text id="2"></text>
            <text id="3"></text>
            <text id="4"></text>
        </binding>
        <binding template="TileWide310x150ImageAndText01" fallback="TileWideImageAndText01">
            <image id="1" src="ms-appx:///Assets/snowday.jpg"/>
            <text id="1">New text</text>
        </binding>
    </visual>
</tile>
```

Note how we set the image on the wide tile. When setting an `image` element's `src` attribute, the URL can start with any of the values from Table 8-3.

TABLE 8-3 URL prefixes for tile images.

URL prefix	Description	Notes
ms-appx:///	Use this to refer to an image file shipped in your app's package.	The three slashes after the colon are required. See Chapter 5 for more details.
ms-appdata:///local/	Use this to refer to an image file existing in your app's local storage folder. Note you cannot refer to images under your app's temporary or roaming folders.	
http:// or https://	Use this to refer to an image that should be downloaded from a web server.	The system can automatically concatenate a query string to the URL indicating the required image scale (80, 100, 140, 180), contrast, and language based on the user's current environment.

> **Important** The system supports JPEG, PNG, and GIF image formats only. In addition, images must not exceed 200 KB, and neither the height nor the width can be more than 1024 pixels. If your image violates any of these rules, the system discards your XML and does not update your app's tile. This can be quite frustrating, because the APIs do not provide you any indication of failure. However, the system will write an error entry to this event log at Applications And Services Logs > Microsoft > Windows > Apps > Microsoft-Windows-TWinUI-Operational.

Placing a badge on a tile

Placing a badge on a tile is similar to how you update a tile's contents. Instead of using `Tile-UpdateManager`, you use `BadgeUpdateManager` to retrieve one of the two `BadgeTemplateTypes`: BadgeNumber or BadgeGlyph. Then you modify the `XmlDocument`, use the document to create a `BadgeNotification`, and hand the notification to the badge updater:

```
XmlDocument xmlBadge = BadgeUpdateManager.GetTemplateContent(BadgeTemplateType.BadgeNumber);
// Passing BadgeTemplateType.BadgeGlpyh to GetTemplateContent returns identical XML as above

XmlNodeList badgeAttributes = xmlBadge.GetElementsByTagName("badge");
badgeAttributes[0].Attributes.GetNamedItem("value").NodeValue = "7";  // Set value to a number

BadgeNotification badgeNotification = new BadgeNotification(xmlBadge);
BadgeUpdater bu = BadgeUpdateManager.CreateBadgeUpdaterForApplication();
bu.Update(new BadgeNotification(xmlBadge));
```

To see the XML schema for badges, go to *http://msdn.microsoft.com/en-us/library/windows/apps/br212851.aspx*. To see the catalog of badge templates, visit *http://msdn.microsoft.com/en-us/library/windows/apps/hh779719.aspx*. This catalog is also shown in Figure 8-4. You use the status string in the first column to have the badge show a glyph. To have the previous code show a glyph instead of a number, change the fourth line of code to this:

```
badgeAttributes[0].Attributes.GetNamedItem("value").NodeValue = "attention";
```

Status	Glyph	XML
none	No badge shown	`<badge value="none"/>`
activity	 ⟳	`<badge value="activity"/>`
alarm	 🔔	`<badge value="alarm"/>`
alert	 ✳	`<badge value="alert"/>`
available	○	`<badge value="available"/>`
away	○	`<badge value="away"/>`
busy	○	`<badge value="busy"/>`
newMessage	 ✉	`<badge value="newMessage"/>`
paused	 ❚❚	`<badge value="paused"/>`
playing	 ▶	`<badge value="playing"/>`
unavailable	◎	`<badge value="unavailable"/>`
error	 ✖	`<badge value="error"/>`
attention	 ❗	`<badge value="attention"/>`

FIGURE 8-4 The badge glyphs you can put on a tile.

To reset a tile back to its static logo or remove a badge from a tile, just call `TileUpdateManager`'s or `BadgeUpdateManager`'s `Clear` method:

```
// Reset the tile back to its static logo & remove its badge:
TileUpdateManager.CreateTileUpdaterForApplication().Clear();
BadgeUpdateManager.CreateBadgeUpdaterForApplication().Clear();
```

Live tiles typically show content that is fresh, and there are occasions when it is better to show nothing at all instead of showing old content. For example, you should not show weather temperatures or stock prices that are seven days old or older. To enable you to automatically remove old content, `TileNotification` objects offer an `ExpirationTime` property. The system automatically deletes a tile notification when its time expires and reverts the tile back to its static logo:

```
TileNotification tileNotification = new TileNotification(tileXml) {
    ExpirationTime = DateTimeOffset.Now.AddDays(7)
};
updater.Update(tileNotification);
```

Animating a tile's contents

There is a quick and easy way to animate a tile using predefined *peek* templates. Each peek template describes two views of a tile, and the Start screen automatically cycles from one view to the other every few seconds. The following XML template is the TileSquarePeekImageAndText01 template:

```xml
<tile>
  <visual version="2">
    <binding template="TileSquare150x150PeekImageAndText01"
             fallback="TileSquarePeekImageAndText01">
      <image id="1" src=""/>
      <text id="1"></text>
      <text id="2"></text>
      <text id="3"></text>
      <text id="4"></text>
    </binding>
  </visual>
</tile>
```

As documented, when the system receives XML containing this template, it shows one square image without text on the top, one header string in larger text on the first line, and three strings of regular text on each of the next three lines on the bottom. Figure 8-5 shows an example of this tile's appearance.

FIGURE 8-5 The contents of a peek square tile (for which the system cycles between the top and bottom automatically).

The system shows the top half of the contents in the tile, waits a few seconds, shows the bottom half, waits a few seconds, and shows the top half again. This cycling happens continuously and automatically while the user is looking the Start screen.

In addition to using peek templates, your app can queue up to five tile notifications to a single tile and the Start screen will automatically cycle through them. You enable queuing by calling Tile-UpdateManager's EnableNotificationQueue method and passing in true. The following code creates five tile notifications and queues them to the app's tile:

```
TileUpdater tu = TileUpdateManager.CreateTileUpdaterForApplication();
tu.EnableNotificationQueue(true);  // Enable queuing up to 5 notifications

// Queue 5 tile notifications to our app's tile:
for (Int32 tileNum = 0; tileNum < 5; tileNum++) {
   XmlDocument tileXml =
      TileUpdateManager.GetTemplateContent(TileTemplateType.TileSquare150x150Text01);
   tileXml.GetElementsByTagName("text")[0].AppendChild(tileXml.CreateTextNode("#" + tileNum));
   tu.Update(new TileNotification(tileXml));
}
```

Offering multiple tile notifications allows apps to cycle through multiple news feeds, email messages, stock prices, or weather temperatures, giving the user a lot of information at a glance. For developers, it becomes a challenge not to provide too much information.

Once you associate a set of tile notifications with a tile, your app can be suspended or terminated; the Start screen will still cycle through the notifications, giving the user the illusion that your app is still running. Consider how power and CPU efficient it is to have only the Start screen do this work for all apps instead of having every app update its own tile by executing code in the background.

If you add more than five tiles to the queue, the system replaces the oldest using a first-in, first-out (FIFO) algorithm. However, your app can replace a specific tile notification by specifying a tag string:

```
TileNotification tileNotification = new TileNotification(tileXml) { Tag = "MSFT" };
```

Now when we want to replace this tile notification, we just specify the same tag string:

```
TileNotification tileNotification1 = new TileNotification(tileXml) { Tag = "MSFT" };
tu.Update(tileNotification1);
```

Tag strings have a 16-character limit, and your app can use tags only to replace or remove tile notifications. Unfortunately, if the user launches your app via its tile, your app will not receive the tag of the currently visible tile notification. So your app can't display different content based on a specific tile notification. If you want your app to navigate to different content, your app can use secondary tiles (discussed in the "Secondary tiles" section).

So far, the methods shown require your app to be running in the foreground to update its tile's content. In addition, your app can implement a background task. (See Chapter 9.) Background tasks can run periodically or when a trigger (for example, a user logon) occurs. Although the system does not allow background tasks to manipulate an app's user interface in any way, a background task's code can update the app's tile or badge, or show a toast notification.

In addition, there are several techniques allowing your app to update its tile's content while no code is running. The next section, "Updating a tile at a scheduled time," shows how to schedule a tile notification to activate itself in the future. The "Updating a tile periodically" section shows how to have the system periodically poll a web server for a new XML template. And, much later in this chapter, the "The Windows Push Notification Service (WNS)" section shows how you can manage your own web server in the cloud that can push XML templates down to your app's tile for a particular user on a particular machine.

Updating a tile at a scheduled time

In your app, you can use `ScheduledTileNotification` to have the system update your app's tile sometime in the future:

```
XmlDocument tileXml =
    TileUpdateManager.GetTemplateContent(TileTemplateType.TileSquare150x150Text01);
tileXml.GetElementsByTagName("text")[0].AppendChild(tileXml.CreateTextNode("Eat lunch"));
ScheduledTileNotification stn =
    new ScheduledTileNotification(tileXml, DateTimeOffset.Now.AddHours(2)) {
        ExpirationTime = DateTimeOffset.Now.AddMinutes(30)
    };
TileUpdateManager.CreateTileUpdaterForApplication().AddToSchedule(stn);
```

Here we schedule a tile notification that activates itself in two hours. Additionally, the tile notification expires 30 minutes from the time it is scheduled. You can schedule up to 4,096 tiles in advance. This is useful if you want to implement a countdown timer.

Updating a tile periodically

Your app can tell the system to get tile notifications from a web server periodically. Here is an example that has the Start screen poll a web server of your app's choosing every 30 minutes for a new tile template:

```
TileUpdater tu = TileUpdateManager.CreateTileUpdaterForApplication();
tu.StartPeriodicUpdate(
    new Uri("http://WintellectNOW.blob.core.windows.net/public/TileTemplates.xml"),
    DateTimeOffset.UtcNow.AddSeconds(10), PeriodicUpdateRecurrence.HalfHour);
```

Your app can, of course, use the URL to pass additional information to the web server in a query string. For example, your app can send a ZIP code to indicate location information that the web server can use to return an XML template targeted for your app's specific needs ("http://SomeWeatherService.com?Zip=98033").

Call `TileUpdateManager`'s `StopPeriodicUpdate` method to have the Start screen stop polling your web server.

In your app's package manifest, you can enable periodic updates for your app's tile. This allows your app's tile to start showing useful information right after the user installs your app. See the Tile Update section on the Application tab in Visual Studio's package manifest designer.

Secondary tiles

In addition to an app's main tile, an app can have one or more secondary tiles on the Start screen. Secondary tiles have the same capabilities as the app's main tile, including badges, peek templates, queuing up to five tile notifications, scheduled updates, periodic updates, and also Windows Push Notifications. When a user launches your app from a secondary tile, the system passes in a launch parameter to your app so that your app can display different content depending on which tile the user tapped. Examples of secondary tiles are stock-ticker apps with several tiles for different stocks or a weather app with a tile for each geographic location. Having a secondary tile launch your app to a specific stock or location within your app is sometimes referred to as *deep linking*.

Because users are always in control of their Start screen, your app can't just add a secondary tile to it. Instead, your app calls a WinRT API that prompts the user to pin a secondary tile to the Start screen. The user can approve or deny this operation. Most apps expose functionality to add secondary tiles through a Pin To Start button in the app bar, but this is not a requirement. Here is an example of how you create a secondary tile for your app:

```
String baseUri = "ms-appx:///Assets/";
String tileId = "SecondaryTile";
SecondaryTile tile = new SecondaryTile(tileId) {     // ID passed to OnLaunched
    Arguments = "Some argument",                     // Args passed to OnLaunched (can't be "")
    DisplayName = "2nd tile-Display Name",
    RoamingEnabled = true                            // Default is true
};
// Properties common to all tile sizes:
tile.VisualElements.BackgroundColor = Colors.Green;
tile.VisualElements.ForegroundText = ForegroundText.Light;   // Dark=#2A2A2A, Light=#FFFFFF
tile.VisualElements.Square30x30Logo = new Uri(c_baseUri + "SmallLogo.png"); // Optional

// Select tile sizes to offer the user:
tile.VisualElements.Square150x150Logo = new Uri(c_baseUri + "Logo.png"); // Mandatory
tile.VisualElements.ShowNameOnSquare150x150Logo = false;

// The following logos are optional:
tile.VisualElements.Square70x70Logo = new Uri(c_baseUri + "Square70x70Logo.png");
tile.VisualElements.Wide310x150Logo = new Uri(c_baseUri + "WideLogo.png");
tile.VisualElements.ShowNameOnWide310x150Logo = true;
tile.VisualElements.Square310x310Logo = new Uri(c_baseUri + "Square310x310Logo.png");
tile.VisualElements.ShowNameOnSquare310x310Logo = true;

// Ask user to create the secondary tile:
Boolean userCreated = await tile.RequestCreateAsync();
```

Because you can't define any settings for secondary tiles in the manifest, you have to specify all the properties in code. Secondary tiles have two string properties, called `TileId` and `Arguments`. When a user launches your app from its secondary tile, the system passes these strings to your app's `OnLaunched` method as members of the `LaunchActivatedEventArgs` parameter. The `TileId` identifies the secondary tile, and the `Arguments` property is a string with a maximum length of 2,048 characters that your app can use to distinguish further between a launch from a primary tile and a secondary tile.[3]

A cool feature of secondary tiles is that they are allowed to roam across all of a user's machines. When creating a secondary tile, its `RoamingEnabled` property defaults to `true`. Now, if the user installs the app on another PC, the secondary tile will appear on the other PC's Start screen automatically. Of course, this requires that the user log in to both PCs using her Microsoft account. Secondary

---

[3] When the user launches your app via its primary tile, the `TileId` property will be set to a value defined in your app's manifest—specifically, the `Application` element's `Id` attribute. Usually, this has a value of "App". At runtime, your app can get this value by querying the `Windows.ApplicationModel.Core.CoreApplication.Id` property.

tiles only roam on first installation. After this, the user can modify the secondary tiles independently on her PCs; this allows the user to have some secondary tiles on one PC but not on a different PC.

The call to RequestCreateAsync shows the user a dialog box like the one shown in Figure 8-6. From this dialog box, the user scrolls through the offered tile sizes and can edit the name displayed on the tile. Your app can also prompt the user to remove a secondary tile from the start screen by calling RequestDeleteAsync.

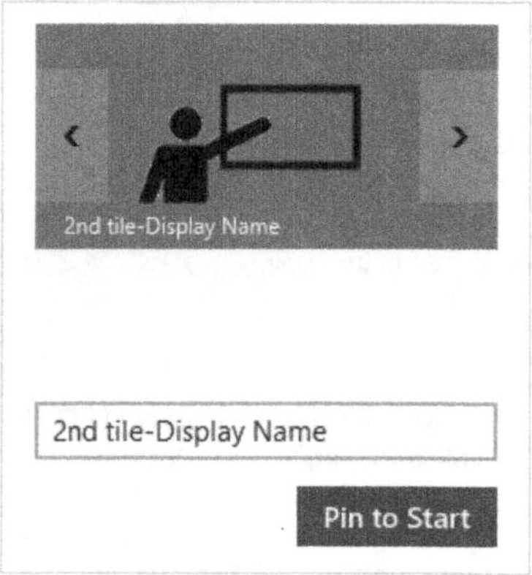

FIGURE 8-6 Secondary tile approval dialog box.

A user can unpin a tile from the Start screen at any time even if its app is not running. Later, when the app does run, it can determine if a particular secondary tile is still pinned by calling this method:

```
Boolean tileOnStartScreen = SecondaryTile.Exists(tileId);
```

And an app can discover all the secondary tiles it still has pinned on the Start screen by calling

```
IReadOnlyList<SecondaryTile> pinnedSecondaryTiles = await SecondaryTile.FindAllAsync();
```

Toast notifications

An app can pop up toast notifications that notify the user of some time-sensitive information. Examples include incoming calls, completion of a download, a printer running out of paper, and so on. Note that the app can always pop up a toast notification; the user does not have to be interacting with the app. Figure 8-7 shows what a toast notification looks like. (The small 30-pixel by 30-pixel logo is shown at the bottom right.) The user can ignore, dismiss, or tap the toast notification. Tapping the toast notification launches its app, bringing it to the foreground. Toast notifications can be accompanied by sound, and they can vary in duration and be tailored for different purposes, such as incoming calls or calendar reminders.[4]

---

[4] Desktop apps can use WinRT APIs to show toast notifications as well. See the sample at *http://code.msdn.microsoft. com/windowsdesktop/sending-toast-notifications-71e230a2/*.

FIGURE 8-7 Example of a toast notification on the desktop.

As with tiles, the user is in control of toast notifications. By default, Windows allows toast notifications to display; however, the user can disable toasts for a specific app by going to the app's Settings pane as shown in Figure 8-8.

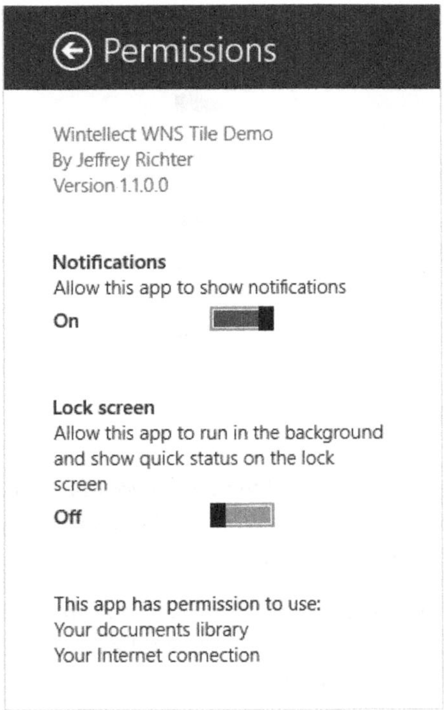

← Permissions

Wintellect WNS Tile Demo
By Jeffrey Richter
Version 1.1.0.0

Notifications
Allow this app to show notifications

On

Lock screen
Allow this app to run in the background
and show quick status on the lock
screen

Off

This app has permission to use:
Your documents library
Your Internet connection

FIGURE 8-8 An app's Settings pane, allowing the user to disable the app's toast notifications.

Users can also manage toast notification settings for all their installed apps and for the system as a whole in PC Settings > Search And Apps > Notifications as Figure 8-9 shows.[5]

---

[5] The Settings charm and Control Panel say *Notifications*, but this setting applies only to toast notifications. Tile and badge notifications are unaffected.

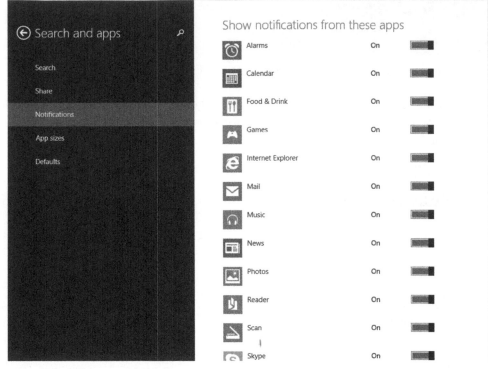

FIGURE 8-9 Controlling apps' notifications from PC Settings.

If you want your app to display toast notifications, you must first enable them in your app's manifest: under the Application section, set Toast Capable to Yes. This is how Windows knows to add your app to the app's permission settings pane and to the PC Settings Notifications pane.

The XML schema for toast notifications is similar to the one for tile notifications. You can find it here: *http://msdn.microsoft.com/en-us/library/windows/apps/br230846.aspx*. To see the catalog of toast templates, see *http://msdn.microsoft.com/en-us/library/windows/apps/hh761494.aspx*.

Here is how to create a toast notification:

```
ToastNotifier tn = ToastNotificationManager.CreateToastNotifier();

// If the user disabled our app's toast notifications, just return
if (tn.Setting != NotificationSetting.Enabled) return;

// Build the toast notification's XML template:
XmlDocument toastXml = ToastNotificationManager.GetTemplateContent(
   ToastTemplateType.ToastImageAndText01);

// Set image and text:
toastXml.GetElementsByTagName("image")[0].Attributes.GetNamedItem("src")
   .NodeValue = "ms-appx:///Assets/snowday.jpg";
toastXml.GetElementsByTagName("text")[0]
   .AppendChild(toastXml.CreateTextNode("This is a toast notification."));
```

```csharp
// Set launch argument:
XmlAttribute launch = toastXml.CreateAttribute("launch");
launch.Value = "Launch argument goes here";
toastXml.GetElementsByTagName("toast")[0].Attributes.SetNamedItem(launch);

// Set duration:
XmlAttribute duration = toastXml.CreateAttribute("duration");
duration.Value = "long"; // or "short"
toastXml.GetElementsByTagName("toast")[0].Attributes.SetNamedItem(duration);

// Set audio sound:
XmlElement audio = toastXml.CreateElement("audio");
var audioA = toastXml.GetElementsByTagName("toast")[0].AppendChild(audio);
var audioSrc = toastXml.CreateAttribute("src");
audioSrc.Value = "ms-winsoundevent:Notification.Looping.Call";
audioA.Attributes.SetNamedItem(audioSrc);
var loop = toastXml.CreateAttribute("loop");
loop.Value = "true";
audioA.Attributes.SetNamedItem(loop);

// Pop up the toast notification
tn.Show(new ToastNotification(toastXml));
```

The XML toast template for this toast notification looks like this:

```xml
<toast launch="Launch parameters go here" duration="long">
   <visual>
      <binding template="ToastImageAndText01">
         <image id="1" src="ms-appx:///Assets/snowday.jpg"/>
         <text id="1">This is a toast notification.</text>
      </binding>
   </visual>
   <audio src="ms-winsoundevent:Notification.Looping.Call" loop="true"/>
</toast>
```

Once the system displays a toast notification, the user can ignore it, dismiss it, or activate it. Most apps only care about the user activating the toast so that the user can perform some action. When the user activates a toast, Windows activates its app and calls the virtual OnLaunched method, and the app can respond however it wants.

```csharp
protected override void OnLaunched(LaunchActivatedEventArgs args) {
   // For a toast notification, args's TileId property equals
   // Windows.ApplicationModel.Core.CoreApplication.Id
   // Query args.Arguments for launch arguments set in XML ("Launch parameters go here")
   ...
```

Usually, an app will not display toast notifications if the app is in the foreground. Doing so is unnecessary because the app already has the user's attention. However, ToastNotification does expose three events that an app can register callback methods with: Activated, Dismissed, and Failed.

When the user activates the toast, the system resumes your app (if suspended), raises the Activated event,[6] and then calls the OnLaunched method. When the user dismisses a toast, the system raises the Dismissed event if your app is running. If your app is not running, the Dismissed event is raised after the user resumes your app.[7] Additionally, your Dismissed event handler is passed a ToastDismissedEventArgs parameter indicating how the toast got dismissed (the user canceled it, the toast timed-out, or your app called ToastNotifier's Hide method). Note that the system raises these events on non-GUI threads, so you must marshal to the GUI thread if you want to update the UI in response to these events. The system will not raise any of these events if your app is terminated; the system will just launch your app and call its OnLaunched method.

When preparing the XML toast template, you get to specify how long the toast should appear to the user before automatically dismissing itself. By default, toast notifications appear for a short duration of seven seconds; the alternative is a long duration of 25 seconds. Typically, you use short-duration toasts for simple notifications that don't require the user to launch your app—for example, the arrival of new email or a social media update. On the other hand, long-duration toasts are more appropriate for events when someone else is waiting, such as when someone is initiating a chat message or there is an incoming phone call.

When displaying a toast notification, the system can also play a sound. To do this, you need to give the toast template an "audio" element. By default, this is a one-time sound, which is appropriate for short-duration toasts such as email notifications or appointment reminders. Although your app can't specify its own custom sounds, you can choose from a predefined set of system sounds. Your app can also specify that the toast needs to play the audio in a loop (loop=true), which requires the toast's duration to be long.

Showing a toast notification at a scheduled time

When your app is in the foreground, the usefulness of showing toast notifications is somewhat limited. The purpose of toasts notifications is to notify the user of something important happening in an app that is not in the foreground. For this, your app can show a toast from a background task that runs when certain events happen, such as logon or a network status change. (See Chapter 9.) Additionally, your app can schedule a toast to pop up at a very specific time—for example, an appointment reminder. Here's how to schedule a toast to display one hour from when the code executes:

```
ScheduledToastNotification scheduledToastNotification = new ScheduledToastNotification(toastXml,
    DateTimeOffset.UtcNow.AddHours(1),  // Delivery time
    TimeSpan.FromMinutes(1),            // Snooze interval (minimum=1 minute)
    2) { Id = "Meeting" };              // Max display count & ID

tn.AddToSchedule(scheduledToastNotification);
```

---

[6] The Activated event's signature indicates that it passes a ToastNotification and Object; however, you can cast the second argument to a ToastActivatedEventArgs and query its Arguments property to see which ToastNotification was activated.

[7] Interestingly, the system raises the Dismissed event before the Resuming event. Thus, you need to be careful with assumptions about the state of your app if it does anything in the Resuming event handler.

We also set a snooze interval that tells the system to show the toast again if the user ignores or dismisses the toast notification. With the recurrence setting of 2, the toast will actually appear three times. You can use the `ToastNotifier` to iterate through the scheduled toasts and remove them from the schedule if they are no longer applicable.

Because it is unlikely that your app will be running when the scheduled toast comes up, the system does not support the `Activated`, `Dismissed`, and `Failed` events for scheduled toasts. When the user taps a scheduled toast, the system calls `UnLaunched` regardless of whether your app was running, suspended, or terminated.

Using the Wintellect Notification Extension Library

Working with the raw XML to create your tile, badge, and toast notifications can become tedious. The code that accompanies this book has a library to help you focus on the notifications instead of the XML.[8] The library gives you type-safety and IntelliSense support. Using the library, the code to produce the XML toast template shown in the previous section looks like this:

```
var toastXml = new Wintellect.WinRT.Notifications.ToastTemplate(
    ToastTemplateType.ToastImageAndText01) {
    Images = { "ms-appx:///Assets/snowday.jpg" },
    Text = { "This is a toast notification." },
    Launch = "Launch argument goes here",
    Audio = new ToastAudio { Loop = true, Source = SoundEvent.LoopingCall },
    Duration = ToastDuration.Long,
};
```

Additionally, the library also checks whether images exist at the specified URLs and that they are in a supported format and size. If a violation is discovered, the library throws an exception right away, greatly improving your debugging experience.

Windows Push Notification Service (WNS)

Table 8-1 listed four ways to update tiles, badges, and toast notifications. In this section, we focus on the last technique, Windows Push Notification Service (WNS).

Periodic updates with URLs go a long way in updating your app's tiles and badges, especially because you can personalize the notifications by using query strings. I already mentioned providing a ZIP code for weather apps. You also can provide a list of stock symbols to adjust the tile to the user's preferences, and so on. Periodic updates suffer from their resolution; they can update no quicker than once every 30 minutes. For some scenarios, you want to notify the user immediately that something has occurred. Examples include flight updates, incoming messages, social updates, and investment changes. WNS sends real-time tile, badge, or toast notifications to a specific user on a specific PC. Whereas periodic updates use a polling mechanism, WNS allows you to push a notification to a user/machine when you need to. Because WNS doesn't waste network bandwidth or CPU cycles for

---

[8] Microsoft also has the NotificationsExtensions library. For more information, see *http://msdn.microsoft.com/en-us/library/windows/apps/Hh969156.aspx*.

potentially unfruitful requests, it is more efficient than polling. This is great news for both your user's battery as well as his network bandwidth.

In addition to tiles, badges, and toast notifications, WNS can also send a raw string to a background task (or to your app if it happens to be running). Your app subscribes to these raw notifications, and because a raw string is an app-defined string payload, your server can send whatever it wants. You'll learn about this more in Chapter 9.

You can see the flow of events for WNS in Figure 8-10. The architecture consists of three pieces: Windows and your app, WNS, and your app's web service. At a high level, here are the workflow steps you need to perform to push notifications from your app's web service to your app on a user's PC:

1. Your app registers itself and the user's PC with WNS; WNS returns a unique-channel URI.

2. Your app then sends this channel URI to your app's web service. Typically, you save all your user's channel URIs in a database of some sort.

3. When your app's web service wants to notify a user of something, it looks up the user's channel URI from the database and sends the desired tile, badge, toast, or raw notification to WNS.

4. WNS then pushes the notification down to the user's PC, which then updates the tile or badge, displays a toast, or invokes your app's background task.

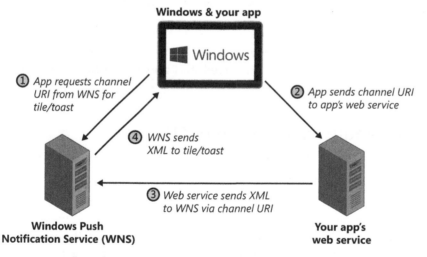

FIGURE 8-10 Windows Push Notification Service workflow.

Registering your app and the user's PC with WNS

Your app registers itself and the user's PC with WNS as follows:

```
PushNotificationChannel channel =
    await PushNotificationChannelManager.CreatePushNotificationChannelForApplicationAsync();
// channel has 2 properties: Uri and ExpirationTime
```

Also, multiple calls to `CreatePushNotificationChannelForApplicationAsync` return the same channel URI. Channel URIs expire every 30 days or so. (`PushNotificationChannel`'s `Expira-tionTime` property returns the channel's expiration time.) So your app will have to periodically renew its channel URI and send the latest URI to your app's web service. The best way to accomplish this is to create a maintenance background task that runs every 25 days or so. (See Chapter 9.)

To update a secondary tile's content or badge, get a channel URI by calling `PushNotifica-tionChannelManager`'s `CreatePushNotificationChannelForSecondaryTileAsync` method. Because users can unpin secondary tiles from the Start screen at any time, you should renew their channel URIs only if they are still present on the Start screen. A typical channel URI looks like this (truncated):

```
https://db3.notify.windows.com/?token=AQI8iP%20tQE%3d...
```

Note that the format of the channel URI is an implementation detail, and there is no need for you to examine or parse it; just send it to your service. As you can deduce from the channel URI string, the WNS client opens a secure connection to `notify.windows.com`. This connection needs to remain open so that WNS can push notifications. It also means that the firewall on the user's PC and poten-tially the proxy server have to allow HTTPS communication to *windows.com*.

If your app is running when WNS pushes a notification, your app can intercept the notification, execute some code in response, and even cancel the notification if it desires. Your app intercepts a pushed WNS notification by registering an event handler with `PushNotificationChannel`'s `Push-NotificationReceived` event:

```
channel.PushNotificationReceived += PushNotificationReceived;
```

In the event handler, the system passes you the notification as a property of the `PushNotifica-tionReceivedEventArgs` argument. Your callback can tell the system to ignore the notification by setting the `Cancel` property to `true`:

```
void PushNotificationReceived(PushNotificationChannel sender,
   PushNotificationReceivedEventArgs e) {

   XmlDocument xml = null;
   switch (e.NotificationType) {
      case PushNotificationType.Tile:  xml    = e.TileNotification.Content;  break;
      case PushNotificationType.Badge: xml    = e.BadgeNotification.Content; break;
      case PushNotificationType.Toast: xml    = e.ToastNotification.Content; break;
      case PushNotificationType.Raw:   String s = e.RawNotification.Content;  break;
   }
   // e.Cancel = true;  // If true (default=false), notification ignored
}
```

An app can call `PushNotificationChannel`'s `Close` method to invalidate the channel. This pre-vents all future notifications from being delivered to the app. It also prevents any tile, badge, toast, or raw notifications from being processed on the PC.

Send the channel URI to your app's web service

Once your app has a channel URI, it needs to send it and its expiration time to your app's web service. The web service is responsible for storing this information and any other information you might need to associate it with the specific user. The service uses this channel to periodically push notifications to the user's PC. The web service should automatically purge any expired channel URIs; avoid pushing notifications to an expired channel URI via WNS.

WNS does not give your app infinite bandwidth to push notifications. WNS has a quota per app that is not documented. WNS returns HTTP 404 (not found) or 410 (gone [channel expired]) errors when channel URIs you send it are no longer valid; your app's web service should remove these from its database and no longer attempt to use them. Unless you're sure it makes sense for your scenario, the app's web service should avoid retrying POSTs to WNS.

To prevent anyone from pushing notifications to your app, you must register your app with the WNS service. You configure your app to use WNS using the Windows Store Dashboard on Microsoft's Dev Center site (*http://dev.windows.com/*).[9] First, you need to reserve an app name in the Windows Store (as discussed in Chapter 11, "Windows Store"). Then, from Visual Studio, associate your app with the reserved name using Project menu > Store > Associate App With The Store. The wizard sets your Store-assigned package identity name and publisher in your app's manifest file. Alternatively, you can use the dashboard to show this information and then you can edit the manifest XML file yourself.

The Windows Store creates a Package Security ID (SID) and Client secret for your package. Your app's web service must authenticate with WNS using these credentials. You get these values by going to your app in the Windows Store dashboard, clicking Services > Live Services Site > Authenticating Your Service. The values will look similar to these:

```
Package Security Identifier (SID)
ms-app://s-1-15-2-84216977-2665019123-2024476369-118581892-194604365-2052745452-3234447176

Client secret
6TbboOHv1mQVIXbm7r/X+Q4PVH9IbxY1
```

You need these values in the next step to authenticate your app's web service with WNS.

Pushing a notification from your app's web service to the user's PC

To push a notification, your app's web service will first have to authenticate with WNS, which will return an OAuth token. The following code demonstrates how to do this:

```
[DataContract]
private sealed class OAuthToken {
   [DataMember(Name = "access_token")]
   public string AccessToken { get; set; }
   [DataMember(Name = "token_type")]
   public string TokenType { get; set; }
}
```

---

[9] This means that you can't use WNS for apps that are not in the store, such as enterprise side-loaded apps.

```
private async Task<OAuthToken> GetAuthenticationTokenAsync(
    String packageSid, String clientSecret) {

    var content = new Windows.Web.Http.HttpFormUrlEncodedContent(
        new Dictionary<String, String> {
            { "grant_type", "client_credentials"},
            { "client_id", packageSid },
            { "client_secret", clientSecret},
            { "scope", "notify.windows.com"]
        });
    using (var response =
        await new HttpClient()
            .PostAsync(new Uri("https://login.live.com/accesstoken.srf"), content)
            .AsTask().ConfigureAwait(false)) {
        return (OAuthToken)new DataContractJsonSerializer(typeof(OAuthToken))
            .ReadObject((await response.Content.ReadAsInputStreamAsync()
                .AsTask().ConfigureAwait(false)).AsStreamForRead());
    }
}
```

WNS returns an OAuth token in JSON format, which the previous code deserializes into an OAuthToken object. The OAuth token (in JSON) looks like this (truncated):

{"token_type":"bearer","access_token":"EgAbAQMAAAAEgAAACoAAJp33aucvS9...==","expires_in":86400}

You can then use the OAuthToken to build the HTTPS POST message:

```
public async Task<HttpResponseMessage> PushAsync(
    Byte[] payload, String channelUri, OAuthToken token) {

    var msg = new HttpRequestMessage(HttpMethod.Post, new Uri(channelUri));

    // Set mandatory information:
    msg.Headers.Authorization = new HttpCredentialsHeaderValue("Bearer", token.AccessToken);
    msg.Content = new HttpBufferContent(payload.AsBuffer());
    msg.Headers.Add("X-WNS-Type", "wns/tile"); // tile, badge, toast, or raw
    // For "wns/raw", the content type must be "application/octet-stream"
    msg.Content.Headers.ContentType = new HttpMediaTypeHeaderValue("text/xml");

    // Set optional headers:
    msg.Headers.Add("X-WNS-Cache-Policy", "cache");
    msg.Headers.Add("X-WNS-TTL", "60");  // Seconds
    // Assign tag label (max 16 chars) to notification; used by device to detect dups.
    msg.Headers.Add("X-WNS-Tag", "SomeTag");
    // Request for Device Status and Notification Status to be returned in the response
    msg.Headers.Add("X-WNS-RequestForStatus", "true");
    return await new HttpClient().SendRequestAsync(msg).AsTask().ConfigureAwait(false);
}
```

You need to add an X-WNS-Type header to indicate the type via four values: wns/tile, wins/toast, wns/badge, and wns/raw. You also have to add an Authorization string with the OAuth access token acquired from *login.live.com*. The last four headers are optional. X-WNS-Tag is the tag we used previously to target specific tiles in the notification queue. Similarly, X-WNS-TTL indicates (in seconds) how long the notification should live before it automatically expires. The cache value indicates what WNS needs to do with a notification if the target machine is offline. The default is to cache one badge and one tile notification, unless your app has tile queuing enabled—in which case, WNS caches up to five tile notifications. The last optional header, X-WNS-RequestForStatus, tells WNS that our web service wants to know the status of the user's PC.

If you set the X-WNS-RequestForStatus request header to true, you get additional information back in the response:

```
X-WNS-NOTIFICATIONSTATUS: received
X-WNS-DEVICECONNECTIONSTATUS: connected
X-WNS-MSG-ID: 354223800B2B76E6
X-WNS-DEBUG-TRACE: BN1WNS1011529
Content-Length: 0
Date: Mon, 08 Oct 2012 20:05:14 GMT
```

The X-WNS-NOTIFICATIONSTATUS response header indicates that WNS has received the notification. If the end user has turned off notifications, this has a status of "dropped." Your app can also exceed the bandwidth of the channel—in which case, the status will be "channelthrottled." WNS returns X-WNS-DEVICECONNECTIONSTATUS if your app's web service asked for it in the request by specifying X-WNS-RequestForStatus. The X-WNS-MSG-ID and the X-WNS-DEBUG-TRACE are used for debugging purposes when you need to ask Microsoft support to trace WNS messages.

To help debug WNS failures, see the following location in the system's event log:

Applications And Services Log > Microsoft > Windows > PushNotifications-Platform

In addition, you (and your users) can see how much network usage an app is consuming for tiles and notifications by using Task Manager's Tile Updates column (as shown in Figure 8-11).

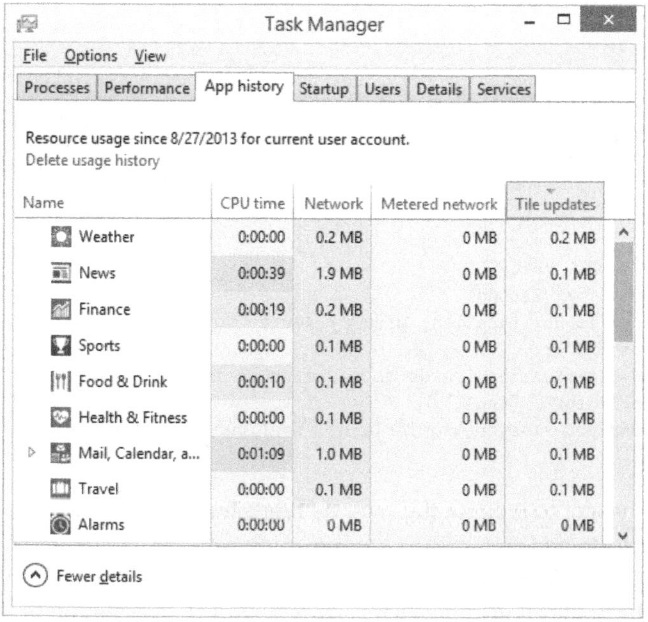

FIGURE 8-11 Task Manager's Tile Updates column shows network bandwidth used for an app's tiles and notifications.

CHAPTER 9

Background tasks

In Chapter 3, "Process model," I explained how Windows Store apps have their threads suspended when not in the foreground. This prevents background apps from consuming battery power. In addition, it prevents apps the user is not interacting with from affecting the responsiveness of the foreground app. Windows provides Windows Store apps that have tremendously powerful features to stay current and provide the latest relevant information to users. We saw good examples in Chapter 8, "Tiles and toast notifications," when we examined how the system can update your tile or show a toast notification even when your app is suspended or terminated. In addition, in Chapter 7, "Networking," I showed how your app could transfer large files even when in the background.

However, some apps need to execute code when suspended in the background or even terminated. Take, for example, an instant messaging (IM) app or a Voice-over-IP (VoIP) app. Users want to receive notifications when contacted by their friends or family. And these notifications still need to come in when users play a game, browse the Internet, watch a movie, or even when the PC is locked or in standby. These apps clearly have advanced requirements when they are suspended or even terminated. In this chapter, I'll show how Windows Store apps can execute code when not in the foreground by using background tasks. *Background tasks are the only mechanism Windows offers that enables your code to run when your app is not in the foreground.*

> **Important** When possible, avoid background tasks; use tile and toast notifications or background transfers instead. Background tasks complicate your app and negatively impact system responsiveness and power consumption. For this reason, background tasks cannot run continuously; they must execute code having short duration. Finally, the user must approve certain background task features, so they complicate the usability of your app too.

Background task architecture

Before diving into all the details, let's explore the Windows background task architecture. If your app needs to have some code execute periodically, you must perform the following steps:

1. Implement the code you want executed as a background task.

2. Decide what triggers your background task code (for example, timer, user logs in, network connectivity change).

3. Add a manifest declaration so that Windows knows how to activate background task code.

4. Register your app's background tasks with Windows the first time your app is activated.

The next four sections explain these steps in more detail.

Figure 9-1 summarizes the interaction between your app, Windows, and your background task code. After your app executes step 4 in the preceding list, Windows waits for the desired trigger event to occur. When the trigger occurs, Windows creates a new process, loads your background task code into it, and calls a predefined entry point. Now, your background task code is executing within this process. When your method completes, the process terminates and Windows waits for the trigger to occur again. Windows will not run multiple instances of a task concurrently.

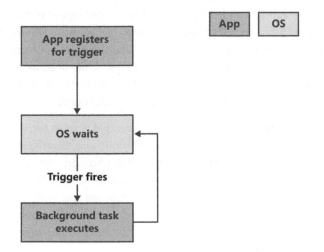
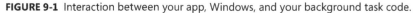

FIGURE 9-1 Interaction between your app, Windows, and your background task code.

> ⚠️ **Important** Because background tasks typically execute in a different process than the app's process and because the app's process might be terminated when the background task code executes, the background task code is not allowed to update the app's user interface. However, a background task can update its app's tiles or badges, or cause the display of a toast notification. In addition, the background task process runs in the package's app container. This means that the manifest's package capabilities and app declarations *do* apply to the background task process. In addition, the background task process can write to the package's data settings and folders (discussed in Chapter 4, "Package data and roaming"), and the package's app can subsequently read this information. Similarly, an app can write to its package data, and its background tasks can read this data. This is the easiest way for an app and its background tasks to communicate data with each other. One process can signal when data is ready by calling `ApplicationData`'s `SignalDataChanged` method, which raises a `DataChanged` event.

Your app must run at least once in order to register a background task and its desired trigger with Windows. Once registered, your app can be running, suspended, or even terminated. When the trigger occurs, Windows starts your app's background task. In fact, some PCs support a very low power state called *connected standby*. In this state, the PC is practically off but is still able to respond to incoming instant messages or VoIP calls. Connected standby is available only on System on Chip (SoC) devices (such as ARM and Intel Clovertrail PCs). A background task is the only way to execute code when a PC is in Connected Standby mode. From an administrator command prompt, run **PowerCfg.exe /SleepStudy** to see which background tasks are registered to run while a PC is in connected standby.

Step 1: Implement your background task's code

Now, let's look at how you implement the code you want executed as a background task. Here is a simple example:

```
namespace MyApp.BackgroundTasks { // NOTE: determines filename "MyApp.BackgroundTasks.WinMD"
   using Windows.ApplicationModel.Background;  // For IBackgroundTask & IBackgroundTaskInstance

   // NOTE: WinRT components MUST be public and sealed
   public sealed class MyBackgroundTask : IBackgroundTask {
      public void Run(IBackgroundTaskInstance taskInstance) {
         // Register cancelation handler (see the "Background task cancellation" section)
         // NOTE: Once canceled, a task has 5 seconds to complete or the process is killed
         taskInstance.Canceled +=
            (IBackgroundTaskInstance sender, BackgroundTaskCancellationReason reason) => {
            // TODO: Tell task it should cancel itself as soon as possible...
         };

         // Recommended: Adjust task behavior based on CPU and network availability
         // For example: A mail app could download mail for all folders when cost is
         // low and only download mail for the Inbox folder when cost is high
         switch (BackgroundWorkCost.CurrentBackgroundWorkCost) {
            case BackgroundWorkCostValue.Low:    // The task can use CPU & network
            case BackgroundWorkCostValue.Medium: // The task can use some CPU & network
            case BackgroundWorkCostValue.High:   // The task should avoid using CPU & network
               // This example records the last trigger time in an application data setting
               // so the app can read it later if it chooses. We do regardless of work cost.
               ApplicationData.Current.LocalSettings.Values["LastTriggerTime"] =
                  DateTimeOffset.Now;
               break;
         }
      }
   }
}
```

For code to execute via a background task, it must be implemented as a WinRT component. In Microsoft Visual Studio, you create a WinRT component by creating a new Windows Runtime Component project. This project simply creates a dynamic-link library file. However, the file extension is .WinMD instead of .DLL. In step 3, you'll register the full name of this class (MyApp.Background-Tasks.MyBackgroundTask) with Windows. Then, when Windows is ready to execute this task, it will try to load a .WinMD file whose name matches the namespace (`MyApp.BackgroundTasks.WinMD`). For this reason, in Visual Studio, you must make sure that the namespace and the output file name match.

After loading the file, Windows creates an instance of the `MyBackgroundTask` class by calling its parameterless constructor. So you must make sure that your class exposes a public parameterless constructor. By default, the C# compiler emits this for you automatically, but it will not do this if you explicitly define a constructor yourself. Then, after creating an instance of your `MyBackground`-`Task` class, Windows casts it to the WinRT `IBackgroundTask` interface and calls this interface's Run method, passing it an object that implements the WinRT `IBackgroundTaskInstance` interface. Each time Run is called, it's passed a new `IBackgroundTaskInstance` object. I discuss the `IBackground`-`TaskInstance` interface more in this chapter's "Background task progress and completion" and "Background task cancellation" sections.

Inside your Run method, you can execute any code you'd like. In the preceding example, I just record the last time the Run method executed in the application data's local settings.

Step 2: Decide what triggers your background task's code

The next step is to decide what event initiates the loading and execution of your background task's code. Table 9-1 lists the main trigger types that apps use and indicates when each fires.[1] The table also indicates each trigger's lock-screen and hosting-process requirements; these columns are discussed later in this chapter.

TABLE 9-1 Background task trigger types.

Trigger	When this trigger fires	Frequency	Requires lock screen	Host process
MaintenanceTrigger	At most, every 15 minutes; requires PC be on AC power.	Can be 1-shot or repeating	✕	BackgroundTaskHost.exe
TimeTrigger	Like MaintenanceTrigger; can run if PC on battery power.	Can be 1-shot or repeating	✓	BackgroundTaskHost.exe
SystemTrigger	See Table 9-2.	Can be 1-shot or repeating	See Table 9-2	BackgroundTaskHost.exe
LocationTrigger	When PC enters or leaves a Geofence.	Always repeating	✓	BackgroundTaskHost.exe
PushNotificationTrigger	When Windows Push Notification Service (WNS) pushes string payload.	Always repeating	✓	BackgroundTaskHost.exe or your app
ControlChannelTrigger	For real-time communication app; not available for JavaScript apps	Always repeating	✓	Your app

---

[1] Some additional trigger types exist for use by hardware manufacturers (`DeviceServicingTrigger` and `DeviceUseTrigger`) and mobile network providers (`NetworkOperatorHotspotAuthenticationTrigger` and `NetworkOperatorNotificationTrigger`).

Maintenance and time triggers

Maintenance triggers and time triggers behave identically: they execute some code at some future time. To allow the system to sleep as much as possible (conserving battery), these triggers fire at most 96 times a day (every 15 minutes). You can configure these triggers so that Windows runs your code just once, or you can have Windows run your code repeatedly (like once an hour).

The difference between these two triggers is that a maintenance trigger executes your code only if the PC is running plugged in on AC power.[2] On the other hand, a time trigger executes your code when the PC is on AC or battery power. Most people think that a time trigger is the better choice because your code is more likely to run. However, users must put your app on their lock screen in order for a time trigger to execute your task's code, and users might decide not to do this. Putting an app on their lock screen is how users indicate that they are willing to let your app's background tasks consume battery power. I'll talk more about lock-screen apps later in this chapter's "Lock-screen apps" section.

Although maintenance and time triggers behave identically, they serve different purposes. You typically use maintenance triggers for nonurgent opportunistic work, such as content indexing and renewing a Windows Push Notification Service (WNS) channel for updating tile, toast, and raw notifications.[3] (See Chapter 8.) On the other hand, you typically use time triggers for urgent work that an end user really cares about—for example, an email program that periodically polls a server looking for new mail messages.

System triggers

The system trigger allows your code to execute when a system-related event occurs. Table 9-2 lists all the system trigger types and their lock-screen requirements.

TABLE 9-2 System triggers and lock-screen requirements.

System trigger type	When trigger type fires	Requires lock screen
InternetAvailable	When Internet connectivity is established	×
NetworkStateChange	When the connection state changes (cost, LAN/WiFi/3G)	×
ServicingComplete	After a newer version of your app is installed	×
OnlineIdConnectedStateChange	When the Microsoft account associated with the logon changes	×
TimeZoneChange	When the PC's time zone changes	×
SmsReceived	When the device receives an SMS message	×
LockScreenApplicationAdded	When the user puts your app on the lock screen	×

---

[2] If a maintenance trigger happens to fire when the machine is on battery, the system executes your code as soon as the PC is plugged back into AC power.

[3] WNS channels expire every 30 days and, as of this writing, I'm not aware of any computer that can last a full 30 days on battery power. Therefore, updating a WNS channel is not something that requires urgent attention.

System trigger type	When trigger type fires	Requires lock screen
LockScreenApplicationRemoved	When the user removes your app from the lock screen	✗
BackgroundWorkCostChange	When the cost of performing background work changes (The Mail app uses this to tell the mail server to push all mail when the cost is low or only Inbox mail when the cost is high)	✓
UserPresent	When the user first generates input after the user is away	✓
UserAway	When the user doesn't generate input for some period of time (usually after 4 minutes)	✓
SessionConnected	When the user logs in	✓
ControlChannelReset	When the network connection is reset and needs to be re-established	✓

Like maintenance and time triggers, system triggers can be single-shot or repeating. For example, perhaps the next time the user logs in (`SessionConnected` trigger type), you might want to perform some task or maybe you want to perform the task every time the user logs in.

Location triggers

The `LocationTrigger` allows an app to execute some code when the user's PC arrives at or leaves a particular location. For example, an app could show a coupon when near a particular store. Apps using this trigger can execute code when the PC is running on battery power or if the PC is in the low-power connected-standby state. For this trigger to work, users must add the app to their lock screen. (See the "Lock-screen apps" section.) When the trigger fires, the task's code can show a toast notification on the user's lock screen. If the user activates the toast and unlocks the PC, Windows activates the app that registered the background task, bringing it to the foreground.

To use this trigger, your app must get a reference to its `GeofenceMonitor` singleton object and give it one or more `Geofence` objects it should monitor:

```
private async Task InitializeGeofenceMonitorAsync() {
   // Get a reference to the app's singleton GeofenceMonitor object
   GeofenceMonitor gm = GeofenceMonitor.Current;
   gm.Geofences.Clear();   // Erase all its Geofence objects

   // Get the PC's current location (requires Location capability)
   Geoposition geoposition = await new Geolocator().GetGeopositionAsync();

   // Register a Geofence whose state changes whenever the PC goes within 1 meter of it
   Geofence gf = new Geofence("InitialPCLocation",                          // Geofence Id
      new Geocircle(geoposition.Coordinate.Point.Position, 1),              // Point & radius
      MonitoredGeofenceStates.Entered | MonitoredGeofenceStates.Exited,     // When task should run
      false,                                                                // Not 1 time
      TimeSpan.FromSeconds(5),                                              // Dwell time
      DateTimeOffset.UtcNow,                                               // Start time
      TimeSpan.FromHours(1));                                              // Duration
   gm.Geofences.Add(gf);   // Add the Geofence object to the GeofenceMonitor's collection
}
```

Then, whenever the system detects the PC entering or exiting a location related to one of the app's Geofence objects, the PC fires the app's `LocationTrigger` background task. In response to this, the background task can call `GeofenceMonitor`'s `ReadReports` method to find out which `Geofence` object or objects have been entered or exited:

```
public sealed class GeofenceLocationTask : IBackgroundTask {
    public void Run(IBackgroundTaskInstance taskInstance) {
        IReadOnlyList<GeofenceStateChangeReport> reports = GeofenceMonitor.Current.ReadReports();
        foreach (GeofenceStateChangeReport report in reports) {
            // This loop processes a report for each Geofence object that changed
            // Each report includes the Geofence object affected, its position,
            // the NewState of the Geofence (Entered or Exited), and the reason why
            // the report was generated (Used or Expired):
            Geofence geofence = report.Geofence;                       // The Geofence object affected
            Geoposition pos = report.Geoposition;                      // The Geofence object's position
            GeofenceState state = report.NewState;                     // Entered or Exited
            GeofenceRemovalReason reason = report.RemovalReason;       // Used or Expired
            // TODO: Process the Geofence object affected here...
        }
    }
}
```

Push notification triggers

`PushNotificationTrigger` is for real-time communication (RTC) apps, such as mail, instant messaging, and Voice over IP (VoIP). Apps using this trigger can execute code when the PC is running on battery power or if the PC is in a low-power, connected-standby state. When a network message comes in, the PC wakes up and executes the background task code. For this trigger to work, users must add the app to their lock screen. (See the "Lock-screen apps" section.) When the trigger fires, the task's code can show a toast notification on the user's lock screen. If the user activates the toast and unlocks the PC, Windows activates the app that registered the background task, bringing it to the foreground.

In Chapter 8, I discussed the Windows Push Notification Service (WNS). In that chapter, I showed how an app acquires a channel URI and sends it to your app's web service.[4] Then, in the future, your service can push an XML template representing a tile, badge, or toast notification to the user's PC. In that chapter, I also mentioned that there was a fourth kind of notification referred to as a *raw notification*. The payload of a raw notification is a string (up to 5 kilobytes) instead of XML. When a raw notification is sent to a PC, the system invokes a `PushNotificationTrigger` background task's code, passing it the string. The code can then interpret the string and decide how it wants to react to

---

[4] Because channel URIs expire every 30 days, create a maintenance trigger task to run with a frequency less than 30 days to update the channel URI with your cloud service periodically.

it: show a toast, ignore it, write something to app data, and so on. Here's how to implement back-ground task code to process the raw notification's string:

```
namespace Wintellect.BackgroundTasks {
   public sealed class PushNotificationTask : IBackgroundTask {
      public void Run(IBackgroundTaskInstance taskInstance) {
         String rawNotificationString = ((RawNotification)taskInstance.TriggerDetails).Content;
         // TODO: Process the rawNotificationString...
      }
   }
}
```

For an example of how your app's web service can interact with WNS to send raw notifications, see Chapter 8. Due to the 5-KB string limit, raw notifications can send only short messages that trigger your task's code to take some action. If you have more data to send to the task, have the task's code make a network request to query the rest of the data. Also, note that WNS push notifications do not guarantee delivery; for example, the client might not be connected to the Internet.

> **Important** When sending a raw notification, the HTTP Content-Type header must be set to "application/octet-stream" and the HTTP X-WNS-Type header must be set to "wns/raw".

The PushNotificationChannel class offers a PushNotificationReceived event. Your app code (not background task code) can register a callback method with this event. When the PC receives a raw push notification, Windows first checks to see if the app that created the channel URI receiving the notification is running in the foreground. If it is, Windows raises the PushNotifica-tionReceived event, passing your callback method a reference to a PushNotificationReceived-EventArgs object. This object's NotificationType property indicates the type of push notification (PushNotificationType.Raw for a PushNotificationTrigger) and the RawNotification property returns the string content. Your app can now execute some code in response to the raw notification. In fact, your app can prevent the PushNotificationTrigger background task's code from executing by setting PushNotificationReceivedEventArgs's Cancel property to true. If the raw notification is not intercepted and canceled, the background task is started so that it can respond to it.

Control channel triggers

Like the PushNotificationTrigger, ControlChannelTrigger is also for real-time communica-tion (RTC) apps and work when the PC is in a low-power, connected-standby state or on battery power. This trigger allows code to execute when data comes in over a socket. Of course, the user must add apps that use this trigger to the lock screen. When possible, it is highly recommended that you avoid ControlChannelTrigger and use PushNotificationTrigger. PushNotification-Trigger is much simpler to implement, and it uses PC resources more efficiently. ControlChannel-Trigger is typically for legacy communication protocols. For these reasons, I do not explain Con-trolChannelTrigger in this book. If you need more information about ControlChannelTrigger, see the "Background Networking" white paper available for download from the MSDN website: *http://www.microsoft.com/en-us/download/details.aspx?id=28999*.

Step 3: Add manifest declarations

Once you have implemented your background task code and decided which trigger you want to use, you must inform Windows of your background task WinRT components. You do this by adding declarations to the package manifest for your app. Figure 9-2 shows Visual Studio's manifest designer with its Declarations tab selected. To add a background task to your app, select Background Tasks and then click the Add button. Then select the trigger you wish to use from the Supported Task Types list. Note that Audio is not a trigger; it allows your app to play audio when it is not in the foreground. For example, the Windows Music app enables this declaration. You'll also notice that Maintenance is missing from the list. If you want to use a maintenance trigger, select System Event (do not select Timer).

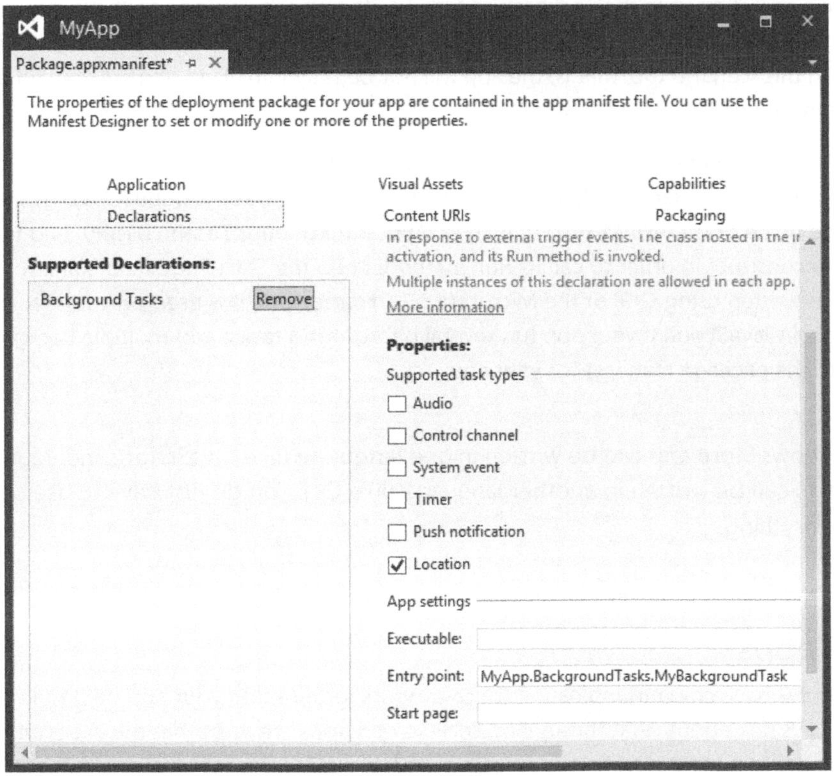

FIGURE 9-2 Adding a background task declaration to your app via its package manifest.

Then, after selecting an item under Supported Task Types, go to the Executable field. This field tells Windows which process to execute when the trigger fires. This process will load your WinRT component's .WinMD file and execute your task's code. There are two options for this field. For most of the triggers, you must leave this field blank, which tells Windows to use its own Background-

TaskHost.exe process. For a `PushNotificationTrigger`, you can leave this field blank or you can specify the name of your own app's executable. If you use the latter, Windows will have your app's process load the WinRT component and run the task in the same process as your app. This is not the recommended thing to do, but it allows your background task's code the ability to access the same state (memory) as your app. However, if your app is suspended, all threads but the thread running the background task code remain suspended, so you must not perform any interthread communication or deadlocks will occur. In addition, because the GUI thread remains suspended, the background task cannot update the app's user interface. If the app's process is not running, Windows will activate it, but the app is not launched with a main view or hosted view activation. The result of all this is that your background task cannot have any expectations of the app's state and, in fact, the app might not have its state fully initialized.

For a `ControlChannelTrigger`, you must not leave the Executable field blank; instead, you must specify your app's executable name and your WinRT component's .WinMD file must load in the app's process. As mentioned previously, the `ControlChannelTrigger` is used for RTC apps, and these apps typically have a socket open in the background task. For the app to respond to the incoming call on the socket, the background task and the app have to share the same process. Everything I said earlier still holds true in this scenario too; that is, the app will not be fully initialized and you should avoid interthread communication.

For the declaration's Entry Point field, enter the full name (including the namespace) of the WinRT class you created in step 1 (for example, MyApp.`BackgroundTasks.MyBackgroundTask`). This tells the host process the name of the .WinMD file to load (MyApp.`BackgroundTasks.WinMD`) and the name of the class to construct in order to call its Run method. Keep the Start Page field blank for Windows Store apps written using C++ or the Microsoft .NET Framework; it is used only for background tasks written in JavaScript. If your app has several background tasks, add multiple Background Task declarations to the package manifest for your app.

> **Note** Your Windows Store app can be written in one language (like JavaScript), and your background tasks can be written in another language (like C#). You do not have to use one language for everything.

Lock-screen apps

Table 9-1 and Table 9-2 have columns indicating which triggers require that your app be on the user's lock screen. Let's talk about what this means. Lock-screen apps are apps that the user considers important. Specifically, when the user is adding an app to his lock screen, he's allowing that app's background tasks to consume system resources even when the PC is on battery power. These apps typically have a real-time networking requirement like a chat or VoIP application. For example, the Microsoft Skype app needs to be on the user's lock screen so that it can inform the user of an incoming call. The Windows Calendar app is a lock-screen app too, but for a different reason: it shows the user some text indicating his next appointment. Showing this on the lock screen allows the user to see his next appointment without unlocking his PC. It also allows calendar reminders to show toast notifications on the lock screen.

Figure 9-3 shows a user's lock screen. The lock screen always shows the time, date, network connectivity, and power status. In addition, the user can configure up to seven apps as lock-screen apps.[5] If an app's tile is showing a badge, the tile's badge logo (a 24-pixel by 24-pixel monochrome image) is shown along with the badge. The badge is, of course, dynamically updatable, while the logo itself is static for the app. Figure 9-3 shows the badge logos and badges for the Mail and Alarms apps. The user can select to see the detailed status for one of his lock-screen apps; this app's tile text appears next to the time. In Figure 9-3, you see the Calendar app is showing the user's next appointment.[6]

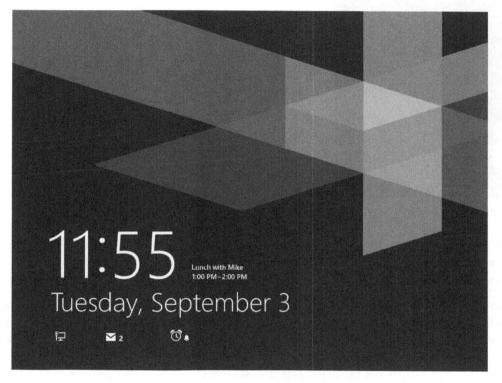

FIGURE 9-3 A user's lock screen showing apps that declare background tasks triggered with lock-screen requirements.

Users control which apps are on their lock screen using PC Settings > PC And Devices > Lock Screen, as shown in Figure 9-4. Here, the user can choose up to seven lock-screen apps. The user can also select one app to see its detailed status and one app to be an alarm app.

---

[5] By limiting the number of lock-screen apps to seven, there is a guaranteed upper limit of resource usage (seven times the resource quota discussed in the "Background task resource quotas" section).

[6] If your app supports secondary tiles, the user can make your app a lock-screen app, choosing to see the secondary tile's badge logo, badge, and wide tile text. For more information, see the MSDN documentation for SecondaryTile's LockScreenBadgeLogo and LockScreenDisplayBadgeAndTileText properties.

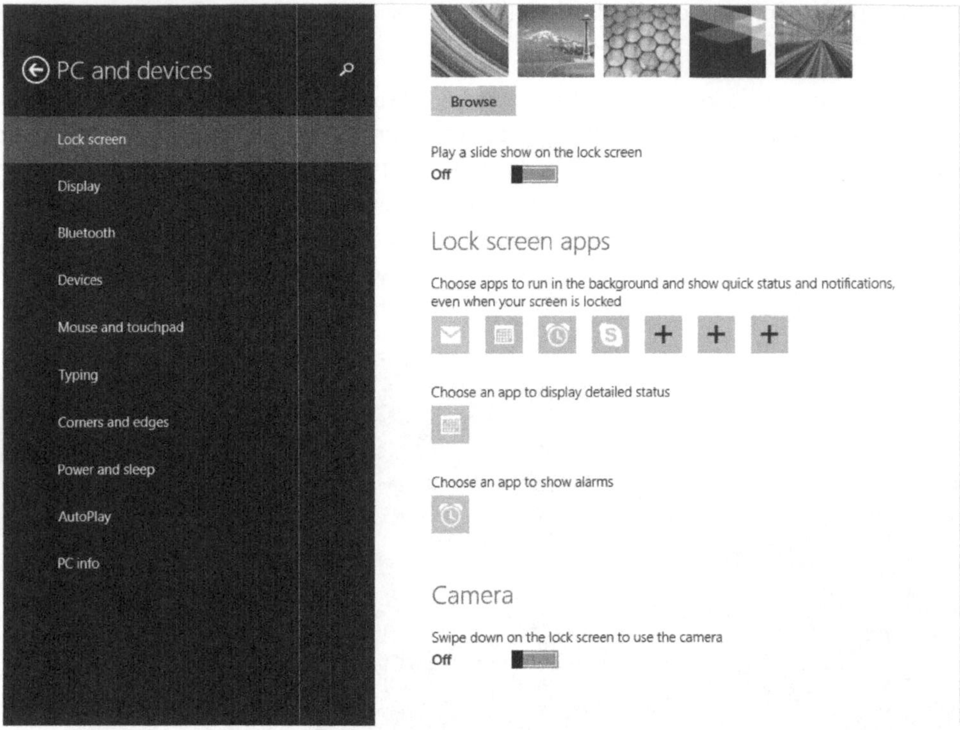

FIGURE 9-4 The user configures lock-screen apps via PC Settings > PC And Devices > Lock Screen.

In addition, when the user is interacting with an app containing a background task with a lock-screen trigger, the user can select the app's Settings charm, select Permissions, and then add or remove the app from the lock screen as shown in Figure 9-5.

So now you see what lock-screen apps look like from the user's perspective. Figure 9-6 shows what they look like from the developer's perspective. If any of your background tasks start via triggers that require the lock screen, you must create a 24-pixel by 24-pixel monochrome image and set the Badge Logo field to the image's package-relative pathname. You might also want to create larger images increased by 140 percent and 180 percent for screens supporting higher dots per inch (DPI). You'll also have to set the Lock Screen Notifications field to Badge on the Application tab of the manifest designer. This causes Windows to offer your app as one of the seven the user can select via the PC Settings Lock Screen Apps section. If your app offers a wide tile and you want to allow the user to see its text on the lock screen, set the Lock Screen Notifications field to Badge And Tile Text. This causes Windows to offer your app as one that can show the user detailed status.

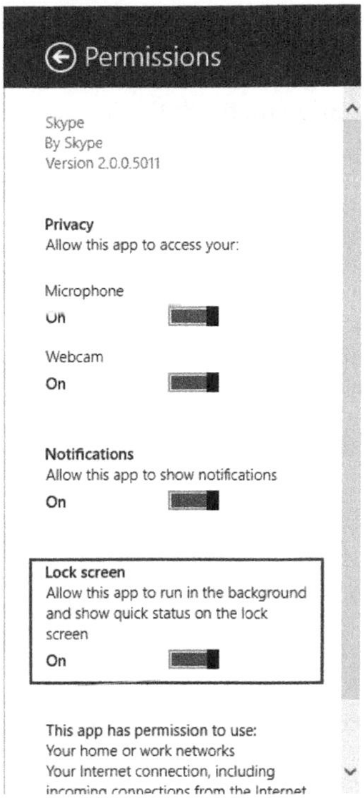

FIGURE 9-5 The user can add and remove the foreground app from the lock screen via its Permissions pane.

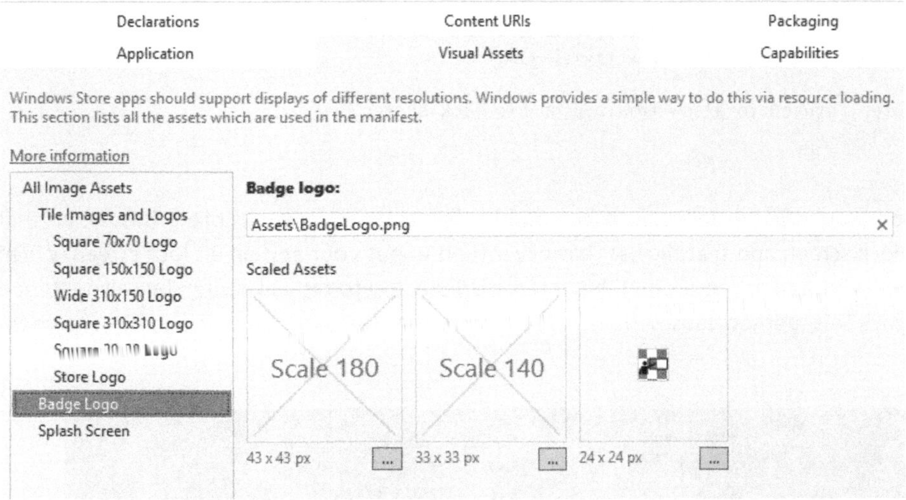

Figure 9-6 Additional manifest requirements for lock-screen apps.

Also, if any of your background tasks display a toast notification, set Toast Capable to Yes as discussed in Chapter 8.

WinRT offers a `BackgroundExecutionManager` class exposing three methods that an app can invoke to help manage its lock-screen status:

```
namespace Windows.ApplicationModel.Background {
    public static class BackgroundExecutionManager {
        // Gets the calling app's lock screen status
        public static BackgroundAccessStatus GetAccessStatus();

        // Prompts the user to add the calling app to his lock screen
        public static IAsyncOperation<BackgroundAccessStatus> RequestAccessAsync();

        // Removes the calling app from the user's lock screen (sets status to Denied)
        public static void RemoveAccess();
    }
}
```

Both the `GetAccessStatus` and `RequestAccessAsync` methods return a `Background-AccessStatus`, defined as follows:

```
public enum BackgroundAccessStatus {
    // The user has never been prompted to add the calling app to the his lock screen
    Unspecified = 0,

    // The calling app is on the lock screen and the PC supports connected standby
    // Only returned if the app declares ControlChannel in its manifest
    AllowedWithAlwaysOnRealTimeConnectivity = 1,

    // The calling app is on the lock screen but the PC doesn't support connected standby
    AllowedMayUseActiveRealTimeConnectivity = 2,

    // The user refused to allow this app on his lock screen
    Denied = 3,
}
```

When your app is first installed, its background access status is `Unspecified`. This means that it is not on the lock screen and that the user has never tried to put your app on his lock screen. When the user activates your app, it can prompt the user to add the app to his lock screen by calling `Request-AccessAsync`. This method causes Windows to prompt the user with the message box shown in Figure 9-7.

FIGURE 9-7 Windows prompts the user to add the app to his lock screen.

If the user selects Don't Allow, the status changes to Denied, indicating that the user has explicitly chosen not to allow your app on to his lock screen. If the user selects Allow, the status changes to AllowedWithAlwaysOnRealTimeConnectivity or AllowedMayUseActiveRealTimeConnectivity. The former means that the app has declared a Control Channel background task and that the PC also supports connected standby. The latter is returned in all other scenarios.

Note that once your app has prompted the user, Windows will not allow your app to prompt the user again. That is, RequestAccessAsync prompts the user the first time your app calls it; future calls to this method do not prompt the user and simply return the current BackgroundAccessStatus. Windows implemented this behavior to prevent an app from pestering the user repeatedly to put the app on the lock screen. If you need to test this functionality repeatedly, you can uninstall and re-install the app or, in Visual Studio's property page for your project, select the Debug tab and then select the Uninstall And Then Re-install My Package option. Of course, an app can call RemoveAccess to remove itself from the user's lock screen; this sets the BackgroundAccessStatus to Denied.

Finally, your app can register background tasks that fire whenever the user adds or removes your app from his lock screen. See the system trigger's LockScreenApplicationAdded and Lock-ScreenApplicationRemoved trigger types.

Step 4: Register your app's background tasks

Once you've implemented your WinRT background task components in a .WinMD file and declared your app's background task in the manifest, you're ready to have your app register the background tasks with Windows itself. Registration provides Windows with additional details about the tasks and when they should execute. Many people want to register their app's background tasks as soon as the user installs the app. However, this is not possible. The user must run your app, and then your app can register its background tasks. In some corporate environments or with original equipment manufacturer (OEM) PCs, the PC might have many pre-installed apps that the user never launches. If Windows allowed registration of an app's tasks upon installation, all these apps' background tasks could run even though the user might not care about some of the apps at all.

Therefore, an app must register its background tasks the first time the app launches. The best way to tell if your app needs to register its background tasks is to ask the system which background tasks your app has already registered by calling WinRT's BackgroundTaskRegistration's static All-Tasks property:

```
Boolean anyTasksRegistered = BackgroundTaskRegistration.AllTasks.Any();
```

If `anyTasksRegistered` is `false`, your app needs to register its background tasks. You register a task by first constructing and initializing a `BackgroundTaskBuilder` as follows:

```
if (!anyTasksRegistered) {
    var btb = new BackgroundTaskBuilder {
        Name = "Some friendly name",      // See the "Debugging background tasks" section
        // Specify the full name of the class implementing the IBackgroundTask interface
        // You could specify a literal string here, but I prefer to do it this
        // way to get compile-time safety and rename refactoring support
        TaskEntryPoint = typeof(Wintellect.BackgroundTasks.SystemTriggerTask).FullName
    };

    // Specify the desired trigger (TimeTrigger, MaintenanceTrigger, SystemTrigger,
    // LocationTrigger, or PushNotificationTrigger). This example uses a TimeTrigger
    btb.SetTrigger(new TimeTrigger(freshnessTime: 60, oneShot: false));

    // Optional: add 1+ system conditions and
    // indicate whether the task should stop if any condition is lost
    btb.AddCondition(new SystemCondition(SystemConditionType.InternetAvailable));
    btb.CancelOnConditionLoss = true;   // System tells task to cancel if any condition is lost

    // Register the task with Windows
    BackgroundTaskRegistration registeredTask = btb.Register();
    // Use registeredTask to Unregister, or if the app wants Progress/Completed notifications
}
```

In this case, I'm creating a `BackgroundTaskBuilder` referring to a `TimeTrigger` that fires every 60 minutes if the PC can reach the Internet. (See the "System condition types" sidebar.) The `TaskEntryPoint` property must be set to the full name of the WinRT component class that implements WinRT's `IBackgroundTask` interface. You could use a literal string here, but I prefer to set this property using the technique shown in the code for several reasons:

- The code will not compile unless I reference the WinRT component's .WinMD file from my project's references. This is important to do because it ensures that the .WinMD file is packaged and deployed in your app's package file. If you forget to include the .WinMD file in your app's package, then of course, the background task won't work.

- The code will not compile if I spell the name of the type incorrectly.

- If I want to change the name of the type implementing the `IBackgroundTask` interface, I perform a refactor rename to change it throughout all projects in the Visual Studio solution.

`BackgroundTaskBuilder`'s `Register` method returns a `BackgroundTaskRegistration` object, which looks like this:

```
public sealed class BackgroundTaskRegistration : IBackgroundTaskRegistration {
   // Properties identifying the Name (assigned by you) and the
   // GUID (assigned by Windows) that uniquely identify this task.
   public String Name { get; }
   public Guid TaskId { get; }

   // Unregisters a task (true=stop now; false=wait until done running)
   // NOTE: You do not have to explicitly unregister 1-shot tasks;
   // they automatically unregister themselves after they execute.
   public void Unregister(Boolean cancelTask);

   // See the "Background task progress and completion" section.
   public event BackgroundTaskCompletedEventHandler Completed;
   public event BackgroundTaskProgressEventHandler Progress;
}
```

System condition types

Frequently, it doesn't make sense to have your code execute just because a trigger occurred. For example, if your app periodically polls a server for new email messages or RSS feeds, you'd probably use a time trigger, but what if the Internet isn't available at this time? Then it doesn't make sense to run your task. To improve the efficiency of the system, you can add system conditions to a trigger. In fact, you can apply several system conditions to a single trigger if you'd like. Note that you can add system conditions to any kind of trigger, not just system triggers. Table 9-3 lists all the defined system condition types.

TABLE 9-3 System condition types.

System condition types	Executes or cancels task based on
InternetAvailable* InternetNotAvailable	Internet availability
UserPresent UserNotPresent	User's presence
SessionConnected SessionDisconnected	Whether user is logged in or not
FreeNetworkAvailable	Availability of a nonmetered network
BackgroundWorkCostNotHigh	Ability to use a lot of CPU and network resources

* Developers frequently forget the InternetAvailable condition. This condition is required so that Windows continues to power network cards; your task will not be able to use the network unless you specify this condition.

When a trigger occurs, we say that the background task is *latched*. This means that the background task wants to run, but then the system checks the conditions to make sure that they're all true. If any of the conditions are false, the system will not run the task. As soon as all the conditions become true, the system will run the task. Also, when creating a BackgroundTask-Builder, setting its CancelOnConditionLoss property to true causes the system to notify a background task that it should stop when any of its conditions change. See the "Background task cancellation" section.

Debugging background tasks

Debugging background tasks can be challenging. For example, if you want to debug your timer or maintenance trigger, you set a breakpoint and wait about 15 minutes until the system invokes your task and hits your breakpoint. This makes debugging a background task quite painful. To improve this situation, Visual Studio has built-in support to help with debugging background tasks. Specifically, Visual Studio allows you to forcibly trigger a background task by using its Debug Location toolbar, as shown in Figure 9-8.

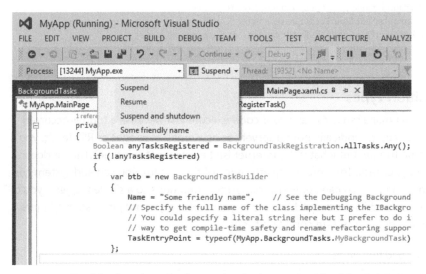

FIGURE 9-8 Forcibly triggering a background task trigger using Visual Studio's Debug Location toolbar.

When your app is running (not stopped at a breakpoint), drop down the list where you find the Suspend and Resume triggers discussed in Chapter 3. If your app has registered any background tasks, the names of the background tasks (as set using `BackgroundTaskBuilder`'s `Name` property) also appear in this list. When you select a background task's name, Visual Studio forcibly invokes it. If you have a breakpoint set, Visual Studio will stop there and offer you the normal interactive debugging experience.

Additionally, event log entries can help you troubleshoot background task issues. You can find them under the following path:

Applications And Services Logs > Microsoft > Windows > BackgroundTaskInfrastructure

There are two logs: Operational and Diagnostic (disabled by default). Make sure you enable Show Analytic And Debug Logs on the View menu.

In addition, Microsoft makes several Windows PowerShell commands available for managing background tasks, as shown in Table 9-4.[7]

TABLE 9-4 Windows PowerShell commands for managing background tasks.

Cmdlet	Description
Enable-AppBackgroundTaskDiagnosticLog Disable-AppBackgroundTaskDiagnosticLog	Enables and disables background task logging in Event Viewer.
Get-AppBackgroundTask	Gets background task information.
Start-AppBackgroundTask	Starts a background task.
Unregister-AppBackgroundTask	Unregisters a background task.
Set-AppBackgroundTaskResourcePolicy	Configures the use of global pools by background tasks. (See the next section.)

Windows tracks battery consumption for multiple days, and you can see the impact that background tasks have on battery consumption with powercfg.exe /sleepstudy.

Background task resource quotas

If your app is running in the foreground while one of its background tasks executes, Windows puts no limitations on the app container's CPU or networking usage. However, if your app is not running in the foreground, its background tasks get restricted CPU and networking usage.[8] As mentioned before, the system makes a distinction between apps that are on the lock screen and apps that are not. Table 9-5 shows how much CPU usage all of an app's background tasks get to share. If your app is not on the lock screen, all of its background tasks share 1 second of CPU usage every 2 hours regardless of whether the PC is running on AC or DC power. If your app is on the lock screen, all its background tasks get to share 2 seconds of CPU every 15 minutes. If your background tasks do not complete in this time, Windows suspends the threads executing your background tasks and resumes the threads when your app's quota replenishes in the next 2 hours or 15 minutes. Unused time does not roll over.

---

[7] For more information, see *http://technet.microsoft.com/en-us/library/dn296421(v=wps.630).aspx*.

[8] Network cards are particularly resource intensive and drain the battery quickly.

TABLE 9-5 Background task resource quotas.

Resource limit	Non-lock screen app every 2 hours	Lock screen app every 15 minutes
CPU (AC & DC)	1 sec	2 sec
Network (DC only) x MB/sec	.625x MB (daily=7.5x MB)	4.69x MB (Daily=45x MB)

When the system suspends your app's background task threads, Windows logs an event in the BackgroundTaskInfrastructure event log. You can also find out on the next invocation of the task's Run method how often the system suspended it by checking BackgroundTaskInstance's SuspendedCount property.[9]

When the machine is on battery power, the system also has a quota for your app's network usage. If the network can transfer 10 MB/sec, when your app is not on the lock screen, it can transfer 6.25 MB every 2 hours, with a maximum of 75 MB per day. If your app is on the lock screen, it can transfer 46.9 MB every 15 minutes, with a maximum of 450 MB per day.[10]

In reality, Table 9-5 indicates what the system guarantees your app's background tasks. However, if there are few background tasks on the machine, your background tasks could use more CPU and network than these minimums because Windows also has a global pool that apps can tap into. This is a problem for testing your background tasks because they might all run successfully if they get more than the app's minimums. However, a user's PC might have many background tasks that deplete this global pool, so your app's tasks have to share the app's minimum resource quota, preventing them from completing their work.

When testing your background tasks, you want to make sure they can run successfully if all they get is the app's minimum CPU and networking usage. As a developer, you can tell Windows to turn off the global pool of resources and force each app's background tasks to share the app's minimum by executing the following PowerShell cmdlet:

```
Set-AppBackgroundTaskResourcePolicy -Mode Conservative
```

You restore the use of the global pool with this PowerShell cmdlet (which will require a reboot):

```
Set-AppBackgroundTaskResourcePolicy -Mode Normal
```

You see how much resources a background task used with this PowerShell cmdlet:

```
Get-AppBackgroundTask -pfn PackageFamilyName -IncludeResourceUsage | fl
```

Finally, your background task can call BackgroundWorkCost's static read-only CurrentBackgroundWorkCost property to determine how much CPU and network resources are available as your task executes. The code shown in this chapter's "Step 1: Implement your background task's code" section demonstrates this.

---

[9] If you want to specifically know if the task was cancelled due to CPU or network usage, you can cast the BackgroundTaskInstance to BackgroundTaskInstance2. This interface exposes a GetThrottleCount property.

[10] These numbers are subject to change with different versions of Windows. Consider them as a rough indication.

Deploying a new version of your app

Beware that previously registered background tasks remain registered when a user installs a newer version of your app's package. So, as you are creating a new version of your app, do not change the names of your background tasks' classes or the name of the .WinMD files that contain them; if you do, your background tasks will just stop working. If you need to alter your background tasks with a new version of your app, register a background task using a system trigger with a ServicingComplete trigger type. This trigger fires just after a user installs a newer version of your app's package. In this task's Run method, you can unregister any old tasks and register any new tasks (with any class name or .WinMD filename changes) you wish.

Use BackgroundTaskRegistration class' static AllTasks property to iterate through all the currently registered tasks and unregister any you no longer want. This code shows how to unregister all of them:

```
foreach (var task in BackgroundTaskRegistration.AllTasks)
   task.Value.Unregister(true);
```

Once this loop completes, you can then register any background tasks the new version of your app requires.

I recommend that your app always register a background task using a system trigger with a ServicingComplete trigger type, even if its Run method does nothing. This allows a new version of your app's package to execute some code after installation, even without the user starting the new version of your app. You can unregister tasks and register new tasks, of course. But this is also useful for upgrading your package's data (as discussed in Chapter 4).

Background task progress and completion

Each background task can notify its app of its progress and completion. Of course, this information is useful only if the app is actually running, not suspended or terminated. Because of this, the notification mechanism is not reliable and an app should not require getting these notifications. However, I will explain briefly how to enable these notifications. The best way to reliably transfer data between an app and its background tasks is to use package data settings or files as described in Chapter 4. If the app and background task are running, one could notify the other of the change by calling ApplicationData's SignalDataChanged method.

First, the app must get a reference to a background task's BackgroundTaskRegistration object. You get this after calling BackgroundTaskBuilder's Register method or by calling the BackgroundTaskRegistration class' static AllTasks property.

Once you have a BackgroundTaskRegistration object, it exposes Progress and Completed events with which you can enlist callback methods. Note that your callback methods are not invoked using the GUI thread, so if you want to manipulate user interface components, you'll have to call a CoreDispatcher's RunAsync method.

Each time a task runs, its Run method is passed a new object implementing the IBackground-TaskInstance interface:

```
public interface IBackgroundTaskInstance {
    // Gets the instance ID of the background task instance.
    Guid InstanceId { get; }

    // Gets access to the registered background task for this background task instance.
    BackgroundTaskRegistration Task { get; }

    // Gets or sets progress status for a background task instance.
    UInt32 Progress { get; set; }

    // Tells Windows that the task isn't done running even if it returns from its Run method
    BackgroundTaskDeferral GetDeferral();

    // The number of times Windows suspended this task
    UInt32 SuspendedCount { get; }

    // Notifies your task instance that the system wants to terminate it now.
    event BackgroundTaskCanceledEventHandler Canceled;
}
```

This interface defines a UInt32 Progress property. When your background task sets this property, Windows raises the Progress event in the app (if the app is running) and passes it the progress value. Your app's callback method receives a BackgroundTaskProgressEventArgs object that has a read-only Progress property returning whatever value the task's code set.

When the task's Run method returns (or when calling Complete on a BackgroundTaskDeferral object), Windows raises the Completed event in the app (if it is running). Your app's callback method receives a BackgroundTaskCompletedEventArgs object that has a CheckResult method. If the task's Run method threw an unhandled exception, this method rethrows it so that you can know if the task ran to completion successfully. Be aware that this mechanism is very unreliable. The Check-Result method works correctly only if the task's Run method executes everything synchronously. That is, it must not be an async method and it must not use a deferral. However, I must say that executing your Run method synchronously is a fine thing to do because a GUI thread does not execute it. In fact, it might even be desirable to execute everything synchronously because this reduces memory overhead and improves performance, which is an important consideration due to limited resource quotas.

Both the Completed as well as the Progress event handler receive the originating registered task as a BackgroundTaskRegistration parameter. This allows the Progress and Completed events to distinguish between potentially multiple registered tasks that all use the same Progress or Completed event-handler methods. For example, an app can register for a maintenance trigger as well as for a system trigger. Both triggers can use the same completed event handler. The BackgroundTaskRegistration's Name and TaskID will be different for each. Along the same lines, both

`BackgroundTaskProgressEventArgs` and `BackgroundTaskCompletedEventArgs` also have an `InstanceId` property that your app can use to differentiate between task instances. This can happen, for example, if you get multiple network changes in a short period of time.

Background task cancellation

While a task is running, Windows might want to cancel it prematurely (before it runs to completion). Windows notifies your task of this by raising `IBackgroundTaskInstance`'s `Canceled` event. Your background task should register a callback method with this event as soon as it starts executing. If Windows wants to cancel your task, it invokes your callback method, passing it a `BackgroundTask-CancellationReason` enum (as shown in Table 9-6) that indicates why Windows wants to cancel the task. Your callback method has 5 seconds to cancel the task or Windows simply terminates the process.

TABLE 9-6 `BackgroundTaskCancellationReason` enum values and their meanings.

Value	Description
LoggingOff	The user is logging off.
Uninstall	The package is being uninstalled.
ServicingUpdate	The package is being updated to a newer version.
Abort	`BackgroundTaskRegistration`'s `Unregister` method was called, passing `true`.
Terminating	Process lifetime management is killing the process. This happens only for tasks running in the app host, not in BackgroundTaskHost.exe.
IdleTask	The Task is "running" but is not using any CPU or network resources. The system cancels it so that the PC can go into a low-power mode.
ConditionLoss	One or more conditions became unavailable.
SystemPolicy	The app has too much resource pressure, such as memory consumption.
QuietHoursEntered	The PC entered quiet hours as set in PC Settings > Search & Apps > Notifications.*

* Alarms and lock-screen call apps do not respect quiet hours. Quiet hours are not engaged if you are actively using the PC. When Quiet Hours starts, background tasks are canceled, and they are restarted when Quiet Hours ends.

Long-running background tasks that appear to be "hanging" to the system can prevent Windows from entering or remaining in connected standby. This has an obvious negative impact on the system's battery life. For example, when Windows is ready to enter connected standby, it waits for several minutes for the background task to respond or give any sign of life by executing some code. If that never happens, Windows considers the task as hanging, creates a dump file, and kills the task. These hangs show up in the Windows Store dashboard. Background tasks can appear to be hanging for different reasons. For example, it can happen because there's a bug in your code where you forgot to complete a deferral or Windows is waiting on a slow or unresponsive Internet connection or server. Hence, the recommendation for background tasks is that they are not long-running: start the task on a trigger, do your work, and exit.

When Windows wants to cancel your background task, set some signal in your Canceled event handler notifying your task code that it should terminate as soon as possible. Here is an example of a task that does this correctly:

```
public sealed class NetworkIOTask : IBackgroundTask {
    public void Run(IBackgroundTaskInstance taskInstance) {
        // I use a CancellationTokenSource to let the task know when Windows wants to cancel it
        CancellationTokenSource cts = new CancellationTokenSource();

        // When Windows wants to cancel the task, cancel the CancellationTokenSource
        // NOTE: Once canceled, a task has 5 seconds to complete or the process is killed
        taskInstance.Canceled += (sender, reason) => cts.Cancel();

        String lastHttpString = null;
        try {
            // This task performs some network operations so task duration is unpredictable
            HttpResponseMessage response =
                new HttpClient().GetAsync(new Uri("http://Wintellect.com/"))
                .AsTask(cts.Token).GetAwaiter().GetResult();

            lastHttpString = response.Content.ReadAsStringAsync()
                .AsTask(cts.Token).GetAwaiter().GetResult();
        }
        catch (TaskCanceledException) {
            lastHttpString = "Canceled";
        }
        finally {
            ApplicationData.Current.LocalSettings.Values["LastString"] = lastHttpString;
            // NOTE: When using a deferral, complete it here so the system knows your task is done
        }
    }
}
```

CHAPTER 10

Sharing data between apps

The ability to share data is extremely useful for users and greatly simplifies the effort required by software developers. For end users, sharing allows a user to use one app to create some content and then use other apps to edit or view the content. For software developers, sharing allows developers to focus on what their app is best at. An app can be great at editing photos but not great at sharing photos with online accounts like Facebook. Or the app might not be great at creating collages of photos or adding photos to a diary. Other apps might be good at these tasks but not good at editing. In addition, via sharing, users can decide for themselves which apps they want to use to complete their task.

In this chapter, I talk about how apps can share data with each other. First, I'll talk about how an app packages data so that it can be shared with other apps. Then I'll show how to share data using the clipboard and how to share data using the Windows Share charm.

One thing to note is that sharing should always be instigated by the user and under the user's control. An app should not try to automatically share some data with another app because this might be a breach of security: the user might not want one app to access the data produced by another app. When we speak of apps sharing data, the app creating the data to share is called the *source app* and the app receiving the shared data is called the *target app*.

Apps transfer data via a DataPackage

WinRT defines a `Windows.ApplicationModel.DataTransfer.DataPackage` class. Source apps construct a `DataPackage` object and initialize it with the data the app is willing to share with a target app. The `DataPackage` class looks like this:

```
public sealed class DataPackage {
    public DataPackage();    // Constructs a new DataPackage object

    // Use to set properties (ApplicationName, Title, Description, Thumbnail, etc.)
    public DataPackagePropertySet Properties { get; }

    // Optional: Use this to indicate why you're sharing the package (None, Copy, Move, Link)
    public DataPackageOperation RequestedOperation { get; set; }

    // Call SetData several times to add the same content in different formats
    public void SetData(String formatId, Object value);
```

```
    // These methods are simple, type-safe wrappers over SetData for common types:
    public void SetText(String value);
    public void SetRtf(String value);
    public void SetHtmlFormat(String value);  // See WinRT's HtmlFormatHelper class
    public void SetBitmap(RandomAccessStreamReference value);
    public void SetApplicationLink(Uri value);
    public void SetWebLink(Uri value);
    public void SetStorageItems(IEnumerable<IStorageItem> value);
    public void SetStorageItems(IEnumerable<IStorageItem> value, Boolean readOnly);

    // When adding HTML with references to content inaccessible to the target app,
    // add each URI and RandomAccessStreamReference to the ResourceMap so the target app can
    // access the content.
    // Example: If HTML has <img src="ms-appx:///Images/Photo.jpg"/> do this:
    // String imgSrc = "ms-appx:///Images/Photo.jpg";
    // ResourceMap.Add(imgSrc, RandomAccessStreamReference.CreateFromUri(new Uri(imgSrc)));
    public IDictionary<String, RandomAccessStreamReference> ResourceMap { get; }

    // Optional: Raised after target app pastes data (source app can delete content if desired)
    public event TypedEventHandler<DataPackage, OperationCompletedEventArgs> OperationCompleted;

    // Optional: Raised after DataPackage is GC'd. This allows the source app
    // to delete content (such as a temporary file) if desired:
    public event TypedEventHandler<DataPackage, Object> Destroyed;

    // Sets a delegate to handle requests from the target app
    // (see "Delayed rendering of shared content")
    public void SetDataProvider(String formatId, DataProviderHandler delayRenderer);

    // Returns a read-only version of the DataPackage object (this is what target apps get)
    public DataPackageView GetView();
}
```

After the share source app constructs an instance of this class, it sets some DataPackageProperty-tySet properties describing the data (ApplicationName, Title, Description, and so on). If the data is going to be shared via the clipboard, the app can set the DataPackageOperation property. The next thing to do is add content to the DataPackage object.

A DataPackage object is supposed to characterize a single piece of content. However, that single piece of content can exist in many different data formats. For example, HTML text would have an HTML format, could have a Rich Text Format (RTF) format, and would have a plain text format. An image could have an image format and a text format that describes the image or a URI format indicating where the image came from.

The source app calls DataPackage's SetData method once for each data format. Each call to SetData adds a format type (a String) and the data (an Object) representing that format to a dictionary. WinRT defines a static StandardDataFormats class with read-only String properties describing the predefined standard formats:

```
public static class StandardDataFormats {
    public static String Text            { get; }  // "Text"
    public static String Rtf             { get; }  // "Rich Text Format"
    public static String Html            { get; }  // "HTML Format"
    public static String Bitmap          { get; }  // "Bitmap"
    public static String ApplicationLink { get; }  // "ApplicationLink"
    public static String WebLink         { get; }  // "UniformResourceLocatorW"
    public static String StorageItems    { get; }  // "Shell IDList Array"
}
```

For the standard data formats, `DataPackage` offers simple, strongly-typed methods that internally call `SetData`, passing in one of `StandardDataFormats`' strings and the formatted data: `SetText`, `SetRtf`, `SetHtmlFormat`, `SetBitmap`, `SetApplicationLink`, `SetWebLink`, and `SetStorageItems`.

However, you are not limited to these standard formats. An app can define its own, custom data format and add this custom format of the content into the `DataPackage` object. Of course, the target app will have to know the same format name in order to get this data out of the `DataPackage` object. There are many recognized data formats described at *http://schema.org* for things such as books, movies, recipes, events, people, places, restaurants, products, offers, reviews, and more. If you want to use one of these formats, check out the NuGet package at *https://github.com/AndreiMarukovich/Transhipment*. This package includes code to support these formats, which simplifies the code you have to write.

> **Important** The order in which an app adds formats to the `DataPackage` is important: it should add the highest fidelity formats first and the format with the least fidelity last. For example, HTML text should have its formats added in this order: HTML, RTF, and then Text. A target app can enumerate the available formats in order. (See `DataPackageView`'s `AvailableFormats` property.) The target app should take the highest fidelity format it supports. For example, if a target app doesn't support the HTML format, it could use the RTF format (if it supports this) or the Text format (if it supports this). Of course, the target might not support any of the formats placed in the `DataPackage` object by the source app; in this case, the target app simply cannot accept any of the content.

Sharing via the clipboard

Since its inception, Windows has supported sharing data via the *clipboard*. The great thing about the clipboard is that it allows users to select exactly what they want shared. The user also decides what app to share it with. As long as the source and target apps have at least one format in common, the data is shareable. Another great thing about the clipboard is that it allows sharing of data between Windows Store apps and desktop apps.

WinRT has a `Windows.ApplicationModel.DataTransfer.Clipboard` class that apps use to manipulate the clipboard. Because Windows has only one clipboard, the class is a static class:

```
// Static class since there is only one system clipboard
public static class Clipboard {
   // Methods called by share source apps:
   public static void Clear();  // Puts an empty DataPackage on the clipboard
   public static void SetContent(DataPackage content); // Replaces any existing content
   public static void Flush();   // Keeps content on clipboard even if app terminates

   // Methods called by share target apps:
   public static DataPackageView GetContent(); // Returns read-only view of DataPackage

   // Raised when contents change (target apps use this to know if paste is possible)
   public static event EventHandler<object> ContentChanged;
}
```

> **Important** To keep the clipboard under the user's control, an app might call `Clipboard`'s methods from a GUI thread only when that app is in the foreground or only if the app is running under a debugger. This prevents other apps or background tasks from erasing or changing the clipboard's contents unexpectedly.

Here is code executed by a source app that creates and initializes a `DataPackage` object and then puts it on the clipboard:

```
private void PutDataPackageOnClipboard(DataPackageOperation operation) {
   DataPackage dp = new DataPackage();
   // Set desired properties:
   dp.Properties.ApplicationName = Package.Current.DisplayName;
   dp.Properties.Title = "DataPackage Title";
   dp.Properties.Description = "DataPackage Description";
   dp.RequestedOperation = operation;        // None, Copy, Move, or Link

   // Add desired data formats:
   dp.SetText(m_txt.Text);                    // Pulling text from a TextBox control

   // Optional: register event handlers:
   dp.OperationCompleted += OnShareCompleted;  // Mandatory for Move so source can delete data
   dp.Destroyed += OnDataPackageDestroyed;

   // Put DataPackage on clipboard. NOTE: The Clipboard makes a copy of the package;
   // changes made to the DataPackage object do not impact what's already on the clipboard.
   Clipboard.SetContent(dp);
}
```

After the source app has placed its contents on the clipboard, the user can switch to another app, making it the target app. From within the target app, the user would initiate the paste operation using some mechanism specific to the target app. Many target apps support paste functionality via an app bar command, via a menu item, or by using Ctrl+V. These are standard mechanisms that users have grown accustomed to, but a target app can adopt any mechanism it so desires.

Once triggered to accept data shared via the clipboard, the target app calls Clipboard's GetContent method to get its DataPackage objects. However, to ensure that the target app cannot change the clipboard's contents, a DataPackageView object is returned; this grants read-only access to the DataPackage, and it looks like this:

```
public sealed class DataPackageView {
    // ApplicationName, Title, Description, etc.
    // NOTE: The Win32 clipboard APIs set no properties.
    public DataPackagePropertySetView Properties   { get; }
    // Why data was shared (None, Copy, Move, Link)
    public DataPackageOperation RequestedOperation { get; }
    // Use these to find out what formats are available or if a specific format is available:
    public IReadOnlyList<String> AvailableFormats { get; }  // From highest to lowest fidelity
    public Boolean Contains(String formatId);

    // Call GetDataAsync to get the data for a specified format
    public IAsyncOperation<Object> GetDataAsync(String formatId);

    // These methods are simple, type-safe wrappers over GetDataAsync for common types:
    public IAsyncOperation<String> GetTextAsync(String formatId); // For plain text, Rtf,  etc.
    public IAsyncOperation<String> GetTextAsync();               // For plain text
    public IAsyncOperation<String> GetRtfAsync();
    public IAsyncOperation<String> GetHtmlFormatAsync();
    public IAsyncOperation<RandomAccessStreamReference> GetBitmapAsync();
    public IAsyncOperation<Uri> GetApplicationLinkAsync();
    public IAsyncOperation<Uri> GetWebLinkAsync();
    public IAsyncOperation<IReadOnlyList<IStorageItem>> GetStorageItemsAsync();

    // When getting HTML, the target can also get references to additional source content
    public IAsyncOperation<IReadOnlyDictionary<String, RandomAccessStreamReference>>
        GetResourceMapAsync();

    // Tell source app what target app did with the content (raises the OperationCompleted event)
    // Note: Many apps don't call this method, preventing OperationCompleted from being raised
    public void ReportOperationCompleted(DataPackageOperation value);
}
```

So now, a target app could execute code like this to read the content of the clipboard and do something with this content:

```
private static readonly String[] s_targetAppSupportedFormats = new[] {
   StandardDataFormats.Html, StandardDataFormats.Rtf, StandardDataFormats.Text
};

private async void OnPaste(object sender, RoutedEventArgs e) {
   DataPackageView dpv = Clipboard.GetContent();

   // Grab the format the source app says has highest fidelity that the target app supports
   String highestFidelityFormat = dpv.AvailableFormats
      .FirstOrDefault(af => s_targetAppSupportedFormats.Contains(af));
   String msg = null;
   if (highestFidelityFormat == null) {
      msg = "Clipboard doesn't contain any formats supported by target app.";
   } else {
      Object data = await dpv.GetDataAsync(highestFidelityFormat);
      msg = "Pasting: " + data;
   }

   // Do real paste operation here (this demo displays a MessageDialog)...
   MessageDialog md = new MessageDialog(msg,
      String.Format("Pasting content from AppName={0}, Title={1}, Description={2}",
         dpv.Properties.ApplicationName, dpv.Properties.Title, dpv.Properties.Description));
   await md.ShowAsync();
   dpv.ReportOperationCompleted(dpv.RequestedOperation);
}
```

Sharing via the Share charm

In addition to the clipboard, Windows Store apps can take advantage of another mechanism to share data between apps: the *Share charm*. Unlike the clipboard, which requires the user to switch to the target app to have it accept the shared data, the Share charm is designed to allow quick, contextual sharing scenarios that the user wants to complete without leaving the source app. The Share charm allows the user to post a video link to a social network, add a link to a reading list app, email a web page URL to a friend, and so on. It can also be used to send a photo to a photo-editing app, making the editing app aware of the photo. But then the user has to launch the photo-editing app explicitly to manipulate the photo. This scenario would be better served by launching the photo-editing app by way of a file type association or a protocol association (discussed in the "File type associations" section in Chapter 5, "Storage files and folders").

For developers, the Share-charm mechanism allows developers to focus on what their app does best. Their source app doesn't have to know how to post entries to a social network, how to maintain a reading list, or how to email something. The various target apps know how to do these things, and the user initiates the action via the Share charm.

The basic Share-charm workflow goes like this:

1.   The source app has some content the user wants to share.

2. The user selects the Share charm by swiping from the edge and selecting the charm, using the mouse to select the Share charm, or pressing Windows+H.

3. The source app is notified that the user selected the Share charm. At this point, the source app creates and initializes a `DataPackage` object, populating it with whatever content the source app has to share. The source app should insert all applicable data formats. The source app gives this `DataPackage` object to Windows.

4. Windows scans the data formats offered in the `DataPackage` object and then looks at all the installed Windows Store apps that have declared support for the data-sharing activation (sometimes referred to as the *sharing contract*) in their app's package manifest file. When an app declares support for the data-sharing activation, it also specifies what data formats the app can understand. From the data formats placed in the `DataPackage` object, Windows determines which of the installed apps can accept these formats and shows a list of these target apps to the user in the Share pane as shown in Figure 10-1.

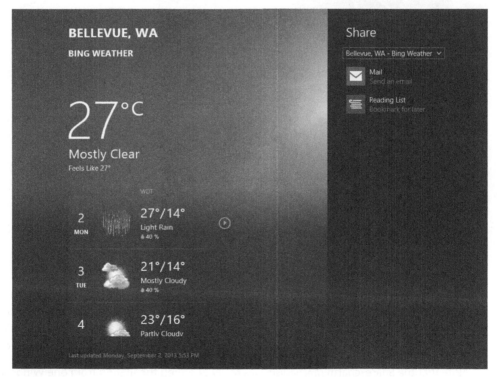

FIGURE 10-1 Sharing from the Weather app shows the Share pane, which lists the share target apps supporting the formats the Weather app has placed in its DataPackage.

5. At this point, the user can select a target app, causing Windows to activate it (via a hosted-view activation). Windows passes the target app a `DataPackageView` object, giving the target app read-only access to the `DataPackage`. The target app will now display some user interface to the user that lets the user know it can access the shared data, and the target app should also let the user know what it intends to do with the shared data (post it, add it to a

collection, email it, and so on). The target app should let the user confirm this action; it should not perform the action without user consent. Figure 10-2 shows the Mail app's sharing hosted view, allowing the user to decide who to mail the data to or allowing the user to tap the Back button, thereby canceling the share operation. The user can also use light dismiss[1] to cancel Mail's hosted view and the sharing operation. Windows controls the top of the pane (the background color, the Back button, and the target app's logo). The rest of the pane is occupied by the target app's hosted-view window.

FIGURE 10-2 The Mail app's hosted view, showing what it intends to do with the shared content. The user can accept or cancel this.

6. Once the user confirms or denies the target app's proposed action, the target app's hosted view is hidden and the user is returned back to the source app so that she can continue interacting with it. The hosted view window is destroyed when the sharing operation is complete.

Note that the Share-charm mechanism was really designed for sharing from one Windows Store app to another Windows Store app; it was not designed for sharing with desktop apps. However, when using a desktop app, if the user selects the Share charm, Windows automatically creates a DataPackage containing a screen shot of the whole desktop and allows the bitmap image to be

---

[1] *Light dismiss* is when the user taps outside the hosted view's window.

shared with Windows Store apps that support bitmap images.[2] For Windows Store apps, the system also creates a `DataPackage` containing a screen shot of the active-view window and makes it available for sharing too.[3] In addition, for Windows Store apps installed via the Windows Store, the system also creates a `DataPackage` containing the URI to the Windows Store app on the Windows Store. The URI is formatted for "Text", "UniformResourceLocatorW", and "HTML Format" so that any apps that support these three formats can accept the shared URI.

Implementing a share source app

It is expected that almost all Windows Store apps will be share source apps. The reason is because almost all apps have some kind of content that is shareable. If the user explicitly selects some content in the app, this is what should be shared when the user selects the Share charm. If the user has not explicitly selected some content, the app should implicitly share something meaningful based on what is being shown to the user. For example, when sharing from Internet Explorer, the URI for the currently viewed webpage is shared unless the user has explicitly selected some text on the page. In this case, the text is shared.

To receive notification when the user selects the Share charm, a share source app must use WinRT's `DataTransferManager` class:

```
public sealed class DataTransferManager {
    // Get DataTransferManager associated with an app's main or auxiliary (not hosted) view
    public static DataTransferManager GetForCurrentView();

    // Raised when the user selects the Share charm when the view is activated
    public event TypedEventHandler<DataTransferManager, DataRequestedEventArgs> DataRequested;

    // Raised when user chooses a target app (rarely used) so source knows the target app name
    public event TypedEventHandler<DataTransferManager, TargetApplicationChosenEventArgs>
        TargetApplicationChosen;

    // Call this to programmatically activate the Share charm
    public static void ShowShareUI();
}
```

First, the app must get a reference to the `DataTransferManager` object associated with its main view or one of the app's auxiliary views via the `GetForCurrentView` static method. Hosted views cannot use a `DataTransferManager` object. Then the app must register a callback method with the `DataTransferManager`'s `DataRequested` event:

```
DataTransferManager dtm = DataTransferManager.GetForCurrentView();
dtm.DataRequested += OnDataRequested;
```

---

[2] By the way, you can create a screen shot of an app using a tablet by holding the Windows button while pressing the volume-down button. This puts a screen shot in the Pictures library's Screenshots folder. On the keyboard, Windows key+Print Screen does the same thing.

[3] An app can prevent its view from being captured via a screen shot by setting its `ApplicationView`'s `IsScreenCaptureEnabled` property to `false`. Apps typically use this to prevent confidential information (like credit card or financial account information) from being captured.

This event is rather unusual in that it is not cumulative. That is, it only ever invokes the most recently registered callback method. It turns out that this is rather convenient. It allows your app to reregister the same callback with it every time your app has a main-view activation (inside OnLaunched, OnFileActivated, OnSearchActivated, or OnActivated) without calling the same callback method multiple times. Alternatively, some apps might register a callback with this event when their App's OnWindowCreated virtual method is called for the app's main or auxiliary view because this method is guaranteed to be called only once for each main or auxiliary view.

For hub, grid, and split apps, you might want to register the callback method when a Page's OnNavigateTo method is called. If you do this, you should unregister the handler when the Page's OnNavigatingFrom method is called because you might be navigating to a page that doesn't register a handler with the DataRequested event. If you don't unregister the handler, the page you navigated away from can't be garbage collected. Also, it will receive DataRequested events even though it is not the page the user is interacting with. Which technique you choose really depends on how your app manages its data for sharing.

Now, if the user selects the Share charm while interacting with your app's view, the DataRequested event is raised, calling your callback method. The DataRequestedEventArgs argument has a single Request property, which returns a DataRequest object:

```
public sealed class DataRequest {
   // Commonly used members:
   public DataPackage Data { get; set; }   // Returns a DataPackage you can initialize
   public void FailWithDisplayText(String value); // Call if app can't share anything now

   // Rarely used members:
   public DataRequestDeferral GetDeferral(); // Call to perform async operations in the handler
   public DateTimeOffset Deadline { get; }   // Indicates when delayed rendering must finish
}
```

You typically implement the callback method as follows:

```
private void OnDataRequested(DataTransferManager dtm, DataRequestedEventArgs e) {
   if (s_nothingToShareRightNow) { // Replace this with your own logic
      // Windows will show this string in the Share pane.
      e.Request.FailWithDisplayText("Select something to share.");
      return;
   }

   // 1. Set some DataPackage properties:
   e.Request.Data.Properties.ApplicationName = Package.Current.DisplayName;
   e.Request.Data.Properties.Title = "DataPackage Tile ";
   e.Request.Data.Properties.Description = "DataPackage Description";
   RandomAccessStreamReference image =
      RandomAccessStreamReference.CreateFromUri(new Uri("ms-appx:///Assets/Planets.png"));
   e.Request.Data.Properties.Thumbnail = image;

   // Optional: Add a URI a target app can use to get back to the content in the source app
   // Requires the source app declare a "datasharingdemo" protocol activation in the manifest
   Uri sourceAppContentUri = new Uri("datasharingdemo:Shared at " + DateTimeOffset.Now);
   e.Request.Data.Properties.ContentSourceApplicationLink = sourceAppContentUri;
```

```
    // Optional: Add a URI a target app can use to get back to the content on the web
    Uri webContentUri = new Uri("http://WintellectNOW.com/");
    e.Request.Data.Properties.ContentSourceWebLink = webContentUri;



    // 2. Add desired data formats to the DataPackage:
    // Target apps supporting "ApplicationLink" and "UniformResourceLocatorW" formats can
    // also get URIs to protocol activate the source app or access the content on the Web
    e.Request.Data.SetApplicationLink(sourceAppContentUri);
    e.Request.Data.SetWebLink(webContentUri);
    e.Request.Data.SetText("Some text");
    e.Request.Data.SetBitmap(image);
}
```

The system must wait for your event handler to return (or for its deferral to complete) before it can show the appropriate target apps to the user in the Share pane. If your OnDataRequested method requires a lot of time (more than 200 milliseconds) to add data formats to the DataPackage, consider delay-rendering the data as discussed in the next section.

Delayed rendering of shared content

It is recommend that apps populate a DataPackage in 200 milliseconds or less. But acquiring some data can be time consuming (for example, if the data needs to be downloaded, compressed, or encrypted). In addition, it would not be good to allocate a lot of memory for some data if the target app is not going to consume it. To address these two concerns, Windows supports delayed rendering of a DataPackage's data format. If it is time consuming or memory intensive to acquire data to put into a DataPackage, use DataPackage's SetDataProvider method. This method allows you to specify a data format and a delegate referring to a callback method. However, Windows invokes the callback method only when the data associated with this data format is requested. This allows the data to be acquired on demand because a target app really wants the data. Of course, you can call SetData-Provider multiple times, once for each different data format.

Here is an example showing how a callback method can perform its time-consuming or memory-intensive task to acquire the requested data:

```
// I made this method 'async' and use a deferral because it's likely that it will want
// to await I/O operations, which is why it is time consuming to acquire the data
private async void DataProviderHandler(DataProviderRequest request) {
    DataProviderDeferral deferral = request.GetDeferral();
    try {
        switch (request.FormatId) {
            case "Bitmap":
                String data = /* Perform memory intensive or await time consuming task here */;
                request.SetData(data);
                break;
        }
    }
    finally {
        deferral.Complete();
    }
}
```

When using this technique with StorageItem objects, you *must* add the file types to the Data-Package's properties first so that the system knows what file types are "in" your DataPackage. This allows the system to quickly identify share target apps that support the specified file types. For example, here is how to prepare a DataPackage to delay-render .jpg, and .png files:

```
DataPackage dp = ...;
dp.Properties.FileTypes.Add(".jpg");
dp.Properties.FileTypes.Add(".png");
dp.SetDataProvider(StandardDataFormats.StorageItems, DataProviderHandler);
```

Implementing a share target app

While many apps can and should be share source apps, very few apps should be share target apps because many apps don't have something to do with shared content. However, there are some apps that make great share target apps. These apps include communication (social networking and mail) apps, note-taking apps, and some apps that can communicate data to devices.

Creating a share target app is pretty straightforward. The first thing you must do is add the Share Target declaration to your app's package manifest. When you add this declaration, you indicate via the Share Description field what your app intends to do with the shared data. This text appears in the Share pane and helps users understand what the target app will do with the data without the user having to activate the target app. For example, the Reading List app shows "Bookmark for later" in the Share pane.

In the manifest, you also indicate what data formats your share target app supports. Examples are "Text", "Rtf", "HTML Format", and "Bitmap". Figure 10-3 shows how to add a Share Target declaration. Specifying anything in the Supported File Types section implies support for the "StorageItems" data format. If you specify Supports Any File Type, your target app will show up in the Share charm if any storage items are in the DataPackage. If you specify certain file types and do not specify Supports Any File Type, your app will appear in the Share charm only if the type of file in the DataPackage matches one of the file types your app supports.

The next thing you must do is define a XAML Page-derived class that shows your app's sharing user interface that allows the user to consent to or cancel the sharing process with your app. If you want, you can have Microsoft Visual Studio jump-start your effort here by selecting Project > Add New Item > Visual C# > Windows Store > Share Target Contract. This causes Visual Studio to produce a basic Page-derived class with some code-behind that will take some of the DataPackage's properties (like Title, Description, and Thumbnail) and display them in the XAML page. When a DataPackageView is given to the target app, the system prepopulates the LogoBackgroundColor and Square30x30Logo properties. (A share source app can change these values if it chooses.) These values can be displayed by the share target app so that the user knows the source app that produced the shared data. The Reading List app shows this source-app branding along with each item. Of course, you'll probably want to customize this page's appearance substantially to meet your app's needs. There is some more work you'll need to do to this page, which I'll discuss shortly.

Use this page to add declarations and specify their properties.

Available Declarations:

Select one...   ▾ Add

Supported Declarations:

Background Tasks

Share Target   Remove

Description:

Registers the app as a share target, which allows the app to receive shareable content.

Only one instance of this declaration is allowed per app.

More information

Properties:

Share description:

Data formats

Specifies the data formats supported by the app; for example: "Text", "URI", "Bitmap", "HTML", "StorageItems", or "RTF". The app will be displayed in the Share charm whenever one of the supported data formats is shared from another app.

Data format   Remove

Data format: Text

Data format   Remove

Data format: URI

Add New

Supported file types

Specifies the file types supported by the app; for example, ".jpg". The Share target declaration requires the app support at least one data format or file type. The app will be displayed in the Share charm whenever a file with a supported type is shared from another app. If no file types are declared, make sure to add one or more data formats.

☑ Supports any file type

FIGURE 10-3 Adding the Share Target declaration to your app's package manifest.

To make this page appear, you have to override your App's `OnShareTargetActivated` method. When the user selects your share target app from the Share pane, Windows activates your app for a hosted view and invokes the `OnShareTargetActivated` method, passing to it a `ShareTarget-ActivatedEventArgs` object. This object has a `ShareOperation` property that returns a `Share-Operation` object:

```
public sealed class ShareOperation {
   // 1. Target app gets DataPackageView to show user what's being shared
   public DataPackageView Data { get; }

   // 2. Target app calls this after the user consents to sharing the data
   public void ReportStarted();    // Keeps source app running, adds share op to progress list

   // 3. Target app calls this to hide the hosted view, letting user go back to the source app
   public void DismissUI();

   // 4. Target app calls one of these after the share operation completes
   public void ReportCompleted();       // Removes share operation from progress list
   public void ReportError(String value);   // Notifies user with toast; updates progress list

   // Methods for extended shares (see "Implementing an extended (lengthy) share operation"):
   public void ReportDataRetrieved();            // Allows source app to be suspended/terminated
   public void ReportSubmittedBackgroundTask(); // Allows target app to be suspended

   // Methods used for manipulating quick links (see "Share target app quick links"):
   public void ReportCompleted(QuickLink quicklink); // Call when share complete; adds quick link
   public String QuickLinkId { get; }               // Contains the QuickLink's Id
   public void RemoveThisQuickLink();
}
```

Inside your OnShareTargetActivated method, you should construct your XAML page, save a reference to the ShareOperation object, and activate the page. Your activation code should execute quickly or Windows will think the hosted view is not responding and kill the whole process (including the main view if it's running). Once the hosted view is activated, your code can access the ShareOperation object's Data property; it returns a DataPackageView object containing the data passed to the share target app. At this point, the code can extract some of its properties and data formats to populate the hosted view's user interface as your app desires.

Ultimately, your app's share target page must show the user what data it is going to consume and what it intends to do with that data. You can allow the user to customize the data, such as adding text in the body of an email, adjusting the subject line, or specifying what data format the target app should consume. When the user is content and ready to let the target app process the data, the user will trigger its acceptance; usually this is done by the user pressing a Share or Send button offered by the page.

Here is sample code demonstrating how to perform a share operation (some advanced features shown are discussed in the next few sections):

```
private async void ShareButton_Click(object sender, RoutedEventArgs e) {
   // Don't suspend source app, add target app to progress list
   m_shareOperation.ReportStarted();

   // Hide hosted view so user can work with share source app right away
   m_shareOperation.DismissUI();

   // TODO: get everything needed from the DataPackageView here...
   for (Int32 second = 0; second < 10; second++) {
      DefaultViewModel["Status"] = "Status: Started - " + second;
      await Task.Delay(TimeSpan.FromSeconds(1));
   }

   // Target app no longer needs source app running; OS can suspend/terminate it
   m_shareOperation.ReportDataRetrieved();

   // TODO: Continue processing (sharing) the data here...
   for (Int32 second = 0; second < 10; second++) {
      DefaultViewModel["Status"] = "Status: Data retrieved - " + second;
      await Task.Delay(TimeSpan.FromSeconds(1));
   }

   // Share is done, report error or success (possibly with QuickLink)
   if (m_chkSimulateFailure.IsChecked.Value) {
      m_shareOperation.ReportError("Share failed.");
   } else {
      if (!m_chkCreateQuickLink.IsChecked.Value) {
         m_shareOperation.ReportCompleted();
      } else {
```

```
        QuickLink ql = new QuickLink {
            // Set mandatory properties:
            Title = "QuickLink title",
            Id = "QuickLink created on " + DateTimeOffset.Now,
            Thumbnail = RandomAccessStreamReference.CreateFromUri(
                new Uri("ms appx:///Assets/Logo.png")),

            // At least 1 of these properties:
            SupportedDataFormats = { "Text" },
            SupportedFileTypes = { ".txt" }
        };
        m_shareOperation.ReportCompleted(ql);
    }
  }
}
```

At this point, the target app should call ShareOperation's ReportStarted method. This method tells Windows to keep the source app running so that it can deliver any delay-rendered content being accessed by the target app. In addition, the system adds an entry to the sharing pane's outstanding share operations list (discussed in more detail shortly). After calling ReportStarted, the target app should call ShareOperation's DismissUI method. This method hides the target app's hosted view, allowing the user to interact with the source app again. The target app's hosted view thread continues performing the share operation.

If the user desires, he can open the Share pane to monitor all the outstanding share operations. If any share operations are in progress, the text "Check progress" appears at the bottom of the Share pane. If the user taps on this text, the Share pane shows the outstanding share operations. Selecting an outstanding operation causes the target app's hosted view to reappear. Your hosted-view page can show the user more specific progress information and also offer the user the ability to cancel the operation.

If the share operation completes successfully, the hosted-view thread should call ShareOperation's ReportCompleted method. This method causes the hosted view and its thread to be destroyed. In addition, the ReportCompleted method removes the share operation from the Share pane's outstanding share operations list.

If the share operation fails, the hosted-view thread should call ShareOperation's ReportError method, passing a string indicating the reason for failure. This method also causes the hosted view and its thread to be destroyed. However, Windows will display a toast notification to the user containing the reason for the failure string and which operation failed to complete. The system will not remove the share operation from the Share pane because the user might have missed the toast notification. If the user later opens the Share pane, he will see "Something went wrong" at the bottom. Tapping on this text displays the list of outstanding share operations. Failed operations show the text "Something went wrong." The user can then select an operation to see the reason for failure and to clear the failed operation from the list. The user will have to retry the share operation from the beginning again to try to get it to work.

Implementing an extended (lengthy) share operation

Sometimes sharing data can be a time-consuming process, especially if the share target app is transferring files. These scenarios are problematic because of Windows Process Lifetime Management (PLM) rules. For example, the system will suspend threads in the target app if the user is not inter-acting with it, preventing the app from completing the sharing operation. So, when performing an extended (lengthy) share operation, the target app must call some additional methods.

Specifically, after the target app has completed its use of the DataPackageView object, it should call ShareOperation's ReportDataRetrieved method. This tells Windows that the target app no longer needs the source app running, thus allowing the system to suspend or terminate the source app. If the target app is going to use the background-transfer APIs (discussed in Chapter 7, "Network-ing") to transfer files over the network, it should call ShareOperation's ReportSubmittedBack-groundTask method. This method tells Windows that the target app can be suspended because the transfer operation is now being performed on its behalf by the background-transfer manager.

Share target app quick links

Some apps have "destinations" within the app itself. For example, the Mail app allows you to send to a specific contact, and a social-networking app might allow you to post to a specific person or group. Users tend to share with the same destinations over and over again. It would be a shame if the user had to share with an app and then select the desired destination repeatedly. It would be better if the user had a way to quickly share with an app's destination. Fortunately, Windows does support this by using a mechanism called *quick links*. Quick links appear at the top of the Share pane.

After a user has successfully shared some data with a target app's destination, the target app can construct and initialize a QuickLink object:

```
public sealed class QuickLink {
    public QuickLink();
    // Mandatory properties:
    public String Title { get; set; }                          // Shown in Share pane
    public RandomAccessStreamReference Thumbnail { get; set; } // Shown in Share pane
    public String Id { get; set; }  // App-defined: passed to target app
                                    // via ShareOperation's QuickLinkId property

    // At least 1 of these properties must be set indicating the data formats
    // and/or file types that cause the Share pane to show this quick link
    public IList<String> SupportedDataFormats { get; }
    public IList<String> SupportedFileTypes { get; }
}
```

Once initialized, the QuickLink object can be passed to ShareOperation's ReportCompleted method. Now, when the user activates the Share charm, if any data formats or file types in the Data-Package match the data formats or files types in a QuickLink, the system shows the quick link's thumbnail and title. If the user selects the QuickLink, the system activates its target app and in the App's OnShareTargetActivated method, it can examine the ShareTargetActivatedEventArgs's ShareOperation's QuickLinkId property. This property returns whatever value was set in the QuickLink object's Id property. The app can use this to quickly share with one of its destinations.

If the `QuickLink`'s `Id` is no longer valid, the target app can call `ShareOperation`'s `RemoveThis-QuickLink` to remove it so that it will no longer appear in the Share pane.

Debugging share target apps

Debugging share target apps can be quite challenging. Sure you can put a breakpoint in the activation code, but when the debugger hits the breakpoint, Windows' light dismiss behavior immediately cancels the share operation. The easiest way to debug a share target app is to run it in the simulator or on a remote PC. In addition, you'll have to launch the app normally first, enabling you to put breakpoints in the share-target activation code. Or you can open the project's properties and select the Project Properties > Debug > Do Not Launch, But Debug My Code When It Starts option.

CHAPTER 11

Windows Store

So here you are. You've developed your app, tested it on all your available systems and on the simulator for different screen sizes, and now you're ready to reap the benefits of all those long days and nights. You want to submit your app to the Windows Store so that users can easily discover it and install it. Also, any updates you make to your app are automatically deployed to your users.[1] In addition, the Windows Store developer portal dashboard gives you a lot of information about your app and its users, such as download volume and reviews, but it also gives you crash data that you can use to quickly close the loop with your customers and give them fixes for your app.

If you want to make money with your app, you have the option of using the Windows Store as a commerce engine. But Microsoft does not force apps deployed via the Windows Store to use its commerce engine; you are free to use other engines, such as PayPal. Microsoft's commerce engine does have a global reach of around 200 countries and over 100 languages and offers several commerce schemes, including trials, in-app purchases, and consumables. I'll discuss the Windows Store commerce engine later in this chapter.

Let's start by taking a quick look at the Windows Store app itself. The main page presents you with a few different promotional sections: a primary spotlight with a handful of noteworthy apps, a section with apps that are recommended for you based on previous purchases and usage of apps, a section with popular apps, new releases, top paid apps, and top free apps. You can browse around in the two dozen categories by selecting the navigation bar on top, and you can obviously search in the Store. You will even find some desktop apps, although you won't be able to install them directly from the Store; vendors can provide a link to where you can download the desktop apps.[2] And, on your website, you can display a link to your app's page in the Windows Store (available for both Windows Store and desktop apps).

When viewing an app, the user is shown the app's description, publisher, category, size, age rating, and a few screen shots. All of this information is provided when a developer submits an app to the Windows Store. The user is also shown the permissions the app needs to run on the system; this information is obtained from the app's package manifest file. When a user installs your app, Windows debits the user's payment method on file (if the app is not free and there's no trial period) and installs the package as discussed in Chapter 2, "App packaging and deployment." This payment method can

---

[1] Users can turn automatic updates off using the Windows Store app's Settings > App Updates > Automatically Update My Apps settings.

[2] Your desktop app will have to pass Windows Certification in order to be listed in the Windows Store.

be a credit card or a gift card purchased online or at a retail store. Once users purchase an app, they can install it on all their PCs.

The Store app shows users only the apps that are installable on their PCs. So if the user is browsing the Store using a Windows RT PC, the Store app will show only apps that can run on an ARM CPU. Similar filtering is applied for user languages and age categories. If the user is using a Windows 8.1 system, he can see and install apps that are built for Windows 8 as well as for Windows 8.1. If both are available, he will see only the 8.1 version. Once the user upgrades his system to Windows 8.1, his apps will upgrade too (if an 8.1 version is available).

Any app can launch the Windows Store app to show a specific app via the ms-windows-store protocol. Here is an example:

```
ms-windows-store:PDP?PFN=PackageFamilyName
```

In addition, you can add some meta tags to your website that, when interpreted by Internet Explorer (when not in desktop mode), cause Internet Explorer to show an app bar button, allowing the user to open your app (if it is already installed) or navigate to your app inside the Windows Store app (if your app isn't installed). For more information about this, see *http://msdn.microsoft.com/en-us/library/windows/apps/Hh974767.aspx*.

I'll start this chapter by walking you through the process of getting your app in the Store, monitoring your app in the marketplace, and updating your app. The second part of this chapter is about the WinRT APIs you can incorporate into your app to use the Windows Store's commerce engine to sell your app and in-app products.

Submitting a Windows Store app to the Windows Store

Before you can submit your first app, you need to register an account with the Windows Store in the Dashboard on the Dev Center. Go to *http://dev.Windows.com* and then select Dashboard. The Dashboard is your one-stop shop for all your Windows Store app needs. It shows your account details, all your apps, their submission status, their crash data, and a financial summary. Registering for a Windows Store account takes a few days, and you can do this before you have your app ready. You register either as an individual or as an enterprise. The Windows Store authenticates both types of accounts. To authenticate an individual account, you as a developer need to give valid credit card details. Microsoft debits your credit card with two small amounts—for example, $0.05 and $0.11. You then enter these two amounts into the Dashboard and, if they match the debited amounts, you are authenticated. For an enterprise account, Symantec is doing the authentication and, because of additional scrutiny, this might take a few days more.[3] If you use the Windows Store's commerce engine, you also have to complete tax forms. Although you can still submit apps to the Store without these forms, Microsoft will not release your app for your users to download.

---

[3] An enterprise account is required if your app requires special-use capabilities (such as Documents Library, Enterprise Authentication, and Shared User Certificates).

Submitting your app

Once you've established a developer account, you can submit an app to the Windows Store. The Dashboard makes this really straightforward by giving you a step-by-step approach for getting your app into the Store, as shown in Figure 11-1. This is where you fill out most of the data users see in the Windows Store.

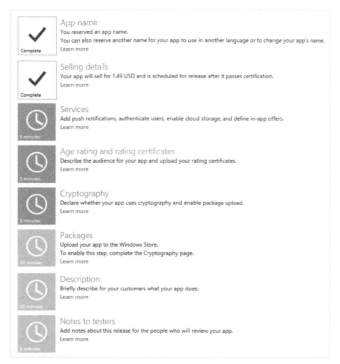

FIGURE 11-1 Steps for submitting your app to the Store.

Let's walk through some of these steps.

- **App Name**   First you have to reserve a name for your app. To prevent spoofing, the Windows Store requires that all app names be unique and that you have the rights to use the name.[4] If you want to localize your app's name, you can provide those translations here as well. You can reserve a name up to one year before actually submitting your app to the Store. If you do not submit an app within one year, someone else can take the name. When you use Microsoft Visual Studio to associate your app with the Store, Visual Studio modifies your app's package manifest file so that your package's display name and app's display name are both set to your app's reserved name.

---

[4]   If you have the rights to a name that is in use by someone else, you can take that up with Microsoft.

- **Selling Details**   On this page, you select your app's price (from $1.49 to $999.99, converted to equivalent values in foreign markets).[5] Choose Free if you do not intend to use the Microsoft commerce engine. Certain apps must be free, such as Windows Store device apps. (See *http://msdn.microsoft.com/en-us/library/windows/apps/hh464909.aspx*.)

  On this page, you also set a trial period that allows users to try your app for a certain period for free. You can choose from Never Expires, 1 Day, 7 Days, 15 Days, and 30 Days. After a user installs your app and the expiration period lapses, the app will no longer run on the user's PCs. Note: you do not have to do anything in your app's code to support trials, although you can create a better user experience by letting them purchase the app once the trial period expires. See "The Windows Store commerce engine" to see how to do this.

  By default, the Windows Store makes your app available as soon as it passes certification. If you prefer, you can specify a specific release date. This page also allows you to set a category and subcategory for your app to help users locate it in the Store. Finally, in the Hardware Requirements section, you indicate what level of DirectX and what amount RAM the user's PC must have to install your app. This is done to prevent users from installing your app on a machine that is not powerful enough for your app's graphics and memory requirements, because this would lead to poor user ratings. Finally, you can indicate that your app is suitable for accessibility.

- **Services**   This page takes you to other pages that give you information about integrating other services with your app, such as the Windows Push Notification Service (WNS), Windows Azure Mobile Services, and Live Connect. You also use this page to define any in-app offers to sell products within your app. The pricing scheme for in-app offers is the same as for the app's pricing. For more detail, see this chapter's "The Windows Store commerce engine" section.

- **Age Rating And Rating Certificates**   This page allows you to set the age rating for your app according to the type of content you display. This page also lets you upload game-rating certificate files.

- **Cryptography**   On this page, you declare whether your app uses encryption technologies (such as SSL). This is required because your app's package files reside in the United States and the U.S. government regulates the export of technology that uses cryptography.

- **Packages**   Use this page to upload your app's package files to the Store. The maximum allowable package size is 8 GB.

- **Description**   On this page, you provide the information users see when viewing your app in the Store app, such as the following:

  - Descriptive text and pictures.

  - Release notes (bug fixes or new features).

  - Recommended hardware for having the best experience with your app.

---

[5] For more information about markets where you can sell your app, see *http://msdn.microsoft.com/en-us/library/windows/apps/hh694064*.

- Copyright, trademark info, and license terms.

- Promotional images if you want your app to be displayed prominently in one of the spotlight sections of the Windows Store app.

- Website and email address for users to contact you with questions.

- URL to a privacy policy if your app collects any information or uses any network capability (as described in Chapter 7, "Networking"). The same URL must also be accessible from your app's Settings pane.

■ **Notes To Testers**, On this page, you provide information that Windows Store app testers need in order to certify your app. The Windows Store team has to be able to test the full functionality of your app; hence, this is where you specify credentials to a test account (which you can disable after your app passes certification) or indicate that your app works only in certain regions. Testers actually read this, so be complete.[6]

Once you've submitted your package for certification, the Windows Store team tests your app. You can find the requirements here: *http://msdn.microsoft.com/en-us/library/windows/apps/ hh694083.aspx*. As you might imagine, a part of this process is automated. On your Dashboard, you can keep track of where your app is in the certification process. (See Figure 11-2.) The Store team commits to having your app go through the process within five days, but it usually takes less time than this.

FIGURE 11-2 The Dashboard showing a Windows Store app's certification status.

---

[6] I actually had two apps fail Store certification and used this section to convince the testers that the app was fine as is. Then both apps passed certification with no changes to the apps themselves.

Testing your app

In the Technical Compliance step in Figure 11-2, your app is submitted to a set of certification tests. Some of these tests are automated, while some of them are performed by an actual person. The automated tests are performed by a tool called the Windows App Certification Kit (WACK). This tool actually ships with Visual Studio and the Windows SDK, allowing you to run the tool yourself before you upload your app to the Windows Store. If the WACK tool discovers a violation in your app, your app will definitely fail certification if you upload it to the Windows Store. So you should use this tool before submitting your app to save you time and effort. You can run the WACK tool on your local PC or on a remote PC. You can even download an ARM version for Windows RT systems. The WACK tool has a graphical UI, but you can also run the command-line version of the tool (AppCert.exe). For details about the kit, see *http://msdn.microsoft.com/en-us/library/windows/apps/hh694081.aspx*.

After you have Visual Studio create a package, the VS Wizard offers you the option of running the WACK tool on the package files. Alternatively, you can start the WACK tool from the Start screen and then specify whether you want it to validate a Windows Store app, desktop app, or desktop device app. WACK needs to start your Windows Store app through a COM API call, which requires elevated privileges; hence, Windows prompts you with a User Account Control (UAC) dialog box before showing you the list of tests, as shown in Figure 11-3. You can run all tests at once, or you can run tests independently, which can save time if you're focusing on removing specific violations. For details on the individual tests and what they do, see *http://msdn.microsoft.com/en-us/library/windows/apps/jj657973.aspx*.

FIGURE 11-3 The required tests for certification in the Windows App Certification Kit.

Clicking the Next button causes the WACK tool to go through the tests. Some of them merely inspect your app's package files, while other tests actually launch your app and simulate user interactions with it; for these tests, you'll see your app appear and disappear a few times. Be aware that some of the tests examine performance, such as the time it takes for your app to launch or suspend. For this reason, it's recommended you close all other applications and leave the machine alone while the tests are running.

Once you've run the tests, the WACK tool generates a report indicating whether your app has passed or failed. Individual test results can be Pass, Warning, or Fail, and only one or more failing tests will result in overall failure. The report shows what tests your app did not pass, with guidance on how to fix it, as you see in Figure 11-4. After your app passes all tests, you can upload it to the Windows Store.

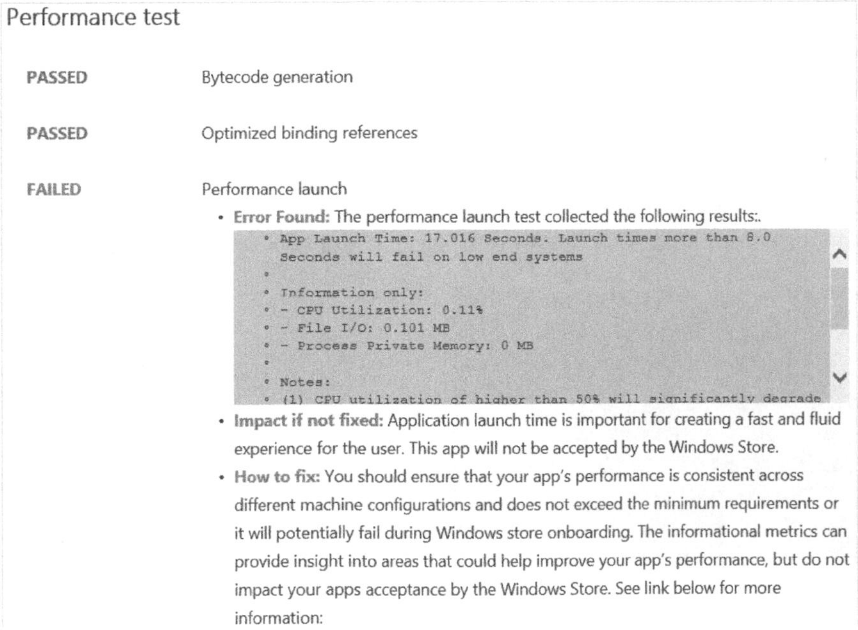

Performance test

PASSED	Bytecode generation
PASSED	Optimized binding references
FAILED	Performance launch

- **Error Found:** The performance launch test collected the following results:.
  - App Launch Time: 17.016 Seconds. Launch times more than 8.0 Seconds will fail on low end systems
  - Information only:
  - – CPU Utilization: 0.11%
  - – File I/O: 0.101 MB
  - – Process Private Memory: 0 MB
  - Notes:
  - (1) CPU utilization of higher than 50% will significantly degrade
- **Impact if not fixed:** Application launch time is important for creating a fast and fluid experience for the user. This app will not be accepted by the Windows Store.
- **How to fix:** You should ensure that your app's performance is consistent across different machine configurations and does not exceed the minimum requirements or it will potentially fail during Windows store onboarding. The informational metrics can provide insight into areas that could help improve your app's performance, but do not impact your apps acceptance by the Windows Store. See link below for more information:

FIGURE 11-4 The WACK tool gives guidance on how to fix failing tests.

There are some common errors made by developers that will either result in delaying or outright failing the certification. I've listed the most common ones here. You can find an up-to-date list at *http://msdn.microsoft.com/en-us/library/windows/apps/jj657968.aspx*.

- Special-use capabilities (Documents Library, Enterprise Authentication, and Shared User Certificates) require an enterprise account. If your app uses any of these capabilities, the Windows Store team looks very closely at your app, ensuring that it uses these capabilities for legitimate reasons. In particular, the Documents Library capability is frequently abused. This is why Visual Studio doesn't show this capability in its manifest designer.

- If your app accesses a network, it must provide a privacy statement as stated in requirement 4.1.1. The reason is because network requests include the client's IP address, which is considered personal information. The privacy policy must indicate what you intend to do with this personal information: discard it, log it, use it to determine a person's name and address, and so on. You must provide the link to your app's privacy policy in the Dashboard (via the Description webpage), and users must be able to get to it via your app's Settings pane. When Visual Studio creates a new Windows Store app project, it turns on the Internet (Client) capability by default, so you must either turn this capability off or provide a privacy statement for your app to pass certification.

> **Important** Section 6.2 of the app-certification requirements mandates that any app that transmits personal information must be assigned a Windows Store age rating of 12 or over. So any app that specifies a network capability in its manifest must be rated for users who are at least 12 years old or your app will not pass certification.

- Make sure you test on all platforms, with and without keyboard, mouse, touch, and with different screen sizes. Also, test the availability of network connections. You can use the simulator to simulate restricted network conditions with roaming and data limits. (See Figure 11-5.)

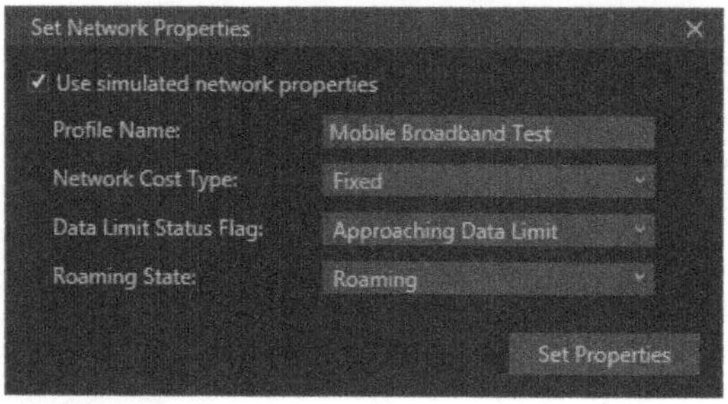

FIGURE 11-5 Use the simulator to test different network settings.

Monitoring your app

Once your app is available to users, you can periodically see how your app is doing by logging in to your Windows Store Dashboard (*https://appdev.microsoft.com/StorePortals*). Here, you will find a wealth of information about all your apps. You can get all the following details:

- **Downloads per day** This report allows you to filter or get specifics by market, age, and gender. You can hone in on the last month or the past 3, 6, or 12 months, and the Dashboard shows how your app is stacking up against the average of the top five apps in its subcategory.

- **In-app purchases** This report shows if your app offers in-app purchases.

- **Usage** This report shows the total usage of your app in minutes per day.

- **Ratings and review**   You can use the ratings and review information to prioritize new features for the next release.

- **Quality**   This report shows you the crash and hang (app unresponsive) rate of your app categorized by the most common failures. User data is automatically uploaded to the Windows Store if users opt In to it via Action Center's Customer Experience Improvement Program. If you provided symbolic debug information (PDB files) when you uploaded your app's package files to the Store, the Dashboard provides you with .cab files for these failures. You can extract the memory dump file (.hdmp) from the .cab file and open it in Visual Studio or Windows Debugger (WinDbg.exe) to debug your app. For more information about post-mortem debugging in Visual Studio, see *http://msdn.microsoft.com/en-us/library/vstudio/d5zhxt22(v=vs.120).aspx*. For information on using WinDbg.exe, see *http://msdn.microsoft.com/en-us/library/windows/hardware/ff538058.aspx*.

Updating your app

After looking at your app's telemetry in the Dashboard, you might have to fix a failure. Or maybe your users are asking for new features that you're ready to add. Once you've built a new release of your app, you need to submit it to the Windows Store. In the App Details section, you create a new release by selecting the Packages link and uploading the new version of your app's package files. At that point, the Windows Store team will validate your app again, just as it did for the first release.

Note that you don't have to change your app's bits for a new release. You can change any of the metadata, such as description, screen shots, price, category, or market, for example. Your app's new release will still have to go through certification, but because the bits haven't changed it will likely go a lot faster. If you update the name of your app, you must submit new app package files too. Make sure you mention the changes in the Notes To Testers page. Any change to your app's information appears as an update to your users.

> **Note**   Developers frequently ask if there is a way their app can know if a newer version is available in order to prompt users to upgrade. Although there is nothing built into Windows to allow this, you can always create your own web server and have your app contact it requesting the latest version of your app that's available. The result can be compared against `Package.Current.Id.Version`.

You can have a Windows 8 version of your app as well as a Windows 8.1 version. There is a restriction around your app's versioning, however. Your app's Windows 8 version number can never be higher than your app's Windows 8.1 version number. The recommendation is to increase at least your app's minor version number for the 8.1 release. This will give your Windows 8 version plenty of room for updates.

If you want to remove your app from the Windows Store, you need to submit a new version of the app and leave all the market options unselected. If your developer account expires, users who previously acquired your app are always able to reacquire it, but your app will not be acquirable by new users. In addition, your app name is released and in-app purchases are disabled if you're using the Windows Store commerce engine. Developers receive email reminders when their accounts are nearing expiration.

The Windows Store commerce engine

Many Windows Store apps are available to users for free. Maybe the app didn't take much effort to develop and the developer just wants to make it available. Or maybe the app is a rich client app over a service that users purchase in some other way (like the Netflix app, which is free because users must already have a valid Netflix subscription) to use the app. Some apps are also free because they incorporate advertising into the app using an advertising SDK, such as the Microsoft Advertising SDK for Windows. Be aware that advertising requires network access, forcing you to provide a privacy statement for your app, and advertising also works only when the user's PC is connected to a network.

Developers can also integrate a commerce engine into their app, which allows them to collect revenue when users purchase the app or any in-app products. The Windows Store provides a commerce engine you can use within your app. However, you do not have to use the Windows Store commerce engine. You can use third-party commerce engines instead. In fact, PayPal offers a commerce engine and an SDK exposing WinRT components, which is available from *http://Services.WindowsStore.com/ PayPal*. If you use a third-party commerce engine, you must list your app as Free on the Windows Store and notify users who the provider is when they make a purchase. (See the certification requirements, section 4.7.)

This section focuses on the Windows Store's commerce engine because it is expected that many developers will use it and because the WinRT APIs to integrate with it are built into the Windows operating system itself.

The Windows Store commerce engine supports many features, including the following:

- Free app trials (time-based and feature differentiated). Providing users a free trial of your app is strongly encouraged because statistics show that users are more likely to purchase an app that they have tried and liked. Users are much less likely to purchase an app before they have the opportunity to try it out.

- A wide range of price points, ranging from $1.49 all the way up to $999.99.

- The ability to accept money in local currencies for 200 different markets around the globe.

- After a user purchases an app, the app can sell in-app products (like the ability to turn off in-app advertising or enabling the viewing of some video). In-app products can expire after some period of time like 1 day, 1 month, 1 year, or never.

If you choose to use the Windows Store commerce engine, Microsoft pays you 70 percent of the first $25,000 and 80 percent for all revenue beyond the first $25,000. Having different versions of your app does not affect this. That is, the total revenue earned does not reset if you create a newer version of your app.

Developers use the Dashboard's Selling Details page to specify the price tier of their app, whether the app offers a trial period, and when this trial period expires. This is also where developers indicate if they want to use a third party commerce engine for in-app purchases. If the developer wants to use the Windows Store's commerce engine, users go to another webpage to specify the list of in-app products they wish to make available. Each product has a string ID, price tier (Free, or $1.49 to $999.99), and details about how long the user can use the product before it expires. Altogether, this information is referred to as the app's *listing information*. An app's listing information is not cached on the user's PC, so an Internet connection is required for an app to gets its own listing information at runtime.

When users purchase an app, they acquire a license for that app. Similarly, whenever users purchase an in-app product, they acquire a license for that in-app product. Windows maintains the user's acquired licenses on the user's PC. In fact, the license information is synchronized across all the user's PCs. This allows the user to purchase an app or in-app product on one PC and, shortly thereafter, the app or product will be licensed on the user's other PCs as well. Of course, the user must be connected to the Internet so that Windows can synchronize the license information. But, once a license is on a PC, an app can always check a license, even if the PC is not currently connected to the Internet.

> **Note** Packages downloaded from the Windows Store are licensed to a user's Microsoft account. This is usually the same account the user uses to log in to her PC. However, they do not have to be the same. In fact, a user can go to the Store app, display the Settings charm > Your Account pane, and change the Microsoft account she used to download packages from the store. I do this when I want to install a package I have already purchased on another family member's PC (where that family member logs in as himself).

The Windows Store commerce engine WinRT APIs

Your app integrates itself with the Windows Store commerce engine by way of WinRT's static `Windows.ApplicationModel.Store.CurrentApp` class. However, when you're developing an app, using `CurrentApp` is a problem because your app can't interact with the Windows Store commerce engine if your app is not in the Windows Store. So, during development, WinRT offers another static class you use instead, `CurrentAppSimulator`. This class' methods are identical to the `CurrentApp` class' methods, but internally the methods simulate the Windows Store's behavior. This allows you to test your app's integration with the commerce engine during development. Here is what the `CurrentApp` and `CurrentAppSimulator` classes look like:

```
public static class CurrentApp(Simulator) {
    public static Guid AppId { get; }   // Your app's Unique ID
    public static Uri LinkUri { get; }  // URI to app's listing in the Windows Store website

    // Call this to download your app's listing information (Internet connection required):
    public static IAsyncOperation<ListingInformation> LoadListingInformationAsync();

    // Call this to examine the app's locally cached license information:
    public static LicenseInformation LicenseInformation { get; }
```

```
// Call these methods to let the user purchase the app or an in-app product:
public static IAsyncOperation<String> RequestAppPurchaseAsync(Boolean includeReceipt);
public static IAsyncOperation<PurchaseResults> RequestProductPurchaseAsync(String productId);
public static IAsyncOperation<PurchaseResults> RequestProductPurchaseAsync(String productId,
    String offerId, ProductPurchaseDisplayProperties displayProperties);

// Call these methods to manage in-app products that expire:
public static IAsyncOperation<IReadOnlyList<UnfulfilledConsumable>>
    GetUnfulfilledConsumablesAsync();
public static IAsyncOperation<FulfillmentResult>
    ReportConsumableFulfillmentAsync(String productId, Guid transactionId);

// Call these methods to get a receipt you can send to a server to validate a purchase:
public static IAsyncOperation<String> GetAppReceiptAsync();
public static IAsyncOperation<String> GetProductReceiptAsync(String productId);

// This method is on CurrentAppSimulator only; call it to initialize the app's listing
// information since the simulator cannot get it from the Windows Store itself:
public static IAsyncAction ReloadSimulatorAsync(StorageFile simulatorSettingsFile);
}
```

If you submit a Windows Store app for certification, it will fail if its code references the Current-AppSimulator class. So, before submitting the app, you must change any code that references CurrentAppSimulator to reference CurrentApp instead. To simplify this, put these using directives at the top of your .cs files and then reference the CurrentApp symbol through the rest of your code:

```
#if StoreSubmission  // In VS, create a "Windows Store"  configuration that defines this symbol
using CurrentApp = Windows.ApplicationModel.Store.CurrentApp;
#else
using CurrentApp = Windows.ApplicationModel.Store.CurrentAppSimulator;
#endif
```

Although you can specify your app's selling details in the Windows Store before submitting your app, there is no way for Windows to download this information until your app is released. So, when developing your app, you need to create a local XML file that describes your app's selling details.[7] You then seed the CurrentAppSimulator class with this information by calling its ReloadSimulator-Async method, passing it a StorageFile object referring to the XML file.[8] Alternatively, instead of calling ReloadSimulatorAsync, CurrentAppSimulator will look for a WindowsStoreProxy.xml file in the %LocalAppData%\Packages*PackageFamilyName*\LocalState\Microsoft\Windows Store\ApiData directory. If CurrentAppSimulator can't find the file in that directory, it will create a WindowsStoreProxy.xml file with default settings.

After CurrentAppSimulator has loaded an XML file, calls to CurrentAppSimulator's Load-ListingInformationAsync method return the simulated listing information (selling details), which

---

[7] It would be nice if the Dashboard offered a way to download the selling details as an XML file, but it currently does not expose this feature.

[8] You should call CurrentAppSimulator's ReloadSimulatorAsync method from within a #if StoreSubmission block of code because your app will fail certification if submitted with a call to this method.

should be identical to the listing information you'd get back from calling `CurrentApp`'s `Load-ListingInformationAsync` method once your app is released.

> **Important** When testing your app, `CurrentAppSimulator`'s *Xxx*Async methods perform their work locally using the XML file; these methods do not perform network I/O; therefore, they will never throw an exception if the PC is not connected to the Internet. However, `CurrentApp`'s *Xxx*Async methods do perform their work by making network requests, so they will throw an `Exception` (with an HResult value of 0x800704CF [ERROR_NETWORK_UNREACHABLE]) if the PC is not connected to the Internet. For this reason, you should always call `CurrentAppSimulator`'s and `CurrentApp`'s *Xxx*Async methods with a try block that catches this `Exception`/HResult so that your app behaves well if the user's PC is offline.

Here is an example of what the XML file must look like:[9]

```xml
<?xml version="1.0" encoding="utf-16" ?>
<CurrentApp>
  <ListingInformation>
    <App>
      <AppId>00000000-0000-0000-0000-000000000000</AppId>
      <LinkUri>
          http://apps.microsoft.com/webpdp/app/00000000-0000-0000-0000-000000000000
      </LinkUri>
      <CurrentMarket>en-us</CurrentMarket>
      <AgeRating>3</AgeRating>
      <MarketData xml:lang="en-us">
        <Name>13a-WindowsStore App</Name>
        <Description></Description>
        <Price>1.99</Price>
        <CurrencySymbol>$</CurrencySymbol>
        <CurrencyCode>USD</CurrencyCode>
      </MarketData>
    </App>
    <Product ProductId="DurableProduct" ProductType="Durable">
      <MarketData xml:lang="en-us">
        <Name>Durable product</Name>
        <Price>2.99</Price>
        <CurrencySymbol>$</CurrencySymbol>
        <CurrencyCode>USD</CurrencyCode>
      </MarketData>
    </Product>
    <Product ProductId="DurableExpiringProduct" LicenseDuration="3" ProductType="Durable">
      <MarketData xml:lang="en-us">
        <Name>Durable expiring product</Name>
        <Price>3.99</Price>
        <CurrencySymbol>$</CurrencySymbol>
        <CurrencyCode>USD</CurrencyCode>
      </MarketData>
```

---

[9] The schema for the XML file can be found at *http://msdn.microsoft.com/en-us/library/windows/apps/windows.applicationmodel.store.currentappsimulator.aspx*.

```xml
    </Product>
    <Product ProductId="ConsumableProduct" ProductType="Consumable">
      <MarketData xml:lang="en-us">
        <Name>Consumable product</Name>
        <Price>4.99</Price>
        <CurrencySymbol>$</CurrencySymbol>
        <CurrencyCode>USD</CurrencyCode>
      </MarketData>
    </Product>
    <Product ProductId="ConsumableProductOffer-Song" ProductType="Consumable">
      <MarketData xml:lang="en-us">
        <Name>Consumable product offer</Name>
        <Price>5.99</Price>
        <CurrencySymbol>$</CurrencySymbol>
        <CurrencyCode>USD</CurrencyCode>
      </MarketData>
    </Product>
  </ListingInformation>
  <LicenseInformation>
    <App>
      <IsActive>true</IsActive>
      <IsTrial>true</IsTrial>
      <ExpirationDate>2013-08-20T04:55:45.7378761Z</ExpirationDate>
    </App>
  </LicenseInformation>
</CurrentApp>
```

The ListingInformation section reflects your app's selling details. Some of these values are retrievable via CurrentApp(Simulator)'s AppId and LinkUri properties. The other values are retrievable by querying properties of the ListingInformation object returned from calling the Load-ListingInformationAsync method. The ListingInformation class looks like this:

```csharp
public sealed class ListingInformation {
    public String CurrentMarket { get; }
    public UInt32 AgeRating { get; }
    public String Name { get; }
    public String Description { get; }
    public String FormattedPrice { get; }
    public IReadOnlyDictionary<String, ProductListing> ProductListings { get; }
}
```

A ListingInformation object contains a ProductListings property that returns a collection of the in-app products your app makes available to its users. The keys are product ID strings (programmatic string values) that allow you to quickly look up a product's ProductListing object. The ProductListing class looks like this:

```csharp
public sealed class ProductListing {
    public String ProductId { get; }          // Programmatic name of product
    public String Name { get; }               // User-friendly name of product
    public String FormattedPrice { get; }     // Price of product
    public ProductType ProductType { get; }   // Unknown, Durable, Consumable
}
```

When developing your app, licenses cannot be obtained. So, in the XML file, you also specify what licenses you want Windows to believe the user has so that you can test your app. You seed the `CurrentAppSimulator` with your app's license and any in-app product licenses via the XML file's LicenseInformation section. Once licenses are available (or defined in the XML file), your app can acquire and validate them by querying CurrentApp(Simulator)'s `LicenseInformation` property. This property returns a `LicenseInformation` object whose class looks like this:

```
public sealed class LicenseInformation {
   // These members return information about the app's license:
   public Boolean IsActive { get; }   // False if side-loaded, trial expired,
                                      // or purchase refunded10
   public Boolean IsTrial { get; }    // True for a trial license
   public DateTimeOffset ExpirationDate { get; }  // For a trial license, indicates expiration

   // This member returns information about each product's license
   public IReadOnlyDictionary<String, ProductLicense> ProductLicenses { get; }

   // Raised when an app or product license changes on the local PC or on another PC
   public event LicenseChangedEventHandler LicenseChanged;
}
```

The `ProductLicense` class looks like this:

```
public sealed class ProductLicense {
   public String ProductId { get; }               // Programmatic name of product
   public Boolean IsActive { get; }                // False if product not licensed
   public DateTimeOffset ExpirationDate { get; }   // For a consumable, indicates expiration
}
```

Note When licenses change using `CurrentAppSimulator`, only the license information in memory is updated; the XML file is *not* updated to reflect the licenses. If you stop your app, restart it, and call `CurrentAppSimulator`'s `ReloadSimulatorAsync` method with the same XML file you used before, all licenses will reset to the state reflected in the XML file.

Note The code that accompanies this book has some very useful classes that can greatly simplify working with the Windows Store commerce engine. The classes allow you to dynamically build at runtime the XML you need to pass to the simulator. These classes support IntelliSense and compile-time type-safety. Having the ability to dynamically construct the XML greatly simplifies testing and enables automated testing of app and product purchase scenarios. In addition, the code automatically updates the XML file as licenses change. This allows you to start with no licenses, acquire new licenses, stop debugging, restart the app, and retain all the licenses you acquired during the previous session.

---

10   Users who want a refund must contact the Windows Store directly; the app developer cannot initiate a refund.

App trials and purchasing an app license

If you offer users a time-based trial for your app, you do not have to write any code. Once the trial period expires, Windows will not let the app launch; instead, Windows prompts the user to purchase the app. But you might want to write code to handle a scenario in which the trial expires while the app is running. In this case, you could write code that prompts the user to purchase the app. If the user purchases the app, the app continues running with all features enabled. If the user refuses to purchase the app, you throw an unhandled exception to terminate the app or let the app run while periodically reminding the user to purchase it.

You can query the `CurrentApp.LicenseInformation.ExpirationDate` property to find out when the app's trial period expires. You might want to show this value to users so that they know when they'll have to purchase the app or stop using it. If you want to offer a feature-differentiated trial, you can simply enable the features after the user has purchased an app license:

```
if (CurrentApp.LicenseInformation.IsActive && !CurrentApp.LicenseInformation.IsTrial) {
   // App is appropriately licensed, enable feature here...
} else {
   // App not purchased & trial expired, app side-loaded, or purchase refunded
}
```

If you want to let the user purchase your app from within it, you can show the user how much it will cost by querying `ListingInformation`'s `FormattedPrice` property. Then, to actually let the user purchase the app, call `CurrentApp(Simulator)`'s `RequestAppPurchaseAsync` method:

```
private async void OnAppPurchase(object sender, RoutedEventArgs e) {
   String msg;
   if (!m_licenseInfo.IsTrial) {
      msg = "App already licensed";
   } else {
      try {
         // Prompt the user to purchase a license for the app
         String receipt = await CurrentApp.RequestAppPurchaseAsync(true);
         msg = m_licenseInfo.IsActive
            ? "App license purchased" : "App license purchase cancelled";
      }
      catch (ArgumentException ex) { msg = ex.Message; }
      catch (OutOfMemoryException ex) { msg = ex.Message; }
      catch (COMException ex) {
         if (ex.HResult != E_FAIL) throw;
         msg = ex.Message;
      }
      catch (Exception ex) {
         if (ex.HResult != ERROR_NETWORK_UNREACHABLE) throw;
         msg = ex.Message;
      }
   }
   await new MessageDialog(msg).ShowAsync();
}
```

The call to `CurrentAppSimulator`'s `RequestAppPurchaseAsync` shows a dialog box you can use to simulate failures you might want to handle in your code. The previous code fragment shows how to properly recover from these failures. If you pass `true` to RequestAppPurchaseAsync, the method returns a receipt if the user purchases the app. If you pass `false`, then RequestApp-PurchaseAsync always returns an empty string, whether the user purchases the license or cancels the purchase. In this case, you can check the `IsActive` property to see if the user purchased the license.

> **Note** You can register a callback method with `LicenseInformation`'s `LicenseChanged` event. Windows raises this event to notify your app of license changes. In fact, it is raised when a trial expires, so you could prompt the user to purchase the app within your callback method. Beware, Windows sometimes waits several minutes before raising this event after a license change occurs.

Passing `true` to RequestAppPurchaseAsync causes it to return a receipt string if the user purchases the license. A receipt looks like this:

```xml
<?xml version="1.0" encoding="utf-8" ?>
<Receipt Version="1.0" ReceiptDate="2013-08-05T20:10:31Z"
        CertificateId="b809e47cd0110a4db043b3f73e83acd917fe1336"
        ReceiptDeviceId="360f3e84-ed66-4f94-bd96-8303ea9da1f9">
    <AppReceipt Id="65626cce-a771-417c-b938-8d29bd1e4c4f"
        AppId="225bdce7-eaa1-4fb9-8d7b-c2d4cb629d1c_gzxgteedtvpx2"
        PurchaseDate="2013-08-05T20:10:31Z"
        LicenseType="Full" />
</Receipt>
```

Receipts are used if your app has a companion web service. They allow your service to verify that the calling client is actually authorized to use some feature or download some content. Also, at any time after the app license is purchased, you can acquire the receipt string by calling CurrentApp(Simulator)'s GetAppReceiptAsync method and then send this receipt to your service. A receipt is signed with a standard XML digital signature, allowing your server to verify that it came from the Windows Store. To learn how your service can validate a receipt, see *http:// msdn.microsoft.com/en-us/library/windows/apps/jj649137.aspx*. You download the certificate used to sign the receipt from *https://lic.apps.microsoft.com/licensing/certificateserver/?cid*=CertificateId, where *CertificateId* is the value of Receipt's CertificateId attribute (a certificate thumbprint). The ReceiptDeviceId uniquely identifies the device the user used to purchase the license, and the AppReceipt's Id uniquely identifies the app receipt, which is guaranteed to be the same across all of a user's PCs.

When a trial expires, the user pays the current price of the app. (This might be different from the price listed when the user originally installed the app.) App licenses are granted as either full or trial. Once a user has a full license, regardless of the price at the time it was acquired (free or paid), it's a full license forever. This includes future versions of the app. If a developer changes an app's price, the price affects new customer purchases only; existing customers are unaffected. If a user installs an app supporting trials and then installs a newer version of an app that does not support trials, the trial is still in effect until it expires; making an app for purchase affects only new users of the app.

Purchasing durable in-app product licenses

An app can sell durable in-app products from within the app itself. These products typically unlock app features for some period of time. For example, your app could sell a durable in-app product that grants the user a special weapon he can use in a game or enables a user to turn off advertising for three days.

To sell a durable in-app product, the developer must first enter these products in the Dashboard under Services. (See Figure 11-6.) You assign each in-app product a Product ID, a Price Tier, a Product Lifetime (either Forever or between 1 day and 365 days), and a Content Type. Users won't see the Product ID; it is a string you use in your code to identify a product. The pricing scheme for the in-app products is identical to the tiered scheme for the app. For each product you add, you'll also have to add a description for it via the Dashboard's Description page.

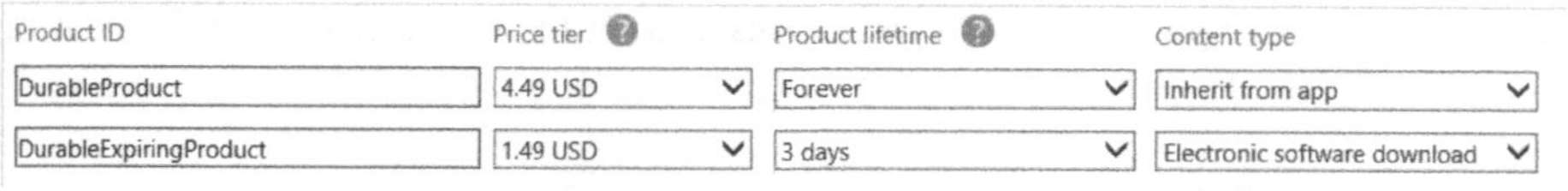

Product ID	Price tier ❓	Product lifetime ❓	Content type
DurableProduct	4.49 USD ∨	Forever ∨	Inherit from app ∨
DurableExpiringProduct	1.49 USD ∨	3 days ∨	Electronic software download ∨

FIGURE 11-6 Using the Dashboard to add a durable in-app product to your app.

The Content Type field is there for tax purposes. You can choose from Inherit From App, Electronic Software Download, Software As A Service, Music Streaming, Music Download, Video Streaming, Video Download, Online Data Storage/Services, Electronic Books, Electronic Magazine Single Issue, and Electronic Newspaper Single Issue. Most of these values are self-explanatory. The default value is Inherit From App, which means that the in-app product falls in the same tax category as the app itself. At the time of this writing, the tax category of all apps is Electronic Software Download, hence there is no difference between leaving the value as Inherit From App or Electronic Software Download. This should be the desired category for the overwhelming majority of in-app purchases. The types that refer to cloud- and online-based services are very specific categories that are taxed differently. If your app uses these in-app products, we recommend you consult with a tax advisor.

To test durable in-app products, you must add them to the XML and then call `CurrentAppSimulator`'s `ReloadSimulatorAsync` method to have it load the XML file. The XML file shown earlier describes two durable in-app products in its ListingInformation section. The "DurableProduct" product never expires (has no `LicenseDuration` attribute), while the "DurableExpiringProduct" product expires every three days.

In reality, these two products work the same way: after a user purchases either product, the license is granted with an expiration date. For a nonexpiring product, the expiration date is 12/30/9999 (effectively nonexpiring), and for an expiring product, the expiration date is the purchase date plus the number of days indicated by the `LicenseDuration` attribute. In your code, you can treat durable in-app products and durable expiring in-app products the same.

Here is how an app determines if the user has a valid license for a durable in-app product:

```
ProductLicense pl = license.ProductLicenses["DurableProduct"];  // Or "DurableExpiringProduct"
DateTimeOffset expirationDate = pl.ExpirationDate; // If you want to show this to the user
if (pl.IsActive) {
   // Product purchased and not expired; enable app feature or content
} else {
   // Product not purchased or expired; do not enable app feature or content
}
```

Your app needs to give the user some way to purchase a durable in-app product. You can get the price to show to users like this:

```
String price =
   CurrentApp.ListingInformation.ProductListings["DurableProduct"].FormattedPrice;
```

And, when the user decides to purchase the product, call CurrentApp(Simulator)'s Request-ProductPurchaseAsync method:

```
private async void OnDurableProductPurchase(object sender, RoutedEventArgs e) {
   String msg;
   var licenseInfo = CurrentApp.LicenseInformation;
   if (!licenseInfo.IsActive || licenseInfo.IsTrial) {
      msg = "Can't license product until app is licensed";
   } else {
      ProductLicense pl =
         licenseInfo.ProductLicenses["DurableProduct"];  // Or, "DurableExpiringProduct"
      if (pl.IsActive) {
         // Product already licensed and not expired
      } else {
         try {
            // Prompt the user to purchase a license for the durable in-app product
            PurchaseResults purchaseResult =
               await CurrentApp.RequestProductPurchaseAsync(pl.ProductId);
            msg = "Product purchase status: " + purchaseResult.Status;
         }
         catch (ArgumentException ex) { msg = ex.Message; }
         catch (OutOfMemoryException ex) { msg = ex.Message; }
         catch (COMException ex) { if (ex.HResult != E_FAIL) throw; msg = ex.Message; }
         catch (Exception ex) {
            if (ex.HResult != ERROR_NETWORK_UNREACHABLE) throw;
            msg = ex.Message;
         }
      }
   }
   await new MessageDialog(msg).ShowAsync();
}
```

The call to CurrentApp(Simulator)'s RequestProductPurchaseAsync prompts the user to complete the purchase of the specified product. The method returns a PurchaseResults object whose class looks like this:

```
public sealed class PurchaseResults {
   public ProductPurchaseStatus Status { get; } // Succeeded or NotPurchased
   public Guid TransactionId { get; }            // Unique ID identifying the purchase
   public String ReceiptXml { get; }             // XML receipt string
   public String OfferId { get; }                // Always "" for durable in-app products
}
```

The most important property here is `ProductPurchaseStatus` because it indicates whether the user purchased the product or not. Here is an example of the `ReceiptXml` (note that Product-Receipt's Id attribute is `PurchaseResults`'s `TransactionId` property):

```xml
<?xml version="1.0" encoding="utf-8"?>
<Receipt Version="1.0"
         ReceiptDate="2013-08-18T16:05:38Z"
         CertificateId="b809e47cd0110a4db043b3f73e83acd917fe1336"
         ReceiptDeviceId="d4ac7873-14dc-4a0f-be9c-375d2700e7f9">
  <ProductReceipt Id="fb61f714-3fb6-4cdd-abd7-d8f19f097804"
                  AppId="Wintellect.WinRTDemo.Store_eqy0cv8ej6g5m"
                  ProductId="DurableProduct"
                  PurchaseDate="2013-08-18T16:05:38Z"
                  ProductType="Durable" />
</Receipt>
```

Also, at any time after the product license is purchased, you can always acquire the receipt string by calling `CurrentApp(Simulator)`'s `GetProductReceiptAsync` method.

Purchasing consumable in-app products

An app can sell consumable in-app products from within the app itself. Consumable in-app products are similar to durable expiring products except that consumable products do not expire based on time. For example, a user might purchase a hint or power up to get past a difficult part of a game. A user can purchase several of these repeatedly; they expire when used (not based on time). Consumable products behave differently than durable products. Consumable products are not licensed, so you do not query `CurrentApp(Simulator)`'s `LicenseInformation` property to see if a consumable product has been purchased. This also means that information about consumable product purchases do not automatically roam across the user's PCs. So your app is responsible for managing consumable products. For example, you must do the extra work yourself to get information about purchased consumable products to roam across the user's PCs. For this, you'll probably want to use Windows' roaming data feature discussed in Chapter 4, "Package data and roaming."

> **Important** Make sure you roam the user's consumable products properly. You will receive customer complaints if purchased consumable products are not available across all the user's PCs. Make sure you test this scenario. Also, a user may uninstall a package and re-install it later. Again, any consumable products previously purchased must remain available after the re-install. You should test this scenario too. You should also amply test the scenario when a user cancels a purchase; do not accidentally grant the user the consumable product and be sure to indicate to the user that the product was not purchased.

To sell a consumable in-app product, the developer must first enter these products in the Dashboard under Services. (See Figure 11-7.) You assign each in-app product a Product ID and a Price Tier. You set the Product Lifetime to Consumable and the Content Type to one of the types previously mentioned. For each product you add, you also have to add a description for it via the Dashboard's Description page.

Product ID	Price tier ❔	Product lifetime ❔	Content type
ConsumableProduct	9.99 USD ⌄	Consumable ⌄	Electronic software download ⌄
ConsumableProductOffer-Song	1.49 USD ⌄	Consumable ⌄	Music download ⌄

FIGURE 11-7 Using the Dashboard to add a consumable in-app product to your app.

To test consumable in-app products, you must add them to the XML and then call Current-AppSimulator's ReloadSimulatorAsync method to have it load the XML file. The XML file shown earlier describes two consumable in-app products in its ListingInformation section: "Consumable-Product" and "ConsumableProductOffer-Song". Functionally, these two consumable products are identical.

Your app needs to give the user some way to purchase a consumable in-app product. You can get the price to show to users like this (which is the same way you do it for durable products too):

```
String price =
    CurrentApp.ListingInformation.ProductListings["ConsumableProduct"].FormattedPrice;
```

And, when the user decides to purchase the product, call CurrentApp(Simulator)'s Request-ProductPurchaseAsync method:

```
private async void OnConsumableProductPurchase(Object sender, RoutedEventArgs e) {
    // NOTE: When the user purchases a consumable in-app product, its IsActive property
    // remains false and the LicenseChanged event is not raised
    String msg = String.Empty;
    if (!m_licenseInfo.IsActive || m_licenseInfo.IsTrial) {
        msg = "Can't license product until app is licensed";
    } else {
        String productId = "ConsumableProduct";
        try {
            // Prompt the user to purchase a consumable in-app product
            PurchaseResults purchaseResult =
                await CurrentApp.RequestProductPurchaseAsync(productId);
            switch (purchaseResult.Status) {
                case ProductPurchaseStatus.Succeeded:
                    // Consumable in-app product purchased
                    // Since app hasn't fulfilled the consumable, Store won't let user buy more

                    // TODO: Integrate product into app (this example increments purchase count)
                    m_ConsumableProductTimesBought += 1;
```

```
                    // Tell the Store the app fulfilled the consumable
                    FulfillmentResult fulfillmentResult =
                        await Store.ReportConsumableFulfillmentAsync(productId,
                            purchaseResult.TransactionId);
                    switch (fulfillmentResult) {
                        // For these cases, assume user purchased our product successfully
                        case FulfillmentResult.Succeeded:
                            msg = "Consumable product purchased. You can purchase it again";
                            break;
                        case FulfillmentResult.ServerError:
                            msg = "There was a problem receiving fulfillment status from the server";
                            break;

                        // For these cases, assume purchase failed (undo product integration)
                        case FulfillmentResult.NothingToFulfill:
                        case FulfillmentResult.PurchasePending:
                        case FulfillmentResult.PurchaseReverted:
                            msg = "There was a problem fulfilling the purchase: " + fulfillmentResult;
                            // This example decrements purchase count
                            m_ConsumableProductTimesBought -= 1;
                            break;
                    }
                    break;
                case ProductPurchaseStatus.NotPurchased:
                case ProductPurchaseStatus.NotFulfilled:
                case ProductPurchaseStatus.AlreadyPurchased:
                    // Notify user that the purchase failed
                    msg = "Failed to purchase consumable product: " + purchaseResult.Status;
                    break;
            }
        }
        catch (ArgumentException ex) { msg = ex.Message; }
        catch (OutOfMemoryException ex) { msg = ex.Message; }
        catch (COMException ex) { if (ex.HResult != E_FAIL) throw; msg = ex.Message; }
        catch (Exception ex) {
            if (ex.HResult != ERROR_NETWORK_UNREACHABLE) throw;
            msg = ex.Message;
        }
    }
    await new MessageDialog(msg).ShowAsync();
}
```

The call to CurrentApp(Simulator)'s RequestProductPurchaseAsync prompts the user
to complete the purchase of the specified product (just like it did for a durable product). Because
consumable products are not licensed, the Windows Store does not update a license for this product.
So your app must record the fact that it has been purchased. In the previous code, I simply add 1 to
an m_ConsumableProductTimesBought field. In a real app, you'd execute code here to integrate the
product into your app (add a hint to the user's collection or grant the user the power up she purchased). Once your app has integrated the product, it must call CurrentApp(Simulator)'s Report-
ConsumableFulfillmentAsync method, passing in the purchase's product ID and transaction ID.
This informs the store that your app has completed integrating the product into itself.

The ReportConsumableFulfillmentAsync method solves the problem where the user purchases a product and then the app terminates because of an unhandled exception or Process Lifetime

Management (PLM) leaving the user in a state where she paid for the product but the app didn't integrate it. The Windows Store remembers the last time the user purchased each product ID. When your app launches, it should call CurrentApp(Simulator)'s GetUnfulfilledConsumablesAsync to get the collection of unfulfilled consumable products and integrate them into the app at this time. The UnfulfilledConsumable class looks like this:

```
public sealed class UnfulfilledConsumable {
   public String ProductId { get; }
   public String OfferId { get; }
   public Guid TransactionId { get; }
}
```

As each consumable product is integrated, call ReportConsumableFulfillmentAsync to grant the user each product she purchased and remove the product from the collection. Only after a product has been fulfilled can the user purchase another instance of the product.

Purchasing consumable in-app product offers

Via the Dashboard, developers can specify up to 200 products to be sellable through their app. However, for some apps, this is insufficient. For example, a music app might sell songs and, hopefully, the library consists of more than 200 songs. By building on the consumable in-app product technology discussed in the previous section, an app can sell a virtually unlimited set of *product offers*.

To sell an unlimited number of product offers, first define a consumable in-app product exactly as described in the previous section. Assign the product a price. And, for testing, add the product to the XML file you'll have CurrentAppSimulator use. For this example, I'm using the "Consumable-ProductOffer-Song" product as in my XML file.

In the previous section, I showed how to call the RequestProductPurchaseAsync method to sell a product. Selling a product offer is identical except you call the overload of the RequestProduct-PurchaseAsync method that takes three parameters. Here is an example that calls this overload to sell a product offer:

```
// Product ID as on Dashboard/XML file (sets price)
String productId = "ConsumableProductOffer-Song";

// App-defined value identifying the offer (song)
String offerId = "Queen-Bohemian Rhapsody";

// Optionally specify a description and image to show the user for the product offer
ProductPurchaseDisplayProperties ppdp = new ProductPurchaseDisplayProperties(productId) {
   Description = "Queen's Bohemian Rhapsody",
   Image = new Uri("http://upload.wikimedia.org/wikipedia/en/9/9f/Bohemian_Rhapsody.png")
};

// Prompt the user to purchase a consumable in-app product offer
PurchaseResults purchaseResult =
   await CurrentApp.RequestProductPurchaseAsync(productId, offerId, ppdp);

// Not shown: Consume the product and then call ReportConsumableFulfillmentAsync.
```

As always, RequestProductPurchaseAsync returns a `PurchaseResults` as discussed in the previous section. However, this time, its `OfferId` property is set to the offer ID value passed in to the RequestProductPurchaseAsync method. Here is an example of what the `ReceiptXml` property returns:

```xml
<?xml version="1.0" encoding="utf-8"?>
<Receipt Version="1.0"
         ReceiptDate="2013-08-18T18:28:36Z"
         CertificateId="b809e47cd0110a4db043b3f73e83acd917fe1336"
         ReceiptDeviceId="11fcf0a3-c434-4fe4-9831-32edd0b66df5">
   <ProductReceipt Id="e4774ee7-965f-4063-af19-9c9d2a18c215"
                   AppId="Wintellect.WinRTDemo.Store_eqy0cv8ej6g5m"
                   ProductId="ConsumableProductOffer"
                   PurchaseDate="2013-08-18T18:28:36Z"
                   ProductType="Consumable"
                   OfferId="Queen-Bohemian Rhapsody" />
</Receipt>
```

APPENDIX

App containers

Users must be confident that Windows Store apps cannot just access any of the user's data or PC resources. So Windows restricts what apps can do on a PC. This appendix explores Windows' security model and how it is enforced.

Windows defines security groups, such as Administrators and Users, and each group has different privileges. When a user is assigned to a group, that individual inherits the group's rights and privileges. For example, if a user belongs to the Administrators group, the user can install desktop apps, change the system time, modify the content of the %System32% directory, and so on. If the user is only a member of the Users group (a standard user), the user cannot perform any of these operations. A standard user, however, can still launch most apps, read files from all over the system, and access certain registry locations.

When a user logs in to a PC with his credentials, Windows starts a logon session for that user and produces an access token. This access token contains the identity and privileges of the user's account. Now, when the user launches an app, that app gets a copy of the user's access token so that Windows knows what the app can do on behalf of the user. Thus, if a user is a member of the Users group, an app running as that user has all the rights a standard user has. Prior to Windows Vista, it also meant that if a user was a member of the Administrators group, all his applications would run with administrative privileges. Hence, any application was able to install other apps, write to the registry or another app's files, send those files anywhere over the Internet, and so forth. From a security perspective, this was far from ideal, and Microsoft introduced User Account Control (UAC) starting with Windows Vista. With UAC, apps launched by a member of the Administrators group run with a standard user token. For more information, you can read *http://msdn.microsoft.com/en-us/library/windows/desktop/bb648649.aspx* and also *Windows via C/C++*, Fifth Edition (Microsoft Press, 2011).

For Windows Store apps, UAC still does not provide ample security. To ensure user confidence with the OS, Windows Store apps must not be able to look into the user's files without the explicit permission of the user. Additionally, to fulfill the promise of clean install and uninstall of Windows Store apps, apps should not be able to clutter the machine's registry or file system. For these reasons, Windows needs to restrict apps from doing things even a standard user can do. Therefore, Windows Store apps run in a very restrictive security sandbox called an *app container*.

To enforce this sandbox, Windows Store apps use another security feature introduced in Windows Vista: *mandatory integrity control*. On a high level, it works as follows. Every process gets a *mandatory label* associated with its access token. For apps or user processes, a label can have three levels: low, medium, and high. By default, a process launched by a standard user gets a medium level and a process launched by an administrator gets a high level. On the other hand, every resource—such as a folder, file, or registry key—has a label as well, with medium being the default level. When an app wants to access a resource, Windows checks the integrity level of the app's process and the integrity level of the resource. In general, a process does not have write access to a resource with a level higher than its own.[1] When you look at the properties of a Windows Store app with a tool like Process Explorer (which is shown in Figure A-1), you see that the process has a low integrity level (Mandatory Label\Low Mandatory Level). Thus, Windows Store apps will not be able to write anywhere on the system, except for their own dedicated location on disk. In Chapter 4, "Package data and roaming," and Chapter 5, "Storage files and folders," you saw that every Windows Store app gets such a storage location on disk that it can use to store state and settings.

The low integrity level prevents apps from cluttering the system, but it does nothing to prevent one app from accessing another app's resources (which also has a low integrity level). To keep apps from accessing each other's data, Windows assigns every app its own Application Security ID (SID).[2] An app will have permission to access a resource only if Windows explicitly allows an app permission by adding the app's Application SID to this resource. You can see this Application SID in Figure A-1; it is the entry with AppContainer in the Flags column.[3] You can find this Application SID back in File Explorer if you navigate to this app's subdirectory in %LocalAppData%\Packages\. When you bring up the Folder properties—for example, the LocalState folder—you'll see that the Application SID has full access to this resource.[4]

Now we know that Windows restricts apps from accessing most of the system. However, apps might still need to do things like access files outside of their sandbox, such as the Pictures library. Because the integrity level and app container restrict the app from accessing these files directly, Windows uses broker processes (for example, RuntimeBroker.exe) to access the files on behalf of the Windows Store app. This broker process runs outside of the app container with a medium integrity level. As a developer, you indicate what resources your app needs by checking capabilities in the app's package manifest file. When Windows creates the process for a Windows Store app, it looks at the manifest file and adds a matching Capability SID to the process' access token for each capability specified. When the app then tries to access a resource, such as a picture in the Pictures library, Windows looks at the process' access token to find the Capability SID, and it creates the broker process that subsequently accesses the required file on the app's behalf. Because of this level of indirection, there is a slight performance penalty for accessing user files.

---

[1] This is, of course, a simplification. Mandatory integrity control provides for execute, read, and write.

[2] An Application SID is derived from the package's family name using an algorithm with no random factors. That is, an app's Application SID is always the same value, even when an app is installed on different PCs.

[3] App containers are mostly used by Windows Store apps. If you run Internet Explorer in enhanced protected mode, it will also use app containers for its tabs.

[4] In Chapter 9, "Background tasks," I discuss how Windows Store apps can have background task code running in their own process (BackgroundTaskHost.exe). Windows assigns this process the same Application SID as the Windows app itself. This means that the background task code is running in the same app container and can therefore share data with its Windows Store app.

FIGURE A-1 Process Explorer showing a Windows Store app's Security settings.

Index

Numbers and symbols

~ (tilde), 39

A

Account Picture Provider app declaration, 33
`Activated` event, 57, 197–199
activating Windows Store apps
    app declarations, 32–34
    hosted view, 53
    launch activation, 44, 50
    main view, 53, 55
    process overview, 49–55
    share target apps, 242
    time considerations, 64–65
    toast notifications, 50, 197–198
`ActivationKind` enumeration, 50, 53, 57
`Add-AppxPackage` PowerShell script, 40–41
Advanced Query Syntax (AQS), 117
age rating for apps, 250, 254
Alarm app declaration, 34
`AlarmApplicationManager` class, 33
`AllowAllTrustedApps` Group Policy setting, 42
animating tile contents, 190–191
app activation. *See* activating Windows Store apps
app containers, 3, 271–273
app declarations
    about, 32–33
    activating apps, 44, 49–55
    adding, 213–219
    listed, 33–34
app development, structuring class code, 70–75
app licenses, 262–266
app logos, 184–186

app packages
    about, 25
    accessing files or folders, 97
    associating with reserved package name, 43
    building, 34–40
    debugging, 46–48
    deploying, 6, 40–44
    manifest file. *See* manifest file
    package data. *See* package data
    Package Explorer desktop app, 45–46
    package files. *See* package files
    package identity. *See* package identity
    privacy policy, 147, 254
    project files, 25–27
    size considerations, 250
    staging and registration, 44–45
App singleton object, 52–53, 57, 61
AppCert.exe tool, 252
App.g.i.cs file, 52
`Application` class
    about, 56–57, 70
    `Current` property, 53
    `OnActivated` method, 54, 107, 238
    `OnFileActivated` method, 104, 106, 238
    `OnLaunched` method, 104, 193, 197–199, 238
    `OnSearchActivated` method, 238
    `OnShareTargetActivated` method, 241–242, 244
    `OnWindowCreated` method, 54–55, 58, 69, 238
    `Resuming` event, 66, 75
    `Start` method, 52
    `Suspending` event, 67–68, 75
    virtual methods, 53–54, 56–57
Application Display Name package property, 29, 43
application models. *See* desktop apps; Windows Store
    apps
Application Security ID (SID), 272

P

About the authors

JEFFREY RICHTER is a cofounder of Wintellect (*http://www.Wintellect.com/*), a training and consulting company dedicated to helping companies produce better software faster. Jeffrey has authored many video courses that can be viewed at *http://WintellectNOW.com/*.

He has also written or cowritten many books about Windows and .NET Framework programming, including *Windows Runtime via C#* (Microsoft Press, 2013), *CLR via C#, Fourth Edition* (Microsoft Press, 2012), *Windows via C/C++, Fifth Edition* (Microsoft Press, 2007), and *Programming Server-Side Applications for Microsoft Windows 2000* (Microsoft Press, 2000). Jeffrey was a contributing editor for MSDN Magazine, where he wrote numerous feature articles and has been the Win32 Q&A columnist, .NET Q&A columnist, and Concurrent Affairs columnist. Jeffrey also speaks at various trade conferences worldwide, including Wintellect's Devscovery, VSLive!, and Microsoft's TechEd and Professional Developers Conference.

Jeffrey has consulted for many companies, including AT&T, DreamWorks, General Electric, Hewlett-Packard, IBM, and Intel. His code ships in many Microsoft products, among them Microsoft Visual Studio, Microsoft Office, and various versions of Windows. Jeffrey consulted with the .NET Framework team for eight years and maintains an ongoing close relationship with that team as well as the Windows team. Most recently, Jeffrey worked with Microsoft to design the new asynchronous programming model supported by C# and Visual Basic. This model is similar to what Jeffrey made available with his Power Threading Library since 2005.

On the personal front, Jeffrey holds both airplane and helicopter pilot licenses. He is also a member of the International Brotherhood of Magicians and enjoys showing friends sleight-of-hand card tricks from time to time. Jeffrey's other hobbies include music (especially jazz and progressive rock from the 1970s), drumming, and model railroading. He also enjoys traveling (which he gets to do quite a bit of) and theater. He lives in Kirkland, Washington, with his wife, Kristin, and his two sons, Aidan and Grant.

 **MAARTEN VAN DE BOSPOORT** is a principal consultant with the Premier Services for Developers division in Microsoft. The Windows division has involved him from the early days of the Windows Runtime to work with partners on showcase apps. He teaches classes on writing Windows Store apps, and in this capacity he has trained hundreds of Microsoft internal and external developers worldwide to write WinRT apps. For the last eight years, Maarten has been consulting for the Windows product group, partnering with all major independent service vendors (ISVs) during Windows operating system (OS) betas to ensure that critical apps would continue to run on the next version of Windows. Maarten has assisted countless ISVs with architecting their software and optimizing their performance for the newest versions of the operating system.

Maarten moved with multiple stops from The Netherlands to the Seattle area in 1997. He appreciates living in the Pacific Northwest with its familiar culture and climate. Early in the morning, Maarten enjoys playing tennis with friends, and it would have been good if he had made up his mind about 20 years ago as to what instrument was best to really play his favorite jazz and bebop tunes. He lives in Bellevue, Washington, with his wife, Brigitte, and his two sons, Jules and Joris.

Now that you've read the book...

Tell us what you think!

Was it useful?
Did it teach you what you wanted to learn?
Was there room for improvement?

Let us know at http://aka.ms/tellpress

Your feedback goes directly to the staff at Microsoft Press,
and we read every one of your responses. Thanks in advance!